D0192553

MEDICINE
on
TRIAL

MEDICINE on TRIAL

....

CHARLES B. INLANDER
PRESIDENT, PEOPLE'S MEDICAL
SOCIETY

LOWELL S. LEVIN
PROFESSOR, YALE UNIVERSITY
SCHOOL OF MEDICINE

ED WEINER
SENIOR EDITOR, PEOPLE'S MEDICAL
SOCIETY

....

THE APPALLING STORY OF MEDICAL INEPTITUDE AND THE ARROGANCE THAT OVERLOOKS IT

Pantheon Books
New York

Copyright © 1988 by the
People's Medical Society

All rights reserved under International and
Pan-American Copyright Conventions.
Published in the United States by
Pantheon Books, a division of
Random House, Inc., New York.
Originally published in hardcover by
Prentice Hall Press, a division of
Simon and Schuster, Inc., in 1988.

Library of Congress
Cataloging-in-Publication Data

Inlander, Charles B.
Medicine on trial: the appalling story of
medical ineptitude and the arrogance that
overlooks it/Charles B. Inlander,
Lowell S. Levin, Ed Weiner.
p.   cm.
Includes index.
ISBN 0-679-72732-9
1. Medical errors—United States.
2. Medical care—United States.
I. Levin, Lowell S.
II. Weiner, Ed.   III. Title.
R729.8.I55   1989
362.1'0973—dc20   89-42987

Manufactured in the United States of America
Pantheon Paperback Edition

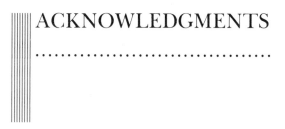

ACKNOWLEDGMENTS

The authors wish to thank the following people, some who have helped to conduct this "trial," and those who also have seen the authors through other, more personal trials as well.

Many thanks to Gareth Esersky, Paul Aron, Laurie S. Barnett, and all those at Prentice Hall Press whose hands (and blue pencils) touched and talents improved our manuscript. Thanks, too, to Gail Ross, our agent, and the staff of Goldfarb and Singer, who helped this book find its way.

We are grateful to Robert Mendelsohn, M.D., Marsden G. Wagner, M.D., and Tom Ferguson, M.D., whose kind words and thoughtful early reading of the manuscript gave us considerable encouragement.

We are indebted to those scholars and scientists, physicians, and laypersons, whose diligent work and research—the "expert testimony" that provides the skeleton and sinew of our argument—truly honors our text and, we hope, is honored by it.

Thanks to the staff of the People's Medical Society, and especially to Perrie Layton, who acted as office traffic cop and occasional keyboardist, and Mike Rooney, who provided the lists of licensure and disciplinary boards that comprise the appendix.

Of course, many thanks to the tens of thousands of members of the People's Medical Society, whose interests and concerns are reflected in this book, and whose dealings with the medical profession were the genesis of this project.

Finally, love and gratitude to our families, who have put up with our general obsession with this subject for at least five years, and our particular compulsion for the past two. All trials have been theirs.

CONTENTS

....

"No one would suggest that doctors and nurses should be superhuman and never make an error or have an accident. But every skill can be performed either competently or incompetently. Insufficient care, sloppiness, and negligence are quite different from occasional accidents."

—Martin Weitz
Health Shock

"They almost killed me, he thought; and he felt his heart pound with dangerous rage. But there was no *J'accuse.* At some point, it seemed to him, human failure melded into and became inseparable from institutional failure, the two together forging such a formidable instrument for failure as to dictate more horror stories than the public ever dreamed of."

—Martha Weinman Lear
Heartsounds

"From inability to let well alone; from too much zeal for the new and contempt for what is old; from putting knowledge before wisdom, science before art, and cleverness before common sense; from treating patients as cases, and from making the cure of the disease more grievous than the endurance of the same, Good Lord, deliver us."

—"The Litany of Sir Robert Hutchison
(1871–1960)"

"An unavoidable conclusion is that the way in which our medical care system has evolved has created conditions that increase the likelihood of damage to the patient."

—Rick Carlson
The End of Medicine

I

OPENING REMARKS

‖‖ FOREWORD

‧‧‧‧‧‧‧‧‧‧‧‧‧‧‧‧‧‧

I warn you. What you will read is not very reassuring. This book presents a grave indictment of American medicine. It is a catalog of ineptitude, malfeasance, gross neglect, indifference, and incredible arrogance. The indictment is not ours. This book is an unabridged exposé of medical mistakes taken directly from medical and public health research. We have culled from this research the bits and pieces of an ugly story to present for the first time a complete picture of this American tragedy. We have organized existing, though sometimes obscure, research in a way that blows away the smoke screen. Critical comments by experts in medicine, epidemiology, and public health have been added to help communicate how serious the situation is. "Serious" is too tame a word. We could with justification call this a conspiracy against the public. One has to wonder why the facts presented in this book have not heretofore been put on public view. Why has the honorable profession of medicine kept the facts of its mistakes to itself? Does the embarrassment of disclosure outweigh the responsibility of medicine first and foremost to protect the patient from harm? Is the profession of medicine so venal that it is willing to risk the lives of people whose trust it enjoys? Can the profession and its institutions be so cynical as to treat patients and the public at large as incapable of understanding what is going on? Or does medicine fear that full disclosure of its hazards would lead to severe legislative reprisals that might spell the end of this freewheeling, self-serving behavior?

There are growing signs that the public has had enough of cover-up and outright deceit. People are not fools, even though they may have been fooled, or lulled, into believing that medical care has been on a steady course of progress, from one medical miracle to another. The overselling and hype about winning the war on cancer is an example. We all want good news about prevention, treatment, and cure of this frightening disease. We have been fed a considerable number of public relations releases about medicine's successes, with little or no effort to portray its downside. But in recent months there has been some disquieting news about chinks in the medical armor. Several celebrated cases of medical mismanagement have made headlines. Government studies raise devastating questions about the qualifications (or lack thereof) of physicians, drug- or alcohol-impaired physicians, misdiagnosis, unnecessary or incompetent surgery, errors in medication, neglect, and high hospital infection rates. It is almost impossible now to watch TV news or read a newspaper without coming across a medical horror story. All of this has stirred peoples' concern for how safe they really are in the hands of their doctor or in the environment of a hospital.

People sense that medicine is both a profession and a business, and that the motives behind these two roles are not always—or even usually—compatible. They sense that physicians may not be the omniscient and totally dedicated care givers that organized medicine's image makers have been advertising. Personal experiences of family and friends drive home the reality of medicine's clay feet.

Physicians and their institutions are aware of these rumblings. Some of them chalk up patient (and now public) dissatisfaction to the failure of doctors to show kindness, consideration, and a willingness to listen and talk to patients. Hospitals feel they can woo back the fearful or disaffected patient with new room decor or gourmet meals. Medical schools are cranking up courses to teach humane care—how to treat patients like (as if they were not) human beings! Yet these signs of professional concern about treating the patient humanely, however well intended, and helpful, do little to get to the heart of serious medical mistakes. The key issue of gross incompetence in diagnosis and treatment remains.

Public misgivings continue to rise. But it has not been easy for people to grasp the full story; to know the extent of the problem everyone faces; to appreciate that one news story or one family member injured by medical care is not an isolated event. It has not been easy to get to the bottom of what causes medical mistakes and why precious little has been done to stop them from occurring. The time has come to pull the curtain back and get a clear view, as harsh and alarming as such a view may be.

Some readers may feel a twinge of queasiness at a public disrobing of the medical priesthood. We have all made investments of trust in our doctors and hospitals. It isn't pleasant to be confronted with evidence of their inadequacies or to learn that the patient's welfare doesn't always top the list of priorities. We feel betrayed. But confronting the facts of this betrayal of trust is the necessary first step on the road to reform. It is also the first step toward the public's regaining control over health care. Experience has taught us that we cannot count on reform generated from within the medical establishment. There are simply too many vested interests in the system trying to protect the status quo. Money, power, prestige, and egos conspire to hold inside-generated reform (and there is some) to marginal, largely cosmetic changes. In such a situation, there is no substitute for an aroused public with access to full information. This book opens the door, but, as the last chapter makes clear, it will be a long struggle on a broad front before the lay public will be given any real power over the way medicine is practiced in the United States. The medical establishment, an entrenched monopoly rooted in deep economic interests, will not simply roll over for reform. And that's not all.

We must overcome our own reluctance to criticize medicine and to challenge our doctors and the laws that protect *them*, not *us*. Real reform will come only when there is true public accountability and active public participation in oversight. It cannot be done for us. It must be done with us.

Though medicine is on trial, we seek reform in this trial, not penalty. Our proposals are intended to strengthen medicine's positive contribution by welding its governance more clearly to the public interest. As we all have a stake in the assurance of high-quality medical care, we must seek solutions that preserve the best of the system while removing its flaws. There was a time when the American medical profession seemed to have broken through on so many fronts, and to have assumed world leadership in making the human condition more pleasant, more pain-free, and more productive than it had ever before been. Perhaps the next golden age of medicine will emerge from a new environment of public awareness and participation in what is done in our name, a new public determination to monitor medicine as a safe and effective human resource.

Charles B. Inlander
President, People's Medical Society

PREFACE

How often one hears it said that America enjoys the finest medical care in the world. This is true in part because it is our parents who first define our heroes for us. As a consequence, public perception of who are positive and who negative role models tends to lag behind reality by a generation or so. While some point out that in modern America the availability of that care to all the people at a fair price leaves something to be desired, few have publicly criticized the quality of that care. In fact we take substantial national pride in our technical accomplishments in medicine and relish the leadership of our medical scientists. There is a special aura about medicine in general and American medicine in particular. The American approach to medical education we believe to be superior to any other, allegedly selecting America's most talented youth and subjecting them to rigorous (although narrow) standards of performance. A select few are privileged to receive the special designation *doctor of medicine*, a degree that admits its bearer to a level of social rights and privilege unprecedented in any other field of endeavor. So special is this recognition that of all those to whom our academic community awards doctorates, in so many varied fields, only the M.D. is considered a "real" doctor. Our doctors deal with the core of life, possessing a unique franchise on services that are often essential for survival. Theirs is a serious business, demanding a unique and complex talent to diagnose and treat disease. They are privy to one's most intimate aspects and have access to an awesome array of powerful interventions affecting both mind and body. And we trust our doctors to use their considerable skills with competence, wisdom, and compassion. Indeed, we do more than trust in our doctors. We have *faith* in them. Often blind faith, especially at those times we are most vulnerable and have no alternatives—or so we think. Our collective anxiety about being without adequate medical care is unlike any other fear of potential deprivation, with perhaps the exception of adequate food and shelter.

Concern about access to educational, legal, and even religious resources pales by comparison with where medicine stands on our list of essentials.

We cannot afford *not* to have faith in the medical care system. It commands us to believe in its integrity. Thus, we tend to avoid information that could erode our confidence in medical care in general, and especially in our own doctor. We allow ourselves to chide the profession for its greed or for failures to communicate or to make house calls. But these weaknesses we perceive as human foibles at a level most of us experience in our own work. They are artifacts of medical practice and are not the central issues of quality.

Doctors over recent generations have established the ground rules for patient behavior, especially regarding the patient's relationship to (and critique of) the doctor. Many of us are taught (or intuit) that it is not good form to play too active a role, never mind a contentious one. Questions to doctors should be polite and deferential, acknowledging their superior knowledge and the wisdom of experience. If we are irritated with the doctor's demeanor in any way or left with any uneasy feeling that something is not right in the care being given, we might save our gripes for relatives or friends. Challenging the doctor is simply too difficult, too embarrassing, too fraught (we believe) with the potential for retribution.

The passive doctor-patient relationship is easily extended to our relationship with the health care system as a whole. This is most true in fee-for-service situations. However, prepaid medical care plans like health maintenance organizations have provided an unplanned benefit; they have to some degree converted certain aspects of the patient-doctor relationship to that of consumer-provider, an economic model that invites more active criticism of the system, at least from the standpoint of costs, convenience, and customer satisfaction. Still, these concerns are usually directed to the business office or customer service representative, not to the doctors themselves. So, fundamentally, nothing has really changed with regard to the patient's right to question the quality of care, its safety, its appropriateness, and its effectiveness. These matters still remain beyond the reach (and certainly beyond the control) of the patient, the customer, the victim of medical mistakes.

Public health officials and clinical epidemiologists have been observing and reporting on the limits and hazards of medical care for years. Their studies mainly are published in scholarly journals and occasionally (when especially dramatic) get reported on television news shows and "specials." The daily press and television pick up on human interest stories of medical mishaps, particularly when celebrities are involved. And, of course, ordinary citizens learn about the tragedy of medical mistakes from personal experience, but have no real way of knowing that tens of thousands of others have been subject to the same abuse.

My colleagues and I set about to correct the inadequate and imbalanced flow of information on medical mistakes. We undertook this task in the belief that creating an informed public is the first step down the road to reforming the medical care system. It is amply clear that the medical care system, on its own, is not capable of significant and sustained efforts to improve the quality of its services. It simply has too much at stake in preserving benefits to its own members. Government's role has not been much more effective, given the overlap of interests between the profession of medicine, the industries that benefit from profitable medical care, and the so-called regulatory agencies, whose members have close links with those they are supposed to regulate.

Real improvements in the safety and quality of care demand public accountability and active public participation in oversight, and the process begins with an informed public. The "social charter" of medicine, found partly in state laws and partly in the unwritten codes of civility and public trust, must be brought to public consciousness and public debate. There is no other viable way to bring the health care system into line with the public expectations for safe, high-quality medical care. People must know what is going on, what is going bad, and what needs to be done to preserve the best of the system while getting rid of its flaws.

Nearly two years of reviewing literally hundreds of studies and commentaries on medical mistakes was a sobering experience. We were appalled at the extent of the problem. All aspects of the medical care process and all dimensions of care were implicated. We were jarred by the data on the seriousness of the consequences of medical mistakes in terms of both human suffering and monetary costs. And there was the galling discovery that the major source of error was not complex, exotic, or mysterious, but commonplace human behavior. Finally and probably most frustrating was our growing sense of the long and continuing history of indifference, cover-up, and tokenism in controlling avoidable medical mistakes. Putting the picture together, we became aware that the whole was indeed greater than the sum of the parts.

It was obvious that the story of medical mistakes could not be presented effectively in a second-hand way. The truly unconscionable state of affairs could best be presented by citing research findings in a straightforward way, with our own comments limited to what is necessary for emphasis, linking, and continuity. Chapters 1 through 12 present the evidence, study after study drawn from the medical literature itself. Interpretive critiques from outstanding medical scholars bear expert witness to the gravity of the situation.

Clearly, any proposed solution to the medical mistake crisis must take an approach that addresses the entire web of complicit factors and forces. They include institutionalized, heavily entrenched attitudes and practices that in many cases will require radical surgery aimed at the very structure of medical education and the medical care system. Other barriers to change are more subtle in their influence. Most crucial is the political will necessary to move toward an agenda for change. In chapter 13 we offer specific proposals for reform in medical education, licensing, regulation of practice, and full and continuous public disclosure of information on the quality of medical care. The latter is the essential factor that can help people regain control of their medical care services.

We have no illusions about a quick turnaround by those who have a vested interest in the status quo, although as the public becomes more vocal in its outrage and more impatient with inaction, the establishment can be expected to offer pious statements of concern and even offer some mild palliatives. *Caveat emptor.* Public pressure must be steadfast in seeking a structure for accountability in medical education and medical practice that is unequivocably and securely under public control. But first the public must overcome its own reticence to criticize, to challenge, and to confront the medical establishment. Our hope is that the evidence of misconduct, malfeasance, and mayhem perpetrated on a trusting public can stimulate and focus public action toward lasting reform.

Lowell S. Levin
New Haven

INTRODUCTION

"The medical profession is unconsciously irritated by lay knowledge."
—John Steinbeck

This book is about lay knowledge. It is about professional knowledge, too—or, rather, the lack of it. Mostly it is about the medical profession's paucity of self-knowledge, and the nonprofessionalism and incompetence that go hand in hand with it. The result is harm and calamity to countless people, patients and medical personnel alike. This book is about what happens when unbridled ego, contemptuous stonewalling, and distorted socialization stand in the way of the public good and the citizenry's right to know.

This book provides what amounts to a profound indictment of many aspects of the way medicine is practiced in America, and of many of those who practice it. We hope to show the range and depth of medical mistakes in this country, and our documentation provides evidence that most medical failures are not the result of bad luck but are rooted in individual incompetence, misplaced emphasis, poor skills, greed, and the failure of the medical profession to acknowledge its weaknesses and correct them. We demonstrate how the medical profession has systematically allowed known incompetents to practice, making mistake upon mistake, threatening life upon life.

Our data were studiously and carefully accumulated, for when non-doctors criticize doctors or the medical profession in general, these people are immediately labeled "irrational" or "antidoctor"; if, in their argument, these same critics cite examples to substantiate their points, they are dismissed as being "anecdotal" and not relying on scientific facts and truths. With that in mind, we have acted as researchers, reporters, and conveyers of information. Indeed, for the most part, the evidence we present comes from the medical literature itself—from physicians, medical educators, medical researchers, and experts in the field of medicine. We cite studies from the world's most respected medical journals, health publications, and books.

What is appalling to us is that the facts we've found have been available to the profession for years. It's been right in front of their eyes, and yet they did not see. That they chose not to see—and then not to act in a responsible, honorable, and humane way—is the only conclusion that makes any sense. If we could find those facts and those studies and understand what they said and implied, the medical profession could—and should—have been able to do so.

That's not to say that all of them were blind. Some doctors and researchers saw and wrote about the dangers. As you read the chapters in this book, in which we've quoted some of these doctors, you'll note the tone of utter frustration in their voices. Here are highly respected medical professionals who have mustered the courage to speak out about problems in hopes that the profession they love will see its faults and heal itself.

To what end? Their pleas and suggestions and well-documented demonstrations of once-and-future hazards have for the most part been ignored or ridiculed, and some of those who spoke out have suffered personal or professional ostracism and calumny and been branded "heretics" or "quacks."

And all the while the experts have gone unheeded, medical consumers have suffered. Unsuspecting consumers have been battered by drunk or doped-up doctors. Their ills have been misdiagnosed by poorly trained physicians. They have had procedures performed on them on the basis of incorrect test results. The list of indignities is almost as long as the list of patients.

This book is a clarification and a condemnation of those indignities. That's all fine and good; there is a place and a need for the bad news to be made public. But that certainly is not enough. After perusing the litany of offenses, surely the question that needs to be asked and then answered is: What can be done to cure medicine?

In the last section of this book we offer that cure, a prescription for change. We are well aware that some within the medical profession will attempt to discredit us and what we propose. Others will deny that a problem even exists. They will say our proposals are radical.

Our proposals *are* radical, but only because they are new and different and forward thinking, and because they shatter the long-held notion that the only people allowed to alter the practice of medicine are the people who practice it. Our "radical" proposals state that the people who should—and, indeed, must—alter the practice of medicine are the people it is practiced on. Our proposals will be considered radical because they are, first and foremost, of, by, and for consumers.

It is not our intention to attack the medical profession just for the sake of angering its defenders or for the joy of slinging stones at Goliath. Our sole purpose in writing this book is to improve the outcome of medicine. The medical world has failed in its attempts to improve and patrol its practice and practitioners, and then has doubly failed in its efforts to cover up the failures.

The facts are out. The ''secrets'' of medical mistakes are presented here for everyone—consumer and provider—to see. To disregard the wishes and the will of the recipients of care is no longer viable; it just can't be done.

It is time for a change. And that change is going to come from the people.

Now, it's our turn.

II

EVIDENCE AND EXPERT TESTIMONY

1

SICK AND TIRED

"It is certain that physicians who harm themselves also directly or indirectly harm their patients."

—Jack D. McCue, M.D.

The doctor is a drunk and everybody knows it. His breath announces the fact. His eyes emphasize it. His hands shake, too, and this is very bad news, because the doctor is a heart surgeon.

The doctor is a drunk and everybody knows it. Only through some quick action and cover-ups have operating room staffs prevented hit-and-run surgical "accidents" from occurring when the doctor sliced and stitched while under the influence. His colleagues are aware of his illness and its dangers; their entire strategy in dealing with it is simply to invoke a kind of professional benign neglect. What they do to keep him from doing harm is to avoid referring their own patients to this surgeon. That's the way these things are done—privately, protected, quietly. Yet, despite this, the doctor is in the hospital every day and he is cutting open patients' chests—sometimes several times a day, conveniently scheduled in between secretive sessions with a bottle, in his office, in his car, poured in a cup of coffee he carries down the hall to a consultation. *Somebody* must be referring patients to him. Besides, anybody can elect to contract his services. His name is still in the Yellow Pages, and it is on the list given out by the hospital to people looking for help in finding a board-certified surgeon.

The doctor is a drunk and everybody knows it—except the patients. And they are the ones who will suffer at his agitated hands. One—and probably more—of them will have to die before this doctor is finally stopped . . . for a while.

What's worse, the doctor is not alone. It may be instructive to place him in the proper perspective:

• Of the doctors in practice today, somewhere between 22,600 and 36,600 are alcoholics, recovering alcoholics, or soon-to-be alcoholics.[1]

• "Alcoholism is a primary disease to which physicians, as a group, seem highly susceptible, and often goes hand in hand with drug abuse," states Stephen C. Scheiber, M.D., director of psychological residency training at the University of Arizona College of Medicine in Tucson, and coeditor with Brian B. Doyle of *The Impaired Physician* (Plenum Press, 1983).[2]

• One study that spanned two decades of investigation found that doctors tend to take more drugs—specifically, tranquilizers, sedatives, and stimulants—than do nondoctors. And it has been known for just about as long that narcotics addiction runs 30 to 100 times higher among physicians than in the general population. According to a 1975 report, "about one out of every six known drug addicts in the United States, England, Holland, France, and Germany is a doctor."[3] While the dramatic increase in drug dependency within the general population over the past fifteen years may have changed this percentage, it remains shocking, even for that time.

• "Between 10 percent and 13 percent of the nation's . . . physicians will have a substance abuse problem sometime during their lives."[4]

• According to David E. Smith, M.D., who is in charge of a California-based chemical dependency recovery facility, drug addiction among doctors is increasing, and "prescription drug abuse by doctors is four times the national average, and their cocaine use has increased tenfold since 1980."[5]

• In fact, a Harvard University study that looked at 500 practicing physicians and 504 medical students found that:

>—59 percent of the physicians and 78 percent of the med students reported they had used psychoactive drugs at some time in their lives (figures higher than among pharmacists and pharmacy students, who might be expected to have even greater access to drugs than doctors and med students).

>—Drugs used in a recreational way by these physicians and physicians-to-be were usually marijuana and cocaine.

>—Drugs they administered to themselves in a course of self-treatment involved tranquilizers and opiates.

>—During the year completed before the study, 25 percent of the doctors had treated themselves with psychoactive drugs and 10 percent had used one of these mind-altering drugs in a recreational manner.

>—10 percent of the physicians admitted current regular drug use occurring once a month or more often.

>—Nearly 40 percent of doctors under age 40 got high with friends.

>—3 percent of the physicians and 5 percent of the medical school students reported that they were drug addicts at some time— and the study's authors believe that the number of drug-taking

physicians in practice will grow as med students take their habits into the world of patients with them.[6]

And this study came on the heels of another, showing that of 133 senior medical students, "noteworthy proportions" had used the following psychoactive substances: alcohol, 96 percent; marijuana, 57 percent; amphetamines, 22 percent; cocaine, 20 percent; sedatives, 17 percent; benzodiazepines (Valium), 37 percent; hallucinogens, 15 percent; and opioids, 40 percent. What's more, according to the researchers, "Twelve percent reported nearly daily use of one or more substances during the last month; a different but overlapping eleven percent reported substance abuse symptoms during the last year."[7]

• And, finally, perhaps the most shocking, sickening, and frightening statistic: The United States "loses the equivalent of seven medical-school graduating classes each year to drug addiction, alcoholism, and suicide."[8]

It is one thing to say that, at a minimum, 5 to 10 percent of physicians in America are incompetent to practice medicine because of addictive, psychological, psychiatric, or other problems. It is another to visualize that percentage, to grasp what it means, to see the big picture. This may be clearer: If one were to accept just the lowest percentage estimate of incompetent doctors, that would mean that patients visit and are treated by one of these ticking time-bomb physicians at least 45 million times every year.[9] Some studies put that figure at 100 million patient visits.[10]

This means 45 to 100 million chances for someone to become a tragic statistic. It is a chilling lottery to win.

Roots

Where does the addicted doctor come from? Where and how does the addiction begin?

According to some theories of psychology, there is what may be called an "addictive personality," described by Scheiber as a "set of character traits all addicts—be they substance abusers or gamblers—seem to share. Some of these traits—the need for recognition, a strong personal drive, high ambition, a sense of separateness from the mainstream of humanity and frequently unfulfilled expectations—seem particularly strong among physicians as a group."[11]

The addictive personality grabs a foothold early on. Alcohol and/or drug abuse is often a way of life—be it a minor or major component—even before the young person becomes the new medical student. Medical school admissions panels are not adept at either identifying or weeding out the addict applicant. Even if they recognize that there is a "problem," they may not consider it overly important. Take, for example, the case of Martha Morrison. (Morrison has written of her own experience in *Finally Free: One Woman Doctor's 17-Year Battle with Drug Addiction,* Crown, 1988.)

Martha Morrison had been injecting drugs for eight years and was totally drug dependent before she filed her medical school application (she'd started taking the painkiller Darvon for migraines when she was 12, and soon after was using and dealing LSD, marijuana, and amphetamines).[12] She had been confined to a psychiatric ward three times before she was a freshman in college. Despite all this, Morrison was admitted to medical school because her premed grades pleased the medical school admissions officials, who were willing to overlook the drugs.[13]

Morrison, as it turns out, was one of the lucky ones: After taking drugs throughout medical school and later (17 years worth of abuse, to be exact, ending when her body simply gave out after her inability to get high on a superloaded addictive regimen of a dozen different drugs a day plus booze —once even injecting pure-grain alcohol), losing 50 pounds, and blacking out three times in six months while driving, she received and accepted help and is now a psychiatrist at the University of Arkansas Medical Center. How many of her patients at the time of her addiction had equally lucky ends is not known.

Morrison's is not an isolated case. While most of the nonmedicinal drug users in medical school are older students (and men in particular), drug-use patterns "appear to have developed in high school and college, and to persist, albeit at a diminished rate, during medical school."[14] The wide use of drugs in a social, recreational way (as alcohol has been utilized for years) occurs especially among those med students and doctors who have grown up since the 1960s.

As medical school students move into internships and residencies, and then into practice, the stress and fatigue of their work load may contribute to new or further drug and/or alcohol use and abuse and psychiatric problems. "Each day physicians encounter stresses that are an intrinsic part of medical practice," writes Jack D. McCue, M.D., Department of Medicine, University of North Carolina at Chapel Hill. "Those who are vulnerable may become unable to practice medicine without the intrusion of seriously neurotic or inappropriate behavior: That is, they become impaired physicians."[15] Like Morrison, they may turn to drink or drugs or both "for sedation, for pain, for detachment, for the high, for euphoria, for fatigue, for depression, for anxiety, to quell feelings of inadequacy."[16] McCue also notes that "up to half the students who eventually graduate need psychotherapy, a smaller but substantial percentage actually receive it. Suicides are second in number only to accidents as a cause of death among medical students."[17]

Harvard Medical School's Edward J. Khantzian, M.D., remarks, "Most substance-dependent physicians' problems represent a condition in which the complex motives involved in choosing medicine as a career have interacted with self-regulation deficits not unique to physicians."[18]

What goes on in the practice of medicine that drives many physicians to drink, drugs, and mental illness? Some of the blame may find its origin early in doctoring life—in the unnatural sleep deprivation and distortion of sleep patterns forced on interns while on hospital duty. Sometimes these young practitioners are "on" as much as 36 to 48 or more hours at a time, leading some observer/critics to wonder whether this is indeed preparation (and preparation for what?) or some sort of frat hazing to see if the "pledges" have the emotional and physical wherewithal—if they have what it takes—to be a member of the club. But it's a hazing that too often backfires, taking doctor and patient together in the recoil. One study conducted at Columbia University[19] noted that when interns were deprived of sleep—as they often are—they:

• Were far less able than usual to recognize arrhythmias based on electrocardiograph readings.
• Suffered significant mood alteration—they showed greater sadness and less energy and confidence. Displays of social affection also decreased.
• Developed numerous psychopathological symptoms, and felt that they had acquired abnormal patterns of thought and perception, along with physiological abnormalities.

Another study, this one conducted by the Department of Psychiatry, Washington University School of Medicine in St. Louis, discovered that of 53 first-year residents, 30 percent had experienced depression during their internship, four had thought of committing suicide, three had actually devised a workable plan to kill themselves, and six who had never before had marital problems suddenly developed them. Thirty-one percent of this group also said that if they had to do it all over again, they would not choose medicine as a career. The researchers, looking for reasons for this large number of depressed and disenchanted young practitioners, found, among other things, that the "onset of their depression generally occurred at the beginning of their internship on a service with a higher number of working hours per week," and that this was something that needed to be and could be changed.[20]

The effects of this traditional trainee sleep deprivation have been likened to what happens to long-run airline pilots who experience jet lag. Rolf Paulson, M.D., in a letter to the *Journal of the American Medical Asso-*

ciation, writes that medical researchers investigating jet lag among fliers would do well to look closer to home: "hospital nurses, house staff, emergency room staff, and others—those who are entrusted in large degree with the care of hospital inpatients." Paulson urges that changes be made in the erratic and counterproductive work hours put in by interns and others, changes that "might reverse some of the major problems in health care in the present and near future."[21] And a panel assembled in the summer of 1987 by New York State Health Commissioner David Axelrod recommended a ceiling of 16 hours per shift for the state's medical residents—a recommendation that led to protests by hospitals and some medical education institutions. Other groups urged weekly and even monthly total work limits in addition to those for consecutive hours on duty.[22]

Lack of sleep among interns on long shifts impairs their efficiency and puts their patients at risk. The long hours at the same time lead to depression, fatigue, and marital problems. These, in turn, lead to drugs or drink, in order to pep up, calm down, or presumably increase clarity of thought to maintain quality levels. They also lead to what one doctor calls "a failure of will," which David Hilfiker, M.D., describes as "the worst kind of mistake," one in which a doctor "knows the right thing to do but doesn't do it because he is distracted, or pressured, or exhausted."[23]

Moreover, the medical student and house-staff training environment "generally neglects the personal growth and development of the physician and fails to provide effective and nonstigmatized assistance during times of stress," writes John-Henry Pfifferling, Ph.D. "This combination of factors, namely, an unaware population subjected to conditions of overwork, neglect of personal growth, and inadequate personal support with unrealistic performance expectations, often leads to inappropriate coping responses and subsequent burnout and impairment."[24]

Then, too, a stressful situation is created when the physician or physician-to-be, in the course of practice or training, uncovers deficiencies in himself, chinks in his "infallible" armor. "Skillful treatment of illness and fear requires reassurance, the most important medicine disposed by a physician," writes McCue. "Reassuring patients effectively, especially when they are excessively anxious, requires special techniques and skills; since these are rarely taught well in medical training, physicians are forced to spend their time doing what they have been poorly trained to do."[25] The gap is galling and, occasionally, debilitating.

Khantzian thinks that doctors' overachievement complex and ego bluster are actually smoke screens and compensation for "self-esteem problems," but that these devices to mask insecurity and uncertainty are insufficient. "Subsequent challenges in life and the insults and disappointments in their work, family life, friendships, and health precipitate crises and make any sense of well-being that their careers provided elusive. At such times of crisis and distress, individuals discover the short-term uplifting and pain-relieving effects of drugs and alcohol.''[26]

Two other factors may contribute to the depression and inability to cope that lead too many doctors down the road to psychological disturbance and substance dependency. One is that many doctors, for whatever reason—money, prestige, ego gratification, external pressures, or a bit of each—are choosing the wrong specialties. For example, one doctor, whose social drinking turned into a binge that ended with his attempted suicide from a sleeping-pill overdose, has been described as "a brilliant neurosurgeon who had no business being a neurosurgeon. There are so many losses (in neurosurgery) that you have to have a hard shell and he had none.''[27] Other doctors, bored, out of their league, depressed at being financially and socially trapped in a subspecialty that provides limited gratification on the one hand and a feeling of isolation on the other, are also prime candidates for "escape" via unacceptable, harrowing, and hazardous routes. (It should be noted for the record that the specialists who most often become drug addicts are anesthesiologists, while those who have family and general medicine practices top the list of alcoholics.[28])

The other, more elemental factor is that too many doctors simply should never have become doctors at all. They drink, take drugs, have mental breakdowns, and burn out quickly—all outgrowths of their basic career misplacement, maladjustment, tension, unhappiness, and fear.

And it is so simple for a doctor to attain and maintain a dependency; as Martha Weinman Lear writes, doctors have always become addicted so easily, "and doctors could stay addicted so gracefully: take out the prescription pad, write the order, a little of the sweet, spacy stuff for Doc's nasty old bursitis.''[29]

While not a dependency or strictly a psychoemotional problem, age can be another component of physician impairment. Not keeping up with current standards, physical infirmity (trembling hands, dimming vision, hearing loss, and others), and mental fuzziness may all afflict the physician whose advanced years are taking their toll. Many of these older physicians are as competent as their younger colleagues, and may be more so because of their years of experience. However, an older doctor who is unable to admit that his professional days are over poses as much of a threat as any other physician with an impairment and impediment to safe and satisfactory practice. Cities and towns in the warm and sunny South and Southwest may have more of such doctors. As a member of Arizona's Board of Medical Examiners explains, "A lot of physicians who come to Arizona to retire like to be licensed. Some like to practice a while, too." This same official explained the difficulty in policing age-impaired physicians: "We don't have any system to let us know who's senile and who isn't. We don't periodically go through our files and look at birth dates. And besides, just because a physician is 75, it doesn't mean he's going to be senile."[30] For the most part, the only person who determines if a doctor is fit to practice is that doctor himself, and he is hardly in a position to make an objective—or frequently even a lucid—judgment.

Signs, Roadblocks, Detours, and Dead Ends

Besides the obvious signs of an addiction or impairment that might be detected by the cautious layperson, there are those that are known to, and by now are familiar to, many medical professionals. The typical picture, says Daniel A. Lang, M.D., of the Los Angeles County Medical Association, usually contains these:

- Occasional unavailability.
- The poorly communicated nocturnal phone order.
- The lapse in judgment.
- Inadequate notes.
- Incomplete medical records.

"From this beginning," explains Lang, "may grow major problems as errors compound; interpersonal relations fail as guilt is projected on others. The conviviality of the professional social alcoholic is lost as the image of the unreliable peer emerges."[31]

In many cases, the doctor has simply lost touch with himself. Not surprisingly, doctors who are alcoholics or are morbidly depressed may not have a tremendous amount of insight regarding their problem. Others may be all too aware of their ruinous slide and preoccupation but may not be able to bring themselves to ask a local colleague or friend for help. These doctors might be willing "to accept aid from further afield, but may not be sure whom to contact or may lack the initiative."[32]

Impaired physicians may lose the sharpness of their skill and, later, that skill itself, but one ability that is not lost—that is, in fact, enhanced— is that of lying. Dissembling, hiding, skulking, covering up, concealing their habit, obtaining surreptitious fixes within the context of their practices—impaired physicians may, out of muddled desperation, become masters of deceit. Martha Morrison, according to writer Dennis L. Breo, was so good at it, she was able to fool her colleagues and professors during eight years of training, "a time when she not only used drugs heavily but also helped teach the medical-school course on substance abuse. She was so good at cover-up that she even fooled her former husband, who was a professor of pharmacology.''[33]

Beyond the personal cover-up are massive and corrupt professional and institutional cover-ups. Even though a doctor may show undeniable, crystal-clear signs of impairment, his colleagues, ''while experiencing growing concern, may hesitate to take action which might be construed as meddlesome or disloyal and instead develop a kind of protective collusion with the doctor.''[34] Linda Fisher, M.D., of the Missouri State Board of Healing Arts, calls it nothing less than a ''conspiracy of silence.''[35] And, citing statistics showing that the public sector is far more concerned about and adept at spotting and censuring impaired physicians than the medical establishment is, Herrington and Jacobson in the *Journal of the American Medical Association* state: ''We do our patients, our professions, and our troubled colleagues no favor by pretending not to see that which is so prevalent today.'' These statistics show that of the 98 alcoholic doctors studied, 49 percent of them had been arrested at least once while drunk, 37.8 percent had been jailed, and 19.4 percent had lost their drivers' licenses—and while these figures and incidents were there for all to see, the public's response to this ''occurred more often and with a larger number of formal indications of disapprobation than did the professional response, as represented by warnings from medical societies and licensing boards, loss of hospital privileges, and actual loss of medical license.''[36]

In *The Malpractitioners,* journalist John Guinther writes: ''Just as policemen rarely if ever report their fellow cops to the authorities for brutalizing a prisoner, many doctors seem to consider it violative of club rules to report a doctor who brutalizes his patients with bad treatment, even though theoretically they are obligated to do so; says the AMA's Principles of Ethics: 'A physician should expose, without fear or favor, incompetent or corrupt, dishonest or unethical conduct on the part of members of the profession.' ''[37] Guinther and many others note the form this ''exposing'' usually takes, and the part hospitals play in this game of cover-up: The incompetent, impaired, and/or dangerous doctor is permitted to resign instead of being fired, thus allowing him to affiliate himself with another hospital, perhaps one in the same city, possibly even the same neighborhood. Not only does the hospital the doctor is leaving never report the doctor's failings, illness, or hazard to the appropriate agencies or to the hospital to which the doctor is going, it may even write a letter of recommendation for him. And even if the doctor is disciplined and fired— even if, in the rarest of circumstances, he has his license to practice in that state revoked—he can just move on to another state. Writes Robert C. Coe, M.D., in a letter to the *Journal of the American Medical Association:*

These physicians migrate. They have certification indicating the granting of a medical degree and thereby have a commodity that is in demand. This commodity is respected, as it should be; therefore, they have an entrée into the licensing procedure. By the very nature of the offense that led to the initial revocation, they fall into a category that makes the use of subterfuge easy in an attempt to regain the social status, mode of living, and income that characterizes the American physician.

This escapism must be stopped. These migrators carry their disease throughout the country. . . . Relicensing *in another state* is not a cure but an entrenchment.[38]

Although most states have "sick doctor amendments" giving state licensing boards the power to stop impaired physicians before they do terminal harm,[39] these statutes are worthless if medical professionals won't report sick colleagues and if hospitals quietly edge addicted, impaired doctors out the back door with their implied blessings and a curse on somebody else's house. When the New York State Health Department, for example, examined the situation within its jurisdiction it discovered "a grave underreporting of physician impairment and incompetence."[40] A further, ironic end-run tactic to avoid informing state agencies about doctors' impairment is the co-opting of the doctor-patient confidentiality relationship; that is, a physician who is treating an impaired physician may conveniently and relievedly consider it a violation of his patient's trust to inform a state agency or anybody else about that impaired physician's mental, physical, or emotional problems. Although it's everybody's business, confidentiality says it's nobody's business—and in that dark cloud of secrecy it remains.

It is also clear that physicians could and should blow the whistle, kindly but firmly, respectfully but definitely, on their age-impaired colleagues, but they usually don't—except, as has been the case, where and when the younger doctors' own finances are concerned and threatened. Robertson tells us of several physician-owned malpractice insurance companies that have "adopted a policy of mandating both a physical examination and a psychological examination of all physicians aged 65 and over," and that this action has been prompted "by their individual and collective claims loss experience."[41] In other words, the major and perhaps the only time doctors get concerned about their older and age-impaired confreres is when it hits them in the pocketbook or stock portfolio. Money talks, even if physicians don't.

There are well-established treatment routes for the impaired physician, not only on the local level but nationally. A handful of magnet rehabilitation centers, to which impaired physicians from all over the country can go, exist in such places as the Mayo Clinic and Atlanta's Ridgeview Institute. In their own localities, doctors may receive help from medical society–sponsored programs. New rehabilitation programs in New York, New Jersey, and Connecticut designed to help physicians overcome their substance abuse include random urine testing for drugs and alcohol without prior notice several times a month.[42]

But these programs are useful only if the entire medical community supports them. "Physicians have a great deal of difficulty saying they have a disease," says G. Douglas Talbott, M.D., who heads Ridgeview,[43] and that points up the problem: If a doctor doesn't know or won't admit that he is ill, and if none of his colleagues will blow the whistle, someone is bound to get hurt—physician first, patient second. It is well known that "impaired physician programs report a low level of self-referrals, and these are not likely to increase significantly."[44]

Only the deepest of fears can force many doctors into a program, and that fear is the loss of the very thing that may have led the physician to drugs, drink, or instability in the first place. As one physician has noted, "The retention of their license is the most important thing to them. They will lose their family or their money, but they want their license. We use that as a coercion to get them into treatment. It's much more effective than anything."[45] It may not be the fear of loss of income that panics these doctors so much as it is the symbolic loss of a self-supposed superiority their breakdowns clearly show they do not believe they have or cannot handle with a clear mind or conscience.

The goal of impaired physician rehabilitation programs—besides the ostensible one of saving a practitioner and getting him back on his diagnostic and therapeutic feet—is professional autonomy. While autonomy may be defined as "the right and capability of the medical staff to act independently of the hospital board in the interest of its membership . . . [by subordinating] the right of the individual to the needs of the group . . ."[46] what it also, and perhaps primarily, seems to mean is, "We damn well better handle or cover up this problem ourselves, or else the government is going to move in, and then our special status and privilege and historically asserted independence all go down the drain." Just as the American Medical Association in 1984 felt compelled to announce a so-called and not very effective "voluntary" freeze of physicians' fees in order to stave off government-imposed pay limits, so, too, the medical profession wants to keep the physician impairment problem safely tucked within the folds of its good old boys system and keep the trust-busting reformers out. Thus, there are glowing statistics of impaired physician programs' effectiveness, claiming anywhere from 50 to 90 percent success rates, depending on the article read.[47] There are doubters, though, and not only among medical consumer groups and some parts of government; in fact, one major study concluded: "Treatment outcome, in general, for impaired physicians has been assumed to be better than for other drug abusers but the studies have lacked adequate controls, need broader outcome measures, and may not be relevant to the new type of [recreational drug] abuser [who primarily uses drugs for euphoria and tends to be a polysubstance abuser]."[48]

What's more, the profession's lust for autonomy means a news blackout beyond its own narrowly defined borders. A survey of impaired physician programs revealed that "medical society programs rarely notify hospitals of physician staff members who are severely impaired"[49]—all in the name of autonomy, of protecting their own. Some view this as arrogance. Others, like Lang, worry that "anonymity begets irresponsibility and invites regression. . . ."[50]

Startlingly, flat-out denial may be organized medicine's latest tactic to keep the regulatory wolves at bay. In a well-positioned 1986 "State of the Art/Review" in the *Journal of the American Medical Association,* the proposal was put forth that physicians might not really have substance abuse problems after all, that since "statements regarding the prevalence of problems with alcohol and other drugs among physicians have often been made without firm empirical support," then "it must be concluded that the prevalence of drug problems among physicians is unknown."[51]

This is dangerous logic—to believe that the problem does not exist until a future study says it does, that the problem's severity is dubious until the statistically significant yardstick is set in place. Although it may put government off the track for a while, it may do the same for impaired physicians who see this as further proof that there is nothing wrong with them. Complicating the matter is that officially sanctioned medical disciplinary boards just can't or won't try to help solve the problem either. For example, Oregon's Board of Medical Examiners, considered one of the best in the United States, "is limited by legal and budgetary constraints from engaging in certain activities, for example, educating physicians about substance abuse."[52]

This is exactly the scenario that worries Martha Morrison, who warns, "If nothing is done to increase alcohol awareness among medical students and physicians, my story will become the norm, and alcoholic [medical professionals] will never get the care they need."[53]

A Postscript on Professions

Although this chapter has concentrated primarily on the impairment problem among physicians, such debilitation is not, among the health professions, solely a doctors' dilemma. For example, according to Madeline

Naegle, Ph.D., R.N., associate professor at Pace University's Lienhard School of Nursing, and chairperson of the American Nursing Association's Committee on Impaired Nursing Practice, who admits her statistics are probably on the low side:[54]

* Of the 1.9 million registered nurses in the United States, about 6 percent have alcohol or other drug dependencies.
* Approximately 100,000 chemically impaired nurses are in the work force.
* From 1980 to 1986, about 1,500 nurses nationally were put on probation for drug-related problems; 1,260 had their licenses suspended; and 1,038 had their licenses revoked.

O'Connor and Robinson, writing in *Nursing Administration Quarterly,* add:[55]

* Of the 10 to 12 percent of nurses with serious personal problems, more than half can trace their difficulties to alcohol and drug abuse.
* And impaired nurses, each making about $18,000 to $20,000 a year, can cost their employers—and, thus, society in general—$50,000 to $75,000 a year in sick leave abuse, health insurance claims, inefficiency in medication and supplies dispensing as well as in patient care, the cost of training and paying replacements, and many other charges.

Naegle further notes that although "conditions such as depression and organic brain syndrome compromise professional ability, data suggest that alcoholism or drug dependence is the most frequent cause of practicing while impaired."[56]

And, like doctors, the nurses leave a trail strewn with clues of impairment for their colleagues to see—if they would only look, or do something when they noticed. It would be difficult for nurses' co-workers not to pick up on the obvious signs that, in many instances, the patients can discern:[57]

* Absenteeism.
* Frequent and unexplained absences from the nurses' station or patient areas.
* Confusion.
* Sloppy, undecipherable record and chart keeping.
* Judgment errors, especially when it comes to the dispensing of controlled substances.
* Mood swings.
* Continual poor hygiene or personal grooming.

- Withdrawal from relationships and development of social isolation.
- Problems with narcotics counts and drug wastage.
- Forgetful behavior that may indicate memory loss or periods of blackout.

Because they are in a position to roam freely throughout a hospital and its storerooms, and because they are in charge of direct patient care and the dispensing of medications, nurses have the means and opportunity to satisfy their motives—doing everything from taking prescriptions that are no longer being used for patients who are off the drugs or have been dismissed and having them filled for themselves to forging signatures to keeping the drugs for themselves and giving patients look-alikes or place-bos.

Pharmacists, too, practice while impaired, and while in that condition may "[dispense] the wrong medication, dispense the wrong strength of a medication, make a labeling error, or fail to detect a serious drug-drug interaction, resulting in injury to the patient."[58]

Doctor, nurse, pharmacist—the impaired practitioner is no isolated, ravaged victim suddenly struck down without warning but rather, as Donald A. Bloch, M.D., director of the Ackerman Institute for Family Therapy, so accurately points out, "the symptom carrier for a malfunctioning work system." He adds that burnout and impairment among doctors, nurses, pharmacists, and others "is never a characteristic of or within an individual but rather, it is a complex of psychological characteristics that reflect features of the larger society"—the medical society, in this case—and that these "wounded healers" have fallen prey to "contextual factors that contribute to the continuation of organizational structures and philosophical viewpoints that foster the burnout and impairment of health professionals."[59]

That is, the system of medical education, of medical practice, of medical discipline is sick, and the participants in that system may and frequently do fall ill from that systemic sickness. The entire chain of medical professions is vulnerable, and as long as it is so, and permitted to be so either by inaction or purposeful action, then vulnerable, too, will be the patient kept in the dark by an autonomous, monolithic, protective structure that persists in flicking off the light of fact and information.

2

·······························

THE MACHINERIES
OF JOY?

" . . . an American Medical Association publication for doctors relates the tale of an engineer who was called in by a doctor whose electrocardiograph was not recording the heart action of a patient. The technician came promptly. He started his check at the electrical outlet and worked back slowly to the connection to the patient in the next room—and found the patient dead. No one had even noticed that the patient's heart itself had stopped."

—Arthur S. Freese in *Managing Your Doctor*

The first true piece of modern patient-care medical technology was the stethoscope. It was back in 1819 that René Laënnec, a French doctor, displayed and demonstrated his crude but effective listening device. A plain long wood tube, it allowed the doctor to remove his ear from direct contact with the patient's chest. This not only replaced an awkward, unsanitary, and frankly embarrassing diagnostic act with one that was cleaner and more refined and *au courant* but also was a symbolic act that neither Laënnec nor any of his contemporaries probably were in the least consciously aware of. From that moment on, the distance between doctor and patient began to grow, and it has been growing in more ways than are measurable ever since.

Today there is an emotional distance, a psychological distance, perhaps even a healing distance that has been placed and left to lengthen between doctor and patient by medical technology. By using—indeed, overusing—this technology, this mechanistic wall that's been building between the care giver and the care-needy, the doctor "retreats further into his scientific cocoon," writes Louise Lander in *Defective Medicine,* her excellent treatise on the malpractice crisis and its roots, "[and] his words and actions become less and less comprehensible to the patient, while at the same time the patient's words and actions become less and less important to the doctor's diagnosis and treatment of his condition."[1]

Author, activist, and radical futurist Jeremy Rifkin believes that we have confused two forms of knowledge—the knowledge of manipulation and the knowledge of essence. "With modern science we have been able to learn more about how things work, behave, and function so that we can use, exploit, manipulate, and control them," he states. "But I don't believe that knowledge has gotten us necessarily any closer to understanding the metaphysics of our existence. . . . All of those invisible aspects of life that we know are important but can't be quantified are left out of the process. It's dangerous when we begin to reduce all of reality to its material components."[2]

To paraphrase one of Rifkin's statements about science,[3] it seems any time anyone criticizes modern medicine and technology, one is sure to be labeled antimedicine, antitechnology, antiprogress, and antiknowledge. This, of course, is partisan polemic and not the case at all, or anything close to the truth. It is entirely possible to be in favor of medicine but still be opposed to the medicine now being practiced, the medicine of power over nature. We need, in Rifkin's view, to move away from the doctrine practiced daily by many, if not most, doctors, the credo of which is "knowledge is power, power is control, control is security," and to replace that with a more humanistic alternative ethic that holds that "knowledge is empathy, empathy is participation, participation is security."[4]

Or, as Robert J. Weiss, M.D., of Columbia University, puts it: "For a profession which considers itself scientific, we have approached in a most unscientific fashion the issue of the appropriate use of technology and treatment. . . . Not only have we not been scientific, we have not been humanitarian."[5]

In *The Way of the Physician,* Jacob Needleman, M.D., talks about a certain basic, essential relationship that exists in cultures other than ours and has existed in them since ancient times. The relationship he discusses is of a simple but deep sort—a helping and healing relationship between one human being and another that outstrips and overshadows all of today's technological achievements and requires no tools of the trade except those of the human (and humane) variety. Needleman worries that our society has lost this one-to-one connection, this empathy or communing or whatever, and that our current headlong and headstrong dash toward a technological imperative is obliterating our ability to tap into and harness the power of this human interaction—a power that he feels may be more important and crucial to our lives than our development and manipulation of machines. "And," he writes, "since it [our overuse of technology] obscures the realities of this other human power, we are prevented from seeing that as the years go by we are gradually losing our possibilities in this realm of human relationship. And without developing these possibilities, we will be defeated by nature far more surely than if we fail to develop our physical technologies."[6]

This too great reliance on technology at the expense of human skills and instincts can be a contributing factor in misdiagnoses. One case in point: A famous 1983 Harvard University study found that one person out of every ten reviewed in the study who died would be alive today if the doctors involved had used their heads instead of their plugged-in devices (see chapter 4). This misguided overreliance also negates the variability of the human animal; in the opinion of Norman Cousins, "the failure of medical technology to make allowances for individual eccentricities can sometimes lead to erroneous pronouncements." He goes on to explain: "Even a cardiograph printout can be seriously misleading. It has happened that literal acceptance of a cardiograph can lead to a mistaken diagnosis of coronary occlusion, with resulting restrictions in life-style and the psychological and physical penalties incurred thereby."[7] Moreover, in the rush (gold rush, it seems) toward the newest, hottest machine in a marketplace atmosphere typified by "technology overkill . . . supply looking for demand,"[8] the value of the machine, its rightful place on the therapeutic menu, and the ratio of benefit to risk or harm is often shoved aside or trampled underfoot. "Medical technology and the system built upon it," state Sidel and Sidel, "have now themselves become an increasingly important cause of disease and disability, both because of the inherent dangers of powerful diagnostic and therapeutic methods and because of their misuse by incompetent and venal personnel and institutions."[9] Or, as Illich puts it: "In a complex technological hospital, negligence becomes 'random human error' or 'system breakdown,' callousness becomes 'scientific detachment,' and incompetence becomes 'a lack of specialized equipment'." Malpractice, he says, has changed—indeed, been allowed to change—"from an ethical into a technical problem."[10]

Lander calls the current desire for a technological fix "medical faddism," and says that what the various medical fads over the years have had in common was "the creation of greater or lesser risk to the patient at a time when the benefit of the new procedure, and whether that benefit can be confidently said to justify its risk, has not been firmly established. The underlying bias of the technological mindset and its activist orientation assumes that newer must be better and that doing more must be better than doing less; hence, the possibility of harm is always a second thought, and one that is only reluctantly entertained."[11]

For those who subscribe to Lander's ideas, it is difficult to swallow what seems to be the medical world's "party line" as stated succinctly by William J. McGill, former president of Columbia University and chairman of the New York State Special Advisory Panel on Medical Practice. "We are now," he says, "in an era of high technology in which medical injury is a risk that must be accepted either in the practice of medicine or in the conduct of hospitalization."[12]

Every procedure has its risk, certainly, and it would be wrongheaded, at best, to refuse to accept the realities of acceptable risk. But it is the magnitude of the crisis, the excessive incidence of injury that worries, frightens, and angers critics of the current trend in technology usage. Burt Dodson, Jr., past president of the Association for the Advancement of Medical Instrumentation, believes that mankind has benefited quite clearly from technology, but "we simply must keep in focus the appropriate role of technology and consider its needs and value within the perspective of the other priorities in health care that may benefit society. . . . It is important as health care professionals that we not become advocates of technology for technology's sake. . . ."[13]

Plugged In

Where the advocacy of technology for technology's sake begins—and, presumably, could be short-circuited—is in medical school. "The medical profession embraces—indeed, endorses—technology with little critical examination," states writer-psychiatrist David Hellerstein, M.D. "It rewards overtesting and overtreating. And, worst of all, it has trained an entire generation of doctors—mine—in certain attitudes and thought patterns that are often detrimental to patient care."[14]

Needleman concurs, adding: "In medical education, the student from the first days is introduced to technological and scientific medicine in a way that almost entirely eliminates . . . the art of medicine. The enormous advances in technology and the need to keep up with them has made it very difficult for people in the process of education to get a feel for the art of medicine."[15]

Not only does this type of early introduction of the eager novice to medical machinery distance the physician from the patient, but it also distances the physician from himself, from his personal history, and from the long history of his profession. This headlong dive toward a technological eddy catches many doctors up in a heady whirl that has little to do with the true art of real doctoring. "Possession of modern, sophisticated technology confers prestige on physicians," writes Kenneth E. Warner, of the University of Michigan's School of Public Health, "and it often contributes to their economic well-being. As a result, hospital administrators want to acquire sophisticated equipment and facilities, both for their own prestige and to attract and hold high-caliber physicians on their staffs. Finally, the public's growing faith in the power of science in general and of curative medicine in particular accelerates the demand for technologically advanced methods of care. In short, technological sophistication is viewed by many—patients, physicians, and administrators—as a surrogate for high-quality care."[16]

Warner goes on to talk about the "social contract" that binds doctors to provide the "best possible care," and this "contract" gives doctors the impetus, the license, to use newer technology in newer ways: "In medically desperate situations—i.e., where the prognosis is poor and reasonable therapeutic alternatives few—physicians are often encouraged to use experimental innovations in nonexperimental settings," he says. "This may result in widespread diffusion of innovations well before their medical efficacy, toxicities, costs, and so on are understood, although early diffusion is not restricted to medical crisis situations."[17]

The medical student sees all this, learns all this, and it becomes part of the action-identity and belief system of the soon-to-be doctor. He becomes a true believer even before he is sufficiently familiar with the belief system itself. "State of the art," in medicine, has become a term that has everything to do with new machines but nothing to do with art at all. What the student learns about technology, whether explicitly or by osmosis or socialization, according to Hellerstein, is that "technology pays":

> Technology gets people grants, promotions, tenure. The surest way to power in a medical center is to ally oneself with technology. . . . In addition, technology reimburses its followers well. The anesthesiologist makes more than the pediatrician, and the internist who performs more procedures to make a diagnosis makes more money than the internist who does only a few. . . . A third lesson, not explicitly stated but obviously followed in practice, was that virtually everyone should be treated. . . . medical students are being swamped by science and technology at the expense of basic healing skills. . . . Technology is often used as a distraction as well—to avoid painful and difficult issues.[18]

Excessive use of technology has a way of desensitizing the user, and especially the young, impressionable medical student, intern, resident, or new practitioner. The technology itself becomes the object of attention, of respect, of value. Test results take on a life of their own and, in composite, can become the proxy of the patient. Thus the intentions and decisions about what is and what needs to be done are between the physician (or team) and the technology.

Basic, intuitive human skills often erode as doctors increasingly are encouraged to turn to machines. "Procedures are good, procedures are very important, but they should be used to confirm and not to establish; they should be used after the interview, after the discussion, not as an automatic part of medical treatment," Cousins says. "Doctors are now being trained to operate high technology, and the interview, which has always been the basis of good medical practice, has now been reduced to about nine minutes on the average. . . . Lawmakers are concerned about the health budget of this country, but if you break down that health budget you see how large a part of it is paid for high technology, a lot of which could have been avoided with a proper interview and exchange."[19]

Physician "nervousness" is also a prime mover in the use of medical machines. It may come from fear of being sued for malpractice or a bad outcome, or from an uncertainty that casts a shadow over the doctor's seeming "infallibility." However, as Weiss admits, "The physician's . . . reliance on technology to relieve his own anxiety about making a mistake by 'missing something' generally contributes little beyond that available from good judgment."[20] To this he adds: "The current level of use may not yet be misuse, but clear evidence from other technologies is that availability tends to promote misuse. This results from both patient expectations for 'scientific intervention' and the physician's need to reduce his own uncertainty. The recent malpractice difficulties have played directly into this physician need, and the overuse of technological testing is now rationalized as defensive medicine."[21]

Weiss here raises an important factor in technological overuse and misuse: patient expectation and pressure. Patients have been led to believe by the medical world's own suspender-snapping public relations that the "new medicine" and latest mechanical breakthroughs will make them whole. So the patients feel it is their right to receive these trendy treatments. Patients have come to see it as their due "to ride in a Cadillac when a Fiat would get from A to B with almost equal effectiveness."[22] Furthermore, people have been led to believe that there is "a new magic in medical technology"; however, the problem is that "scientific medicine is not only not miraculous but that its apparently magical technology robs the patient of his humanness while it subjects him to iatrogenic risk. . . ."[23]

But it's the doctors who have primarily bought into the "gee whiz," "new and improved," magical, and quasi-religious feelings about the cascade of equipment in a big way. "How can one begin to change the practitioners' almost superstitious acceptance of technology when all the forces are pulling in the other direction?" asks John M. R. Bruner, M.D. "Perambulating the aisles of gadgets at the technical exhibits that finance our specialty society meetings, one is drenched with importunities to believe that only a widget with on-board microprocessor and trend display is appropriate to the image of the truly modern anesthesiologist. While the boondoggle of continuing education provides seminars and meetings in exotic locales on almost every topic (except skeptical moderation), the busy practitioner is not going to pay to travel and lose time from work to be harangued on cost containment and on 'what's *old* in good patient care'."[24]

What is clear is that doctors see technology, with its jargon and its mystique and its capacity to distance, as a control mechanism. If the doctor-patient relationship as it exists today is—at least in some doctors' minds—one of power over subservience, the new technology becomes a tool to that end by creating a medical technocracy. As George Bugliarello of the Polytechnic Institute of New York points out, "Attempts at reform must begin by recognizing that some of the new techniques, such as very expensive imaging, tend to reinforce the traditionally dominant role of doctors and hospitals in health care. For this reason, they are readily accepted in the health-care industry." But, he adds, "On the other hand, there are other techniques . . . that can give greater autonomy to the patient, enabling him to place less reliance on doctors and hospitals. For that very reason, however, the development of such techniques is bound to be impeded."[25]

The Soul of a New (and Also Old) Machine

Despite Food and Drug Administration (FDA) regulation of medical devices introduced to the marketplace, many machines become defective in practice. In fact, many of them are dangerous and/or worthless to begin with. "Checks have shown," one writer claims, "that as much as half the new equipment coming into hospitals is defective—defibrillators that could kill both patient and doctor if used as delivered, defective anesthesia machines, and even such simple things as poorly designed lamps that are electrical hazards."[26]

The FDA publishes a monthly report of problems that have been reported to them involving medical devices. A review of these one-time harrowing experiences leads to the realization that quality control is not what it used to be, and that the hazards of technology gone awry are the same as they ever were. What follows are a few randomly chosen examples culled from several issues of the FDA publication, *The Device Experience Network Report* (also known as the DEN report):

• "Death of a dialysis PT [patient] was reportedly caused by the loss of blood due to the failure of a connector in an arteriovenous fistula implanted in the left upper arm of PT."[27]

• Linear accelerator: "Machine rotated in one direction on its own (gantry rotated). Beam stopper pushed against the phantom which was in PT's position. Pushed hard enough to crush the equipment—would have crushed PT."[28]

• Anesthesia gas concentration monitor: "Failure mode of the transducer crystals yields anesthetic concentration readings which are grossly low. Since the device is designed to be used as a real time monitor during surgery, this failure could prompt an anesthesiologist to increase his vaporizer setting to compensate for the error, thus inadvertently overdosing the PT."[29]

• Defibrillator: "On 6/13/85 responded to a cardiac arrest on a golf course. PT was in coarse fibrillation. Paramedics defibbed once. OK. Decided to use R-2 pads to get a more direct charge on PT. As they were placing R-2 pads in place, unit discharged spontaneously giving 2 paramedics a charge. A 2nd attempt was made and again unit discharged spontaneously. PT died. Paramedics hospitalized."[30]

• Fetal cardiac monitor: "Machine shuts itself off without giving an audible alarm. The result is lack of record of events from time the recording stopped until stoppage is discovered. This lack of information can be critical, affecting PT care decisions. Lack of documentation can have serious effects on care outcome and in court proceedings."[31]

• Subclavian catheter: "Catheter became disconnected at the junction of the plastic hub and silicone elastomer catheter as the nurse was withdrawing the catheter. If the catheter tip had not been salvageable it could easily have become an embolism and cost the patient his life."[32]

• Silicone gel-filled breast prosthesis: "In 10/75, reporter had a bilateral subcutaneous mastectomy and had a job modification prosthesis inserted. She has had trouble with this implant. In 2/84, she had pain in left arm and had surgery on 7/28/84. Over 17 tumors found. Both implants were ruptured, with free-flowing silicone throughout."[33]

• Infusion pump: "A PT death resulted from mix-up of . . . model 960 infusion pump and model 965 infusion pump. Model 960 is adult version, and model 965 is pediatric version. Complainant claims devices look too much alike making mix-ups possible. A child died in 3/83 when a nurse dialed in a hyperalimentation procedure on an adult device rather than a pediatric device."[34]

Dozens of similar, but not always as dire, incidents fill the monthly FDA DEN reports. And these are just the ones that have been reported. (A December 1986 survey by the U.S. General Accounting Office found that 53 percent of health care professionals were totally unaware of the FDA's system for reporting problems, despite repeated FDA publicity campaigns.[35]) Sometimes it is just the tip of a tube or the end of a wire that breaks off, remaining in the patient and requiring surgical removal. Other times there are intraaortic balloons that do not expand or deflate, mislabeled ingredients, failed cardiac pacemakers, faulty timers on radiation therapy machines, and unsterile solutions. Hairs, dirt, and even a live silverfish have been reported in supposedly sterile, contaminant-free devices and packaging. The DEN report is nothing less than a numbing litany of breakdown, incompetence, carelessness, and poor or nonexistent forethought, often shocking, sometimes surprising—and, frighteningly, only the tip of the iceberg considering that there are 1,700 different kinds of medical devices in existence, in the guise of some 40,000 commercial brands and models.[35]

Sometimes the tragedy of technical malfunctions is more on the order of "a thousand little cuts." One must wonder (and shudder) each day at the number of people whose blood pressure readings are provided by machines that have been in service for years but rarely, if ever, recalibrated. How ironic it is that butchers' scales are monitored more aggressively by government agencies than medical devices are.

From addenda to the reports, it is clear that the FDA hasn't the time or the manpower to investigate all the horror stories it receives. In fact, it frequently appears that the FDA has little or no interest in investigating these incidents; often the individual reports of a failed this or a malfunctioning that are followed by the boiler-plate paragraph, "This report has been evaluated and sent to the district office for their information. No follow-up or additional information is expected by the CDRH (Center for Devices and Radiological Health)." Reported complaints seem to receive only cursory concern. Equipment that is faulty in either original design or action or both, patient care technology that rolls down the factory assembly line in defective or slipshod shape, continues to go to market and then goes haywire in institutions all over America, often hurting patients and sometimes leading to their deaths.

What also is made obvious by the FDA reports is how big a role human error plays in technological hazard. At the factory, people make mistakes while manufacturing machines. An electrocardiograph machine ought to be but is not any more immune to being a lemon than an automobile is. At the hospital, clinic, or doctor's office, the misuse of highly sensitive, potentially life-altering technology is not unusual. And when an ill-trained technician joins forces with the badly designed, poorly calibrated, or ungrounded machine, proper diagnosis and treatment are a hope at best.

It is clear, as Paul L. McGurgan, a customer engineer for Hewlett

Packard medical products, says, that "potential hazards to the patient arise if the operator is unfamiliar with the operating modality of his instrument."[37] McGurgan goes on to report a survey of users of cardioversion equipment, which delivers electrical shocks to the heart to counteract irregular beats. These users reported that "52 percent of those participating in cardioversion procedures (physicians, nurses, and various medical technicians) were unable to predict the actual operating mode of their instrument after an initial cardioversion effort."[38] That is, once the machine had been used, they could not predict what setting the machine would return to in preparation for its next use—a potentially critical piece of knowledge during an emergency when every second counts. McGurgan concludes that hospitals "should take the initiative to ensure that resuscitation team personnel are adequately trained and thoroughly familiar with the operating procedures of their equipment, as well as proceed with lobbying efforts to encourage manufacturers to develop standardized labeling that will facilitate the identification of the operation of the instrument."[39] It is truly disturbing and even shocking that such training and standardization are not commonplace, but rather some distant ideals merely to be strived for.

Thomas S. Hargest, of the Medical University of South Carolina, has outlined in the industry journal *Medical Instrumentation* the many links along the long and winding communication chain when the operation of medical equipment is being taught, and especially those junctures with the greatest potential for fostering misunderstanding, error, and patient harm. "The effort begins when the engineers who built the equipment first face the challenge of writing the technical manual," he says. "How this effort is, or is not, accomplished has a continuing effect on operation of the equipment, even after the manual and equipment are out of production. There is little doubt that considerable improvement can be made in writing operator manuals."[40]

The next point of instructional transfer occurs with the sales staff, which goes out and pitches the product to institutions and medical practitioners. Here, "new problems surface," because "the information the sales staff absorbs may not be exactly what the engineers intended it to be." Hargest elaborates: "The sales staff consists of many individuals of diverse backgrounds, and though perhaps with similar degrees, neither their training nor their aptitudes are identical. Some will understand well and teach well; some will understand well but be less proficient in teaching; some will not understand at all."[41]

"Unfortunately," Hargest says, "by the time the different levels of skill of the sales staff are apparent, the equipment has reached the hospital; no matter how well or poorly the sales staff are prepared, they must educate future users of the equipment."[42]

Then, the picture—and the process of education—becomes even more complicated. As Hargest explains, "In some hospitals, company representatives will be asked to do the in-service training themselves. In others, they may train in-service nursing personnel who will, in turn, train other staff members."[43] Or else other people will train other people to train other people. The line gets longer and longer—and the patient is at the very end of the tortuous line. It's the medical world's version of the old parlor game, Whispering Down the Lane; the recipient of the last malformed bit of information is the patient. This is not only annoying but it is also a potential threat to proper use of technology because, as Hargest points out, "information transferred most accurately is that with the smallest number of transfer points."[44]

Then, too, the mode of instruction varies from hospital to hospital, group to group, instructor to instructor, company to company. The teaching may be done in person or via videotape, audiotape, or slide show. A personal instructor may or may not use audiovisual aids. The teaching may be on an individual level or a group basis. Sometimes it includes hands-on experience, sometimes not.

What's more, Hargest says that "most nursing schools fail to include even an introductory course in instrumentation. . . . Unfortunately, for this omission, hospital in-service programs must pay the price of greater staff unease, lessened understanding, increased training time, and a lower level of overall efficiency."[45] This is especially so since "nurses need to know what [a machine] is, and how it is cleaned and calibrated."[46]

And finally, there is the amazing fact that physicians are not required to be certified by any independent professional organization to show they know the proper use of the medical devices they operate, and therefore "patients cannot thus be reassured about the instrumentation in the user's hands."[47]

As medical technology moves ahead into a misty future, new concerns confront us, the recipients of technologized medical care. There are the problems and issues surrounding avant-garde biomedical devices. The various artificial hearts are the chief current examples and are clearly problematical, especially in the areas of medical device failures, the blood clot–forming properties of the devices, the material used in them, and the infections resulting from implants.[48] There are ethical concerns and quality-of-life considerations as well; many critics, like George Annas, professor of health law at Boston University, have called for a moratorium on both the permanent and the temporary use of artificial hearts because "of the devastating effects they have had on their recipients, because there is no guarantee [that temporary hearts] will not be permanent [if a human replacement is not available for transplant], we have yet to develop an ethically acceptable method of allocating human hearts to those with artificial hearts, and there is no room in our health care system for an extreme and expensive medical technology that is useless because it does not increase the total number of lives saved by heart transplants."[49] This is a heady, complex, heated issue, as is the identification, maintenance, and/or replacement of aging and obsolescent medical devices.[50] So, too, is the investigation and subsequent start-up of clinical trials on newer devices that seem to be used frequently or excessively despite little or no proof that they improve outcome and that they may, in fact, be the sources of increased mortality and morbidity. The Swan-Ganz catheter, a device used to measure blood flow pressure in the heart, is currently at the center of such a controversy, with some critics attributing large numbers of injuries and deaths to its unnecessary overimplementation "without firm evidence or an acceptable clinical trial establishing that, in the overwhelming number of patients, the benefits of their use exceed the risks."[51]

Then, too, there is the new trend toward the reuse of single-use medical devices. That is, items designed by their manufacturers to be used once and only once and then disposed of are instead being cleaned up, fixed up, and reused by hospitals on patients—usually without the patients' knowledge, and with no firm studies on efficacy and patient safety. Hospitals do it to cut their costs and improve their bottom line. In a survey of one hospital's lab technologists, nurses, technicians, and other pertinent employees, "31 percent reported reprocessing/reuse of cardiovascular catheters and catheter guide wires; 18 percent cited breathing circuits used in respiratory therapy, and 17 percent reported biopsy needles. A second IHPA [Georgetown University's Institute for Health Policy Analysis] survey, of central service and respiratory staff, turned up even higher percentages: manual resuscitators, 44 percent; orthopedic devices, 39 percent; and anesthesia face masks, 30 percent."[52] One hospital, according to Alan L. Otten of the *Wall Street Journal,* admits reusing catheters up to 45 times.[53] But many practitioners and hospitals won't admit that they reuse the single-use devices because they are afraid that if anything ever did go wrong, an injured patient would have a very strong legal liability case against them.

The debate for and against reuse is one of strong vested interests—hospitals wanting to cut costs versus manufacturers wanting to sell more replacement products. So the information available from either side must certainly be viewed as tainted. But the FDA is concerned, and its concern, says John Villforth, director of the FDA's Center for Devices and Radiological Health, "is that as more devices are reprocessed by people with less experience in processing techniques, the possibility of adverse effects to the patient increases."[54] Yet the Food and Drug Administration's seeming concern is a hollow one, and of little consolation for those at risk. When six U.S. senators petitioned the FDA to regulate the reuse of hemodialysis filters—which in some medical care sites have been reused 40 or 50 times, causing dizziness and other side effects—the FDA refused.[55]

There can be no argument in support of a Luddite mentality. Medical technology is here to stay, and in many cases that is a good thing. But in one, key, all-encompassing way, there is something very bad to be said about it. As Jacob Needleman has pointed out to other doctors:

> It was not science you believed in, it was man. But today it is science you believe in and science, great as it is when it is good, is less than man, far less. When science was new to you, you believed in using it—but you were so very careful about it. . . .
>
> But now science is no longer new for you. You no longer put it to the test when you act. More important, it no longer puts you to the test. It has swallowed your mind. There is no longer a creative struggle in you between your own intuition and the whole of science.[56]

3

....

‖SLEEP OF THE DEAD

"The causes of anesthetic death are all too often mundane and obvious and rarely require much, if any, scientific investigation to establish them, provided a truthful account of the facts can be obtained."

—R. Macintosh, M.D.

Anesthesiologists really like the airplane analogy. They enjoy trotting it out when they talk or write about their work, not only because they think it accurately depicts their work but also probably because it makes their job seem a tad more romantic and heroic to people at cocktail parties (who aren't too sure what anesthesiologists do for a living, anyway); after all, anesthesiologists don't practice surgery, the stuff of fiction and myth, although they do make more money.

In the airplane analogy, the anesthesiologist casts himself as the pilot, or the copilot or, at the very least, the navigator of a sophisticated flying craft. It is his job—his art, as he sees it—to guide the flight, make many on-course corrections, and keep the craft stable and the ventilation system functioning. He works at a piece of complex machinery with a multifaceted control panel adorned with a multiplicity of dials, gauges, and alarms. If the passengers experience turbulence, he is there to iron out the bumps and bring his charges in for a safe, smooth landing.

It's a nice analogy, as far as those things go. But an editorial in the medical journal *Lancet* doesn't think it goes very far or very deep at all. "How many anesthetists can remember near misses due to pilot error during periods of personal fatigue?" the editorial wonders, rhetorically, presuming a positive response from nearly all. It asks further: "How many types of anesthetic machine would be grounded by order if they were flying machines?" Here, too, the editorial expects few negatives.[1] And, we wonder, wouldn't there be a public outcry and government investigations and commissions if as many as 10,000 people a year were dying in commercial airline crashes in the United States—just as 10,000 people a year in this country have been reported to be dying of anesthesia administration?[2]

Anesthesiology is not airplane flying. It is a medical discipline that, while doing better than it used to, needs a lot more improvement, public and government scrutiny, and imposed or self-imposed house cleaning.

Anesthesiology is definitely not airplane flying. For one thing, the anesthesiologist rarely goes down in flames with the ship.

Prelude to Problems

The number of deaths due wholly or partially to anesthesia is large, although if statistical percentages are used to gauge the problem it doesn't seem all that bad: Somewhere in the neighborhood of 1 to 2.5 deaths per 10,000 people exposed to anesthesia is the figure usually given. But one should not be lulled into complacency by statistics. "Analysis of current mortality estimates and safety monitoring expenditures," writes J. H. Philip, M.D., of the Department of Anesthesia, Brigham and Women's Hospital and Harvard Medical School, "suggests that the current standard of practice does not provide 'reasonable care'."[3] And these statistics do not even take into consideration anesthesia-related injuries, for which "even the lowest estimates suggest cause for concern."[4]

At least 80 percent of all anesthesia-related mishaps are due to human error. "In my view," writes William K. Hamilton, M.D., of the University of California at San Francisco, "error is near the 90 percent end."[5] And in the most recent of a series of analyses of the use of anesthesia, Jeffrey B. Cooper and associates noted that only "4 percent of the incidents with substantive negative outcomes involved equipment failure, confirming the previous impression that human error is the dominant issue in anesthesia mishaps."[6]

But here's what's worse, according to a consensus among experts: At least *half* of anesthesia deaths are *preventable,* given existing medical knowledge and accepted anesthesia practice.[7] These wholly preventable deaths as well as injuries are, Cooper adds, the result of "inappropriate management of the anesthesia or failure to follow accepted practices. Many estimates of the extent of preventability are much higher, although dissenting views exist."[8] Eighty percent has been mentioned by some researchers as a high-end percentage of preventability.[9]

(It should be noted here that hard numbers are hard to come by in the study of anesthesia-related injuries and deaths. That is because often the death or injury may be attributed to other causes. For example, "doc-

tors may write on a certificate 'death due to appendicitis' if a patient dies
in the operating room from an anesthetist's error while undergoing the
operation to remove an 'abnormal' appendix.''[10] And sometimes good,
helpful records are not kept. Other reasons include the occasional difficulty
in determining cause of death [if autopsies are not performed, the cause
may go undisclosed forever] and the lack of a system set in place and
designed for compiling and reporting anesthesia-related deaths or injuries.
In the United States, there is one more important reason for the scarcity
of solid, perhaps implicating, statistics: "the malpractice climate eliminates all incentive for reporting injuries or even studying the problem.''[11])

Are You Experienced?

Education and training certainly seem to play key roles in the development
and persistence of the problem. Cooper and his colleagues found in their
1984 study that "inadequate experience of one form or another was the
most frequent associated factor cited among all incidents." Even more
significant, of those cases that were determined to have substantive negative outcomes (SNO)—meaning that the results of the anesthesia mishap
led to death, heart attack, cancellation of the operation, or an extended
stay in the recovery room, intensive care unit, or hospital—13 of 14 "involving some form of drug overdose were associated with some directly
relevant form of inexperience or inadequate training." Add to that the
fact that the errors due to inadequate knowledge or training were not, as
one might expect or hope, mistakes made exclusively by medical students,
interns, new residents, or other novices on the service. Rather, in "16 of
the 38 SNO incidents in which the need for additional training was cited,
it was a staff anesthesiologist or nurse anesthetist whose skills or knowledge
were deficient."

Finally, Cooper and colleagues uncovered this ultimate little tidbit of
information, which boldly underscored the contention that poor supervision was a major factor in anesthetic errors. They found that the "most
frequent deficiency" was "absence of the supervisor when a trainee was
managing a case or involved in a crisis for which he clearly lacked the
experience or skills needed to respond appropriately." What's more, and
worse, is that on many occasions, when the supervisors did happen to
show up, they "provided inaccurate or superficial guidance.''[12]

Training, too, is surely the primary point of concern in any critical
discussion of the role, reliability, and safety of nurse-anesthetists. These
medical professionals are not M.D.s with years of supposed quality education and broad technical knowledge and ability. They are, instead,

nurses who have received six months or so of additional training to learn the basics and a bit more of how to administer anesthesia. But then they are permitted to act as certified solo stand-ins in hospital settings where an anesthesiologist is not available. Often, they run the whole anesthesia show when an anesthesiologist, in pursuit of the most patients and the most dollars possible, has booked himself to preside over many operations happening at the same time in different hospitals miles apart, and thus tosses one or more jobs to nurse-anesthetists. Many a preoperative surgical patient has been led to believe that the anesthesiologist who visited him and asked him questions about his health would be the one who would be present at the operation, administering the anesthesia—only to be wheeled into the operating room to find an unfamiliar nurse-anesthetist there. The worry is that should something occur that is beyond the ken of the nurse-anesthetist, the patient could be in serious trouble if no other anesthesiologist is available or if the anesthesiologist of supposed record is unreachable by telephone.

Training is also of concern as anesthesiology breaks down into minutely focused subspecialties. There are those who dispense anesthesia only during heart operations, for example, or only during brain surgery or kidney surgery, and who are supposedly experts in those areas. But are they really so expert, wonders Mark C. Rogers, M.D., professor and chairman, Department of Anesthesiology and Critical Care Medicine, Johns Hopkins Hospital. His concern is that these anesthesiology specialists' periods of specialty training are too brief to be complete—only six months or a year to learn the intricacies not only of anesthesia but also of the heart or brain or of certain common as well as esoteric diseases they will be seeing and interacting with. They need to know all of that, but can they in such a short time? "Can we accomplish in one year of specialty training what others do in two or more years of fellowship?" Rogers asks rhetorically and pessimistically of his fellow anesthesiologists. "Are our trainees so superior to those in other specialties or are we such superior teachers that it is easier for us to achieve identical goals in half the time?"[13]

Contemptible Sleep

The troubled doctor-patient relationship rears its often insolent head in matters of anesthesiology.

For one thing, an anesthesiologist should visit an in-hospital patient at least one day before an operation is scheduled to take place so that important information about allergies, heart problems, family history, blood pressure, etc., can be duly noted and taken into account. But, instead, anesthesiologists often slip into the hospital room during the late hours of the night before the operation, make brief introductions, and ask cursory questions of a person who is tired, frightened, possibly tranquilized, and undoubtedly distracted to the point of forgetfulness. Even these quick consultations don't always take place. Many patients first "meet" their anesthesiologist or nurse-anesthetist only at the moment they are wheeled into surgery, mere minutes before the cutting begins. This does nothing for the confidence of the patient; for the anesthesiologist, it may only reinforce attitudes of contempt, superiority, and infallibility—and of a complacency that kills. Unfortunately, some of the best anesthesiologists are also among the worst at caring for their charges. They are so busy and so wrapped up in their jobs and their business, they simply don't have the time—or think to take the time—to treat their patients as vulnerable human beings.

This condescending attitude by anesthesiologists toward the people whose lives they control is further indicated by the events surrounding the establishment of the Anesthesia Patient Safety Foundation. Formed in October 1985 at the American Society of Anesthesiology's annual meeting, the nonprofit foundation has as its expressed goals "to encourage development of programs and information exchange to reduce the incidence of anesthesia-related mishaps. . . ." A noble goal, to be sure. As reported by the *American Medical News,* the weekly informational organ of the American Medical Association, "Included among the constituencies of the Anesthesia Patient Safety Foundation are groups primarily interested in anesthesia safety—anesthesiologists, nurse-anesthetists, hospital administrators, professional liability insurers, anesthesia equipment manufacturers, and attorneys." There are also hopes that the board might include representatives from the American Hospital Association and the Joint Commission on the Accreditation of Hospitals.[14]

On perusing this list of participant groups, one may notice the absence of one particularly interested party—namely, the patients, the only group whose name actually appears in the foundation's title. This foundation, like many others of similar bent, simply decided, in a very typical medical fashion, that what was good for "patient safety" would benefit little from input by those whose safety was in question. This is yet another example of an Olympian complex held by professional creatures who consider themselves godlike. In the business of caring for mere mortals, they consider these mortals unfit to know the secrets of fire.

To Err Is Human

What exactly are anesthesia practitioner errors, their range and scope, and their levels of preventability and culpability?

Most of the best information and statistics available are derived from studies and surveys conducted at Harvard Medical School over the past decade and a half by Jeffrey B. Cooper, Ph.D., Ronald S. Newbower, Ph.D., James H. Philip, M.D., and their colleagues. Others also have done good work under difficult circumstances, but Cooper and his colleagues have staked their claim to this territory.

Among the errors during anesthesia that are essentially human mistakes, the list is certainly long enough and scary enough; what follows is only a sampling:[15]

• *Syringe swap.* Syringe swap refers to "incidents in which two syringes were inadvertently confused or interchanged and the wrong drug nearly or actually administered."[16] Cooper's 1978 report showed that the wrong drug was actually administered more than five times more often than near-misses occurred.[17] Syringe swaps can occur when a doctor reaches for one syringe but grabs another. Sometimes, however, swaps take place because there is not now, nor has there ever been, nor is there ever likely to be a professionally mandated or standardized order of laying syringes on a work surface. Each doctor may like a different lineup of syringes and other tools of the trade on his worktable. So, if a nurse, used to working with many anesthesiologists, lays out a tray of syringes and related gear in the configuration that Doctor A likes, when in fact it's Doctor B who is going to be in attendance, big troubles can ensue. Also, if anesthesiologists substitute for one another during the operation (not an uncommon occurrence) each may assume that items are ordered his way. It may not be his—and, if so, it certainly won't be the patient's.

• *Ampule swap.* Here, the containers of anesthetic agents are confused, misidentified, and then wrongly administered, for many of the same reasons that syringe swap occurs. "The anesthesiologist's work table may contain ten different drugs in syringes and ampules for administration during the case," Robert E. Johnstone, M.D., points out. "The similarity in size and design of ampules of different drugs and names that sound alike (such as methyldopa, dopamine, and levodopa) causes more confusion." Methods of preventing such swapping errors, Johnstone says, include keeping items in order, accurately and clearly labeling syringes, making sure to double-check the contents of the syringe before injecting, and coding syringes by color or size.[18]

• *Drug overdose.* This tragic mistake includes errors of judgment—

pure human-error medical mistakes—as well as those of a more technical nature.

• *Unintentional or premature extubation.*   Premature extubation refers to "cases in which a patient's trachea was extubated [flow tube was removed] sooner than was clinically indicated and where the interviewee clearly described a failure to follow accepted practice."[19] Upon premature or erroneous removal of a tube, the patient may have difficulty breathing or may inhale his or her own vomit—especially if the operation is performed when the patient's stomach is full—and that can lead to a horrible death by suffocation.

• *Wrong choice of drug.*

• *Wrong choice of airway management technique.*

• *Hypovolemia.*   This "refers to incidents in which fluid replacement was not properly managed . . . in the presence of unambiguous clinical indication as judged by the interviewee."[20]

• *Disconnections of intravenous lines, breathing circuits, and other attachments.*   These are often human errors. But even when there is a mechanical problem, if it is missed or overlooked by the anesthesia operator, it is a clear case of malpractice.

How can so many potentially life-ending incidents occur? The list of factors most frequently cited in anesthetic mishaps and near-mishaps and anesthesiologist or nurse-anesthetist error include:[21]

• Failure to perform proper checkout/history.
• Inadequate experience with anesthesia.
• Inadequate familiarity with equipment or device, surgical procedure, or anesthetic technique.
• Poor communication with surgical team, laboratory, and other personnel.
• Haste, or insufficient preparation.
• Inattention or carelessness.
• Fatigue.
• Excessive dependence on other personnel.
• Teaching activity under way.
• Supervisor not present often enough.
• Poor labeling of controls, drugs, etc.
• Apprehension.
• Boredom.

Johnstone adds another hazard: noises in the operating room. He claims that these beeps and buzzes, bells and blips, hums and hisses "are intense enough to cause irritation and physiologic changes in exposed personnel and to interfere with speech communication.''[22] And that can certainly interfere with patient safety.

None of the above frequently cited factors in mishaps and errors can be considered minor infractions or piddling oversights—not when anesthesia has been described by researchers as ''chemical coma''[23] and the administration of anesthesia as ''continuous resuscitation during ongoing administration of lethal drugs''—drugs that can stop normal breathing, reduce the function of all internal organs, including the heart, and lead to permanent brain injury or death.[24] Even something as seemingly minor or picayune as ''boredom'' or ''apprehension'' can be responsible for acts or nonacts that push an anesthetized patient off his precarious life-or-death perch.

The levels of damage that may realistically be inflicted upon a human being who is the victim of an anesthesia-related ''significant negative incident'' are numerous, and thus they have been classified as to order of severity, as follows (in descending order):[25]

- Catastrophic
    —Loss of life or major organ.
- Profound
    —Permanent organ injury, partial functional loss.
- Severe
    —Transient injury, increasing level or duration of care: infection, transient respiratory failure, transient renal failure.
    —Reparable injury: corneal damage, nerve damage, broken teeth.
    —Psychological injury: awareness during surgery.
- Undesirable
    —Discomfort: pain, nausea, vomiting.
    —Psychological distress: anxiety, fear, excessive waiting.

(Although the so-called ''undesirable'' effects, above, are not life-threatening from the patient's point of view, physical discomfort and psychological distress are not just minor irritants or inconveniences. Try to tell the victim of avoidable pain and suffering that such medical assault and battery is no big deal. And what, indeed, may the long-term consequences affecting the patient's quality of recovery be? It is no wonder that so many patients subjected to unnecessary pain and anxiety develop chronic medical phobia, a cynical attitude toward physicians and hospitals as uncaring, even brutal.)

Cardiac arrest is another possible complication of anesthesia. The results of a 15-year study conducted by Richard L. Keenan, M.D., and C. Paul Boyan, M.D., of the Department of Anesthesiology, Medical

College of Virginia, Virginia Commonwealth University, showed that about 2 patients out of every 10,000 given anesthetics suffered cardiac arrests. Further exploration revealed that patients in the "pediatric age group had a threefold higher risk than adults, and that the risk for emergency patients was six times that for elective patients." Human error in dispensing the anesthetic was predominantly responsible for these heart attacks: "Failure to provide adequate ventilation" was the root cause of almost half of the anesthetic cardiac arrests, and another third resulted from "absolute overdose of an inhalation agent." And although the prior seriously ill condition of a cardiac arrest victim was implicated in 22 percent of the cases, "errors in anesthetic management could be identified in 75 percent."[26]

Taylor, Larson, and Prestwich[27] also studied unexpected cardiac arrests during anesthesia and surgery, and noted that "cardiac arrest in the operating room occurred frequently in patients of good health who were having relatively routine surgical procedures." Taylor, Larson, and Prestwich's concern was that despite the use of monitors, there was often a delay in the diagnosis of cardiac arrest. They found that the cardiac arrests were often due to insufficient oxygen being administered during anesthesia. Even when successful resuscitation was accomplished it frequently occurred "only to show the stigmata of irreversible central nervous system damage in the recovery period."[28] The facts, results, and conditions illuminated by the study were deemed "dismal."

What can be done to reduce the human errors involved with anesthesia? Cooper and his colleagues suggest a list of remedies, all of them simple, obvious, and inexpensive. They are:[29]

- Additional training.
- Improved supervision/second opinion.
- Specific protocol development.
- Equipment or apparatus inspection.
- More complete preoperative assessment.
- Equipment/human factors improvements.
- Additional monitoring instrumentation.
- Other specific organizational improvements.
- Improved communication.
- Improved personnel selection procedures.

Any corporation in America, looking at its assets, its liabilities, and even its bottom line, would have instituted these measures. The oft-cited comparison, the airline industry, has done most if not all of these things. Why hasn't anesthesiology? What will it take? How long will it take until it does? And isn't it astounding that an institution as prestigious as Harvard Medical School had *no* mandatory standards for *minimal* patient monitoring during anesthesia until mid-1986—and that this so-called ''major patient safety/risk management effort'' included measures as simple as continuous monitoring of breathing, pulse, blood pressure, and heart rate, as well as an anesthesiologist's or nurse-anesthetist's presence in the room throughout the entire operation?[30] And isn't it disturbing that these simple steps, which should have been instituted years before everywhere, are to be found almost nowhere?

Iron Pumping

Difficulties with anesthesia-related equipment, when compared to practitioner mistakes, are a small proportion of the problem. They represent less than 5 percent, in some studies.[31] But machine errors in anesthesia are often intricately intertwined with human errors. If the machine is too complex to be understood, with too many buttons and alarms and monitors, and a mistake is made because of this, who is to blame? Is it the fault of the machine for being too complicated, the fault of the operator for lacking familiarity with the machine, the fault of the inventor for designing such a complex tool, the fault of the hospital administrator for buying it, or the fault of the hospital's engineer or technician for not having the savvy, the time, or the will to keep it in good shape? Machine error may be the result of a long chain of miscalculations. And, after all, human beings make machines, run them, and care for them. There is faulty anesthesia technology. But usually the mistakes involved can be traced to at least one human being.

A brief background, courtesy of Peter J. Schreiber, writing in the May–June 1985 edition of *Medical Instrumentation,* may be helpful at this point:[32]

• Until 15 years ago, anesthesia equipment was of simple design and used technology that had not changed for decades, with predominantly pneumatic components.

• Many of the designs had originated in hospitals, and physicians were frequently named as the inventors.

• Basic anesthesia machines were supplied by approximately ten companies, with an array of additional companies supplying accessories, connectors, and adapters.

• During the 1970s the anesthesia equipment industry underwent changes rarely experienced by established industries. The elimination of flammable anesthetic agents from the operating room permitted the use of electronic components and monitors on a wide scale, the introduction of additional powerful liquid anesthetic agents required technology for their safe handling, and the rapid increase in the acceptance of automatic ventilation initiated the design of increasingly complex ventilators.

• During the same period the possible health hazards of daily exposure to trace concentrations of anesthetics were recognized and, in response to this potential problem, anesthesia systems were equipped with waste gas elimination systems.

Today only two companies make anesthesia machines. The rest have dropped out of the business because of concern about liability suits and because of the limited market in a time of cost cutting for machines that can cost anywhere from about $20,000 to as much as $75,000 each. The cost element is the strongest consideration. Some hospitals can't afford new machines and the $1,000 or so per machine for annual maintenance. At other hospitals, stockholders would rather see that money go into the profit pile instead of the capital outlay pile (unless it's a "sexier" and profit-making capital outlay pile, such as into a new CAT scan or nuclear magnetic resonating machine). So, older anesthesia machines (some 10 or even 20 years old) stay in use longer—perhaps, longer than they should. They are patched up, added to, and worked over, which leads to many of the problems. As Schreiber notes:

> Components for an anesthesia system are normally supplied by different manufacturers. In addition to the manufacturers who supply the devices, an entire industry exists to supply adapters and connectors, both for the physical connections between the various components of the system and the connection of the system to the patient. The same industry supplies adapters that can be used to modify the anesthesia equipment as originally supplied by the manufacturer. The physical arrangements and connections between the various components are sometimes left to the decision of the physician or hospital. . . . It can be assumed that an average of eight manufacturers contribute to an anesthesia system; none of them is involved in the final arrangement, and the arrangement may change frequently when components are inserted or removed to adapt the system to different procedures.[33]

There are no laws determining what should and should not be on an anesthesia machine, and no standards for compatibility of components. There is no uniformity or standardization within the profession. This can be dangerous, especially when one considers that an anesthesia machine "may contain 50 to 100 different controls, as many as 50 displays and indicators, and more than 20 different alarm functions."[34]

Ironically, while the vast array of monitors, bells, and whistles are intended to keep the operator on top of things, their very presence, and the operator's belief and faith in their technological accuracy, efficacy, and reliability, can give the operator a false sense of security. This may lead him to grow complacent and overlook the obvious, to downplay what his five senses tell him, and to make critical mistakes—with swift and disastrous consequences. Moreover, Gordon R. Neufeld, M.D., editor-in-chief of *Medical Instrumentation,* remarks that when a patient is in an unstable, deteriorating state, the operating room is already in chaos. Bells and alarms going off only add to the confusion and make things worse. He recommends that anesthesia machine alarms should be "user-friendly" and not contributors to anxious moments in the operating room (OR).

But most important for patient safety are not the technological sentries but the human ones. "The anesthesia team becomes the consciousness of the patient and must remain the 'eternal watchdog,' aided by, but not dependent on, monitors and warnings," Neufeld writes. "Technology allows man to orbit the earth as well as to operate on and resurrect the heart. The important point is that the technology does not do the job for man, technology allows man to do the job."[35]

Many of the mechanically related problems may also be educational and training problems. As James P. Welch of Massachusetts General Hospital's Department of Anesthesia and Biomedical Engineering makes clear, "There is evidence that many anesthesiologists have not been properly trained to conduct a procedure that identifies common hazardous equipment failures." He goes on to say that anesthesiologists and nurse-anesthetists need to know their equipment inside and out, because so much is riding on them. Not knowing how to fix a malfunctioning machine or machine part during an operation can be disastrous. "Yet," he notes, "because few training programs include formal instruction on equipment design or use, the anesthetist's knowledge of equipment is often based entirely on experience."[36] Furthermore, only one comprehensive reference textbook on anesthesia machine design and function is available to anesthesiologists.

"No one would attempt to fly an airplane without being thoroughly familiar with the specifics of that airplane," Schreiber has been quoted as saying. "The same consideration applies to many types of life-support equipment today. We should learn as much as possible from the [airline] industry, and from the industry's accident prevention measures."[37] These should include formal training programs with mandatory updating and refresher courses.

Schreiber and others also have recommended that standards of practice for the specialty of anesthesiology be established by the Food and Drug Administration. As set forth in the Federal Food, Drug, and Cosmetic Act, and its Medical Device Amendments of 1976, the FDA regulates only the safety of the equipment. Yet even in this limited role the FDA has not given a stellar performance. Instead of placing anesthesia machines in the category of Class III devices, in which products must undergo presumably stringent safety testing by the FDA before they can be marketed, these machines have been assigned to the far more lax Class II. This class requires some performance standards for anesthesia machines, but the FDA "has not yet begun the process of promulgating a mandatory performance standard for them, nor have they been considered by the FDA to be among the high-priority items for the development of standards."[38]

Schreiber's idea for FDA determination of practice standards has met with a predictably cold shoulder from his colleagues, who don't want outsiders to tell them what to do, and who would rather just handle it themselves. Edward Richards III, director of the Institute of Preventive Law in Medicine, believes that "critical care professionals should establish their own regulations and enforce them through the professional societies"—an idea that doctors can only love. On the other hand, Richard also thinks that practitioners should be required to have certification to use machines, and ought to get specific certifications for specific machines, in order to "do away with the idea that you can sell this complicated equipment to anyone who can write a check for it."[39]

Other equipment problems facing the anesthesiologist include excessive gas pressure, insufficient gas flow, deficient oxygen concentration, excessive anesthetic concentration, and miscellaneous mishaps. "Essentially every piece of equipment and interconnection that the anesthesiologist uses may fail."[40] The failure may be exacerbated by the fact that "awareness of infections and pollution hazards of anesthetic machines requires frequent disassembly and cleaning of parts, so there is a possibility that the equipment may be reassembled in a faulty or incomplete manner."[41]

Ultimately, though, even the most meticulous care of the machines may not do the trick, for "anesthesia equipment frequently functions in an all-or-none fashion, and even regular maintenance will not identify or prevent all problems."[42] Even standardization of equipment or the arrangement of the components, or the retirement of old and obsolete equipment, may not be enough. New equipment may not be the answer either. As Cooper notes: "More technology does not necessarily mean better or safer patient care. In fact, anesthesia may be reaching a point of diminishing returns. . . . It is wise to remember that the ultimate safety feature in anesthesia is a trained, vigilant anesthetist. Any technological solution that disregards this fact or that diminishes the importance of the patient-anesthetist relationship is a step in the wrong direction."[43]

Still when one considers the many faults in training, the recurring lapses in vigilance, and the sad state of the doctor-patient relationship, one realizes that the anesthesia pipeline may be a vicious circle.

More Problems

Not all anesthesia difficulties fall neatly into the categories of human or technological mistakes. (Even those two categories don't fall neatly into the categories.)

For example, there is the way the anesthesia agent itself is viewed by the professionals who use it. Many doctors view the chemicals as harmless if used properly. "Until recently," writes Arthur S. Keats, M.D., "pharmacologic events were not even conceived as applying to anesthetic drugs in man. The recurrent opinion has been that anesthetic agents themselves are not lethal except when misused."[44] These doctors see no possibilities of iatrogenic problems lurking within these anesthetics—which is just the way iatrogenesis can be spawned. It doesn't make sense for these physicians and experts to deny the danger; after all, "were there no ill effects attendant to anesthetics, there would be no need for experts to administer them."[45] Furthermore, when no danger is suspected, no research is conducted looking into how anesthetics work and how deaths from anesthetics can be prevented. When nothing is looked for, knowledge dies—and so may patients.

Positioning trauma is yet another anesthesia-related iatrogenic possibility. "Incorrect positioning of a patient during anesthesia," Britt, Joy, and Mackay tell us,

> may cause trauma to nerves, spinal cord, eyes, skin, muscles, tendons, ligaments, and appendages and malfunctioning of the respiratory and cardiovascular systems. These untoward events are all preventable. Nevertheless, they still constitute a major proportion of postanesthetic complications, even though they have been observed since shortly after the introduction of ether and their true etiology has been known since the end of the last century.[46]

When the patient is under the influence of an anesthetic, he can't complain about pain caused by the way he's been placed on the operating table. The results of these "postural insults" can be severe: nerve damage can occur after less than an hour in a bad position. Unnatural stretching of the body or other poor patient positioning can lead to problems. That is why an "understanding of the anatomy of the peripheral nervous system and of the physiology of the respiratory and cardiovascular systems is essential for the avoidance of potentially injury-producing positions," and why "it is the anesthesiologist's duty always to protect the patient from all of these hazards before permitting the surgeon to proceed."[47]

Although nonflammable gases, introduced over the past few decades, have reduced the incidence of the worst anesthesia-related incidents—fires and explosions—they still do occur. Some gases may be volatile, and can ignite if raised to a high enough temperature or if subjected to light sources, sparks from electrical equipment or static electricity, or other dangerous sources, with catastrophic results.[48]

Hepatitis related to the anesthetic halothane[49] and particles of glass shredding from the anesthetic-holding ampules with "the potential for intravenous injection of . . . glass particles"[50] are two other possible, but rarer, problems.

Architectural, construction, and contracting errors may contribute, and have in the past contributed, to serious "epidemics" of anesthesia-related deaths and injuries. Something as "simple" as a construction worker placing the wrong label on a gas outlet can cause the unsuspecting practitioner to cause the death of an unsuspecting patient. One of the best known of these occasionally occurring cases took place in 1976 and 1977 at Suburban General Hospital in East Norriton Township, Pennsylvania.[51] There, eleven newly built emergency room treatment cubicles were equipped with labeled oxygen outlets that were in fact plugged into nitrous oxide (laughing gas) lines, while four outlets clearly marked as being sources of nitrous oxide were in reality administering oxygen. At least five people died. It took nearly seven months for any of the medical staff to notice that something wasn't quite right and attribute certain hard-to-explain deaths to it. It took one patient turning blue while receiving "oxygen" in front of the hospital's chief anesthesiologist to bring the problem to light.

Stephen L. Liston, a professor of otolaryngology at the University of Minnesota, suggests (perhaps partially with tongue in cheek) that he has discovered "one of the causes for the occasional breakdown in communication between the anesthesiologist and the surgeon": ear wax. According to Liston, he has been asked "to remove ear wax from the external ear canal of anesthesiologists on so many occasions that I have become convinced that this is an occupational hazard of their profession. It would seem that wearing the molded ear pieces that connects to the stethoscope leads to a build-up of ear wax in the same manner that we see in some patients who wear hearing aids."[52]

The relationship of a patient's age and medical condition to successful anesthesia outcome is certainly a serious consideration. It is clear that people in end-stage diseases or extremely poor health comprise a large proportion of nonerror anesthesia deaths.

Among other serious anesthesia-related concerns is the use of anesthesia in dental offices, frequently by untrained or undertrained dentists. Only about 20 states have laws restricting use of anesthetics to those trained in administering them. But what does training mean? The director of the Academy of General Dentistry has been quoted as saying, "Some dentists take a weekend course in it [anesthesia dispensing]"; if trouble arose, they "wouldn't have any idea how to get out of it."[53]

Then, too, dentists, M.D.s, and others who work around anesthetics are themselves subject to anesthesia-related health problems. Despite "scavenger" equipment that sucks up waste anesthetic gas leaking into the atmosphere during a procedure, anesthesia is absorbed by the practitioners and other personnel. "Chronic exposure to trace concentrations of anesthetic gases, primarily halothane and nitrous oxide," an American Dental Association study found, "has been linked to an increased incidence of liver, kidney, and neurologic diseases, miscarriages in female personnel and spouses of male personnel, and a greater incidence of birth defects."[54] The main sources of excessive gas levels are "high-pressure leaks in a pipe or cylinder and the work practices of the anesthesiologist"[55]—that is, a machine problem or an incompetent or sloppy practitioner.

However, the problem goes beyond damage to medical or dental personnel—the problem gets passed on to the patient as well in a different way. One researcher is quoted as believing that scavenging is important because "there are a lot fewer sleepy anesthesiologists in scavenged operating rooms, and they're making better decisions and having a lot more energy at the end of the day."[56] But what of the anesthesiologist or dentist in a nonscavenged or insufficiently scavenged office or operating room? How sleepy is he? How good are his decisions? How safe are his patients?

This much is clear. Despite a statistically low anesthesia-related death rate and a somewhat more prevalent injury rate, there is much to be done to make anesthesia as safe as it can be and to prevent the vast number of incidents that are absolutely preventable. To do less would be unconscionable. It is time for the public and health advocates to take a good look at anesthesiology, the medical practice that is "hidden behind the operating room doors and cloaked in a cloud of soporific vapors," where it has "remained relatively remote from public attention, medical instrument manufacturers, hospital administrators, insurance companies, and other physician groups." Until that time, improvements will continue to arrive at the anesthetizing station "in a slow and, often, piecemeal fashion,"[57] and unnecessary mortality and morbidity will persist.

4

....

SEEING THINGS

"Physicians think they are doing something for you by labeling what you have as a disease."

—Immanuel Kant

In theory, at least, diagnosing illness has been the medical profession's strongest suit. Even before they had the tools to aid in the fight against certain conditions, it seemed that doctors could divine what they were up against. They might have been helpless in combating the disease, but their training let them presume they were on top of things, that they were informed—both by the book and through their intuition and experience—and could in turn soothe and inform the patient and the patient's family.

Today, all of that—accurate diagnosing, informing, and soothing—resides in a very problematic universe. And, as medical care has become more sophisticated, more technology bound, and more capable of finding things wrong with patients (including things that aren't there—the "non-disease diseases"), medical professionals have gained the tools to act and to treat, but in the process have lost the elemental tools of listening, observing, and diagnosing. Ronald P. Rapini, M.D., scorns this trend in the pages of the *New England Journal of Medicine;* he believes that the education and practice of medical students and primary care physicians "should emphasize diagnosis, not treatment. Once a diagnosis is made," he says, "a physician can always look up the treatment somewhere. If physicians cannot make a diagnosis, they are hopelessly doomed to trial-and-error or symptomatic therapy."[1] And their patients are doomed to feel the effects of this groping in the dark.

By discovering (or, as some see it, by inventing) an avalanche of new diseases, conditions, syndromes, and symptoms, physicians make it difficult for themselves to pinpoint anything with precision, for there is so much to choose from and, thus, so many possible diagnostic errors and traps to fall into. They have made it worse, though, by denying uncertainty, failing to communicate well with patients, wielding self-determined superiority, and leaping before looking.

So despite the advances that have been made (or, more likely, because of them), the level of misdiagnosing of disease in the United States— errors of both commission and omission—is far too high. And that means the amount of malpractice and unnecessary treatment, the number of forced drug dependencies and disrupted or ruined lives, is disgraceful, immoral, and certainly, at the very least, unprofessional. Of the top five reasons Americans sue their doctors for malpractice, the number one reason is failure to diagnose cancer, number three is failure to diagnose fractures or dislocations, and number four is failure to diagnose a pregnancy-related problem.[2]

Why are mistakes in diagnosis—missing what's there, finding what isn't—happening at such wholly unacceptable rates, despite medicine's advances and its assurances to the contrary?

Now You See It, Now You Don't

Misdiagnosis as a medical way of life begins early. Medical students and interns make lots of errors in diagnosis during physical examinations; some studies show that the incidence of such errors is 40 percent or more, with errors of commission comprising about 7 percent and errors of omission 25 to 35 percent.[3] A 1983 Houston Veterans Administration Medical Center and Baylor College of Medicine study found residents made errors 13.1 percent of the time, while interns made mistakes 15.6 percent of the time. And, according to the study, "approximately two-thirds of all patients examined had at least one error noted."[4]

Wiener and Nathanson found that despite five years of medical training, interns and residents made large numbers of errors during standard physical examinations, which could be classified as follows:[5]

ERRORS OF TECHNIQUE
1. Poor ordering and organization of the examination.
2. Defective or no equipment.
3. Improper manual technique or use of instruments.
4. Inappropriate performance of the examination (i.e., when required patient cooperation or other prerequisites were not present).
5. Poor bedside etiquette, leading to patient discomfort or embarrassment, or overt hostility.

ERRORS OF OMISSION
  1. Failure to perform part of the examination.

ERRORS OF DETECTION
  1. Missing a sign that is present.
  2. Reporting detection of a sign that is not present.
  3. Interpreting normal physiological or anatomic variation as abnormal.
  4. Misidentifying a sign after detection.

ERRORS OF INTERPRETATION
  1. Failure to understand the meaning in pathophysiological terms of an identified sign.
  2. Lack of knowledge of or use of confirming signs.
  3. Lack of knowledge of the value of a sign in confirming or ruling out a diagnostic entity.

ERRORS OF RECORDING
  1. Forgetting a finding and not recording it.
  2. Using illegible handwriting, obscure abbreviations, improper terminology, or poor grammar, and doing incomplete recording of findings.
  3. Recording a diagnosis and not the sign detected.

These, though seemingly innocuous, are or can be major errors—any one of them leading to a course of treatment that could harm a patient. Of course, these were "greenhorn" interns and only slightly more seasoned residents. They are new at the game. They have a lot to learn. That they make their mistakes on trusting patients, and that these mistakes may not be caught by more experienced physicians until it is too late (if ever), are certainly disquieting facts. But they are the facts of life in medical training to which many if not most patients admitted to medical school-affiliated hospitals must submit. More disturbing is that although there is a decreasing incidence of error with each year spent in medical training, the Baylor study still shows that "the number of errors in the final year remains significant." What's more, too high a level of misdiagnosis "also exists among experienced private practitioners and university-affiliated attending physicians."[6]

In fact, experienced physicians show signs of alarming diagnostic weakness in their ability to estimate probabilities and in their lack of knowledge about the risks that can occur as a result of an operation or procedure. For example, a study published in the *Journal of the American Medical Association* looked at doctors' accuracy in estimating the probability of disease. Accuracy in such instances is, of course, important because these predictions often determine the type and number of diagnostic tests ordered and performed, the medication prescribed, and the course of treatment. The researchers chose ten doctors—board-certified or board-eligible medical school faculty members—and had them examine patients complaining of sore throats at a university student health center. The physicians recorded their estimates of the probability of these patients having strep throat. The doctors were also to note what treatment they would institute, and they were to do this before lab results on the throat cultures were made available to them—something that doctors in private practice do all the time.

The results: In 81 percent of the cases, the doctors overestimated the chance that the patients' throat cultures would be positive for strep. In reality, only 15 people out of the total of 308 (4.9 percent) given throat cultures showed positive for streptococcal infection. What's worse, and highly indicative, is that doctors—basing their actions on faulty predictive abilities—actually started 104 patients on drug therapy for strep throat, when in fact only 8 of them actually had the condition. "If overtreatment is defined as the use of antibiotics in culture-negative patients," wrote the research team, "the physicians' probability overestimation was associated with substantial overtreatment."[7]

Add to this a 1985 study from the University of Washington's Department of Family Medicine.[8] Researchers there attempted to discover how well physicians knew the risks involved and the complications possible in ten surgical and invasive diagnostic procedures. The importance of accurate knowledge of these risks and complications is crucial if physicians are to make the proper treatment decisions and to prevent or handle the problems that can arise during these procedures. In other words, if a doctor knows that a certain procedure has a high risk or a high level of complications, he might try an alternative procedure with less risk and a lower level of complication. Seems simple. However, among the 128 doctors surveyed—all members of the Washington State Medical Association—the results were not good and less than comforting. Of the total responses given to this test of knowledge:

- Only 27 percent were correct.
- 26 percent underestimated the dangers.
- 27 percent overestimated the dangers.
- A startling 21 percent admitted no knowledge as to the dangers.

Equally astonishing, these researchers also found "that for each procedure at least one physician explicitly stated that the complication in question 'never occurred' or had a rate of 'zero' or 'none'." Furthermore, the study points out that of the many doctors who made "gross underestimates" of the potential risks of and complications possible in a herniorrhaphy (the surgical repair of a hernia), many were doctors who performed the procedure on a regular basis.[9]

The researchers stated that being board certified didn't improve accuracy, and neither did the number of years in practice or whether the doctor was a surgeon or a general practitioner. They appeared "similarly ignorant."[10] The researchers concluded that:

> The possible consequences of not knowing this information are readily apparent. If physicians underestimate the risks of a procedure, more patients may be subjected to the procedure with the associated increases in morbidity, mortality, and health care costs. It seems likely that if physicians knew that the risk of death among elderly men undergoing herniorrhaphy was actually much higher than they currently estimate, fewer elective hernia repairs would be carried out on such patients. The converse may also apply: If risks are overestimated, we may tip the balance of clinical decision against the use of the procedure, thereby depriving our patients of a valuable therapeutic or diagnostic alternative. The magnitude of some of the commonly made errors in estimating these risks suggests that their effects may be of great clinical significance and have substantial impact on health services.[11]

Dead Men Do Tell Tales

Postmortem, a person speaks loudly. Ironically, the corpse is often treated by members of the medical profession with more interest and concern for detail than the live person was. Coroners and hospital pathologists are discovering that too many cadavers on slabs before them are victims of medical incompetence, especially in the area of diagnosis.

When researchers examined 100 consecutive cases in which autopsies conclusively proved the victims had suffered heart attacks, then looked back at the records to see if doctors had diagnosed heart attack, they were shocked to discover that only 53 percent had been diagnosed. That is, nearly half of all heart attacks had been undiagnosed or misdiagnosed. This 47 percent failure rate was deemed "appalling" by the researchers— a strong, emotional opinion seldom seen in the dry, stuffy, coldly authoritative pages of medical journals. The study went on to say that it was "particularly disturbing when it is considered that the myocardial infarction was the cause of death in two thirds of the cases. . . ." And even more unnerving was the discovery that "half of the cases were managed by cardiologists."[12] What good are experts if they're not expert—or even close?

A nationwide, 32-hospital study that compared 1,800 "clinical" diagnoses made on living patients to "anatomical" diagnoses made at autopsy found the error rate was nearly 20 percent. About half of those mistakes probably led directly to the patients' deaths. According to a report by Washington University in St. Louis, one of the institutions participating in that national study, the most common medical problems overlooked and the rate at which they were overlooked were:[13]

- Pulmonary embolism—nearly one in two.
- Peritonitis—nearly one in two.
- Pulmonary abscess—nearly four in ten.

These statistics were similar to those of a 1983 study at Boston's Brigham and Women's Hospital and Harvard Medical School. In it, researchers found that doctors missed certain diagnoses in dying patients up to nearly one-fourth of the time and that one in ten people would have lived had diagnoses been made and made correctly.[14]

An autopsy-based survey at St. Joseph's Hospital in Tucson came up with about the same figure—20 percent of missed major clinical diagnoses.[15] And in a Northwestern University Medical School review of 2,537 cases it was determined by autopsy that in 10 percent of the patients "serious primary disease leading to death of the patient was not diagnosed correctly. . . ."[16] The researchers also found it "significant" that "64 percent of all autopsies disclosed one or more important undiagnosed diseases or surprises that were unsuspected before death."[17]

There are other such studies with similar results. To put things in some sort of perspective, if these averages were seen as school grades, the doctors involved would at best be squeaking by with a C-plus, and at worst would be flunking. Is that really good enough? Would the public accept that sort of on-again, off-again accuracy from other practitioners involved in life-or-death situations?

Why the mistakes, misdiagnoses, oversights? Joel E. Dimsdale, M.D., of the psychiatry department at Harvard Medical School's Massachusetts General Hospital, writes, "We make diagnostic mistakes when we lack sufficient knowledge, when we are careless in evaluating a patient, when our laboratories are in error, or when our interpretations of laboratory findings are in error." To these, Dimsdale adds another, often overlooked culprit, one that "can lead to profound errors in medical diagnosis"—"the physician's feelings about the patient or his illness."[18]

Looking at several case histories of misdiagnosis and the role the doctor-patient relationship may have played in them, Dimsdale shows[19] that a common thread running through them is physician discomfort; that:

• When the patient came from a group (racial, professional, or otherwise) with which the physician was uncomfortable, his abilities to piece together the differential diagnosis plummeted.

• When the patient's behavior made the doctor feel uncomfortable or angry, the doctor was unable to reach a diagnostic conclusion that he should have been capable of reaching by virtue of training and experience.

• When the patient was too close to the doctor, when he was a colleague with whom he worked, the doctor's decision-making ability was also impaired.

• When the patient's illness itself made the physician uncomfortable, he had difficulty acknowledging the presence of the illness and referring the patient appropriately.

Physicians are unable or unwilling to acknowledge that these patient-generated feelings lead to misdiagnoses. These attitudes stand in the way of any improvement in the crisis of diagnosis, and certainly of the doctor-patient relationship in general. The potential for the encroachment of social, cultural, or racial bias in physician decision making, judgment, and even commitment cannot be underplayed. Such biases are deeply rooted and not easily changed. Here we can rely only on careful monitoring of physician services and on a patient population that knows the potential for this risk, knows its rights to responsible diagnosis and treatment, and knows how to redress its grievances. With the growing number of AIDS patients, particularly among stigmatized groups such as homosexuals, bisexuals, and intravenous drug users, the importance of the physicians' social prejudices looms large.

Add to this the most common thread, the most oft-repeated physician-centered flaw seen in most surveys on the subjects of misdiagnosis, maldiagnosis, and nondiagnosis: that doctors are relying far too heavily on new technology and not enough on what their own eyes, ears, noses, fingertips, brains, and intuition should be telling them. Presumably they've had instruction on how to use those basic and quite effective human tools in the first place. "Lab tests and diagnostic machines wouldn't be so dangerous if doctors weren't addicted to the quantitative information these tools provide," writes Robert S. Mendelsohn, M.D. "Since numbers and statistics are Modern Medicine's language of prayer, quantitative information is considered sacred, the word of God, indeed, the *last* word in a diagnosis. Whether the tools are simple, like thermometers, scales, or calibrated infant bottles, or complicated, like X-ray machines, EKGs, EEGs, and lab tests, people and doctors are dazzled into crowding out of the process their own common sense and the qualitative judgment of doctors who are real diagnostic artists.''[20]

Ironically, there are problems as well stemming from the reluctance (or inability) of some physicians to apply good quantitative analyses. Those physicians suffer from a statistical phobia or find it difficult to believe in the results of careful clinical trials or large probability sample studies if these results are at odds with their own (far more limited) experience. Although medical schools offer some limited training in epidemiology and biostatistics, these subjects are always near the bottom of the popularity scale. They are simply not seen as clinically relevant.

X Marks No Spot

If the miscues and missed clues uncovered by autopsies are shocking, the accuracy rate of those who read X-rays is even worse.

Whereas 10 to 20 percent was the range of clinical misdiagnosis found at autopsy, nearly every published study puts the mistake rate of X-ray readers at 20 to 40 percent. In one research project, ''despite more modern equipment and facilities, more refined techniques, and presumably more advanced approaches to the teaching of radiology,'' it was seen that radiologists working at Harvard University ''disagreed on the interpretation of chest radiographs as much as 56 percent of the time. Moreover, there were potentially significant errors in 41 percent of their reports.''[21] In addition, according to the same article, by Leonard Berlin, M.D., ''studies have shown that up to 20 percent of colon tumors are missed in the lower gastrointestinal series. In a recent study at the University of Missouri, an error rate of 30 percent was reported among staff radiologists for chest radiographs, bone studies, gastrointestinal series, and special procedures.''[22]

The total population of the United States when Berlin wrote his paper was 240 million. He estimated that 144 million of those people would undergo a radiological examination that year, and he arrived at the mind-boggling conclusion that about 43 million people would have their X-rays misinterpreted and, thus, their illnesses possibly misdiagnosed.[23] Even when X-rays are read a second time, only about a third of the initial errors are discovered.[24]

Why these errors? Some, like Rhea et al., claim that ''there will always be errors when humans perceive and interpret an image.''[25] Still, one has to be concerned that such a contention might distract us from acknowledging and doing something about the excessively high current rates of error. We have a long way to go before we need worry about the irreducible minimum rate of error. This seems to be merely a rationale for bad or sloppy practitioners.

More likely the problem is haste, in addition to undertrained and underskilled interpreters. "Ideally we may prefer that a radiologist study a radiograph for five or ten minutes, review the patient's medical history and physical and laboratory findings, consult with the attending physician, and finally examine the patient personally before rendering his decision; however, we all know that such a practice is virtually nonexistent," says Berlin. "In most hospitals, particularly when there is no radiology teaching or residency program, a single radiologist will render his interpretations of a stack of radiographs quickly, without recourse to the patient's records and the attending physician's consultation. In such an environment, errors are more commonplace; yet it is exactly this type of situation which provides the 'standard' against which most radiologists are measured today."[26] The sheer amount of X-rays taken—the excessive use of radiography as a result of so-called defensive medicine, sheer greed, or the continued attitude among physicians that many X-rays are "routine" as part of a patient diagnostic package deal—is probably contributing to these hasty and cursory readings and to reading errors.

Additionally, Swensson, Hessel, and Herman hypothesize that mistakes and oversights occur because "the radiologist terminates his visual search prematurely, e.g., upon detecting what he considers to be a key finding, without thoroughly examining the remainder of the film. Studies of radiologists' eye movements during interpretation confirm that large areas of the film are never examined. . . ."[27]

Misread X-rays either lead to incorrect, unnecessary treatment or postpone needed procedures. If 43 million Americans are having their X-rays misinterpreted every year, it is no simple national dilemma. It would seem to be nothing less than an epidemic.

Mental Breakdown

People with real or alleged psychiatric or behavioral disorders are being misdiagnosed—and harmed—to an astonishing degree. Many of them do not have psychiatric problems but exhibit physical symptoms that may mimic mental conditions, and so they are misdiagnosed, put on drugs, put in institutions, and sent into a limbo from which they may never return. Others may be considered mental cases because the doctor simply can't explain in a biomechanical way what's wrong with the person. This false assumption of psychological illness based on nothing more than uncertainty, insecurity, and ignorance is "probably the most common error made in medicine."[28] On the other hand, the physical illnesses of psychiatric patients go underdiagnosed or undiagnosed. In more ways than one, the psychiatric patient is an afterthought, a stepchild of society, stigmatized and held in low regard.

A study of 215 patients sent to a medical-psychiatric inpatient unit, in research undertaken by the medical-psychiatric unit and consultation-liaison service at St. Mary's Hospital and Medical Center, and the department of psychiatry at the University of California School of Medicine, San Francisco, found that further tests "resulted in a therapeutically important alteration of the referring diagnosis in 41 percent."[29] Furthermore, of the patients sent to this psychiatric unit with a tentative diagnosis of "untreatable dementia," an amazing 63 percent in reality had treatable conditions.

Robert S. Hoffman, M.D., the author of the study, points the finger at the process whereby "a primary physician applies a preliminary diagnosis of mental disorder, which is decisive in determining the patient's subsequent course."[30] In other words, a physician—general practitioner, family practitioner, internist—with little knowledge of psychiatric or behavioral disorders makes a stab at what he thinks is wrong with the patient, and puts the person on a track he or she should not be on. Very often the problem isn't mental at all, but rather an underlying physical condition the physician had been trained to look for, diagnose, and treat—but missed. Worse, according to Hoffman, was how often the supposed psychiatric or behavioral problems were due to nonpsychiatric medications prescribed by the doctor, who then never considered the drug as a possible cause of the difficulty. These were not minor drug reactions either—apathy due to depression or delirium was the most common symptom—but, according to Hoffman, "in only 3 of 13 patients with toxic deliria were medications suspected as a causative factor despite the fact that the patients were known to be taking drugs of well-recognized psychotoxic potential."[31]

Hoffman concluded on a note of warning:

> If the misdiagnosis rate in our series accurately reflects the situation in other communities, many such patients are wrongly being labeled as demented and treated accordingly. The consequences in terms of the cost of medical care and institutionalization, to say nothing of the human suffering involved, are immense. The limiting factor for such patients appears to be inadequate assessment rather than incurability.[32]

In another study, when 131 randomly selected patients at the Manhattan Psychiatric Center were examined, it was found that "approximately 75 percent of the patients reevaluated may have been wrongly diagnosed when admitted to the center," and that "frequent misdiagnosis of schizophrenia caused severe harm to many patients who were inappropriately given powerful drugs, such as neuroleptics, that mask symptoms and may cause irreversible side effects."[33]

Misdiagnosis in a psychiatric setting tends to err on the side of the psychiatric rather than the physical. The assumption is that the problem is mental and signs indicating it might be physical are often disregarded as being unlikely. It can be a disastrous assumption. "Making a mistaken diagnosis of schizophrenia—as opposed to taking schizophrenia to be something else—is the more dangerous error," says William Carpenter, director of the Maryland Psychiatric Research Center. "Generally, if you miss the diagnosis of schizophrenia, other treatments are not likely to do a patient much harm. But the reverse is not true. If you make the mistaken assumption of chronic schizophrenia, the patient may never recoup his losses."[34]

According to experts in the field, the neuroleptic drugs given to schizophrenics, or those assumed to be schizophrenics—Thorazine is the best known of these drugs—can cause grave, permanent side effects like tremors and spasms, and can foil any attempts at reexamination and rediagnosis. Then, too, the danger of "prescribing neuroleptics to patients who are actually depressed . . . is that their depression may not be relieved, and can worsen."[35] Misdiagnosis, and misprescribed drugs, the Manhattan study showed, can lead to suicide.

Other studies and surveys indicate the same level of misdiagnosis:

• Researchers at McLean Hospital in Belmont, Massachusetts, delved into 49 geriatric psychiatry cases and discovered that "medical factors were implicated as a direct cause of psychiatric symptoms in 12 cases, with a probable relationship in 8 and a possible relationship in 4. Of these, 7 involved adverse effects of drugs, most of which were given for nonpsychiatric indications."[36] It was also seen clearly that "when the major medical problem improved, the chances of psychiatric improvement were greater."[37]

• And a paper produced at the University of Ottawa and Ottawa General Hospital demonstrated that 43 percent of psychiatric patients had one or several undiagnosed physical illnesses, that in nearly 20 percent of these "the somatic pathologic condition alone was the cause of the psychiatric disorder" and that "physicians other than psychiatrists missed one-third and psychiatrists one-half of the major medical illnesses in patients they referred."[38]

The reverse side of this misdiagnosis coin is that of errors of omission. Whereas primary care physicians may wrongly be determining that patients have mental illness when they don't, they are equally adept at underestimating true psychiatric difficulties. In fact, a 1984 meeting of the Association of American Medical Colleges was told that primary care physicians are so unskilled at determining psychiatric problems, they overlook 90 percent of those staring them right in the face.[39] This meeting was also given the suspected reason for the misdiagnoses and underdiagnoses: ". . . patients receiving psychiatric care from primary physicians are likely to receive no more than 15 minutes of interview time and are then sent home with medication."[40] But the root of the difficulties goes even further back: "At the core of the problem is the poor training that most medical students receive in psychiatry"; in medical schools "less than half of the teaching of psychiatry is done by psychiatrists" and "of 205 family practice residency programs studied, 25 percent did not require a psychiatry rotation and 20 percent used nonphysicians to teach specialized psychiatric material that would ordinarily be the responsibility of a physician."[41] And this can lead to related, unfortunate situations, like the one shown by Rose et al., in which physicians rarely considered depression as a possible root cause of bowel disorders among patients they were seeing but instead immediately assumed there was something organically wrong with the patients. In fact, further study showed that among patients who were determined to be depressed "no organic disorder was detected in 64 percent" of those who came in with abdominal pain or irritable bowel syndrome. "That depression is common in gastrointestinal outpatients is not always appreciated," wrote the researchers, and pointed out that this lack of appreciation often led to unnecessary investigations and surgery.[42]

It all comes down to this: Doctors are making big and plentiful mistakes in diagnosing both physical and mental ills—or nonills—and people are being hurt because of it. More examples:

• During a test, 80 doctors could find only half the lumps hidden in silicone models of female breasts. Might this 50 percent error rate have something to do with the fact that even though they knew they were being tested and observed and were told to treat the models as though they were real in a real examining situation, the doctors spent a mean time of less than two minutes examining these "breasts" for cancerous signs before coming up with their misdiagnoses?[43] Had they been real breasts, the untreated breast cancer implications are enormous. Meanwhile, this information dovetails with that of earlier and concurrent studies showing that breast cancer is the source of a very large number of malpractice suits against primary care physicians specializing in family practice, obstetrics/gynecology, general surgery, and internal medicine—suits based not on faulty or catastrophic courses of treatment but rather "based on delayed diagnosis or misdiagnosis." Some of the areas of diagnostic error leading to these suits had to do with:

> —Doctors accepting a negative mammogram as the only evidence they felt they needed to rule out cancer. In fact, mammography is not fail-safe. The doctors should have known this but instead relied too heavily on technology, and by doing so they delayed performing important and even potentially life-saving biopsies.
>
> —On the flip side, doctors not following up on detected breast irregularities, including those shown in a positive mammogram.
>
> —Doctors inadequately evaluating nipple discharges.
>
> —Doctors ignoring patients' repeated breast complaints.[44]

• Of general hospital admissions, 20 to 40 percent involve "individuals with serious drinking or drug problems, most of them alcohol, as do 10 to 15 percent of ambulatory cases and 40 to 60 percent of emergency room visits"—and yet the actual diagnosis of alcohol or drug use or dependency is made in fewer than 5 percent of cases.[45]

• In 1986, Sen. John East of North Carolina killed himself, and in his suicide note he blamed his doctor for failing to diagnose his hypothyroidism—a failure that ruined his health, made his life too painful to live, and was the reason for his self-inflicted death.[46]

• A 48-year-old Maryland woman was told she was dying of multiple myeloma, a particularly deadly cancer, and had only 12 months to live. She underwent chemotherapy with the drugs melphalan and prednisone, made arrangements for her own funeral, broke off with her fiancé, quit her job, and spent some psychologically devastating time in a cancer ward surrounded by dying people—then found out she had never had cancer. In fact, one of the doctors involved in the case had noted on her chart that he did not believe she had multiple myeloma and should by no means be treated for it. However, the next time she showed up at that doctor's office for a checkup, his senior partner, without doing further tests, started her on a chemotherapy regimen. This was such a departure from acceptable practice and did so much harm that the junior doctor actually acted as a witness for the plaintiff at her malpractice trial. After five weeks, the chemotherapy treatments were stopped. A later, special examination at Memorial Sloan-Kettering Cancer Center in New York showed that she did not have multiple myeloma and never had. She is now "obsessed with the disease, and according to testimony at her [malpractice suit] trial the chemotherapy increased her chances of getting it."[47]

• Similarly, a former auto worker in St. Louis was told by two pathologists that he had adenocarcinoma of the esophagus, a rare form of cancer. The two doctors made their diagnoses based on a biopsy. The man underwent an operation that involved the removal of a rib and portions of his esophagus and stomach. It was only after the surgery that the doctors discovered that he had never had cancer at all. Despite a $2.5 million malpractice judgment in his favor, the man has been and probably will always be in constant pain, is unable to work, and, in the words of his attorney, "The man's body is a total disaster."[48]

These are just a few stories and studies, pulled at random from the authors' files—files of research, and of personal letters addressed to the authors directly or to the People's Medical Society. The letters are far too numerous to indicate any progress in the area of diagnosis/misdiagnosis, and far too numerous to publish here. One People's Medical Society member wrote in a letter of her years of headaches, tingling fingers, and balance difficulties. She was diagnosed by a string of doctors as having everything from a pinched nerve to infection of the spinal fluid, multiple sclerosis to "it's your nerves, honey"—all the while slowly becoming a quadriplegic until it was finally discovered that she had a brain tumor, benign and operable. She is still trying to regain the physical skills she lost during those years of agony, and she writes: "If only those doctors had told me or my husband that they didn't know what my problem was and had sent me to someone else, I might have found out sooner and not had to go through what I did. Doctors have to realize that they are not 'gods,' and have the guts to tell a person that they don't know what the problem is."

States Joseph Lipinski, a psychiatrist at Harvard Medical School: "Some people would like to pretend misdiagnosis has gone away. But it hasn't. And the human wreckage is outrageous."[49]

5

SCHOOL FOR SCANDAL

". . . in these days when a student must be converted into a physiologist, a physicist, a chemist, a biologist, a pharmacologist, and an electrician, there is no time to make a physician of him."

—Andrew MacPhail

"The child is father of the man."

—William Wordsworth

Long before the person who, for better or for worse, has become a doctor can lay so much as a cold stethoscope on the person who, for better or for worse, has become a patient, those four-plus years of learning and on-the-job training known as the American medical education transpire. During these years the knowledge, the habits, and the attitudes of physicians are mined and molded. Any discussion about medical education and what makes a doctor a doctor (and what makes a doctor a doctor who makes mistakes) invariably ends up sounding like food scientists debating the properties of something like monosodium glutamate: Does the product add a new flavor, or does it merely emphasize the properties already present?

A sort of corollary to that might be: Is medical school—and, thus, the medical profession—attracting the right people? Does it even know who the right people are? Is it bringing into the fold of its secret handshake society too large a percentage of the wrong people, who will go on to become inept and possibly even dangerous practitioners?

Any admissions process should be as harrowing for the admitters as it is for those admitted. For admissions panels or committees in medical schools, it is even more pressure filled: There are very few slots for very many seemingly qualified young men and women (mostly men, mostly white). Those who are admitted must not only uphold what is seen as the good reputation of the school but should also evolve into the kinds of doctors who will make their alma mater and the medical good old boys network proud. And, to a large extent, these admissions committees are successful—severely shortsighted and limited though their definition of "successful" may be. They are excellent judges of stick-to-itiveness; most medical schools in the United States have very few dropouts and failing students. In general, getting in means staying in and making it through.

But there are gaping flaws in the medical school admission process, flaws large and numerous enough for critics in and outside the medical profession to call for the schools to do some serious rethinking about what medical school admissions criteria ought to be.

Premed

What sort of student is presently sought by medical school committees and rewarded by admission? According to Cynthia Carver, M.D., the process of medical school selection "results in academically oriented, competitive and intelligent young people being chosen. Characteristics such as warmth, sensitivity or ability to communicate and listen do not weigh heavily."[1]

Furthermore: "The personal values that students bring with them to medical training set the stage for the way they eventually will practice medicine," say the medical writing team of Michael B. Rothenberg, M.D., and Jo Rothenberg. "Medical school admissions committees select groups of students who seem to share certain compulsive, competitive, and egocentric traits. When those students enter into curricula that not only reinforce those traits, but also add to them the expectations of omniscience and omnipotence, then it appears that the people who are responsible for those curricula are, to a large extent, influencing the professional values and capabilities of many of our doctors."[2]

It's a matter of like attracting like, and becoming one.

For a long time medical schools, in their admissions process, have keyed in on students who graduated from college with high grades in the sciences—biology and chemistry and what is considered the "premed" track. The rationalization is that these are the only people who can weather the bitter storm of graduate education and become doctors. Of course, this sentiment is held by those who themselves slogged through biology and chemistry and premed courses when they were younger, and who now are in a position to reward the new generation of mirror images (and, in the process, honor themselves, protect themselves, and reinforce the worthiness of their own dicta and training) by admitting them to medical school.

In this way, the broadly educated person whose background is in the liberal arts—the scholar, if you will—finds himself or herself at a substantial disadvantage whenever and wherever he or she wants to go to medical school. Those held in favor are those who have studied little else than the sciences. They may even have left undergraduate school before the fourth year because of the opportunity to hop from one extremely focused scientific lily pad to another, without wetting their toes in the mainstream of the studies of human endeavors.

The President's Commission for the Study of Ethical Problems in Medicine and Biomedical and Behavioral Research reported in 1982 that "although most medical schools require premedical training in such fields as biology and chemistry, few require humanities or social and behavioral science courses." When the commission took a look at the entering classes for all medical schools in the United States in 1979–1980, the outlook wasn't very hopeful. Less than 8 percent of the new doctors-to-be had majored in the humanities or social and behavioral sciences, or other, similar nonscience disciplines. "Thus," the commission concluded, "it may be that the undergraduate experiences of most successful applicants are deficient in the exposure to the social sciences and humanities that could help sensitize them to the concepts and skills essential to becoming effective and responsive communicators."[3]

"Students interested in medicine but unwilling for whatever reason to pursue science majors may be discouraged from competing for places in medical schools," state Dickman et al. in the *Journal of the American Medical Association*. "Admissions committees in medical schools continue to weigh 'scientific aptitude' more than any other factor in their admission process."[4]

And for no really good reason. In the Dickman survey, students in medical school who had not majored in science as undergraduates were compared with those who had done so (the latter comprising at least 75 percent of medical students today). Grades, clinical performance, and national board medical examination scores of three medical school classes at the State University of New York at Buffalo were looked at. The results: "Examination scores revealed no significant differences across three class replications. Residency selection among graduating seniors was also independent of undergraduate major." The recommendation: "It is suggested that admissions committees, premedical advisers, and students reconsider their attitudes about the necessity of concentration in the natural sciences before entering medical school."[5]

In most cases, a personal interview is held in conjunction with the medical school application process. Here, too, there are serious problems. As Keill and Willer remark, "Research on the admissions process indicates that interviewers and decisions of admissions committees on the desirability of certain applicants may be biased by the applicants' academic credentials.''[6] That is, an applicant who shows poor communication skills and no tendency toward compassion (two elements in the all-important doctor-patient relationship) may still get a slot in school because he fulfills the mirror image requirements.

If the personal interview carries any weight at all, then, it does so not by confirming to the interviewers that ''This is a person with a great future in caring,'' but rather that ''This is one of us.'' The trouble is, though, that he or she might *not* be one of them, but just somebody who is good at interviews. Take, for example, the case of the pseudonymous med student, Tim Morton, who tells his true story in Peter MacGarr Rabinowitz's *Talking Medicine.*[7] Morton had fared poorly in his first attempt to get into medical school; he suffered for having had low grades in his freshman year in college (Harvard) and for being an English major, not a science major. He also was idealistic, and he cared about caring. His interview at the medical school of the University of Washington was a disaster. After his rejection, he graduated from college, and the only employment he could find was emptying garbage cans at a state park.

Then his interest in a medical education was rekindled, and he sought the help of a professor and family friend. She explained to him that ''most of getting into medical school was politics, in the sense that you have to present yourself in the most favorable light and appear to be the sort of person that the medical school is looking for.''[8] She urged him to take more college courses with impressive-sounding scientific titles, to strive to get the top grade in each class (the grade being more important than a true understanding of the subject), and to get good letters of recommendation. This family friend advised Morton that med schools ''aren't interested in greenhorn idealistic people who want to change the system— they want people who understand that the system is there because it is the best possible system.''[9] He fudged on his application to make it look better than it really was; he did this by listing ordinary scholarships as ''honors.'' Disregarding his own true feelings, he answered questions on the application form in ways he thought the admissions committee would approve of. He expressed no opinions. He regurgitated a party line. He felt morally bankrupt doing this, but he wanted to be a doctor, and to attain that goal he played the game.

Coached for his interview by friends who were already first-year med students, Morton put on a false front and struck a phony pose, and breezed through the interview. Although he felt certain that the second interview had gone worse than the first, he received his acceptance a month later.

Perhaps, on the one hand, Tim Morton's story can be seen as a victory for the liberal arts faction. After all, he was an English major who did get in. But, more seriously, it ought to be seen as a not atypical bamboozling of an admissions panel. Who knows what kind of people are getting into medical school, if play acting counts for so much? And how does this portend for the future of medicine—or the patients of doctors who can lie so well?

The President's Commission for the Study of Ethical Problems in Medicine and Biomedical and Behavioral Research reported in 1982 that among the "suggestions for changes in selection criteria" there was one that favored "individual assessments, either through interviews or psychological tests, for an applicant's predisposition toward humane service."[10] This brings up another real concern: the psychological makeup of the medical school applicant and admittee.

"There is ample evidence," report Keill and Willer, "of higher-than-average rates of substance abuse, psychiatric hospitalizations, and suicide among medical students."[11] Rothenberg and Rothenberg acknowledge studies in the medical literature that show that "episodes of depression or emotional distress are experienced frequently or severely by one-third of the interns and that about one-quarter of the interns experience suicidal ideation."[12] It is terrible to have such things happen, but they do happen. Medical school is full of pressure, or the student can be made to feel that it is.

More ominous and, certainly, more directly affecting the welfare of patients, is Keill and Willer's finding that "most students who do experience psychiatric problems eventually do complete their medical education . . ."; and that "the long-term effect of problems experienced during the medical school career are unknown."[13] Not all psychiatric conditions are permanently debilitating and complete recoveries can be made. But it is a very big red flag waving wildly just out of sight of patients. It is practically impossible for a patient to find out how well a doctor did in school (we all would like to be treated by someone who did well rather than someone who just squeaked through). Imagine, then, how much less likely the doctor is to admit to having had psychiatric problems in med school . . . and after.

Granted (and luckily for unwary patients everywhere), the number of psychiatrically at risk medical school applicants is small. What is frightening, though, is the profile of the psychiatrically afflicted applicant or student: "The student most likely to have problems," Keill and Willer tell us, "is a white male who is entering medical school directly out of his undergraduate college." In other words, this description, we are further informed, "sounds like the typical medical student."[14]

Class and Clinic

Once admitted to medical school, the green, eager, and impressionable student learns the trade and is indoctrinated into the "union." "The training program," writes Cynthia Carver:

> is disease oriented, with life-threatening or rare conditions receiving the most attention, and the acquisition of skill in doing procedures . . . and using diagnostic machines . . . being prized. The day-to-day ills of the public are ignored as "minor problems." The promotion of health and the prevention of disease are almost entirely neglected. Techniques for the relief of symptoms such as pain, fatigue, or anxiety are not emphasized.[15]

The patients seen by the students are extremes. Many have exotic diseases, are seriously ill, or are bedridden. Few have ordinary ailments or are ambulatory. This is just the opposite of a typical general practice. "In most medical schools, well over 50 percent of the teaching is done on 'horizonal' rather than 'vertical' patients," note Sidel and Sidel. As Jack Gieger has commented, "It's like teaching forestry in a lumber yard."[16]

Adds Carver:

> If you don't see pimples and headaches and low back pain in your training, you develop neither interest in these symptoms which affect millions, nor the skills to treat them. If the emphasis in your training is on diseases like "systemic lupus erythematosis," which the average general practitioner may not see in a lifetime of practice, then quite naturally you will tend to select a specialty in which you are likely to see more of the weird and wonderful rarities, because they are presented to you as the true focus of interest and excitement in medicine. . . . The direction in which the student is pushed is inexorably towards specialization and complicated technology.[17]

It is here, during these years of schooling, that medical students are trained to believe "that for every symptomatic action there is an appropriate and opposite therapeutic reaction, and that they are supposed to find it and prescribe it."[18] It is here, during this time, that the students learn "to look upon human beings as objects for study rather than as persons with whom they must work collaboratively to solve problems," write Sidel and Sidel. "Students come to reject as 'imaginary' or unworthy of their highly skilled attention those problems for which they can offer no technological fix. They think of themselves as a specially privileged class.''[19]

During the first two years, students learn the medical three Rs: reading, rote, and regurgitation. ''Although there is clearly a need to know a great deal of factual information, many critics contend that students spend too much time memorizing and not enough time learning problem-solving and observation skills,'' concluded the President's Commission. ''Especially during the first two years of medical school, intellectual thought may be stifled because the expectation (as reflected in examinations) is that students should simply memorize and regurgitate facts rather than learn to apply information and concepts to solving problems.''[20] Furthermore, through this regurgitation and rote learning about normal and abnormal structure and function, ''students are taught about bodies as though the minds, emotions, and lives associated with those bodies were irrelevant.''[21]

Here, too, during this time, the young doctors pick up and incorporate into their newly acquired physician persona the attitudes of doctoring shown and set forth to them by superiors and role models. The President's Commission expressed concern about how and from whom these new physicians receive attitudinal lessons. ''Due to the large number of medical students, limited faculty, and the need for clinical training to occur in small groups, medical schools typically draw a substantial proportion of their clinical teachers from the surrounding community,'' the commission noted. ''Control over what such part-time faculty teach, how it is taught, and the coherence and consistency of the material may be limited. It is particularly difficult to monitor or control the attitudes and implicit values projected by this diverse, numerous, adjunct faculty to ensure that they foster the desired attitudinal changes.''[22]

''Students are taught about legal consent but not ethical consent,'' Robinson writes in an article aptly and chillingly titled ''Are We Teaching Students that Patients Don't Matter?'' ''They may see or participate in concealment of medical mistakes and learn to practice deceit,'' he went on. ''The use of unconscious females for gynecology training may encourage the wrong attitudes to patients. Trainee GPs may learn that the doctors' rights are more important than those of the patient.''[23]

A Hunter College School of Social Work study looked at the mechanisms used by medical school graduates in a clinical setting for ''defining and defending the various mishaps which frequently occurred.'' The researchers found that these novice internists had learned three techniques:[24]

• *Denial.* ''. . . the negation of the concept of error by defining the practice of medicine as an art with 'gray areas,' the repression of actual mistakes by forgetting them and the redefinition of mistakes to nonmistakes.''

• *Discounting.* When the young doctors could not deny that a mistake had occurred, they externalized the blame, placing the onus for the error on either medical or nonmedical bureaucracies, or on their superiors or subordinates. They even blamed the disease itself. And, too, they blamed the patient. The point was to show to others and rationalize to themselves that the mistake was due to circumstances beyond the young doctors' control.

• *Distancing.* "When they could no longer deny or discount a mistake because of its magnitude, they utilized distancing techniques."

The same study points out, "The whole system of accountability during a graduate medical specialty training was found to be a variable, and, at times, contradictory process. The house staff ultimately sees itself as the sole arbiter of mistakes and their adjudication. House staffers come to feel that nobody can judge them or their decisions, least of all their patients."[25]

Or, as H. Jack Geiger, M.D., notes, "Medical students, physicians-in-training in hospitals . . . learn very rapidly that you will get in deep trouble for lack of technical competence—and properly—but that you will not get in *nearly* the same degree of trouble for lack of compassion, for lack of explaining, for lack of accountability."[26]

The Root of Some Evil

The problem of medical school tuition is a serious one. Very few medical students graduate from school and go into practice without facing tens of thousands of dollars of debt. According to a research economist at the Center for Health Policy Research at the American Medical Association, the average debt of graduating medical students in 1971 was $5,000. In 1980, it was $17,200. By 1984, it was $26,500.[27] Statistics from the Association of American Medical Colleges show that in 1985, 87 percent of medical school seniors carried a debt averaging $29,943; 38.6 percent of those owed more than $30,000; and 12.8 percent owed more than $50,000.[28] The 1986 figures show that 82 percent of med school graduates were saddled with an average debt of more than $33,000.[29] The ramifications of this indebtedness extend far beyond individual students' checkbooks. All of medical practice may be affected, and so almost certainly is the safety of patients.

It is a concern among many that the cost of a medical education could make it a profession open only to the wealthy. Furthermore, it is worrisome that in order to pay off their loans, medical school graduates may, in ever-increasing numbers, stream toward only the best-paying specialties and the most lucrative geographical areas instead of opting for a general or family practice in an area perhaps devoid of doctors and just as devoid of people with enough money to pay doctors. Medical researcher Gloria J. Bazzolli underscores the threat when she warns that ". . . anesthesiology, radiology, and surgery may become more popular as debt loads increase," because ". . . indebtedness has a statistically significant effect on specialty choice. . . ."[30] Additionally, with the cost of education rising and the availability of financial aid decreasing, large numbers of minority students may not be able to get into or stay in medical school, or even consider medicine as a realistic career goal. This can only destroy the diversity and pluralism necessary to keep medicine vital and honest and responsive to many publics.

More frightening still is the flip side to doctors going into lucrative subspecialties; that is, the possibility that the high costs of medical education may force many students "to decline the opportunity to further their medical education beyond absolute minimum requirements."[31] Hardly optimistic news for those who will be treated by these new, minimally educated doctors. Another negative response to financial pressures may lead physicians to increase their patient loads, thus providing less attention to more patients at probably higher prices. As Sidel and Sidel so accurately point out, "Any society with a fee-for-service medical-care system that permits its physicians to enter practice with this level of indebtedness at the very least subjects its physicians to extraordinary temptation and at worst leaves itself open to high levels of laboratory tests, surgery or other unnecessary or dangerous professional services performed largely because physicians must pay off their crushing debts."[32]

We are all of us—doctor and patient alike—at risk of becoming economically influenced victims. Without a solution, what is currently good about medical education may go down the tubes, and patients may be harmed beyond any conscionable limits.

Changes

There is little doubt that much needs to be done to improve American medical education. Whether it requires a fundamental stem-to-stern overhaul, or simply some fine-tuning here and there, is central to the debate. Critics and supporters abound, but amid the gnashing and wailing some calls for important alterations in medical education must be heard, considered, and instituted. (For our recommendations, see chapter 13.)

Cynthia Carver suggests that laypersons—not just doctors and administrators—sit on the medical school interview committee because, after all, "it is the layperson who is the future patient."[33] She also is aware—

and she is not alone here—that the ivory tower medical education in a way disassociates the young doctors-to-be from the real sociological concerns that affect people's health, and this must be changed. The limited, biomechanical, conservative orthodoxy of medicine creates blind spots in doctor training. "If you are not taught and have no opportunity to see how nutrition, occupation, socioeconomic status, emotions, stress, and family problems affect what diseases people get and how they progress, you will not be interested in these factors, in how they contribute to disease or in how they can be altered," Carver says.[34]

In addition, much more emphasis must be placed on the teaching of prevention in medical school. Considering its importance, its proven effectiveness, and its cost-cutting nature, it is stunning that less than 2 percent of a medical student's time is taken up with this subject.[35]

Some critics suggest that students ought to be required to attend and pass courses in ethics (since, according to a survey by the Association of American Medical Colleges, of the medical students questioned, only 5 percent had ever taken courses in ethical problems in medicine, and less than 3 percent had taken courses in medical law[36]) as well as in doctor-patient communication and even in literature and humanities. The latter would seek to instill sensitivity in the students and to remind them that there is a universe of words and thoughts and deeds out there beyond *Gray's Anatomy* and the intensive care ward. Other observers think that no medical school should accept students straight out of undergraduate school, but should require at least a year off in between, to be spent in self-education, travel, public service, or other experience-broadening endeavors.

Medical schools at Harvard University, Southern Illinois University, and the University of New Mexico have experimented lately with upgrading their programs to make them more intellectually stimulating and, perhaps, more cognizant of the things that go into a doctor-patient relationship that don't plug into the wall or find their way onto a hospital's computer printout bill. Also, beginning with its September 1986 class, Johns Hopkins University School of Medicine dropped its requirement that incoming students take and do well on the Medical College Admissions Test (MCAT), which is sort of the College Boards of medicine; the university claimed to have felt that having to prepare for and take the test discouraged applying undergraduates from taking humanities courses, getting involved in extracurricular activities, or looking for part-time jobs, so they could take more science courses to bone up for the MCAT. Meanwhile, beginning with its fall 1987 freshman class, the University of Pennsylvania dropped rigid course requirements for admission to its medical school, replacing them instead with proofs of proficiency. In other words, a student need not have taken biology courses in undergraduate school, so long as he or she has acquired the necessary knowledge. As the President's Commission noted, ''Efforts to recruit caring and humane individuals into professional schools are unlikely to be successful if the educational regimen is not conducive to these values.''[37]

But Sidel and Sidel believe that little change and improvement can be made ''without removing medical education and postgraduate training from their current control respectively by the Association of American Medical Colleges and by the American Medical Association and the specialty boards.''[38] The President's Commission adds that the biggest obstacle to any reform efforts is the difficult if not impossible transformation of the attitudes or the reshaping of the behaviors of existing professionals.[39] The Sidels may have a solution, though: ''The fact that so much of this training is financed by public funds provides a powerful lever for taking the decision making out of the hands of these special-interest groups and putting it under public control.''[40]

Robert Mendelsohn dreams of a New Medical School, one that will include a Department of Ethics and Justice. It will also have a department devoted to iatrogenic (doctor-caused) disease, in which researchers ''will be paid to find out how medical care does more harm than good, and how proposed new treatments might prove harmful.[41] In this New Medical School, generalism and not specialization will be the order of the day, and the faculty and role models will be not only medical doctors but also alternative practitioners such as osteopaths and chiropractors.

The most crucial change apparent in Mendelsohn's New Medical School would be the kind of student who would be admitted to it. This school would steer clear of the ''too compulsively achievement-oriented'' applicants, the types who ''lose contact with the genuine goals of medicine and become wrapped up in competition and in the application of technology to *subdue* rather than restore the balance of Nature.'' To that end, the New Medical School would ''look for people who are comfortable being with people rather than doing something for or to them.''[42]

Perhaps Mendelsohn's School is just a pipe dream. Or maybe it really can happen—if fought for. ''The question for the future,'' writes Rocio Huet-Cox in *Reforming Medicine,*

> is whether we, as a nation, are willing to continue accepting small, potentially inconsequential changes in the medical education health care system, or whether we are willing to challenge the powerful conservative institutions of medical education and to demand that they be responsive to our health needs. In large measure, those same medical institutions are supported through taxpayers' dollars. It is our health that is at stake. How many more decades can we wait?[43]

6

BLOOD, SWEAT, AND FEARS

". . . Let your own discretion be your tutor: suit the action to the word."

—*Hamlet*, Act 3, Scene 2

We are a test-crazy society. As much as we think we hate tests, we love them, and we love taking them, because we think they prove something. In school, we take tests to see if we are smart or stupid by society's standards. We take tests to get jobs or acquire promotions. In our spare time, we flip through popular periodicals and take tests to determine if we are success-oriented, or understanding parents, or perfect (and, preferably, imaginative) lovers. We take medical tests to find out if we are healthy or diseased in the eyes of the medical profession.

All these tests, no matter what type they are, feed our desire to know, our desire to trust the competency of the tests, our desire (or, at least, our willingness) to believe the results, and, often, our consent to changes based on the results. We think they prove something, and we may act accordingly to satisfy their conclusions. We let them define us.

In school or on the job, too great a reliance on both the test and the test's interpreters can dramatically and sometimes tragically change the course of one's career. In magazine tests, the damage is slight: A bad outcome may merely ruin an afternoon or burst a wishful-thinking bubble.

In medicine, though, too great a reliance on tests at the very least raises the cost of medical care. But worse than that, tests can cause pain or send a patient down the wrong therapeutic path. In the worst-case scenario, tests create the conditions for a patient's death. The errors of medical tests and laboratory results—mistakes of commission, mistakes of interpretation, mistakes of belief in tests on faith—join with a damaged doctor-patient relationship and the overcompensating of doctors for their uncertainties, and the net result can be a patient in jeopardy.

Testing, 1, 2, 3

"When I go to a doctor," says Robert J. Weiss, M.D., "I want that physician to be able to make some judgments about whether or not what I am complaining about may be serious. . . . What often happens today is the substitution of the laboratory test for clinical judgment. We often find that students treat the chart. . . ."[1]

Treat the chart . . . frequently, for so little reason, and with such little regard for benefit versus risk. As a conservative estimate, about two-thirds of all medical tests are worthless and of no help to the patient, Thomas Preston, M.D., points out in *The Clay Pedestal.*[2] He goes on to say that the person who gets the routine number of tests upon admission to the hospital—approximately 20 or more—has less than a 36 percent chance of being found normal by all the tests, even if that person is perfectly well. Statistical abnormalities pop up, and to the medical big-game hunter an abnormal reading means a hidden disease. "Excessive testing in people who are normal is the primary source of mistaken diagnoses," claims Preston.[3]

Robert Mendelsohn, M.D., likes to tell of his favorite study, the "one in which 197 out of 200 people were 'cured' of their abnormalities simply by repeating their lab tests!"[4] This might even be considered a humorous anecdote except for the implications: that as "more and more lab tests, X-rays, and consultations are performed, the chance of error goes up exponentially"[5]—and "most diagnostic procedures that result in severe injury or death are due to *carelessness.*"[6]

What seems to be happening here—as it is happening in other areas of the medical care industry—is that physicians are turning away from what their five senses, their common sense, and their brains would tell them if they let them or if they were educated to respect themselves and their innate intelligence and humanity. Instead, they huddle around technology and rote, using those instead of thinking.

"Medical tests can't give doctors definite yes or no answers," Rex B. Conn, M.D., professor of pathology and laboratory medicine at Emory University School of Medicine, has said. "They should help guide medical judgment, but they shouldn't overshadow the other aspects of medicine." Then, too, says Marion Laffey Fox, R.N., coauthor of *A Patient's Guide to*

Medical Testing, "A good, careful clinician—experienced at examining patients, asking questions and *listening*—can often uncover disease more accurately than any test performed on those patients."[7]

Griner and Glaser concur: "False-positive results from unnecessary tests may lead to costly and sometimes harmful interventions. Skills in history taking and physical examination, obviously important for the practice of medicine, may suffer from overreliance on tests."[8] They also state that the elimination of hands-on laboratory classes in most medical schools is to blame in large part for keeping med students from understanding how tests work, what they can do, and the limitations of their usefulness.

If young doctors are given a broader and better education, they should learn, in the words of Maryann Napoli of the Center for Medical Consumers, that "all this testing is sometimes absolutely useless—since, for many diseases, medicine's diagnostic capability has progressed well beyond its ability to provide successful treatment."[9] Or, as David B. Reuben, M.D., is quoted as saying, physicians "must not equate the ability to know with the need to know. The latter may at times be a luxury that is neither beneficial nor affordable."[10]

Out of Order

Why do physicians order the tests they do, in the manner they do, and in the numbers they do? The reasons are numerous and multifaceted. In fact, when George D. Lundberg, M.D., added up all the answers he'd received from other doctors over the years, he came up with this:[11]

Confirmation of clinical opinion	Medicolegal need
Diagnosis	CYA (cover your ass)
Monitoring	Documentation
Screening	Personal profit
Prognosis	Hospital profit
Unavailability of prior result	Attempt to defraud
Previous abnormal result	Research
Question of accuracy of prior result	Curiosity
	Insecurity
Patient-family pressure	Frustration at nothing else to do
Peer pressure	To buy time
Pressure from recent articles	"Fishing expedition"
Personal reassurance	To establish a baseline
Patient-family reassurance	To complete a data base
Public relations	Personal education

Ease of performance with ready availability	To report to an attending physician
Hospital policy	Habit
Legal requirement	Others

Zieve points to two others. He says, first, that sometimes doctors play a kind of free-association tag: "A vaguely remembered association between a clinical state and a given test or between two tests may be the stimulus for the request, without a clear recognition of its applicability to the particular clinical circumstances being faced at the moment."[12]

The worst abuse of all may be the unnecessary repetition of tests—repetition that frequently is ordered by physicians who want test results to gibe with their own "feelings" about the case. In other words, the doctor will order tests and keep ordering tests until they begin to indicate something the doctor wants them to indicate. It's man versus machine in a match of diagnostic egos. Then, too, tests are often performed more frequently than the tests are supposed to be repeated, and far more often than the change in the patient's condition (or alleged condition) warrants. These tests, and repetitions of these tests, may even go on after the "abnormality" has disappeared. Also, as Zieve points out, "Often only one of a complex of tests is abnormal and merits following, yet the entire complex is repeated each time, when the one test is all that is required.[13]

"Most patients," one study has found, "enter [a] hospital without having had laboratory tests done. When prehospitalization laboratory tests had been performed, however, a high rate of subsequent duplication was found."[14] The most unnecessarily repeated tests—a result of hospital policies—were blood tests and urinalysis.

Test ordering is excessive in teaching hospitals, where "the house officer with a hectic schedule may resort to test routines that, although they make life easier and require the house officer to make fewer decisions, have no inherent logic," report Griner and Glaser. They go on to state that in a teaching setting, "the problem is further compounded by attending physicians and consultants who abrogate responsibility for close supervision of the more routine aspects of patient care once diagnostic and treatment strategies have been developed.[15]

Wong et al. in two *JAMA* articles on lab tests agree, and see the problem as one of considerable misuse. They note that the number of tests has risen over the past two decades at a rate of 10 to 15 percent a year. They also remark that, in teaching hospitals,

> ordering of diagnostic tests is often delegated to the most junior member of the team—a physician in the first year of postgrad-

uate training or even a third- or fourth-year medical student. Their test-ordering behavior is largely determined by "protocols" or "routines" that the house staff have developed without consideration of efficient use of the laboratory tests. These protocols then are passed on to successive groups and serve as a major source of "education" for the house staff in laboratory testing.[16]

According to Wong and Lincoln, medical students also face "criticism from attending staff for failure to obtain a particular test but not for ordering unnecessary tests . . . ,"[17] and add: "Misuse of laboratory tests represents at best a waste of scarce resources and at worst may lead to poor patient care by missing the mark or by generating false leads. Hospitals and clinical laboratories need to develop methods for quality control of test-ordering practices."[18]

Thus it can be seen that institutional mandate, physician habit, and the "legend" of the test-ordering practices ("passed on from resident to resident and to medical student as a kind of folklore . . ."[19]) are major reasons for the overuse, inappropriate use, and abuse of laboratory tests and test ordering.

"Much of the preference for the new, more complicated, more expensive procedures comes about not because medical knowledge has grown so much but because it has grown so little," one critic has written. "In many cases it is thought that one procedure is superior (in a purely technological sense) to another, but what one would really like to know is *how much* superior it is in terms of *end results*."[20]

A Yale University School of Medicine study found that there is a "diversity in approaches to diagnosis"—that there is no one, standard, generally approved methodology, but, rather, that diagnoses are made via routinized whims of personal preference. Because of this diagnostic free-for-all, "team management of cases may result in excessive ordering of tests" and some of this overordering of tests can be attributed to "each physician's tendency to want to add something to the patient's work-up to justify the consultation."[21]

And, presumably, to justify a fee. As a 1986 Harvard University School of Public Health study showed: "Doctors in groups that charge patients for each aspect of their treatment are more likely to order certain tests than their counterparts at large medical organizations that charge a fixed fee for health maintenance. . . ."[22] Doctors in big group practices who charge for each service they provide tend to order 50 percent more electrocardiograms and chest X-rays than doctors who work for HMOs or other prepayment plans. Said one researcher: "Our data suggest that for certain high-profit, high-cost tests, there may be increased use in fee-for-service as compared with prepaid practices. The method of payment itself seemed to influence test use."[23]

Lack of empathy is yet another cause of overuse and abuse of tests. Physicians "often do not know what their 'little tests' and procedures are like for patients," Carver explains. "The doctor who orders the tests rarely has to watch; thus he or she doesn't know what proportion of patients finds the examinations extremely unpleasant . . . most doctors-in-training are young, healthy people who have no idea what being a patient is like."[24] (This is the same truth that drove Martha Weinman Lear to write in *Heartsounds:* "Not that I wish illness upon [doctors], may you never have illness, but perhaps it would teach doctors something they do not know. . . . A required course at all medical schools: no one graduates without two consecutive semesters of chronic, debilitating sickness."[25])

Then, too, there is "serendipitomania," which has been described as "the common habit of ordering all of the laboratory tests in hopes of 'falling into' a disease."[26] This method of medical Easter egg hunting is often aided and abetted by "certain practices of the laboratory [that] can also be identified as contributing to misuse of tests."[27] For example, "Many hospital laboratories . . . use comprehensive laboratory test request forms that list virtually the entire inventory of available tests; tests are ordered by checking off boxes next to the test names. Such forms . . . are an open invitation to the user to check off excessive numbers of tests. [One] comprehensive request form listed the four thyroid function tests; perhaps because of doubt about how to make an appropriate choice, the user often ordered all four tests to avoid making a wrong choice."[28]

"One of the most unfortunate abuses of the laboratory is related to gamesmanship on the part of the doctor ordering the tests," declares Russe. "Because of a desire to impress the attending physician with his erudition," he explains,

> the consultant may order unusual or little-known studies on the patient. Such studies are frequently of limited value in establishing a diagnosis or modifying therapy, but they clearly put the consultant one up on his peers. If the laboratory is able to comply with the consultant's suggestion and perform an obscure test, very likely the result will be of questionable validity since no one has done that procedure before. This spurious abnormal value can then be pounced upon by the gamesman, leading to a spiraling of more tests ad absurdam.[29]

Physicians frequently use the excuse of "defensive medicine" when ordering numerous tests. They say it is better to order more tests than are necessary than fewer, from a future lawsuit standpoint. But in a study published in the *Journal of the American Medical Association,* researchers found that "medicolegal considerations [fears of malpractice litigation] were cited as a contributing factor for only 1 percent of all tests ordered, and even in those it was not necessarily the sole factor."[30]

This defensive nervousness, coupled with the love of ordering tests, especially high-tech tests, is often at the root of what is known as the "cascade effect"—a chain reaction of one test forcing the use of another and another and another . . . until the patient is either harmed in some way, has his or her hospitalization extended unnaturally and unnecessarily, or has his or her bill run up enormously. Mold and Stein, for example, tell of the case of a 59-year-old man who went into the hospital for a hernia repair. The man had a history of coronary artery disease, along with some other lung and esophageal conditions, which gave him some chest discomfort. However, his family physician had ascertained that his coronary artery disease was stable. Still, on admission, the man was examined by a cardiologist, who suggested that the surgery be delayed until the man could be put on the treadmill of a cardiac stress test to see if he was fit to undergo the hernia surgery.

This is where the cascade effect took hold, and the man's stay in the hospital became a set of circumstances that were seemingly beyond everybody's control. Sent down to have the stress/exercise-tolerance test, the man had to wait six hours at the heart station for it. "During that time he became anxious, agitated, and angry, and had some mild chest discomfort," report Mold and Stein. "Because of the discomfort, the test was not done, and the patient was transferred to the telemetry unit because of the possibility that he was having preinfarction angina."

Now things really got bad. The man was now so angry—no wonder; he'd come in for a relatively simple hernia operation—and had worked himself up to such a state that he began to have more chest pains, and these were showing up as negative changes on the EKG. So he was whisked away to the cardiac care unit, where they put him on intravenous nitroglycerin and gave him orally a drug to prevent a heart attack, even though there was no sign of a current or impending heart attack in any of his blood samples. The poor man then underwent coronary arteriography, in which a probe was snaked through his arteries to his heart to determine if there were any major blockages of the coronary arteries. He had had this procedure done once, nine years before; now, the new arteriogram showed not only that he was not in any danger of having a heart attack but in fact that his coronary artery condition had actually improved since that first examination nearly a decade before. So, now, did the man have his operation? Report Mold and Stein: "At that point the hernia repair could not be performed because of a full operating-room schedule, and it had to be rescheduled for two weeks later.'' He eventually had that operation, with no complications.[31]

This man's story is not unique. Mold and Stein tell of uncomplicated pregnancies becoming very complicated because of the addition of a fetal heart-rate monitor, leading to interventions and catastrophes—or, at least, cesarean sections—never imagined by any of the participants. Cascade events occur frequently enough to be of concern; any time physicians become powerless in the face of a chain reaction of tests gone amok, the system needs reassessment. The cascade effect is the result of practitioners who take incomplete histories (''the exercise-tolerance test was ordered because writing an order for the test was perceived to be easier than spending the time necessary to obtain enough of the patient's history to assess adequately the seriousness of the chest pain''[32]), who don't think hard about what tests mean or might predict, and who order tests promiscuously, without a specific goal in mind. ''That is, the test should be ordered to obtain the answer to a question that will make a difference in the care of the patient,'' write Mold and Stein. ''It is vital to remember that the adverse effects of a test or procedure include not only allergic reactions, the discomfort of injections, and cost, but also such risks as increased anxiety and false positive results that may propagate an unwanted and harmful cascade.''[33]

Not all physicians are guilty of overordering tests. In fact, some underorder, and the fault lies not in the stars but in the specialty: Internists and pediatricians order too many, surgeons not enough. While in some instances less is more, that's not the case in medicine. With too few tests, there can be a ''failure to respond to clues to underlying disease that are provided by first-level tests.''[34] The underordering of tests is not so much healthy conservatism as it is unhealthy ineptitude—not a money saver, to be sure, but highly costly . . . in the extreme.

Some of the blame for excessive and inappropriate test ordering must be laid squarely on the shoulders of patients, who have been oversold on the virtues of medical intervention, or want to see some ''results'' for their money, hoping those results will result in some action. As Napoli says, many people ''equate extensive testing with excellent medical care.''[35] She adds: ''One reason we may so readily accept tests is that we may be underinformed about their accuracy, risks, and value.''[36] Frivolousness coupled with lack of information leads to what one sees in the overuse of ultrasound tests during pregnancy, tests that may not be indicated or valuable as much as 30 percent of the time. Why are so many unnecessary ultrasound tests performed? Not only is it frequently physician mandate or pressure but, according to a story in the *New York Times,* ''The ultrasound pictures make curious additions to baby albums . . . but many of them serve no medical purpose.''[37]

The medical test as snapshot album souvenir—courtesy of the eager to please (and even more eager to bill) physician.

The Misinterpretation of Dreams

What good is the most sensitive, accurate test if the doctors can't read it or see the reality between the facts? And how dangerous can misreading be? Robert Mendelsohn gives some examples:

> . . . once you submit to a physical examination, your doctor might interpret some minor abnormalities—real or bogus—as *pre*-conditions of some serious illness, requiring, of course, serious *pre*-intervention. A minor fluctuation on a blood sugar test might be interpreted as *pre*-diabetes, and you'll get some medicine to take home. Or the doctor may find something—maybe a stray tracing on the EKG caused by a passing jet plane—that leads him to believe you have a *pre*-coronary condition. Then you'll go home with a *pre*-coronary drug or two, which while fighting your *pre*-condition will mess up your life. . . .[38]

Underscoring Mendelsohn's contention is a study, published in the medical journal *Lancet,* that looked at 200 patients "who had had one or more unexpected, unexplained abnormal results in a biochemical profile on admission to hospital. . . ." The study, according to its authors, "concentrated on the possibility that such results might be indicative of pre-symptomatic disease. . . ." Under many circumstances—perhaps under typical circumstances—doctors might read these surprise results, jump to some heady conclusions, and begin treating patients tagged by these tests as having "preconditions." What the *Lancet* study showed, though, was that after a reassessment 5 years later, only 3 patients of the 200 actually had developed the conditions it was predicted they were going to develop.[39] In other words, an error or miscalculation or misinterpretation of some sort occurred in the tests of 197 of 200 people tested—197 people who had nothing wrong with them, 197 people who might have been treated, medicated, or operated on needlessly.

Errors of interpretation may occur early in the testing process for a variety of reasons, such as technical miscues like improper collection of specimens (which leads to unusual data from which faulty judgments are made) or overstaining or understaining the specimen slides. Carelessness of either the laboratory or the medical staff can result in potentially devastating mistakes. On the labs' part, "failure to transmit a significant laboratory value or X-ray interpretation appropriately constitutes a dereliction of duty.'' On the medical staffs' part, ''failure to notice (i.e., receive) the result or not to look for it is equally negligent.''[40] It is vitally important, believes William O. Robertson, M.D., that the initiative be taken ''to assure that lab medicine, pathology, and radiology communication are prompt, clear, concise, and immediately recognizable if abnormal . . .'' and that the professionals involved avoid the use of illegible handwriting or confusing abbreviations.[41]

Moreover, direct errors of commission influence the interpretation process, even in so-called ''simple'' tests. Take, for example, the common and ubiquitous Pap smear. Sampling and reading errors by physicians, cytotechnicians, and pathologists are rampant in this country, undermining whatever reliability the test has. Statistics show that in the United States, a false-negative rate of as much as 36 percent and a false-positive rate of 15 to 20 percent are considered acceptable by the medical powers that be. Moreover, according to one official of the International Academy of Cytology, ''a 95 percent accuracy rate could be achieved through the combined efforts of both doctors and pathologists,'' but that ''many physicians and pathologists are inadequately trained to perform Pap smears [because of] educational programs offering substandard training in cytology [and because of] persons in the field 'who haven't bothered taking the time' to master their discipline.''[42] Overworked technicians who, because they are tired or burnt out from looking at thousands upon thousands of slides, miss results staring them straight in the face, and that is another serious, preventable situation.

There is a long list of other reasons for misinterpretation of tests. Among others, Zieve mentions:[43]

• Physiological variation (''the variable responses one finds on retesting a given individual at different times'').
• Overinterpretation of test values.
• Unawareness of extraneous factors that influence tests (''extraneous'' refers to ''factors, alterations, or effects that do not influence test results under normal or ideal circumstances, but which may affect the results in patients with various and sundry abnormalities besides the one primarily measured by the test'').
• Uncritical acceptance of published opinions regarding the comparative value of tests supposedly measuring the same function, unnecessary use of tests, unnecessary repetition of tests, and failure to interpret tests in relation to the clinical findings.

But perhaps chief among causes of physician misinterpretation of test results is an ignorance or misunderstanding of how tests work—and how human beings work to affect the results of these tests; these physicians have an "unfamiliarity with procedures or with physiologic factors affecting them," Zieve claims, adding, "Clinicians interpret most tests they use without knowing how the tests are performed or the assumptions utilized in calculations."[44] What a good doctor, who truly cares about his or her patients and the meaning and results of tests, should know about them includes, among the most important:[45]

- Reliability of the method or the analytical equipment with which the test is done.
  - Technical skill of laboratory personnel.
  - Effectiveness of laboratory quality control.
  - Standards of normal values for the test in the performing laboratory.
    - Extraneous factors affecting results.
    - Interdependence of variables related to the patient and his disease.
    - Sensitivity and specificity of the test.
    - Cooperation of the patient.

What physicians often do not know is the range of normal readings and how the laboratories arrive at these alleged norms for each test. Surprising as it may seem, there is no internationally or even nationally agreed-upon "norm." Each laboratory may have its own set of numbers for what it considers normal—an entirely different set of numbers and an entirely different range of normal values from the lab right across the street. So-called "normal" values and "normal" ranges are merely those values and ranges that that particular lab has come up with using a specific (and often small) population. For example, a hospital laboratory may, to acquire the "normal range" numbers it needs, gather up blood or urine or whatever from the doctors and nurses in that hospital—a population that may not in any way be representative of the United States population as a whole or the hospital's patients in particular. It is a biased sample, and certainly not random enough to be considered scientifically valid— and yet it is used, and physicians make clinical judgments and devise therapeutic options using these possibly flawed but seemingly authoritative numbers. Furthermore, it is not uncommon for sample figures to have been gathered decades ago or longer, thus leading doctors to devise clinical strategies or diagnostic scenarios based on the dated values of an ever-changing human race. Another flaw altogether is the very concept of "normal." Some people are perfectly healthy even though they do not fall between the gunsights of the rigid and predetermined "normal range." Consistently registering numbers that fall only a slight fraction outside the "normal range" as determined by the laboratory's flawed sampling may doom a perfectly healthy but slightly and statistically unusual person to a life of unneeded medications and procedures performed by medical personnel who operate "by the book," even if they don't know what the book means.

"Ideally, the physician should know which reference population was used to define the range of normal for a test," says Richard K. Riegelman, M.D., of George Washington University Medical Center. "This information is rarely available, however."[46] Riegelman also states that in interpreting test results, doctors need to remember, but frequently forget (or never learned), that:

• *"Outside normal limits" does not equal "diseased."* "When test results are just outside normal limits, patients are especially likely to be disease-free. Maintaining the distinction between 'outside the range of normal' and 'diseased' is central to the correct use of laboratory tests."[47]
• *"Within normal limits" does not equal "disease-free."* ". . . Many tests in common use do not do a good job of separating those with disease from those without disease. In addition, a test may be useful in diagnosing some diseases and useless for others."[48]
• *Changes within normal limits may be pathological.* "Despite the wide range of normal, most individuals maintain their own test level within much narrower bounds. . . . Thus, past test results are important in evaluation of current findings. . . . Normal limits drawn from an entire population may be much less important than changes even within normal limits for an individual."[49]
• *"Within normal limits" does not equal "desirable."* "The range of normal reflects the test values of a reference population believed to be free of disease at the time the test was done. These values may be higher than desirable and may indicate an increased tendency of members of the reference population toward development of disease in the future. For instance, the weight and cholesterol levels of Americans are often said to be, on the average, higher than desirable and to contribute to the development of heart disease. Failure to recognize the distinction between 'within normal limits' and 'desirable' . . . may have important therapeutic as well as diagnostic implications."[50]

In other words, people are different, and applying hard and fast rules across the board is bound to lead to failure and could possibly lead to harm. If the doctor doesn't know the patient, or he or she doesn't seek to learn about the patient, problems arise, resentments grow, and dangers lie at every turn.

Lab Errors While-U-Wait

With the advent of newer, more compact, computerized, and generally affordable technology, physicians have opened up their own laboratories in their own offices to use on their own patients. Not only does having the analyzing equipment right there in the next room speed up the results (meaning that therapy may be initiated far more quickly than it would be if results had to be delivered or mailed from a commercial lab), in many cases it also frees the physician from dependence on hospital laboratories and outside vendors. Mostly, though, having an in-house lab with near-immediate results is a great profit-maker for the doctor—"a way for physicians to generate additional revenue without seeing more patients and without doing more work."[51]

Studies have shown that these home-grown labs—between 40,000 and 100,000 of them, compared with 13,000 hospital and independent labs—are notoriously poor at what they do. In one wide-ranging study, an investigator found that "physician-office labs perform less accurate work, use fewer safeguards to minimize erroneous results, and employ fewer personnel with training in clinical laboratory procedures than do licensed clinical facilities."[52] Why? Because the thousands of in-office labs throughout most of the nation are "exempt from a broad spectrum of mandatory federal, and sometimes state, regulations that govern licensed clinical labs and establish standards for quality control."[53]

This investigation, concentrating on labs in California, discovered that:[54]

• ". . . 44 percent of the employees in these unregulated labs have no formal education or training to perform lab analyses."
• ". . . fewer than 30 percent of the physician-office labs . . . have formal quality control programs."
• "Though 20 percent of the results reported by unregulated laboratories were as accurate as those reported by regulated laboratories, the remaining 80 percent were significantly less accurate. . . ."

Herbert Derman, M.D., a president of the College of American Pathologists, has said that "physicians are trained very little, if at all, in [laboratory] quality as measured by accuracy and precision. Of course, conscientious people will do conscientious work, and most of their work may be quite good. But even conscientious people need to have information, and in doctors' offices, lab work tends not to be done by the most experienced of persons."[55]

Study after study shows that small, in-office laboratories tend to have a greater variability in test results than do large, regulated labs. A recent study[56] looked at the situation in Idaho, where clinical laboratories are regulated "except those in which licensed physicians personally perform tests on their own patients." What happened in Idaho is that the state's Laboratory Proficiency Committee and the Division of Health Laboratories "began to hear stories of patients placed in jeopardy by erroneous laboratory test results from uncontrolled small hospital laboratories and private physicians' office laboratories."[57]

When these departments looked into the problem, they found that "the laboratory was the responsibility of either a nurse, a medical technologist, or an individual without formal training [and] that many of the individuals staffing physicians' office laboratories in Idaho have had little or no post–high school education."[58] Further examination uncovered significant testing error rates, and "only 26 percent of laboratories supervised by nurses and 42 percent of those supervised by 'others,' including staff trained on the job . . . were found to have acceptable programs and records."[59]

Other problems in office labs that the Idaho study identified include:[60]

- Lack of quality control in laboratory testing procedures.
- Lack of knowledge concerning quality control in the laboratory.
- Lack of adequate procedure manuals.
- Lack of preventive maintenance.
- Lack of knowledge concerning laboratory safety.
- Inability to assimilate or understand information concerning the quality assurance guidelines that pertain to physician office laboratories.
- Laboratory staff turnover, resulting in someone with inadequate training being responsible for test analyses.

The scandal of all this is not merely the quick-buck, slipshod nature of many of these labs, but that "performance levels could be improved through simple, relatively inexpensive interventions," the researchers concluded.[61] Yet this is not being done. Further, there is no federal regulation of laboratories in doctors' offices, and only three states—Idaho, Wyoming, and Pennsylvania—now have comprehensive regulations covering situations in which employees other than a doctor in that doctor's office laboratory perform test analyses. And yet, according to an article in the *Wall Street Journal,* despite Pennsylvania having "some of the nation's toughest rules for doctor's-office labs . . . its officials say they have never disciplined a doctor for faulty testing."[62]

This is a significant problem—one that the medical profession and allied health fields simply cannot wait any longer to address seriously.

Ray of Hope?

"X-rays are like cars," medical writer/critic Arthur S. Freese explains. "Primarily safe and valuable in the hands of the competent and conscientious operator, but lethal weapons in the hands of the irresponsible, inadequate, or badly trained technician."[63]

The use of X-rays for diagnostic testing as well as for many therapies is well established and, frequently, soundly based. It is said that 13,500 lives a year could be saved if all women over the age of 50 years would have mammograms taken annually.[64]

However, this ray of light has its dark side. Human error, negligence, unnecessary use, excessive use, technological error—all contribute to an atmosphere that is fraught with apprehension and mistrust. Take, for example, this very same lifesaving mammogram. Negative results provided by mammography are wrong between 5 and 69 percent of the time; that is, cancer is there when the mammogram says it isn't. In one study, of 48 "negative" mammograms of women who later turned out to have breast cancer, one-third had cancers that were clearly visible in the X-rays, but had been overlooked or misread by the X-ray personnel or physicians.[65]

As it is with medication, so it is with X-rays: The bad often rides the coattails of the good. As John W. Gofman, M.D., and Egan O'Connor declare in their provocative and seminal text, *X-Rays: Health Effects of Common Exams,* "Ionizing radiation, even at extremely low dose rates, breaks human chromosomes and inflicts enduring chromosomal injuries."[66] And with more than 300 million medical and dental X-ray exams, taken each year, that is a great deal of chromosomal carnage. The young are more apt to suffer radiation-caused problems than the old. Infants are highly sensitive (". . . a newly born child is about 300 times more sensitive than a 55-year-old to induction of cancer by radiation. . . . "[67]), 5-year-old children are "about five times more likely to get later radiation-induced cancer than an adult given the *same* radiation dose at age 35 . . . ,"[68] and 10-year-olds may be at the greatest risk of all.[69]

The X-ray/cancer connection is certain and strong; what is less known to the public is its extent when the use is excessive or faulty. According to Gofman and O'Connor:

• About 78,000 people every year get cancer from medical and dental X-rays. That means that in a single generation, radiation will induce 2,340,000 cancers.[70]

• Radiation can cause every major kind of cancer imaginable, including the kinds that account for about 90 percent of cancer deaths in America.[71]

• "There is no X-ray exam which exposes only one cancer-prone organ. Every exam increases the risk of several types of cancer. . . ."[72] As an example, Gofman and O'Connor mention an X-ray look at the ribs—a radiological "peek" that can lead to cancer of the lungs, kidneys, stomach, and, in women, breasts. The risk is greater if the patient is a smoker, because smoking acts as a multiplier on other factors.[73]

Women are also in the X-ray danger zone when they are pregnant. Weitz writes that X-rays "given to pregnant women during the 1950s and 1960s caused between 5 and 10 percent of all childhood cancers in North America and Western Europe."[74] In addition, irradiating the embryo can cause major birth defects, including small head size, mental retardation, skeletal deformities, and eye and heart defects. Radiation can cause "nonspecific infant mortality during the first year of life, and often during the first week."[75] Leukemia during the first 15 years of life—and other cancers throughout adulthood—may also be the result of X-rays of the stomach and pelvic areas during pregnancy. The age of the mother has no effect on the damage to the embryo.[76]

Another radiation hazard endangering mostly women is the increasingly common screening of school-age children for early signs of scoliosis, a curvature of the spine that can cripple and sometimes leads to death. In an aggressive and well-intentioned attempt to spot this defect before it goes too far, state and local governments and school districts may have gone too far themselves.

In the screening process, young children are examined, usually by doctors provided by the government or school. Those students who doctors believe are likely to have or develop scoliosis are then referred on for further examinations. Many of these further examinations, and the periodic checkup that may ensue, include X-ray pictures of the spine.

But do the dangers of the screening process outweigh the benefits afforded those who undergo the tests? In New Jersey, which had mandatory scoliosis screening, 773,000 public and private school students were examined in 1983 (the last year for which data are available). Of these, 16,000 were thought by the screening doctors to require further testing. Of these, 4,600 were X-rayed. And of these, only 817 ever received braces or surgery for scoliosis. In other words, 3,783 students, all at an age when X-rays can do the most harm, received doses that were unnecessary.[77]

In another scoliosis survey, this one conducted by the Food and Drug Administration, 256 X-ray units in 28 states were examined. Of these, just a shade over half used the best methods recommended for cutting down unnecessary exposure to radiation, only 58.6 percent of them used gonad shields, and a meager 7 percent of the units used breast shields. The FDA went on to report that while "as many as 14 percent of the children in screening programs were found to have scoliosis . . . the incidence of this disease in the general population is only 4.5 percent."[78] That is, there is overdiagnosis and misdiagnosis going on, leading to unnecessary X-rays—and frequent X-rays, too. Gofman and O'Connor relate the facts about the excessive radiation by female scoliosis patients during the Milwaukee Brace treatment, a common scoliosis therapy that exposed these young girls to as many as 22 X-rays over an average three-year period—and raised the number of them at risk of breast cancer from 140 to 290 per million, or a 110 percent increase.[79]

Some may say that these are the risks we take for the benefits we derive from ionizing radiation. They are wrong, at least in degree. True, an X-ray that is undeniably necessary and that years later may lead to a cancer is an even-up trade-off. The key word here is "necessary." Gofman and O'Connor and others believe we are being overdosed to death by X-rays, and that "a three-fold larger reduction would be achievable with some additional effort—all without losing any of the benefits of the diagnostic information."[80] And the savings in potential lives lost would be enormous.

Overdose: Playing the Field

Upon entering a clinic or hospital, one assumes that at the very least the people who work in these places know how much radiation is emitted from their machines, where that radiation is supposed to go, and how to aim it to get it there. These are not safe assumptions. According to Gofman and O'Connor, "The dose used for the same exam commonly varies 10-fold, often 20-fold, and even up to 100-fold, from one facility to another, and even from room to room in the same facility. A patient can unknowingly step into a cancer risk 10 or 20 times greater than . . . *average* entrance doses."[81]

How can this be so? What makes it so is laxity and negligence, and an attitude either that machines can't be wrong or that no harm can be done even if the machine is a "little" off. Using that theory, technical error becomes an impossibility. Human error is, ergo, negated. Similarly, patient safety becomes a nonevent. According to Weitz, in one study about a third of all the X-ray machines examined by the researchers needed to be repaired because they were giving off too much radiation. The same study found that inept technique caused between 5 and 10 percent of all X-rays to be retaken.[82]

"It turns out that even offices which are confident that they *do* know their . . . doses are often seriously mistaken," say Gofman and O'Connor. That's because these offices calculate the dosage from information in manuals and from what the dosages ought to be. However, this blind belief that "calculations are an adequate substitute for measurement" is shattered when the direct beam measurements are taken, and the dosages come in as low as one-tenth and as high as four times what they are supposed to be.[83]

Even more shocking is the fact that "the dose from diagnostic radiology can be reduced by a factor of ten or more if all conditions were optimized,"[84] and that is a significant amount of damage that could be avoided.

Some radiologists think they can prevent radiation risk by fractionating the dose. In other words, instead of giving one large dose, which might entail some hazard, they can give a few smaller doses that add up to the same dose but with less risk. Fractionating *may* reduce or eliminate nausea and other immediate and temporary side effects of high-dose radiation, "but with respect to delayed and deadly effects such as cancer, there is definite evidence that dividing a dose does *not* reduce the risk."[85]

A patient may ask clinic, office, or hospital radiologists just what level of X-ray dose he or she is receiving but is advised not to hold his or her breath until an answer is forthcoming. There is the flawed practitioner-patient relationship to blame, of course. Then, too, there is something else. The Mayo Clinic's Joel Gray, M.D., is quoted as saying: "My feeling is that if they won't tell you, they don't know, and if they don't know, they could be among the facilities delivering a hundred times the necessary dose."[86]

Field reduction should be teamed with dose reduction. Field is the size of the area of the body that is exposed to the X-ray. Patients are frequently exposed to radiation over a wider field than is necessary. Radiology technicians often collimate (line up and size up) to film size instead of to the body part that is being X-rayed, so that the area exposed to radiation is larger and the risk of organ and chromosome damage is needlessly increased. Weitz says that "half of all conventional X-ray examinations expose patients to unnecessary radiation because the X-ray beam is larger than the area of the film."[87] Gofman and O'Connor add that collimation to body part, instead of film size, can significantly reduce the dose that an infant receives—"a direct five-fold reduction in the infant's risk of later lung cancer from the exam."[88]

Beyond the errors of collimation and radiation overdose are other human errors—for example, the introduction of contrast material can be dangerous, not only because intravenous and intraarterial injections are tricky procedures even for the experienced, but also because contrast media can be toxic, and if a medical professional fails to "introduce the compound into the body in the right concentration at the right place at the right time," the botched results can be fatal.[89]

And beyond the purely human errors involving radiation are those mistakes related to technology. There are frequently tragedies like the one that occurred at the East Texas Cancer Center early in 1986, when a computer malfunction, according to an Associated Press report, "apparently caused excessive radiation doses for two cancer patients . . . causing the death of one man."[90] The problem was a "software glitch," and "what the computer screen indicated was going on was not what was going on," explained one doctor involved in the case. The events were as follows:

> In the case of [a] 33-year-old man, the operator began radiation treatment with the equipment after correcting an operator-entry command. The machine shut down immediately and flashed a malfunction message, Mr. Free [Bob Free, an investigator with the Texas Bureau of Radiation Control] said.
>
> The operator believed the patient had not received the treatment and reset the machine, he said. But the patient had experienced something like an electrical shock and was rolling off the table when the second dosage caught him in the shoulder and neck, Mr. Free said.
>
> Mr. Free said representatives of the clinic and manufacturer examined the machine and determined there was no electrical or other hazard. As a result, the machine was put back into use.
>
> Three weeks later, the same error was made on [a] 66-year-old man . . . confined to a wheelchair and suffering from emphysema [who] died . . . after receiving an excessive dose of radiation. . . .

The same make and model machine had malfunctioned the year before at a Georgia treatment center; it "unleashed a large radiation dose . . . on a patient undergoing treatment for breast cancer . . . [created] a deep, discolored hole [below her collarbone] 'between the size of a quarter and a half-dollar' . . . [and] destroyed a vital nerve center and robbed her of the use of her left arm."

Similar horror stories of radiation misuse and overuse, mistakes and negligence, technical and human errors, abound. So long as X-ray machines remain incorrectly calibrated—causing the need for retakes, and thus adding to the excess radiation—and so long as dose rate, beam size, and duration of the patient's exposure to the beam are poorly and incompetently effected and monitored, there will continue to be X-ray–related deaths all out of logical, predictable, scientific, and humane proportion. So long as no one cares, so long as hospitals remain loose in their sentinel responsibilities, so long as manufacturers gloss over flaws in their machines, and so long as "no one checks on the individual doctor who may have the [money] with which to buy a used X-ray machine, or who may even just rent one[91]" and not know exactly how to use it—we will continue to see future generations suffer the wounds of burns we inflict on ourselves today.

Gofman and O'Connor write:

Aside from cessation of cigarette smoking, the authors . . . are aware of nothing on the horizon which would eliminate as many cancers as the single action of reducing the dosage in medical and dental diagnostic radiology. . . . In terms of economic resources, the services of well-trained and independent radiologic physicists to check and adjust equipment (including film developers) would be far less costly than the enormous medical bill for 1.5 million cancer casualties.[92]

7

CUT AND RUN

"The knife is dangerous in the hand of the wise, let alone in the hand of the fool."

—Hebrew proverb

There is an old saying that surgeons bury their mistakes. Another one says that surgeons bury only half their mistakes—the other 50 percent they just keep performing operations on.

It would be nice if one were able to disabuse the people who believe these old sayings of their belief in them with cold, hard facts to the contrary. But there is a great deal of truth to those old saws about current sawbones.

Was This Trip Really Unnecessary?

If one wishes to split hairs on the matter, unnecessary surgery is technically not a medical mistake. When greed controls the impulse to operate when an operation is not called for, as is often the case in unnecessary surgery, such an operation is certainly a grossly unethical and immoral act, but not a medical mistake per se. There are two ways, though, in which the concept of error does come into play in unnecessary surgeries: first, when a physician, from ignorance or uncertainty or a mind clouded by the need to make big and quick bucks in order to pay off school or practice or drug-related debts, really is not aware that the operation is unnecessary; and, second, when mistakes, negligence, and pure malpractice happen during what is clearly an unnecessary operation to begin with—a situation in which one terrible miscalculation is piled atop another, like the house that Jack built.

Sometimes a patient's problem can be taken care of either surgically or medically. In such cases, one is as good as the other in doing the job. Taking the nonsurgical route, however, usually means smaller fees for the doctors involved. Watching, waiting, and listening haven't the billing strength of aggressive or invasive procedures. "Considering all this, an average physician may easily rationalize the need for surgery" writes Herbert H. Keyser, M.D., in *Women Under the Knife*. "He loses sight of the possibility that the surgery might be unnecessary."[1] Keyser adds that patients "for whom the advice to operate was not unethical but yet was *questionable* can be found regularly in most hospitals."[2]

Just how prevalent and potentially destructive is unnecessary surgery? Robert G. Schneider, M.D., a board-certified internist with a subspecialty in cardiology, proposed this equation in 1982 (and the figures are certainly higher today):[3]

Total number of annual operations in the U.S. = 20–25 million.
Overall mortality rate for all major surgery = 1.33 percent.
Unnecessary surgery estimates = 15–25 percent.
    Up to 50–60 percent for some
    operations.
    40–80 percent and more for
    tonsillectomies and hysterectomies.

15–25 percent unnecessary operations multiplied by *20–25 million operations* equals 3 million to 6.25 million unnecessary operations. Multiply that figure by the *1.33 percent mortality rate,* and the total number of unnecessary deaths (approximately) per year in the U.S. comes to 40,000 to 83,000.

"In 1974, the Senate investigation into unnecessary surgery reported that American doctors performed 2.4 million unnecessary operations causing 11,900 deaths and costing about $3.9 billion," writes Martin Weitz in *Health Shock*. "It has been calculated by Professor John McKinlay, a noted critic of medical waste, that more deaths are caused by surgery each year in the United States than the annual number of deaths during the wars in Korea and Vietnam, which were considered national tragedies."[4]

Keyser contends that of the currently estimated 35 million operations a year, "at least 15 percent, or 5 million, are unnecessary."[5] He cites hysterectomies, dilation and curettage, and cesarean sections as the most overperformed unnecessary procedures—all inflicted upon women, interestingly. And cesareans—which are four times as risky as nonsurgical delivery—are on the rise. Already accounting for 21.1 percent of 3.7 million deliveries in the United States, the incidence of the operation is increasing at a rate of about 1 percent a year, when in fact the number could easily and safely be halved, according to one study. While defensive medicine, and the mistaken attitude held by physicians and patients that once a cesarean, always a cesarean, are given as the main reasons for the high numbers of the procedure performed, one of the authors of the study has a different view: "The bottom line, I think, is that a cesarean is often much easier for an obstetrician," says Stephen A. Myers, M.D., of Mt. Sinai Hospital in Chicago. "They don't have to stay up all night waiting."[6]

According to a National Institute for Health Statistics report, of the 750,000 hysterectomies performed in this country each year, 22 percent are unnecessary and "in only 10 percent of the cases were the indications for a hysterectomy so clear-cut that all doctors would agree to perform the operation."[7] To which Keyser adds: "It is a safe assumption that doctors who do most of their hysterectomies on women under 40 are practicing improperly."[8] And if anyone should think that the high number of hysterectomies performed is somehow unrelated to sexist thought and behavior on the part of physicians, one need only read the following, quoted by Gena Corea, about a cancer conference in which the assembled surgeons

> had agreed that they rarely hesitate to remove an ovary but think twice about removing a testicle. "The doctors readily admitted that such a sex-oriented viewpoint arises from the fact that most surgeons are male," [*Medical World News*] reported. "Said one of them wryly, 'No ovary is good enough to leave in, and no testicle is bad enough to take out'!"
>
> Does this mean women might be undergoing unnecessary surgery?[9]

The House Select Committee on Aging determined and reported that "at least 23 percent of the 1 million [cataract lens] implants performed may not be necessary," mostly because of fraud, abuse, and waste that takes the form of high markups and manufacturer kickbacks and other enticements.[10]

Circumcisions have also come under fire recently as procedures unnecessary except for those for whom it has traditional religious significance. Side effects, including excessive bleeding and infection, occur in 1 in 500 circumcised infants.[11] Another side effect possible in the 1.5 million annual circumcisions in the United States (representing 80 percent of all male newborns) can be "trauma"—that is, damage to the penis. And not minor "trauma," either. Two infants in an Atlanta hospital in 1985, for example, joined the six or eight others on record as having suffered disfiguring burns while undergoing circumcision via cauterizing needles used to burn off the foreskin. According to one news report, "The burns to one of the infants were so severe that his penis was destroyed. A sex change operation has been performed so that the child will be raised as a female, according to a lawsuit filed on behalf of the child's parents. . . ."[12] The lawsuit charges that "Baby Doe is now a female person, who has been rendered sterile and completely incapable of reproduction, and who will require medical monitoring and hormonal therapy throughout the remainder of her life."[13]

Such an incident is horrific and tragic under any circumstances; that such a thing could occur as a result of applying new technology while attempting to avoid a surgical knife and the resultant possibility of loss of blood is certainly an unhappy irony; and that this awful surgical mistake and assault on the life of a newborn would occur during circumcision, a procedure that even the American Academy of Pediatrics and the American College of Obstetricians and Gynecologists think is medically unnecessary[14] only heightens the shock and sadness of the situation.

"Given the number of situations in which it is realistically possible for medical injury to occur, an ominous amount of it does," writes John Guinther. "Assuming, minimally, that 70 percent of all treatment is of a routine nature, in the remaining 30 percent of contacts, the injury rate is as high as 1 in 4 and the negligent rate about 1 in 12, not a very comforting thought for anyone with a complex illness requiring intensive or surgical care."[15]

Amid all the discussion about surgery that is unnecessary or otherwise, appropriate or otherwise, one needs to consider the place of elective surgery in the scheme of things. An elective surgery is one which the patient elects or chooses to have on his or her own; it is not an emergency or a medical imperative. Guinther explains that while the "line between an elective and an unnecessary operation can be a fine one," to his mind the essential difference is this:[16]

> A *proper* elective procedure is one for which there are substantial medical indications that the patient will benefit from it.
>
> In the *unnecessary* operation, there are no medical indications that the operation should be performed and there may be indications that it should not be performed.

One must also weigh the place the concepts "unnecessary" and "medical mistake" have in elective surgery when one considers the scene that unfolded in Los Angeles County during the first 35 days of 1976. At that time, physicians staged a work slowdown and withheld all but emergency services. Elective surgeries were canceled. The local newspapers regularly ran alarmist stories that could only have led readers to believe that the slowdown was seriously and dangerously affecting the public's health. It was certainly affecting the public's health—but only for the better. Roemer and Schwartz found that "the doctors' withdrawal of services—consisting in large part of elective surgical procedures—appears to have caused relatively slight inconvenience to the people of Los Angeles County."[17]

But that is only part of it—the researchers also found that "the withholding of elective surgery . . . was associated with a significant reduction in the county's overall mortality experience, compared with the previous five years."[18] To be perfectly accurate, there was "a virtually steady decline"[19] of deaths during the length of the slowdown—and as soon as the work action ended and elective surgeries resumed, "there was a substantial jump in the mortality rate."[20] These statistics, wrote Roemer and Schwartz, "lend support to the mounting evidence that people might benefit if less elective surgery were performed in the United States," and that "much elective surgery performed in the United States is of questionable value," which can only lead to the conclusion that "greater restraint in the performance of elective surgical operations might well improve U.S. life expectancy."[21]

This is not an isolated occurrence, either. In 1973, when doctors went on strike in Israel and elective surgery was stopped, the country's death rate plummeted 50 percent, while a 52-day doctors' work stoppage in Brazil in 1976 led to a 35 percent mortality rate decline.[22]

How and why are unnecessary surgeries and needless deaths occurring?

• Incompetence, pure and simple, is one reason.
• Greed has already been mentioned as a contributing factor.
• Doctors failing to keep up with new medical developments that make some surgical procedures obsolete may also be implicated.
• On the other hand, doctors who are on the "cutting edge" of surgical innovation and experimentation may be performing operations that aren't ready to be performed yet, with the patient as an unwitting (or at least underinformed) guinea pig. "It seems true," writes Ruth Macklin, Ph.D., in the *American College of Surgeons Bulletin*, "that surgery, compared with other areas of medical practice, subjects fewer innovative procedures to prior review and sustained clinical investigation. . . . Patients and surgeons alike would benefit from a proper scientific approach to new surgical procedures, instead of the method of 'trial and error'."[23] Adds a *New York*

Times editorial: "A new drug must be proved safe and effective before it can be sold. So must a new medical device. But there is no Government agency that regulates new surgical procedures, just an ad hoc assessment system. . . . That's an inconsistency that needs to be resolved, maybe by having the Government insure that all operations receive proper peer review."[24]

• Surgeons' need to find enough work to make a living is another reason for the proliferation of unnecessary surgeries. Too many surgeons being propelled from medical schools is a major underlying problem. The Graduate Medical Education National Advisory Committee (GMENAC), created in 1980 by the Secretary of Health and Human Services, looked at the United States' need for physicians and projected that there would be a surplus of 70,000 doctors by the year 1990, and that the number of surgeons in the marketplace would exceed marketplace needs by 40 percent. Current figures tend to bear out the concern generated by these projections. "In 1949, when the American population numbered 148 million, about 9 million surgical operations were performed; in 1975 there were 20 million operations for a population of 211 million," Lander writes. "The number of operations performed, in other words, had increased 122 percent, while the population had increased but 43 percent, or, if you prefer, the rate of operations had risen from 61 per 1,000 population to 95."[25]

More recent figures from 1971 to 1977 show that "the number of operations increased 34 percent while the population increased by only 6 percent," and the "supply of surgeons increased between 1971 and 1975 at a rate of *seven* times that of the general population."[26] Keyser states that numerous studies have demonstrated that

> as the number of surgeons in a community increases, the number of operations tends to expand to fill their time. In 1977, with 100,000 surgeons available, there were 20 million operations. By 1982, the number had risen to more than 34 million. During that interval the number of surgeons increased by 15 percent, although the population increased by only 4 percent.[27]

• The big ego of a surgeon who wants to strut his stuff can lead to unnecessary operations, too. The problem, according to Hugo Tristam Englehardt, Jr., Ph.D., is that "one can be enamored of the pleasure of performing difficult and involved procedures which have the allure of requiring particular scientific and technological competence, to the neglect of the more simple and mundane procedures which have greater and more widespread benefits for patients."[28]

• Then, too, there are surgeons who are indiscriminate and callous in their practice and with their subjects. They will operate on anybody at anytime, no matter how old, how young, how sick, or how fragile the patient is, or how unlikely the chances are that the surgery will be successful or that the patient will survive it. Some surgeons will operate as readily on an infant as on an adult, even though they know—or ought to know—that "a child less than a year old has the same risk of death from surgery as a person aged 60 to 70 years old. . . ."[29] Not much has changed from 1922 when William D. Haggard, M.D., in an editorial entitled "The Unnecessary Operation," remarked: "There are regrettably some unconscionable pothunters who will operate on anybody that will hold still. Every hospital should eliminate that kind of man."[30]

Every hospital should have done so back then, and should do so today, but that didn't happen and it isn't happening now. Many hospitals don't want to eliminate those kinds of doctors. Such surgical opportunists run up nice charges that hospitals can add to their profit sheets. Many hospitals do mouth platitudes meant to indicate their desire to improve conditions. They set up, or in most cases are mandated by law to set up, peer review and quality assurance committees to look at and judge surgeons and the way they operate.

All fine and good, except for one slight problem: "Abuses often go unchecked at those hospitals," Keyser insists, "because peer review is ineffective and, in some cases, nonexistent."[31] Furthermore:

> Peer review at certain hospitals is a sham, particularly in obstetrics and gynecology, which has an inherent problem all its own. For example, when a uterus is removed because it has prolapsed (fallen down) too far into the vagina, the appropriateness of the surgery depends upon the extent of the prolapse or the patients' symptoms. The uterus itself will be structurally normal. Nor is abnormal tissue expected with D&Cs [dilation and curettage] or when babies are delivered by cesarean section. In these cases, the review committee's judgment must be based on the history and physical findings recorded in the chart to see whether the agreed-upon standards have been met. When the doctor writes the "correct" words, the chart will "pass" whether the words are true or not.[32]

But, deeper and more indicative of systemic rot and/or misplaced priorities is the tolerance of unnecessary surgery and surgical error that pervades the educational process and the practice atmosphere of the people who cut open other people for money. How is a doctor to improve his skills and sharpen his awareness and concern—and eliminate questionable, inappropriate, unnecessary surgeries—when the American College of Surgeons has allowed "a margin of error of 12 percent before it [leveled] a charge of unnecessary surgery"?[33] Twelve percent is not nothing nor is it some abstract statistic. It is 12 people out of every 100 having surgery, when it is the surgeon's motives—and those of his professional groups—that should be going under the knife.

Slice and Dice

Unnecessary procedures and the mistakes that occur during them are only a portion of the entire surgical error picture. Sidel and Sidel quote one well-connected physician as admitting that "errors in judgment or technique concerning either the anesthesia or the surgery, or a combination of the two, contribute close to 50 percent of the mortality in the operating room."[34]

So much of the problem originates in the medical school curriculum. For example, James L. Breen, M.D., no less than a president of the American College of Obstetricians and Gynecologists, has expressed his regret that obstetrics and gynecology "is the only specialty that allows a physician to perform major surgery with only 18 months of surgical training, much of that representing other than actual operating room experience."[35] Perhaps if obstetricians and gynecologists did very little in the way of surgery, this deficiency in their education might not set off an alarm of any great magnitude. Unfortunately for all concerned, of the ten most frequently performed operations in America (as of 1982, the last year for which good statistics are available), five are performed solely on women and frequently if not usually by obstetricians and gynecologists. They are: dilation and curettage (number 2 on the list), cesarean section (3), hysterectomy (5), bilateral destruction or occlusion of fallopian tubes (6), and oophorectomy and salpingo-oophorectomy (9).[36]

Breen points the finger of blame at a number of medical school practices, and is concerned that ob-gyn surgical novices are receiving too little information and experience not only about their own area of discipline but about others that may relate and interact with theirs as well. "Is it realistic to assume," he wonders, "considering the limited amount of time devoted to gynecologic surgical training, that gynecologic surgeons are well versed in urologic, gastrointestinal, and vascular surgery?"[37] This lack of knowledge can lead to complications that the ob-gyn surgeon cannot, within his education and experience, handle competently. And this in turn could lead to delays while a surgeon who *can* handle the problems is found and put into service—or it could end up with the ob-gyn surgeon trying his hand at it anyway, hoping for or expecting the best.

Breen, who states for the record that "most residents today are surgically handicapped because they suffer from a case of the 'deficits'," also singles out as a major problem the "all too common practice of the second-year neophyte acting as the sole teacher of the first year innocent."[38] The visually impaired leading the blind.

Lack of surgical hands-on experience is a major health and safety concern today, and it is not restricted to the medical school years. Sidel and Sidel note that "because of the relatively large number of doctors practicing surgery in the United States in proportion to its population, and because of their maldistribution, many surgeons perform only a few operations a week—this though most surgeons themselves believe that surgeons should average about ten operations a week in order to maintain their skills."[39] Because of the present and future surgeon glut, while the number of operations is growing every year, the number performed per surgeon is dropping—in 1974 each surgeon in the United States did an average of 217 operations annually; by 1983, that figure was 161—and this means a greater chance of disaster for the patient on one of these doctors' tables.[40]

We are not suggesting or endorsing the idea that surgeons should, and have a right and social responsibility to, crank up the ol' surgery machine merely to avoid becoming rusty. That sort of thinking leads only to excuses for unnecessary surgeries. Rather, the course of choice, some believe, is to limit the number of surgeons and allow them to maintain a schedule that keeps them technically proficient but not necessarily prolific. Otherwise, the results can be dire, as was shown in a 1984 study by the Department of Health and Human Services' National Center for Health Services Research. This study found that hospitals that perform surgical procedures infrequently "have substantially higher death rates for patients than do those that perform high volumes of the same operations. . . ." When the researchers looked at nine types of operations—abdominal artery surgery, gall-bladder surgery, certain operations on ulcers and the large bowel, arthroplasty of the hip, two kinds of hip fractures, and two types of lower-limb amputations—they discovered that patients "had about a 13 percent greater chance of dying if their operations were performed in hospitals that performed relatively few operations."[41] That adds up to between 3,100 and 3,800 excess deaths directly related to procedures performed in low-volume hospitals—in just one year, and in just those nine surgical categories. Two years later, the Veterans Administration shut down about a third of its 51 heart surgery departments in V.A. hospitals after an audit of 21 of these units when higher than average mortality rates turned up this information: Of 134 patients who had died after surgery, more than half were victims of "preventable errors," due at least in part to too few open-heart operations performed at these facilities.[42]

In Cleveland, where respected medical institutions have a worldwide reputation for heart surgery, an exposé series by the *Plain Dealer* in 1983 found that not only did most open-heart surgery units in that city "violate government and professional standards for patient safety," and not only were open-heart units "virtually unregulated in Ohio, leaving patients with little way of knowing which open-heart units are substandard and possibly dangerous," but also that "6 of Greater Cleveland's 10 open-heart units failed to perform 200 annual operations, the recommended number for surgical teams to develop and maintain optimal surgical skills. . . . One hospital did just two in 1979—with one death."[43]

What's more, the *Plain Dealer* series reported that two area hospitals "allow[ed] doctors to perform surgery even though the surgeons [didn't] have the professional qualifications recommended by a committee of the nation's top heart specialists."[44]

But this is no worse, it seems, than the situation at Harlem Hospital in New York, which was cited and fined by the State Health Department "for allowing an unlicensed physician to perform a routine operation in which complications developed that led to the amputation of the patient's leg."[45] No supervising doctor, no one who might have known how to deal with those complications, was anywhere around. And the fine levied against the hospital by the state was $125,000, later reduced to $39,000. Hardly more than a slap on the wrist for grossly unethical and unprofessional behavior that led to the loss of a patient's limb.

There are other, even more bizarre, abuses. Hospitals and surgeons have permitted medical supply manufacturers' representatives—with or without medical degrees—to participate in and, frequently, take charge of operations utilizing their company's equipment. There are any number of people walking around today—and a number of others who never made it through the operation—whose cardiac pacemakers were implanted by cardiac pacemaker salesmen.

In looking around for the prime culprit in preventable surgical error, at least one study[46] has implicated poor judgment by surgeons. "Such problems included reaching wrong diagnoses, delaying needed surgery, performing unnecessary or overly extensive surgical procedures, or ignoring trouble signs because of overconfidence or misplaced optimism."[47] The study found that in "90 percent of the errors of therapeutic commission, the mistakes were those of unnecessary, contraindicated, or technically defective surgical activity."[48]

And defective medical teamwork, as well. "All too often hindsight suggests that detailed training for the procedure itself and careful attention to handling its possible complications has not been implemented," writes William O. Robertson, M.D. "Again and again, what should have been routine has been overlooked; frequently the OR team has never run through a 'disaster drill'; on occasion, the staff nurses may not have been trained in dealing with complications of a particular surgical procedure."[49]

"All too often," Robertson states, "while extensive medical consultation has been fully taken care of, appropriate surgical consultation is not sought. Here, too, the opportunity for surgeons to work together in advance would seem worth taking advantage of."[50]

When looking for the root causes of the epidemic of "surgical misadventures" in the United States, one must return again and again to the weaknesses inherent in the medical education system, to doctors' egos and egotism-as-veiled-uncertainty, to physicians' distorted need to be autonomous and independent vendors, and to the breakdown of the doctor-patient relationship.

As Lander explains it:

> The surgeon is in a powerful position to minimize both psychic and somatic problems by providing the patient with explanations, concern, and reassurance before surgery, and warmth and interest afterward. It is most likely, however, that he will appear rushed, unconcerned, and aloof throughout, for he most probably regards the essentials of his work as taking place only when he is assuming an active, decisive stance above a supine, totally passive body, largely concealed by surgical draping, a person reduced to a thing. When that body regains consciousness and begins attempting to function as an active human being, the surgeon will probably continue to concern himself only with its thingness—attending to the state of the wound but hardly noticing the state of the person in whom he created it . . . the surgeon's focus on the technological, the thingness of medical practice as opposed to the humanness of sickness, is but a refinement of the stance of modern medicine generally. . . . He feels much more comfortable maneuvering the hardware of the modern medical scientist.[51]

As long as disclosure laws do not exist (or, if they do exist, do not have teeth), as long as mortality and morbidity statistics are not made readily available or available at all to the public, and as long as the medical profession covers up for its faulty own despite review committees designated to weed out the bad practitioners, surgery will be a crap shoot for the person who needs it or thinks he needs it, or wants it or thinks he wants it.

8

BUGS IN THE SYSTEM

"... there are substantially more nosocomial infections each year than hospital admissions for either cancer or accidents and at least four times more than admissions for acute myocardial infarction."
—Robert W. Haley, M.D.

If ever anybody has earned the right to be spinning in his grave, it is Ignaz Semmelweis. Even after 100 years and total vindication, his theories and teachings still are not given enough attention by the people in the medical professions, a fact that highlights their extremely poor judgment and patients' incredibly bad luck.

Semmelweis was the nineteenth-century Austrian physician who observed young mothers in hospital wards dying of childbed fever and as a result postulated the theory that these women were being killed by germs passed from sick patients to healthy ones on the hands of doctors. Simply by washing the hands between patient contact, or between morgue and autopsy work and patient contact, Semmelweis told his colleagues, deadly infections would be cut down if not cut out entirely. The good doctor's colleagues ignored him, and he died without convincing them that when patients put their lives in physicians' hands they were jeopardizing those lives.

Eventually Semmelweis was recognized as a prophet without honor in his own profession and was elevated to his rightful position as a medical pioneer; the medical world and its clients lived happily and infection-free ever after.

Except that isn't what happened.

Despite Semmelweis's century-old discovery and warning, what could the venerable, spinning physician think when an article in a professional journal, in this day and age, is capped by the headline "Hand Washing Prevents Infection,"[1] as if this were some new discovery? Or that a study of intensive care units found that "hand washing occurred after only 41 percent of . . . contact,'' and that the ''basic concepts of infection control in the medical intensive-care unit were frequently ignored, particularly by physicians.''[2]

And hand washing is just the tip of the infection iceberg. Isolating infected patients, assuring sterile technique, and keeping a vigilance over matters of personal hygiene are all crucial steps toward as infection-free a medical environment as possible—and all of these are in various stages of failure or disregard in hospitals and other health care settings throughout the United States today.

It makes one's head, no less than Dr. Semmelweis's, spin.

Hands Across America

Some facts about nosocomial (hospital-originated) infections:

• There are no fewer than 100,000 nosocomial infection-related deaths annually in America, and some estimators say that conservative figure may reflect only a third of the fatalities. About 2 million hospitalized patients a year—that is, between 5 and 10 percent of the hospital patient population—acquire a nosocomial infection.[3]

• Nosocomial infection rates are highest in large teaching hospitals and lowest in nonteaching hospitals. While this almost certainly reflects the fact that the large hospitals attract the sickest patients, it also underlines the point that where there are more people with direct access to the patients there are consequently larger problems of maintaining necessary sanitary discipline, and infections spread more readily.[4]

• More than 100,000 hospital patients annually in the United States acquire nosocomial bacteremia—the presence of bacteria in the blood—and, according to Richard E. Dixon, M.D., mortality rates ''range from 20 percent for patients who do not develop shock, to greater than 80 percent for those who do.''[5]

• Treatment-related infection is now ''the principal cause of morbidity and the second leading cause of death in the population undergoing hemodialysis,'' explain Yu et al., ''with infection of the vascular-access site with staphylococcal bacteremia the most serious infectious complication.''[6]

• Infection is the most frequent cause of death in cancer patients.[7]

• Pneumonia, which Podnos, Toews, and Pierce point out is now the most common hospital-acquired infection leading to death, occurs in 0.5 percent to 5 percent of all in-hospital patients and in 12 percent to 15 percent of patients ill enough to require intensive care,[8] has a high morbidity and mortality rate (20 percent to 50 percent), may be responsible for 15 percent of all hospital-associated deaths, and may be introduced into the lungs by way of contaminated respiratory therapy equipment or simply by breathing the air filled with droplets of infection from other patients or medical personnel coughing, especially in the close quarters of intensive care units.[9]

• And beside the human cost of such infections, there is the matter of rising heath care financing. Researching their last book, the authors found statistics indicating that from 1983 to 1984 nosocomial infections accounted for 15 percent of all hospital charges and ended up adding, at a minimum, $1.5 billion to America's medical bill. Since then, those numbers have already become old news. More recent findings indicate that in 1985 the excess charge to the American medical bill due to nosocomial infections had risen to about $2.5 billion annually,[10] and, as said before, the true figure may actually be double that because about a fourth of all infections acquired in the hospital don't show up until after the patient is discharged. Then work-related expenses and costly readmission to the hospital can be factored in. Robert Haley, M.D., director of the Division of Epidemiology and Preventive Medicine at the University of Texas Southwestern Medical School, states flatly that nosocomial infections are adding "an unnecessary $4 billion a year to our national health bill."[11] Garibaldi et al. put the figure yet higher: They claim that surgical wound infections alone (of which there are more than a million each year in the United States) "add an average of seven days to the usual hospital stay of surgical patients and cost more than 10 billion dollars in direct and indirect expenses."[12]

Considering this toll in lives and dollars, it might be expected that at least the very minimum of remedial actions might be taken. But, when Milhap C. Nahata, Pharm. D., asks the question, "Have we made significant progress in preventing infection by hand washing in the last century?" his own response has to be "Not really."[13] A two-word death sentence for possibly tens of thousands—a death sentence that is commutable, preventable, if only care and concern were taken to eliminate callousness and negligence and gross medical errors.

"We consider that hand washing is necessary after even minor contact with patients or support equipment," Albert and Condie assert, "because even the limited contact that occurs with taking the pulse, blood pressure, or oral temperature, or just touching a patient's hand, can result in transfer of organisms that can be recovered up to 2.5 hours later."[14] Or, as David Rimland, M.D., puts it, "infected and colonized patients act as reservoirs, with transient carriage on the hands of personnel implicated in transmission from patient to patient."[15]

Hand washing is recommended after contact with every patient by both the Centers for Disease Control and the American Hospital Association. It is certainly the single most important preventive against the spread of nosocomial infections. And yet, despite the clear message, and the simplicity, importance, and efficacy of washing one's hands, it "seems to be a procedure that is ignored or at least underemphasized in our present system of medical training."[16]

If we are to avoid nosocomial infection incidents like the one in Houston in the fall of 1985, when 1 baby was killed and 25 others were made ill in an infant intensive care unit when doctors and nurses failed to wash their hands,[17] the fear of infection and the awareness of the basic units of prevention need to be drummed into the heads of medical students and those educated in the allied health fields—people who should really already know its importance.

"Unfortunately," says hospital epidemiologist Timothy R. Franson, M.D., "infection control isn't taught as stringently as we might like. Most medical schools don't teach practical prevention, stressing things like hand washing."[18]

William Schaffner, M.D., a president of the Society of Hospital Epidemiologists of America, says, "Hand washing is something your mother told you to do. People think it couldn't possibly be important in the hospital anymore. There isn't a doctor in the world who isn't focused on high technology, so simple things tend to be overlooked."[19]

Correcting this simple act of "overlooking" could avert disasters in many if not all aspects and specialties of health care. For example:

• Weinstein and Young state that in the practice of ophthalmology "conscientious hand washing between patient contact is remarkably effective in halting the transmission of such diseases [as viral and bacterial eye infections]."[20]

• Hand washing is absolutely vital in the hospital nursery, because the major mode of infection transmission to infants is on the hands of the medical personnel they come in contact with.[21]

• Surgeons could avoid patient-contact infections if they "scrubbed" for ten minutes of "constant friction, soaping, and repeated rinsings,"[22] as well as keeping those cleansed hands away from faucet handles and other bacteria-ridden objects.

• Laboratory workers could help stop the spread of some infections if they remembered to wash hands before leaving the lab area.[23]

• The three types of patient most at risk from hand-carried infections are newborns, surgical patients, and those with catheters.[24] Studies have shown that among newborns, especially, herpes is transmitted nosocomially through handling by medical personnel.[25]

• It has been found that dentists and dental hygienists can transmit herpes from their hands to patients' mouths. One dental hygienist in Pennsylvania contracted a patient's herpes through an open skin rash on her hand, and then passed the virus on to 20 other patients over a four-day period. The researchers recommended that "gloves be worn by dental personnel with suspicious lesions on their fingers, and that patients with lip lesions delay dental treatment until the ailment clears."[26]

Wearing gloves would help contain or eliminate a number of hand-carried infections. It is not always practical for certain health care workers to slip on gloves, especially when those gloves are needed most, such as during an emergency. It is understandable that a patient in a life-or-death situation must not be kept waiting while medical rescuers snap on a pair of surgical gloves before touching the gasping victim. However, "inconvenient" and "time-consuming" are insufficient alibis for health workers to use in nonemergency situations. By putting on gloves, workers who handle and insert certain invasive instruments, such as endotracheal tubes, may not only prevent infecting a patient, they may actually prevent *themselves* from being infected *by* the patient.[27]

But even gloves aren't the answer if the hands beneath aren't well scrubbed, or if the physician performing the procedure or surgery is a carrier of infection. Studies show that bacteria can infect surgical patients by traveling a route out through a glove puncture during an operation. Van den Broek et al. have reported just that, relating how the virulent *Staphylococcus epidermidis* microorganism passed from a carrier surgeon's hands through a hole in one of his surgical gloves into cardiac surgery patients' bodies, and went on to colonize heart-lung machines, blood, catheters, the surgical wound—and ended up causing an epidemic of prosthetic valve endocarditis, a heart-based infection and inflammation of the area surrounding a replaced heart valve.[28]

The No-no's in Nosocomial

Hand washing, though a critical and basic preventive measure, isn't the only infection stopper, nor are dirty hands the sole starters of all nosocomial infections which, when combined, may be "among the ten leading causes of death in the United States."[29] And even cautious investigators believe that "human error is often partly responsible for the problem."[30]

Catheters, and especially urinary catheters, are good cases in point. These devices are ready pathways for bacteria to slide from the outside world right into the waiting inner areas that are highly susceptible to infection, but it is not some mere natural unavoidable occurrence that causes urinary tract infections to account for 42 percent of all nosocomial infections, making it the leading hospital-acquired infection (followed by surgical wound infections, 24 percent; nosocomial pneumonia, 10 percent; primary and secondary nosocomial bacteremia, 5 percent; and all others, 19 percent.[31]) Epidemiologist Stephen Gluckman, M.D., has been quoted as saying that it is possible that catheters are "misused or kept in for too long."[32]

These urinary catheter nosocomial infections are particularly dangerous, too: It is clear that even "apparently innocuous urinary tract infections of any cause can have important delayed morbidity."[33] Even more, Platt et al. determined that "the acquisition of urinary-tract infection during indwelling bladder catheterization is associated with nearly a threefold increase in mortality among hospitalized patients. . . ."[34]

In addition to intravenous infusion devices and respiratory therapy equipment, hemodialysis units and equipment are also of special concern in the spread of nosocomial infections to those in already weakened and vulnerable states. Among the many ways infections occur here, "faulty dialysis technique has resulted in epidemics of disease in some units and probably contributes to a low level of endemic infection problems as well."[35] The hepatitis B virus is particularly implicated, and is virulent, fast-spreading, and dangerous to those susceptible, including the hospital workers themselves. One survey of more than 300 dialysis units showed "an HBV [hepatitis B virus] attack rate of 6.2 percent for patients and 5.8 percent for staff." These are not minor outbreaks, either. Bryan reports that some dialysis units have reported high mortality rates—and that's just among the medical personnel—all because of "lapses in aseptic technique," such as contamination of wounds, improper technique, and certain unsterile conditions.[36]

Nosocomial infections can also pass to patients via the procedural chain of the food services department, due to any one or more of the following—nearly all of them with their roots in human error, and any one of them preventable through proper education and management, caring, and an average amount of common sense:[37]

- Lack of hand washing.
- Poor personal hygiene.
- Faulty patient-care technique.
- Inadequate refrigeration (the culprit in nearly half of all nosocomial salmonellosis outbreaks).
- Inadequate cooking.
- Inadequate reheating.

• Holding food in warming devices at bacteria-incubating temperatures.
• Using contaminated raw ingredients in uncooked foods.
• Improper cleaning of equipment.

Mallison points the finger at another institutional work area cum breeding ground: hospitals' central service departments, those units responsible for processing, storing, and dispensing hospital supplies and equipment. "The role of the CSD in the prevention of nosocomial disease is clear," he writes, "because improperly sterilized or disinfected reusable items—including endoscopic equipment, thermometers, bedpans and urinals, respiratory therapy and anesthesia supplies, equipment for aspiration and suction, pressure transducers, and surgical instruments—have been directly responsible for the transmission of infection."[38]

But food services and central services are not the only areas implicated. The list of hospital departments responsible for failing to contain nosocomial infections because of persistently poor and unprofessional hygiene practices is a scandalously long one: intensive care unit, pharmacy, laundry, laboratory (where workers need to be admonished not to keep their lunches in the same refrigerators as the ones that contain serum or other specimens[39])—and the list goes on. And so do unfortunate incidents:

• An outbreak of *Pseudomonas aeruginosa*—a pathogen with a high case-fatality ratio—in a premature nursery caused by contaminated resuscitation equipment in the delivery room.[40]
• Death due to infection after a rubber-band hemorrhoidectomy.[41]
• The death of an Idaho woman from rabies after receiving a corneal transplant from a man who had undiagnosed rabies.[42]
• A Legionnaires' disease miniepidemic in a Rhode Island hospital that led to examination and suspicion of, and mobilization against, the hospital's cooking and drinking water, but that was later found to be caused by the never examined or suspected "heavily contaminated" water in the hospital's cooling towers.[43]

Another area in which one would think the greatest of care should and would be taken is the operating room (OR). Yet here, too, laxity, negligence, and uncaring and unthinking behavior can and do put patients in jeopardy and lead to unnecessary and preventable nosocomial infection episodes. According to Harold Laufman, inherent in the problem of OR infections is "the pervading effect of human failure. The danger associated with unskilled, poorly trained, or untrustworthy personnel who may abuse an otherwise satisfactory environment constitutes an insidious, but perhaps the most important, aspect of hazard control in the operating room."[44]

Some of the more common abuses, oversights, and carelessness of OR workers include:

- Leaving a door open to the corridor while operations are in progress.
- Permitting unrestricted opening and closing of the operating-room doors as people come and go.
- Not covering long hair, sideburns, or beards.
- Allowing technical, nursing, and anesthesia-administering personnel to circulate in and out of operating rooms while wearing short-sleeve shirts.

"No matter how particulate-free the air may be that is blowing into a room, the particulate biologic matter that inevitably is circulated around the room is quantitatively in direct proportion to the number and movement of people in the room and the amount of exposed hair and skin," Laufman states. "Shed particles tend to mount exponentially when excessive numbers of improperly covered visitors are present and when unnecessary activity of people occurs, including the flapping of drapes, towels, and gowns as well as any other maneuver that may unsettle previously shed particles from horizontal surfaces."[45]

Sometimes even when care is taken to eliminate a potential cause of nosocomial infections in the OR, it backfires, presumably because not enough research and testing has gone into the efficacy of such measures. Laufman thinks one of these measures, a tacky mat that has "been widely promoted and used in front of the doors leading to the surgical suite on the pretext that they prevent the tracking in of dirt from common corridors"—sort of a flypaper concept—not only doesn't remove bacteria from operating room personnel's shoes but in fact may transfer bacteria already stuck on the mat onto the shoes of new arrivals. No such neat high-tech marvels are necessary. Simple mopping up between operations (along with regularly scheduled cleaning of the corridors outside the operating room) is "an unsurpassed method" of fighting bacteria on the floors.[46] So why isn't it done? Is it the lower cost of a mat as compared with the salary and supervision of a housekeeping employee with a mop and bucket? But what really, ultimately, is the cost?

And what incentive is there for hospitals to keep their operating rooms clean? The threat of some sort of punishment? Not likely. Take the case of an operating suite at Middlesex General–University Hospital in New Brunswick, New Jersey, which was found by state Department of Health inspectors to have "unsanitary conditions"—conditions like dust in a vent and holes in the suspended ceiling. Was there a fine? Did someone get called on the carpet? Did the institution risk losing its license? All that happened was that the operating suite was closed for half a day to give the housekeeping staff time to clean up the cited failings. That's it. And the only penalty or inconvenience to be felt by anyone involved was felt by the sick people in the hospital, who had their operations bumped from Thursday to Friday or Saturday. Everybody got their operations—46 in one day because of the rescheduling—with no loss of income to the hospital. In fact, by keeping patients in a day or two longer, the hospital might actually have benefited financially. It certainly wasn't penalized.[47]

Getting Back—or Going Backward?

Fighting nosocomial infections is a mixed bag of effectiveness. In practically anything related to health and medicine, the best offense is a good preventive defense. Eliminating or controlling nosocomial infections is no exception. According to Haley et al. in their major study of infection prevention, the establishment by hospitals of intensive infection surveillance and control programs was "strongly associated with reductions in rates of nosocomial urinary tract infection, surgical wound infection, pneumonia, and bacteremia. . . ." Such a surveillance program would include a system of organized inspection undertaken by a "trained, effectual infection-control physician, an infection-control nurse per 250 beds, and a system for reporting infection rates to practicing surgeons."[48]

When Haley and colleagues examined hospitals with just such programs in place, they found that the hospitals' infection rates were reduced by 32 percent. However, even though the Joint Commission on the Accreditation of Hospitals mandates infection-control units, very few hospitals have effective programs. Most are understaffed and lack expert supervision.[49] Such ineffective programs have demonstrated an overall infection rate *increase* of 18 percent.[50] Thus, during the mid-1970s only 6 percent (out of a possible 32 percent) of America's nosocomial infections were actively prevented, despite ostensible concern and money thrown at the problem. By the early 1980s the prevention figure had barely moved and was only at the 9 percent level.[51] Also, the Haley study found that these infection surveillance teams' stock contribution to infection control—environmental culturing, during which samples of bacteria are collected from hospitals' walls and floors and are identified—was ineffective.[52]

Antibiotics have been flung wholesale at the encroaching infections— approximately one-third of all hospital patients are given antibiotics, and 200 million prescriptions for antibiotics are dispensed in the United States every year[53]—in the simplistic and misguided belief that might makes right and that there is safety in numbers. This kind of thinking, unfortunately, frequently has resulted in more harm than good. As the authors have written:

> Typically, when there is a rash of infections, hospitals haul out the antibiotics to do away with the monsters that the antibiotics themselves have nurtured. And it may work for a while—until the aftereffects set in. Not only do patients have bad reactions to the drugs, but there is a rapid development of strains of bacteria resistant to the antibiotics that were once effective against these organisms. The amount of penicillin required to treat an infection today is 50 times greater than it was 30 years ago.[54]

Moreover, Alfred E. Buxton points out that "some antibiotics used to treat life-threatening diseases change the host's flora, predisposing to colonization with multiple-drug-resistant bacteria, while others impair host defense mechanisms."[55] Martin J. Blaser, M.D., remarks in an editorial in the *Annals of Internal Medicine* that, for example, "when a *Salmonella* strain (especially if it is antibiotic resistant) is introduced into a population, persons receiving antimicrobial agents are at higher risk for acquiring infection, subsequently becoming ill, and having severer manifestations of the illness. During a large milk-borne salmonellosis outbreak in Chicago," he adds, "illness was six times more likely among exposed persons who had received antibiotics during the prior month than among those who had not." Blaser also implicates antibiotic overkill and the creation of resistance by bacteria with leading to epidemics of nosocomial acute diarrheal illness.[56]

On the other hand, sometimes the antibiotic arsenal is mobilized against armies that aren't even there. It is common knowledge that patients are receiving too many antibiotics too often inappropriately with too little evidence of actual infection. (Sometimes they are given antibiotics prophylactically to prevent infections, with variable results.) And despite this knowledge little has changed in the two decades since Beaty and Petersdorf wrote of "the astounding estimate that antibiotics are given on the basis of proper indications in only one of ten instances," and that "the use of antimicrobials to cover surgical patients, patients with viral infections, and other so-called 'infection-prone' individuals constitutes a leaky umbrella at best and may be distinctly detrimental." To the two researchers, the "most important principle in the prophylaxis of iatrogenic disease, however, is to administer drugs only when they are needed, and to perform diagnostic procedures only when they are likely to yield meaningful information."[57]

To help in this, pharmacists could, but seldom are asked to, join in antibiotic surveillance and control programs. They know the antibiotic utilization of the hospital as a whole and per individual physician, and may be able to assist infection control programs in pinpointing overuse and improper use leading to the creation of resistant strains of bacteria. Pharmacists can participate in continuing education sessions for physicians on the proper use of antibiotics and "may also provide the physician with research data on new agents, the cost of these agents, and the efficacy of such agents as they become available."[58] But pharmacists' inclusion in these courses and in decision making is, in most hospitals, hardly a foregone conclusion.

So, the last line of defense comes down to disinfectants. The theory here is, "If we can't prevent germs, we'll swab and mop them out of existence." Unfortunately, even if disinfectants were that effective and powerful, it would be difficult to eradicate microorganisms that have gotten toeholds on supplies and equipment. But the trouble is that disinfectants *aren't* that effective and powerful.

In fact, some hospital and other health care facility disinfectants do not disinfect at all. In the summer of 1986, articles appeared in newspapers reporting that Reagan administration budget cuts had four years earlier forced the shutdown of the only federal laboratory designed to test the potency and efficacy of disinfectants.[59] The federal government believed that the states would pick up the responsibility (and the tab) for testing disinfectants, but only Florida, North Carolina, Mississippi, and Virginia did so. Thus the country was left with no national independent, unbiased testing facility for gauging the effectiveness of disinfectants.

Martha E. Rhodes, M.D., assistant commissioner of the Florida Department of Agriculture and Consumer Services, has been quoted as saying that some 15 to 20 percent of disinfectant samples analyzed in her state were ineffective—so ineffective, in fact, that "two or three samples were received by the state laboratory in Tallahassee with large numbers of bacteria growing in the disinfectant that was supposed to kill them."[60] What, then, is growing—unknown, unsuspected, and unchecked—in the disinfectants sold in the other 46 states, purchased by hospitals and health care facilities that have nothing to go on but the exaggerated sales claims and skewed testing data provided by the disinfectant manufacturers themselves, trying to push their product in an extremely competitive marketplace?

Until a federal agency once again accepts the task of testing, running the risk of disinfectant-related nosocomial infections will be a fact of life— or death.

Nosocomial infections may never be eliminated. Hospitals are full of people who carry infections that can and do spread. But if not total eradication, then control and containment are acceptable . . . and attainable. The only thing keeping hospitals and other facilities from meeting at least the 32 percent reduction in infections—or even half that, or a third of that—is the lack of will and determination of hospital administrators systematically to enforce sanitary protocols already on the books. Thirty-two percent sliced off even the most conservative figure of annual nosocomial infection deaths would mean more than 30,000 lives saved—the high estimate would mean 100,000 people living instead of being killed by hospitals' home-grown and well-nurtured bacteria.

9

A TASTE OF OUR
OWN MEDICINE

"I firmly believe that if the entire *materia medica* as now used could be
sunk to the bottom of the sea, it would be all the better for mankind—
and all the worse for the fishes."

—Oliver Wendell Holmes

Bob East, a popular, prize-winning photographer for the *Miami Herald,* a
lively man with a dapper, Daliesque handlebar mustache, was in the operating room. It was March 1, 1985. The fate that ironically flings arthritis
upon gifted musicians and atrophying disease upon strong and swift ath-
letes had given this visual artist cancer of the eye—his camera eye. And
the eye was about to be removed. Already a victim of fate, Bob East was
about to become its casualty.

To relieve pressure against the cancerous eye, the surgical team
tapped 50 milliliters of fluid from East's spine, saved it in a container for
reinjection, and put the vial aside. The vial was unmarked. This was the
first mistake.

Meanwhile, an employee of a local Miami eye institute arrived in the
OR, carrying a tray. The tray was to be used to carry East's eye to the
institute for study. With the tray was a vial of glutaraldehyde, a tissue
preservative. The vial was unmarked. This was the second mistake.

During the operation, a nurse saw the unmarked vial on the tray,
asked what was in it. Someone, from behind a surgical mask, replied
"CSF"—cerebrospinal fluid. This was the third mistake. The vial of glutaraldehyde was duly marked "CSF." This was the fourth.

The rest is a sadly predictable story. When the time came to reinject
the CSF, the glutaraldehyde was injected instead into East's spine. Immediately, his blood pressure plummeted, his pulse slowed to a near stop,

his breathing ceased. No one knew why he'd suddenly taken a turn for the worse—until the resident from the eye institute returned and wondered aloud where his glutaraldehyde had gone.

Five days later, Bob East's wife had her brain-dead husband removed from life support. He was gone in minutes.

Two weeks later, Fred Hicks, Sr., of Fairview, Tennessee, a patient at Vanderbilt University Medical Center, was given juice mixed not with his medication but with a liquid air freshener. Both the medicine and the oil of wintergreen air freshener were green, were liquids, were in similarly shaped bottles, and were sitting together in the same refrigerator—a refrigerator that was supposed to be reserved for medications only. In the hospital for minor cataract surgery, Hicks, 81, was dead within hours.

And then there was Lillian Cedeno. The 21-year-old woman with cancer of the sinus and facial bones had entered Albany Medical Center Hospital for treatment on February 27. She was also six months pregnant. During the procedure, Cedeno received the cancer-fighting drug Vincristine—but it was mistakenly injected into her spine instead of given intravenously. Lillian Cedeno first became paralyzed, then slipped into a deep coma, breathing only with the assistance of a respirator. On March 16, her baby was delivered by cesarean section. Lillian Cedeno never knew it. She also never knew that her premature baby girl died of a heart attack 24 days later. At 6:14 P.M., May 24, 85 days after the faulty injection, Lillian Cedeno was pronounced dead. Later the doctors would list the cause of death as cancer.

These three well-publicized medical mistakes of early 1985 gave the American public a fleeting glimpse of a national scandal. Perhaps many readers and viewers thought they were being made aware of a few tragic and isolated uncommon occurrences. Others, more savvy or more suspicious, thought or knew that those deaths were just the tip of the iceberg.

Both groups were wrong. These unnecessary and preventable deaths were merely the tip of the tip of the very uppermost tip of an iceberg that itself is sitting on a glacier. The only difference between those victims and the tens of thousands of others like them every year is that those three got some ink and a little media time. But it didn't do them or anybody else any good.

Accidents can happen. Nobody's perfect. But accidents with drugs happen far too often in hospitals and other health care facilities—often enough, in fact, to be nothing more or less than the fruits of negligence, ignorance, carelessness, and systemic rot. And perfection is not the point. Responsibility is.

Speaking of the Bob East case, Sheldon J. Schlesinger, a Ft. Lauderdale attorney, was quoted as saying, "It occurs all the time and there is an inadequate focus on the problem. Hopefully, as a result of this case medical procedures will be more stringent and lawyers will not be blamed for filing malpractice cases."[1]

Stanley M. Rosenblatt, a Miami malpractice lawyer, concurs: "I don't see what happened to Bob East as an isolated case. Time and time again I see instances of poor communication between doctors and nurses result in horrible tragedies."[2]

Poor communication, limited education, sloppiness in practice, mistakes in prescribing and dispensing, and the basic dilemma of an overmedicated America are some of the major components of the rampant medication error epidemic present in the American medical system today.

On Something

What is a medication error? How does it occur? A medication error, according to Louise Lander, "is a broad classification of mishap that can mean the patient got a drug when he shouldn't have or got no drug when he should have, got the wrong drug, got the wrong dose of the right drug, or got the drug by the wrong route (e.g., intravenously instead of by intramuscular injection or by mouth) or in the wrong site (e.g., on the right foot instead of the left). (Getting a drug earlier or later than the doctor ordered is not considered an error.) The effect of a particular medication error can range from essentially zero to death, depending on the characteristic of the drug and the condition of the patient."[3]

Medication errors also include "failure to monitor for side effects; failure to initiate proper monitoring; and simple technical errors with decimal points, abbreviation, legibility, and verbal orders."[4] To the list, Illich adds that patients may "get an old or a contaminated batch [or] a counterfeit . . . and still others receive injections with improperly sterilized syringes. Some drugs are addictive, others mutilating, and others mutagenic. . . . Subtle kinds of poisoning thus have spread even faster than the bewildering variety and ubiquity of nostrums."[5]

Basically, though, errors occur "because of a lack of knowledge, substandard performance or because of defects in the system."[6]

And the scope of the problem? Davis and Cohen, whose book *Medication Errors: Causes and Prevention* is a classic in the field, state that the range of errors in hospitals that are not using the far more efficient and protective unit-dose system of pharmaceutical distribution ranges from 5.3 percent to 20.6 percent, with an average of 11.6 percent. Rounding off the average to a 12 percent medication error rate, and applying that to a hospital with 300 patients, the arithmetic looks something like this:[7]

300 patients × 365 days = 109,500 patient days.

Each patient receives about 10 doses of medication a day =
     1,095,000 doses of medication administered annually.

131,400 medication errors are committed annually.

360 medication errors are committed daily.

And that's just one average-size hospital.

"For the disbelievers," writes Davis and Cohen, "let us select an arbitrary figure of 1 percent, a much lower figure than any reported by studies in nonunit dose hospitals. Such an error rate would mean 10,950 medication errors annually, 30 medication errors daily. Clearly, even with a low medication error figure, the number of errors is alarming."[8]

As William O. Robertson, M.D., puts it, "Murphy's Law seems to be constantly in action in our hospitals."[9] This is no minor breakdown, either; for "with the average hospitalized adult receiving an average of 13 different drugs on multiple occasions (for children the number is 7), the opportunity both for the unexpected and for error is enormous."[10] It would be bad enough if healthy people were somehow exposed to this many drugs at one time—"polypharmacy" is the name for it—but, as Lander points out, "Hospitalized patients are especially vulnerable, partly because they are relatively older and sicker than other patients, partly because they are made to consume a large number of drugs during their illness."[11]

A remedy seems obvious. "One method of cutting down on adverse reactions is to cut down on drug use," as one Boston University researcher stated the case clearly.[12] To which Robertson adds, "Since the likelihood of error is an exponential function of the number of actions taken, keeping the number of drugs prescribed to a minimum is essential in an effective risk management strategy."[13]

But it is not as simple as all that. By merely suggesting this seemingly minor and much needed alteration—reducing the amount of drugs manufactured, prescribed, dispensed, and injected or ingested—one attacks and proposes the undermining of almost all of current medical practice. To be careful and conservative with medication is a subversive concept indeed, even though, as Illich notes, "some experienced clinicians believe that less than two dozen basic drugs are all that will ever be desirable for 99 percent of the total population; others, that up to four dozen items are optimal for 98 percent."[14]

"One out of every six visits to the doctor is made by people with illnesses that the doctor can do nothing about (colds, coughs, flu)," Martin Weitz tells us, "yet the great majority of these patients receive drug treatment."[15]

"Some 60 to 80 percent of the complaints doctors see are emotional in origin," writes Arthur S. Freese. "These could be treated without drugs, but [that takes] time and understanding"—something in short supply in medical encounters these days. So: "It's quicker and less troublesome to get rid of the patient with the mutually satisfying act of writing out an Rx."[16]

The patient, then, takes drugs that may not be and probably are not effective against what is really ailing him. As the drugs fail to cure the problem, the patient thinks the worst about his condition. The doctor, on the other hand, "recognizing that there is no disease present, begins to form a picture of the patient as a 'crock,' a nuisance who upsets his time schedule or—what's worse—refuses to cooperate by getting better. As the doctor continues to fail with drugs, he feels increasingly helpless and angry, so he increases the dosages of drugs, making them stronger."[17] And then the medication errors really start.

Lander agrees, adding that "the physician is part of a subculture in which maximizing the number of patients he sees is the socially accepted route to a yacht and a country estate, and wielding his prescription pad with a professional flourish is an appreciably more efficient means to that end than attempting to talk things out."[18] And this is even more so now since in the past two years doctors have begun selling prescription drugs to the patients instead of sending them to the pharmacist to fill the order. Despite the possible conflicts of interest—that it would behoove physicians to overprescribe or only prescribe those drugs they keep stocked in their offices' back room—and despite the dangers of keeping a pharmacist, who might pick up on a prescription or dose error, out of the prescribing picture, the trend is far too monetarily appealing—somewhere between $10,000 and $40,000 in yearly additional income from selling the drugs they prescribe—for doctors to worry.[19]

But more than money is involved: It is dominance and ego, the assertion of professional certainty (or, rather, masked uncertainty) over human interaction and interrelationship. Says Lander: "Writing a prescription, because it is something that only a physician can legally do, gives him psychological satisfaction as an exercise of his unique power, and receiving a prescription gives the patient psychological satisfaction as a gift of that unique power. . . . But the prescription, a thing, easily comes to substitute for the dialogue, the relationship, that might have made it unnecessary."[20]

One person who saw the problem and the struggle firsthand from both sides—as dispenser and as receiver—was Hal Lear, M.D., whose bout with heart disease and the medical system found him in many a hospital bed accepting many a medication. Writes his widow:

He realized then—something else he never had realized before—
what huge emotional investment doctors make in the orders they
wrote. It was utterly gurulike: Give the patient the green pill
and say, "This is going to help you." And in fact the red pill
might work every bit as well, maybe better, but the guru's omnipotence is now tied to the green pill. If the patient asks for
something different, that is a challenge to medical authority and
must, like all such challenges, be faced down. This is annoying,
he thought. Worse than annoying: this is bad medicine. These
people do not listen to the patient. They are too enveloped in
their own authority.[21]

Reaction Shots

Drugs, though useful—frequently lifesaving—are strong potions, and even
when working "miracles" to clear up a specific condition they may actually be causing yet another one, or may even ironically be causing the
very condition they are supposed to be curing. Drugs may also erode the
general state of one's health. Destroying the village in order to save it is
the apt military metaphor.

It is known that about 40 percent of people undergoing medical care
suffer side effects from the medications given them,[22] and these reactions
can leave a person "blind or deaf, afflicted with kidney, liver or brain
damage, bone necrosis, ulceration of the bowel, intestinal hemorrhage,
skin scars, extreme sensitivity to sunlight, or other disabilities that may
last for months or years."[23]

Lander adds:

Introducing the chemistry of medication into an individual's internal ecology is intrinsically risky. Drugs (even aspirin) are inherently toxic and, at dosage levels that vary widely among
individuals, will produce a toxic reaction. And practically any
drug will in some people produce a hypersensitivity, or allergic,
reaction, a danger that is unpredictable unless the reaction has
occurred before. Either type of reaction may be as trivial as a
transient skin rash, as final as death. If the drug is injected, there
is an intensified risk from the greater concentration and more
sudden introduction of the drug, and the additional risks of infection from unsterile equipment or improper cleansing of the
skin. If the drug is given in the form of intravenous fluid, there
is the risk of death from pulmonary edema (filling up of the lungs

with fluid) and the risk of a wide variety of lesser complications from such a drastic alteration of the individual's internal chemical environment.[24]

Some examples of side effects, common and otherwise, drawn at random (the selection pool is so vast and deep) from the medical literature, include:

• Attacks on the gastrointestinal tract—mouth, esophagus, stomach, small and large intestines, and pancreas—and such attacks are common: "nearly all oral drugs have gastrointestinal side effects," and "surveys of hospital inpatients show that 20–40 percent of all side effects of drugs affect the gastrointestinal tract." These gastrointestinal symptoms often reduce patient compliance. They also may be signs of drug-induced diseases, ones that have "pathological changes that do not resolve immediately the drug is withdrawn."[25]

• Drug-induced myopathies (muscle disorders), including myasthenia gravis and related conditions.[26]

• Cataracts in children receiving high-dosage oral prednisone daily for chronic asthma.[27]

• Diseases of the liver—cell necrosis, hepatitis, impairments of bile secretion—which account for 8 percent of adverse drug reactions because the liver is a sort of central clearinghouse for drugs, metabolizing and excreting them.[28]

• Systemic lupus erythematosus, of which 10 percent of diagnosed cases are caused by medications taken for other diseases. The medication-induced lupus is "clinically indistinguishable from the spontaneous disease that it mimics,"[29] is "an elaborate example of pharmacological provocation of an illness," and is caused by more than 40 drugs.[30]

• Drug reactions diametrically opposite to the stated intent of the drug's action. Among these are: the long-term use of analgesics to relieve muscle contraction headache "actually feeds rather than helps the pain";[31] tranquilizers used to control schizophrenics "may actually be causing serious mental and emotional problems that are unrelated to the original disorders";[32] "the commonest drugs to cause cardiac arrhythmias are those that are themselves used to treat rhythm disturbances."[33]

And on and on, in fistfuls of studies, reports, and articles. One may well argue that unpleasant to life-threatening side effects are the justifiable risks one takes while trying to derive the benefits of certain medications, and that there is no blame to be placed when a drug reaction occurs when those benefits have been deemed and accepted as greater than the risks. This may be so. However, so many of these "acceptable risks" are preventable, and need neither be "acceptable" nor "risks." At the very least, prolonged morbidity and other negative outcomes associated with drug-induced illnesses can be avoided by early recognition by physicians of what is indeed a drug-induced illness, a situation occurring so frequently "that physicians in clinical practice should consider it as a diagnosis at least once a day."[34]

The trouble is, as Seidl et al. have explained, "Most physicians are ill-informed about adverse drug reactions."[35] As a group, physicians have a "lack of knowledge of the pharmacology, pharmacokinetics, and chemistry of the drugs [they prescribe], and of the physiologic factors in both health and disease that predispose to drug reactions. . . ."[36] Laurence A. Savett, M.D., has shown that the consequences of physicians failing to diagnose a drug-induced illness, or failing to diagnose it soon enough, can lead to persistent illness, recurrent illness, unnecessary examinations and tests, prolonged and inappropriate treatment, and future jeopardy from the drug.[37]

Among other obstacles to recognition and appropriate treatment of adverse drug reactions and drug toxicity, according to Kenneth L. Melmon, M.D., are:[38]

• The physician's "failure to set a therapeutic end point for the drugs he uses. When a therapeutic end point is not predetermined, a toxic end point is often reached."
• Lack of therapeutic objectives, leading to lack of therapeutic effect. If "therapeutic objectives have not been predetermined, lack of efficacy is difficult to recognize, and a useless (but potentially toxic) agent will continue to be administered."
• The physician's "overly hopeful expectations of drug therapy," especially when combined with the physician's "low index of suspicion." Melmon expands upon this point:

A physician is naturally reluctant to think that his treatment contributes to a patient's disability. It is easier to attribute new symptoms to an extension of an underlying disease than to obvious or occult drug toxicity. . . . Too frequently, laboratory data or new symptoms that do not "fit" into the anticipated course of a disease are ignored.[39]

But ultimately, and most profoundly, adverse drug reactions, iatrogenic drug-induced illness, and toxicity are symptomatic of the most gaping flaw in a systemic breakdown. "We are a pill-taking society," Melmon writes, echoing Illich and Mendelsohn and so many other concerned colleagues and observers. "A major cause of preventable drug reactions is that too many pills are prescribed."[40]

Prescription Proscriptions

"Contrary to their accepted image and contrary to what the public rightly expects," John Pekkanen tells us, "doctors often know very little about the drugs they are prescribing. Too often all they know is precisely what the drug companies want them to know."[41]

This, obviously, does not make for good, safe, efficient prescribing. It can lead to the ordering of the wrong drugs, too many or too few, too large or too little a dose. Pharmacists do a better job overall in knowing how to prescribe than physicians do,[42] and, along with nurses, pharmacists ought to be monitoring physicians' prescribing performance as a way to prevent catastrophes—if physicians' egos and power drives would ever permit such observation and correction. But it is necessary. One university teaching hospital looked into pharmacists' complaints and found that "less than 25 percent of orders for intravenously given solutions contained adequate instructions for subsequent administration of fluids."[43] This sort of thing can and does lead to confusion in the pharmacy, uncertainty among the nursing staff, waste of supplies and money for the hospital—and, most important, danger to the patient. All avoidable. Avoidable, too, is the increased length of stay in the hospital caused by inappropriate drug prescribing—a difference of two days longer than for those who received proper therapy.[44]

Oftentimes a function of physicians' lack of pharmacological knowledge, combined hazardously with their drive to assert what they believe is proper and beneficial, is polypharmacy, which, according to Lander's excellent definition, is "the prescribing of multiple medications [which] creates a risk that is greater than the sum of risks from the individual drugs, because the chemistry of their interactions creates new dangers."[45] In other words, overkill.

Polypharmaceutical problems in a hospital setting may begin with an incomplete, less-than-thorough physical examination and history that may fail to uncover prescription medications or over-the-counter drugs being taken by the person being examined. When this lapse occurs, hospital patients may soon be getting duplicate drugs or chemical disease fighters that are antagonistic to other medications with active ingredients already being taken. And the resulting drug-drug interaction can wound and kill. This is how Libby Zion died.

Zion, 18, daughter of writer Sidney Zion, suddenly came down with a 101-degree fever and an earache, probably as a result of an infection at the site of a wisdom tooth that had been extracted a few days before. The Zions called up their long-time family physician, who told them to take Libby to the hospital. The doctor, instead of joining them at the hospital as they thought he would, spoke by phone with physicians there, and they decided that Libby Zion had a virus that was going around. By this time, her fever was about 103. The family doctor and all the hospital personnel involved in the case told the worried parents to go home, their daughter was in good hands, and she'd be well taken care of.

What happened next is what killed Libby Zion. She was taking Nardil, an antidepressant. She told the admitting physician that she was taking it. It was written on her chart. Despite this, and for no apparent reason, she was given Demerol, a painkiller that can be fatal when taken with Nardil. She also never received the antibiotics that were ordered. The only things she received were Tylenol and Haldol, a tranquilizer. The Nardil and Demerol mixed sent Libby Zion into a psychotic state, violently thrashing about on her bed. Nurses requested that the intern on duty examine the patient, but the intern did nothing but order, over the phone, that Libby Zion be put in a straitjacket, and then tied down to the bed by her wrists and ankles. At 6:30 A.M., the first time Zion's temperature had been taken since 2 A.M., it was 107.6 degrees. Cold compresses did nothing. Libby Zion went into cardiac arrest, and died at 7:30 A.M. Cause of death was listed as "acute pneumonitis." The intern, who had neglected to see Libby Zion for the four final hours of her life, was promoted to residency status.

Lawsuits were filed by the Zions. A grand jury looking into the matter issued a report denouncing the actions of the hospital and medical professionals involved. The hospital was persistent in its denials of wrongdoing; at one point it even attempted to blame the whole incident on cocaine use by Libby Zion, but the toxicologist who performed the autopsy was not able to confirm the presence of any cocaine in the body. Finally, three years after the incident, New York Hospital, one of New York City's most prestigious, admitted its fault in the matter, was fined $13,000 by the state, and was ordered to submit a monthly report explaining the cause of death of all admitted patients who die there within 24 hours of entering the hospital. Other penalties were also imposed. The grand jury commented that New York Hospital was probably typical, and that unsupervised interns and residents were too much in charge everywhere.

(As a footnote to all this, it is an interesting twist of fate that as this settlement and much of the story of Libby Zion was being put to rest, artist Andy Warhol died of complications following gallbladder surgery at this same hospital, leading to a New York State Health Department inquiry and report that accused New York Hospital's staff of inadequate and incomplete presurgical examinations and tests, faulty supervising by the nursing staff of a private duty nurse, and other deficiencies. Dan Jacobson, of United Press International, reported the Zion-Warhol coincidence this way: "Many of the violations in that case, which the hospital has admitted, are similar to those in the Warhol case."[46])

Another—perhaps the major—cause of polypharmacy is, as Kurt Kroenke, M.D., has labeled it, "polyphysician": "Where physicians gather, opinions gather likewise," he says.[47] Polypharmacy is a scenario of "conflicting, competing, and incompatible drug orders written by multiple physicians for a single patient," Robertson makes clear. "As many as nine different physicians have been involved in writing orders for one patient during a single 24-hour period!"[48]

Sometimes, and especially among polypharmacy's key target group— America's senior citizens—the onslaught of drugs is so great that these people become medication freaks: prescription junkies, Rx addicts. Researchers at the Cornell Medical Center in New York uncovered what they called "iatrogenic dependence." They concluded:

> In pursuit of symptomatic relief from unrecognized depressions and from the chronic ailments of advancing age, the elderly receive many medications from numerous physicians. Therapeutic interventions are often duplicated or contradictory and result in the coadministration of tranquilizers, sedatives, and analgesics. The result may be dependence which the patient and physician fail to recognize or to diagnose in the presence of withdrawal symptoms.[49]

Another problem: doctors' poor handwriting. It used to be a joke. No more. As much as harmful overprescribing and polypharmacy are perfect examples of the current medical educational and practice ideological infrastructure, so are illegible handwriting and unclear oral orders indicative of the communications breakdowns that are rampant and seemingly intrinsic to the system. Poor handwriting may be, as an American College of Legal Medicine was told, the most common cause of drug overdose.[50] And an unclear oral medication order can lead to tragedy, as it did, for example, in a Louisville, Kentucky, children's hospital when a doctor ordered (or thought he ordered) 0.8 milligrams of morphine sulfate, but the nurse heard (or thought she heard, or wasn't sure if she heard) 0.8 cubic centimeters of the drug. Thus injected with an overdose ten times greater than the requested amount, a 17-month-old baby girl went into "profound shock with decreased cardiac output" and shortly afterward died.[51]

"A poorly communicated order is the seed or the fertilizer for errors—the sole cause of an error, or the stimulus for the lack of knowledge or poor performance by other health professionals which results in an error," write Davis and Cohen. "All too often the nurse or pharmacist, who is at the interface with the patient where the error occurs, is assigned the blame and the reporting responsibility for an error which was caused by the physician's poor communication."[52]

Davis and Cohen also remarked that illegible handwriting has an indirect error factor, too: by making progress notes, consultations, and histories and physicals difficult if not impossible to read or understand, physicians set the stage for other subsequent physicians and health care workers to ignore, avoid, or discount these important documents.[53] Also, illegibility on hospital medication orders can necessitate an almost 20 percent "callback rate." That is, the pharmacy has to send the prescription back to the ordering physician for clarification; thus, time and money and many tempers—if not lives—are lost.

"Short of grafting a typewriter onto each physician's writing arm or granting 'continuing medical education credits for handwriting accomplishments,' no simple remedy is obvious," writes Robertson,[54] who goes on to say that complicating the matter is that not all the indecipherable nature of orders has to do with writing: "One Washington hospital, priding itself on the accuracy, legibility, and completeness of its order sheets, was stunned to discover that approximately 14 percent of orders of non–intensive care medical patients were verbal orders. With so many similar-sounding names of medication, such practices are fraught with problems."[55]

Who or what is to blame for as much as 58 percent of the information on hospital charts—and 80 percent of doctors' signatures—being illegible? One must take to task personally the 40 percent or so of physicians whose handwritten or oral orders are indistinguishable from alien scrawl. Most of the blame, though, Davis and Cohen assert, should fall on the medical educators and hospital administrators who tolerate the sloppy writing as a fact of life, and on nurses and pharmacists and other health care workers who have to read illegible orders every day but do not raise a ruckus or document the problem.[56]

Another extremely serious prescription-writing error involves the incorrect computation of drug dosages. This is not uncommon; in fact, it is far too common for anyone's good. These dosage errors may originate with the physicians, the pharmacy, or the nursing staff, and may include:

• Mistakes in arithmetic.
• Misplaced decimal points.

• Confusion with or misunderstanding of and inability to work with the metric system.

• Poor judgment manifesting itself as a belief in and prescribing of a totally wrong-size dose.

For example, a study of six hospital emergency rooms showed that antitetanus shots were used incorrectly 23 percent of the time—6 percent of patients received too little medication, risking the possibility of contracting the disease along with its 45 to 55 percent case-fatality rate; 17 percent were overtreated, risking adverse drug reactions.[57] And, the researchers discovered, "patients at higher risk for tetanus (those with tetanus-prone wounds who had never been given a complete initial course of immunizations) had the lowest likelihood (27 percent) of receiving correct antitetanus treatment."[58] Why did these computational/judgment errors occur? The physicians may very well not have had any idea what the recommended dosage is, and simply did not bother to look it up; or, in the case of excessive administration of the antitetanus drug, the physicians, in their zeal to be sure to wipe out the possibility of tetanus even if it meant administering a bit more than necessary, did not think about or in fact may have been ignorant of the risk of overtreatment. "Finally," the study states, "patient-care surveillance systems are lacking in most emergency rooms, and physicians do not learn about treatment except in cases with a serious adverse outcome."[59]

Another typical example of computational error is evident in results of a study of dosage sizes in an infant intensive care unit. The results: "1 in every 12 doses computed by 95 registered nurses contained an error that would result in the administration of an amount that was 10 times higher or lower than the dose ordered." What's more, "the error rate was no different for experienced or inexperienced nurses."[60] Experienced nurses simply felt absolutely confident in their skills and instincts, and believed they were right—even when they were absolutely dead wrong.

Five years later, a similar study[61] showed remarkably similar results: a 6.3 percent error rate in computing drug doses, and magnitudes of error that were either ten times too much medicine prescribed or ten times too little. Here, too, those with the most experience made the most dispensing errors—and these were major, potentially lethal errors: Assuming a 6.3 percent error rate, and assuming that a baby "who is sick enough to be in hospital for ten days receives on average ten doses of medication per day," one is faced with the startling and rather sickening conclusion that "approximately six of these doses would be erroneous, and three would result in gross overmedication or undermedication."[62] Two points came out of this study: (1) that "it may be hazardous to rely on experience as a factor that should minimize errors,"[63] and (2) that "all medical personnel involved in the ordering and administration of drugs should be taught computing skills and be evaluated routinely."[64] That this is not already the case is irresponsible and shameful. In fact, one group of researchers— who discovered a 40 percent drug infusion error rate among a pediatric intensive care unit's personnel, with 93 percent of those errors being classified as serious—provided the personnel with programmed calculators. Problem eliminated. How many people would be spared drug overdose or underdose if this simple, common-sense remedy were effected throughout the entire medical system?[65]

Finally, any discussion of medical mistakes in the area of prescribing medication would be incomplete if it did not touch upon the use—over-prescribing or inappropriate prescribing, really—of antibiotics. Promiscuous antibiotic prescribing and use is one of the key underlying causative factors in hospital-induced infections because it creates organisms resistant to the antibiotic's strength—this at a time when antibiotic agents that stop the spread of staphylococcus infections are losing their power to do so, and no truly antistaph agent has been developed in nearly a quarter century—"merely chemical modifications of drugs we already have." One of the last, if not the very last, drugs to which staph is sensitive is Vancomycin. It costs $800 a day, causes deafness and kidney disease among its set of horrible side effects, and if staph ever become resistant to it, through overuse or abuse, we're all in big trouble.[66]

Physicians, and especially surgeons, abuse antibiotics, and, in the process, abuse their patients. "Irrational prescribing of antibiotics is but a common example of the doctor as activist-technologist, expected by himself and his society to act upon his patient's body, rather than to teach the patient how to give his body's intrinsic healing powers a chance to act," is the way Lander puts it. Irrational prescribing practices include "prescribing an antibiotic for a viral illness, prescribing an antibiotic without taking a culture, prescribing an antibiotic by telephone without examining the patient, and prescribing an antibiotic prophylactically when the efficacy of such prophylaxis is dubious."[67] This sort of irrational prescribing, this antibiotic treatment given without acceptable indication, according to what Jack D. Sobel, M.D., told an infectious disease conference sponsored by the American College of Emergency Physicians, may be the most important cause of the rise over the past decade of iatrogenic yeast infection, also known as *Candida vaginitis.*[68]

Mendelsohn notes that too many physicians prescribe penicillin for conditions penicillin can do nothing about. "Since penicillin works almost exclusively against bacterial infections," he says, "it's useless against viral conditions such as colds and flu. . . . What [penicillin] can do is cause reactions from skin rash, vomiting, and diarrhea to fever and anaphylactic shock."[69] Stamm et al. told the New York Academy of Medicine in 1981 about the case of a 51-year-old man with chronic bursitis who received from a doctor, in response to the patient's complaint of sore shoulders, several administrations of 1.2 million units of procaine penicillin intramuscularly. There was no justification for such a medication regimen, stated the researchers: "Why penicillin was given on several occasions to a patient afflicted with chronic bursitis is perplexing. Did the physician in question believe that a penicillin-sensitive bacterium was the etiologic agent of the inflamed bursa? Or is penicillin here being employed as a placebo and as a potentially dangerous one at that?"[70]

Ken Harvey, M.D., notes that many clinicians like to give their patients broad-spectrum antibiotic drugs, which he calls "the refuge of the diagnostically destitute." These doctors have a fondness for this type of antibiotic "because in theory it doesn't matter what you treat, if you have a broad agent it will kill all germs. The danger of using broad spectrum antibiotics to treat any infection," Harvey says, "is that you are selecting out resistance on a broad front. If they're active against 20 microorganisms, then all those 20 are being put under selection pressures to become resistant."[71] Soon, there won't be anything left to fight these organisms with.

It is becoming increasingly clear that, as reported in a 1983 edition of *Internal Medicine News,* most antibiotic misuse is related to surgeons' inappropriate use of prophylactic antibiotics, i.e., antibiotics pumped into a patient to prevent the occurrence of an infection that might happen, not to fight an infection that's already there. The article stated that numerous studies have shown at least 50 percent of surgeon-prescribed prophylactic antibiotics are administered when:[72]

- No infection is present.
- An incorrect drug is selected.
- A less expensive drug could have been selected.
- The dose is excessive.
- The duration of treatment or prophylaxis is excessive.

In fact, one study has shown that "70.9 percent of prophylactic antibiotic administration to surgical patients was irrational on the basis of proved efficacy," and overall, "only 7.6 percent of prophylactic therapy was rational."[73] The use of antibiotics in this manner, though, has not abated.

The basic fault, as it is in many medication-related problems, is one of physician education, or lack of same. Wang observes that "prescribing patterns are largely determined by educational experiences," but that education appears to be less than satisfactory because "physicians simply don't know enough about prevalent organisms and available drugs to use them intelligently.''[74] Calvin M. Kunin concurs: ''Instruction in infectious disease and antimicrobial therapy has been severely curtailed recently in most medical schools''; but he sees it as a problem that goes further and deeper in its roots and ramifications than classroom and lecture hall deficiencies. The problem of the overuse of antibiotics, Kunin states, ''is part of a larger problem of overuse of medical care facilities, diagnostic tests, and other drugs.''[75]

The overuse and abuse of antibiotics is no minor, inconsequential matter, for ''what is hanging in the balance is not only the control of infectious disease but the incredible advance of medical science itself. Today, most organ transplants, surgery, and cancer therapy are dependent on antibiotics. If these drugs are rendered useless, the risk of patients acquiring resistant infection will increase, and make these modern medical procedures dangerous.''[76]

Dispensing with the Formalities

To read a certain monthly column in a magazine for the nursing profession is to read some pretty eye-opening material. Called ''Medication Errors'' and edited by Michael R. Cohen, R.Ph., this feature is nothing less than a public *mea culpa* in the form of an advice column, a chance for a nurse or two each month to reveal a mistake she made or nearly made while dispensing medication. The nurses are offered and accept (readily, it is to be assumed) complete anonymity; one can see why when one reads between the lines of some of the titles: ''Don't Identify Drugs by the Appearance of Their Containers: Read the Labels,''[77] ''Don't Use Abbreviations that Can Be Misinterpreted,''[78] ''Check the Patient's Identification Band Before Giving a Medication,''[79] ''Check the Doctor's Order Sheet Before Giving the First Dose of Medication.''[80]

What becomes apparent over the course of six months' or a year's reading of this column is that even when the prescribing process is performed to perfection, there is a multiplicity of potential foul-ups in the dispensing process involving the pharmacist at one end and the dispensing nurse at the other. Most of these dispensing errors are preventable. ''In some cases,'' Davis and Cohen say, ''closer attention to the work at hand, or more concern with professional responsibility, would have prevented the error.''[81]

Some of the basic dispensing errors are:

• Failure to read labels.
• The mislabeling of medications (causing ''wrong drugs to be ad-

ministered, wrong route of administration to be used, drug overdoses and underdoses, and much patient apprehension''[82]).

• Misreading prescriptions (or incorrectly hearing them in the case of oral orders).

• An ill-informed nursing staff or others filling prescriptions on their own, without a pharmacist's assistance from the hospital pharmacy after hours.

The wrong drugs administered to the wrong people in the wrong way are the classic components of the dispensing error scenario.

When Barker et al. studied medication errors in nursing homes and small hospitals, they found error rates of 12.2 percent in the long-term care facilities and 11 percent in the hospitals—both about double the medication-error limit standard of 6 percent. They also concluded that:[83]

• Nurses were ''unaware of the vast number of errors in which they were involved.''

• The most frequent error was omission—forgetting to dispense the required medication. This accounted for 81.9 percent of all drug errors in hospitals, 41.5 percent in the nursing homes.

• Number 2 on the error list was the dispensing of unauthorized drugs—44.8 percent of all errors in the nursing homes, just 9.7 percent in the hospitals—including 140 doses associated with orders that were technically inactive because they were either out of date or unsigned.

• Wrong dose, wrong route, and wrong dosage form were also found to occur in these facilities.

A better working relationship between doctor, pharmacist, and nurse, a relationship not of blind trust or of blind mistrust but of open-eyed reality, could eliminate a good proportion of these errors.

Under the general heading of errors of medication dispensing are faults of production on the part of the pharmaceutical companies—and especially those of labeling and package design. (The more basic questions of this industry's conscience, ethics, greed, and territorial imperative are the raw materials for many other books.)

Wang and Turndorf believe that within the error rate of medication dispensing—''one out of every six or seven times medication is given''— it is probable that ''packaging or labeling similarity of drugs which have different functions may have contributed to these preventable errors.'' They add: ''In reviewing incidents and reports of errors in administering medications, it became apparent that errors were made because of similarity in size, shape, or color of containers holding markedly different drugs, difficulty in reading labels, confusing appearances of container packaging of the same medication, as well as failure to read the label."[84]

Brand name sound-alikes and spell-alikes cause dispensing errors, as do label and package look-alikes. They are tragedies just waiting to happen. Robertson recalls that in the 1920s, "when $HgCl_2$ (mercuric chloride) was used as a diuretic, the tablet was shaped in the form of a coffin and the container had *Poison* imprinted on the glass itself. Today, drugs are no less potent. . . . "[85] But frequently they are less well—and less honestly—labeled. In fact, with many drug brand names sounding so much alike, making disastrous drug-dispensing mistakes very possible, there is even more of a reason (more than sheer economics) for doctors to order and prescribe in generic rather than brand (sound-alike) names. Identity foul-ups could be far less likely, if not virtually eliminated, with this approach. Standards of medication identity need to be promulgated and applied to ensure maximum discrimination between potential sound-alike and look-alike products.

No one would deny that when used properly, drugs are effective and often critical for sound care. The problems occur when they are not used properly, which is often enough to kill a stadium's worth of people each year and sicken many more than that.

But the problem goes even deeper than that—to motives, tendencies, and basic belief systems. "The general problem has very little to do with whether the Food and Drug Administration is or is not sufficiently vigilant or whether the profit motive does or does not induce the pharmaceutical industry to attempt to market unsafe drugs," Lander explains. "Any drug therapy, however relatively safe the medication and however apparently appropriate its administration, involves some measure of risk. And collective risk increases over time with the increase in the number of people being medicated, the number of products available for that purpose, and the tendency to equate medical care with taking medicine."[86]

To which Swarth adds:

> . . . rather subtly the individual citizen was taught to forgo the major responsibility for maintenance of his own health. To wit, no individual, as was the custom before World War II, could have a follow-up on such a simple matter as his urinalysis without first consulting a physician. This exerted considerable impact in destroying an individual's ability to care for himself. Likewise a mother was taught to no longer go to the drug store for ten cents worth of camomile tea or dried raspberries to control her baby's colic and instead to consult a pediatrician. . . . In other

words, by limiting the means by which persons might deal directly with their own illnesses, we have bestowed a real monopoly of health care upon physicians and at great social and economic costs.[87]

10

ALTERNATING CURRENTS

"There is a need in fulfilling the requirements of medicine to use professionals other than physicians. The concept that the doctor, the physician, is the only professional who can exist in the execution of the functions and requirements of medicine is idiocy."
—Harold M. Schoolman, M.D.

Of all the mistakes made by physicians and the medical world that hurt the American people, one of the most powerful and pervasive is their erroneous belief that they alone practice medicine.

The truth of the matter is that physicians practice a specific and limited type or school of medical treatment, which uses as its guide a certain belief system they themselves have defined and they themselves have had the good fortune and political clout to have dominate the scene.

But there are other, nonphysician practitioners, whose belief systems—and therapeutic and patient care successes—go back as far as the roots of medical establishment history. In fact, some of these practices *are* the roots of modern medical practice, but they have been and are still attacked and vilified in questionable public relations efforts and suppressed by the modern medical establishment for reasons that often have little or nothing to do with the sanctity of science or the good of the public.

"Doctors are not the only 'professional' health care providers," notes Lori B. Andrews, J.D., of the American Bar Foundation.[1] Rather, the development of health care services has been channeled "by granting an exclusive practice privilege and high status to practitioners relying on a particular approach to health care, a disease-oriented intrusive approach rather than a preventive approach."[2]

The thrust of arguments against a physician monopoly is not intended to disparage the medical establishment or to raise alternative practitioners to the level of heroes. Establishment medicine provides many essential and effective benefits; nonphysician medicine can and frequently does do harm. There are able practitioners in both camps. Stephen Barrett, M.D., defines quackery as "that which claims too much."[3] If he is accurate, there is quackery and there are quacks aplenty in and out of establishment medicine.

Truly, the debate ought to be about safety and choice, about who should and shouldn't be permitted to provide health care and why. It is not really and should not be about one belief system versus another, for the belief that a sick person should get well—by whatever means—ought to be at the heart of any and every system. In fact, that belief ought to be a unifying factor. No one school of thought ought to blackball another if *together* they can provide the building blocks of diagnosis and treatment—while the practitioner-patient relationship provides the mortar. That's the way it is in China: Practitioners of the two "competing" systems of medical care, modern Western and traditional Chinese, are trained in the ways of the other. "This solution has the advantage of making available to the patient those elements of either system which might be of help," note Sidel and Sidel. "Where such a combination does not exist, there is danger that the patient may be deprived of a symptom-relieving or even lifesaving method from either the 'regular' or the 'alternative' system."[4]

"If organized medicine stops the growth activity of allied health manpower, there are two social costs," explains Princeton University political economist Uwe Reinhardt. "One is, of course, that patients will lose access to an alternative provider who often is more accessible and quite probably cheaper. The other social cost, which is not even talked about, is this—you are precluding large numbers of Americans from exercising entrepreneurship in health care."[5]

Reinhardt readily admits that risks do exist in pursuing the care of nonphysician practitioners instead of that of M.D.s. "It could be dangerous, but then you have to go by the principle that I thought organized medicine always went by, and that is that we should have a free market in health care," he says. "And a free market is dictated by the principle of *caveat emptor,* let the buyer beware. After all, you have consenting adults transacting with one another, and patients ultimately bear the cost of malpractice, and therefore should have the right, in my view, to decide are they willing to take this risk or not."[6]

Establishment medicine, at least superficially and for public consumption, avows and maintains belief in a free market system—so long, it seems, as it remains the only market and is left free to do as it pleases. The choice and comfort of many sick people thus become at best a tertiary concern.

Past as Prelude

How M.D.s ascended to the catbird seat of medical practice is a story rooted in luck, hard work, and fervent political machinations.[7]

At first, despite their desires to be considered historically and effectively above the mass of multifaceted "health" purveyors, such as botanical practitioners and apothecaries, physicians simply weren't much better in helping people get well. In fact, they were often worse. Whereas herbalists and the like treated their patients with medicinal concoctions and corporeal manipulations and utilized the placebo effect to the utmost, physicians' repertoire included bloodletting and blistering and other invasive procedures that, in the name of curing, could and often did finish off already weakened patients. Moreover, the medicines used by the physicians back then were no different from those used by all the other practitioners. Physicians tried to shape medical practice laws of the states to favor themselves and their method of treatment and school of thought, but they could not show that their ways of thinking and doing things were better than those of the alternative practitioners. They did not merit the exclusive keys to the franchise, and rightly were not given them.

Not until the latter part of the 1800s did M.D.s finally have the ammunition they needed—advances in the medical approach to disease fighting, and an alignment with scientific principles at a time when "science" and "scientific" were excellent buzzwords. Medical science took on and defeated many of the most virulent and mass-death-dealing infectious diseases, cholera, typhoid, and diphtheria among them, through the discovery and use of antiseptics and vaccinations, as well as drugs like ether that gave surgery greater safety and increased successes.

Soon, despite the effectiveness and soothing, even healing, properties of various alternative methods of health care, physicians were victorious in getting those franchise keys and acquiring state government-legislated lockouts of nonphysicians. They were able to impose "science"—or what they claimed was science—across the land, and were successful in closing schools of medical and health care training that didn't jibe with their new wave way of thinking.

And so it is more or less unchanged to this day—except for a few not so minor details. For example, numerous nonphysician treatment modes—acupuncture, chiropractic, and even homeopathy, to name just three—have been shown to be effective health-providing systems, despite the doubts and aspersions cast on them by M.D.s. Furthermore, whereas medical practice hit its stride in the fight against infectious disease, most of those ills have been conquered or controlled. In the fight against chronic diseases, establishment medicine, with its emphasis on disease fighting rather than health promotion and prevention, has not fared as well. And beyond, the establishment has actively overseen a "medicalization" of nondisease human activities, like childbirths, and brought this most natural of developments under the exclusionary and protectionist umbrella of medical science.

In other words, while there is certainly and probably always will be a need and a place for establishment medical practice of one type or another, there seems little justification today for that establishment to maintain its franchise alone. Other practitioners have shown their ability to offer alternative care on their own or in conjunction with (or as adjuncts to) the M.D.s.

Yet the physicians still wield the power and political clout, via state medical societies and national organizations like the American Medical Association (AMA), to keep the antiquated medical practice acts in place. "The 'bottom line'," according to one AMA document, "is election of legislators friendly to AMA positions."[8] This is curious, for should not the bottom line be the best and most complete care options for the patient?

Battle Lines

"But to what extent is opposition from doctors more a matter of money than scientific judgment, a war over medical turf?" asks TV documentary host Marty Goldenson.[9]

"The articulated justification for licensing is protection of the public, but it is usually the profession itself that seeks licensing, often as a way to insulate itself from economic competition," writes Lori Andrews. "Professionals can use licensing to gain status, increase income [by] restricting entry into the profession (for example, by controlling the pass rate for the licensing exam) and, to a certain extent, to freeze the technical requirements for the occupation so that professionals who have paid the cost of entry will not be driven out of the business by competitors using advanced or alternative methods."[10]

For possibly the first time since the end of the nineteenth century, and certainly for the only time post–World War II, physicians are eyeball-to-eyeball with potential patient-stealers at the same time that there is a physician glut as well as reduced remuneration from third-party payers and a rise in prepaid health plans, like health maintenance organizations (HMOs).

In addition, as Goldenson points out, "More Americans are forsaking physicians, embracing instead alternative practitioners. Since 1975, the use of midwives is up 300 percent. Chiropractors say they've now had visits from two of every five citizens. Podiatrists claim to be the fastest-growing health profession. All manner of psychotherapists are putting psychiatrists on the defensive."[11]

Physicians look around them and see:

• That pharmacists have organized to get the right to write prescriptions[12] and to check customers' blood pressure.

• That, in Iowa, a law was passed allowing chiropractors to "draw blood for diagnostic purposes, do physical examinations and routine lab tests, and offer nutritional advice."[13]

• That while 73 percent of Americans claim satisfaction with their physicians' treatment and relief of pain, nearly an identical number—70 percent—held the same high regard for the ministrations of their chiropractors, 69 percent for consulting nutritionists, and 83 percent for those who used the services of faith healers.[14]

• Not only the handwriting on the wall but also the typeface on the printed page: that 75 percent to 80 percent of adult primary care and 90 percent of pediatric primary care services could safely be delegated to alternative health professionals."[15]

• In their own journals, colleagues noting that because alternative healers usually have limited treatment options, "they concentrate on the most important treatment option of all, the healer-patient relationship," and they ask: "Could alternative healers despite their weaknesses be, in effect, showing the medical profession the path to more effective healing—direct communication with patients?"[16]

Seeing all this, the medical profession has not moved "to combine nonallopathic with allopathic approaches to health care."[17] Instead, in what may turn out to be a major medical mistake and tactical blunder, the medical profession has fought hard to strengthen its hold and fundamentally support the medical licensing laws that protect it. The dynamic duo of medical lobbyist and state legislator has cooperated in attempting to shut down all care-giving or information- and/or opinion-giving "outsiders." "Vitamin dealers, health food store owners recommending certain foods and food supplements, and abortion counselors have been prosecuted for the unauthorized practice of medicine, and publication and distribution of a book has been enjoined as violating the Medical Practice Acts," Andrews writes. "One state medical disciplinary board committee has opined that if Atari or Apple began to market diagnostic software to the general public that action might violate the medical licensing laws."[18]

Mutual aid groups—organizations of lay people suffering a common ailment who help and support each other—tread a fine line: one step too far in the direction of providing certain services to their members and they've violated the medical practice laws. Physicians who want to help these groups by offering them free technical medical advice are often scared away by fears of being charged by licensing boards and their professional organizations with aiding and abetting the unauthorized practice of medicine. And the doctor glut will only make things worse: more suits for unauthorized practice filed by the physicians against the unlicensed alternatives.

Medical practice acts in numerous states seem to restrict the treatment of nearly every human flaw or quirk to physicians alone; the wording in various acts across the country legally delivers unto M.D.s those who suffer everything from "infirmity" to "blemish." Even the vague term "condition" is the sole venue and opportunity of the physician, whether he or she can do anything to improve that "condition" or not, or even whether he or she has ever been trained to treat that particular "condition" or not.

The restriction to physicians of so many acts and rights is so thorough and broad that in some states everyday practitioners like dentists, nurses, pharmacists, physical therapists, oral hygienists, osteopaths, and even veterinarians have to get special exemptions under the law so that they can do their jobs and not be accused of practicing medicine without a license. In other states, doctors have been successful in getting legislatures to require that barbers, cosmeticians, masseuses, ear piercers, and even shoe fitters get special exemptions under the medical licensing laws to practice their crafts.[19]

Apparently to squelch, eradicate, or at least pen in its competitors, the medical establishment has gone heavily to the mat against some of them. Nutrition writer and health activist Gary Null authored a series of articles that seem to show that the AMA, in violation of the Sherman Antitrust Act, allegedly plotted "to first contain, and then eliminate the profession of chiropractic in the United States."[20] Null's portrait is one of a medical profession competitively and economically fearful of another treatment system, the second largest health care delivery system in the United States, acting in ways detrimental to the health care quality and options of the public.

It is a portrait that the federal courts agreed with in August of 1987. U.S. District Judge Susan Getzendanner, ruling in favor of four chiropractor plaintiffs in their 11-year-long antitrust suit against the American Medical Association, cited the AMA's "systematic, long-term wrongdoing and the long-term intent to destroy a licensed profession." She said that the AMA's actions were manifested especially by a physicians' boycott designed "to contain and eliminate the chiropractic profession" by "labeling all chiropractors unscientific cultists and depriving chiropractors of association with medical physicians. . . ." By the AMA, in their policies, forbidding physicians from referring patients to chiropractors, accepting referrals from them, or even lecturing to them, chiropractors were not being allowed to compete freely in the health care marketplace. The AMA had also created a Committee on Quackery in 1962, the sole purpose of which seemed to be the destruction of the chiropractic profession. Judge Getzendanner also implicated the American College of Surgeons and the American College of Radiology as coconspirators with the AMA. At an earlier stage of the case, five defendants—The Illinois Medical Society, the American Hospital Association, the Chicago Medical Society, the American Osteopathic Association, and the American Academy of Physical Medicine and Rehabilitation—had reached a settlement, one that included affirmation of the rights of chiropractors.[21]

Besides chiropractors, physicians have had publicized and prolonged skirmishes with osteopaths as well as with more outré unorthodox practitioners. It might be instructive and illuminating to take a brief look at the whys and wherefores of two less publicized but crucial and indicative turf wars right in their own backyard: the M.D.s versus nurse-practitioners and physician-assistants, and the M.D.s versus midwives.

First Aides

The fight by M.D.s against nurse-practitioners and physician-assistants currently seems to boil down to this: According to the physicians, the N.P.s and P.A.s just don't know their place and, moreover, maybe they just don't have a place.

Some of the cross-resentments, especially in the case of the nurse-practitioners, have a long, historical footing. Doctors have acted in the superior role, probably because of their longer education, higher salaries, and greater acquired prestige, but it is nurses who have given most of the direct provider-to-patient care. It is the nurses who have altered erroneous treatment protocols in order to save lives and save doctors' hides, and the nurses who frequently are on the receiving end of scorn for many events that are out of their control. A lot of the resentment and rivalry between the two camps, states the President's Commission for the Study of Ethical Problems in Medicine and Biomedical and Behavioral Research, has its roots in the fact that "typically each health profession carries out its own educational program in isolation from the others. Thus although doctors and nurses eventually practice together, they are rarely trained explicitly to collaborate. As the role of nurses has expanded to include substantial portions of what was traditionally the exclusive domain of medicine, there is an increased need to clarify and coordinate the roles of the two professions."[22]

Of late, many nurses have become advocates of independent or nurse-controlled nursing, in which they can "both manage and practice . . . fix their own hours and set their own fees . . . (and) develop a continuing relationship with their clients."[23] Further, nurses claim that what they do

> can be different from, and complement, doctors' work. Doctors tend to see patients who are ill or injured and in need of immediate attention. Nurses can keep watch over peoples' health from month to month; they can monitor long-term problems like emphysema, diabetes, heart disease, arthritis, or Parkinson's disease. And they can do routine physical exams to spot minor ailments before they become major ones. Certain groups of the population—especially children, the elderly, and women, all of whom need regular exams—are the nurses' natural constituency.[24]

Beyond this move toward an independence of sorts in practice and economic matters, nurses have been forced by certain legalities to assert themselves in ways that doctors may view as insubordinate or even mutinous. Now that the courts are "increasingly reluctant to hold attending physicians liable for an R.N.s negligence," nurses are beginning to feel that to cover themselves legally, each nurse is obliged "to alert a patient to what she deems to be inappropriate or substandard physician care and to intervene in a doctor's treatment decisions."[25] This does not endear the new nursing spirit of independence (read "defiance") to many physicians.

Into this roiling cauldron add a pinch of nurse-practitioner. And, for good measure, a dash of physician-assistant. Then watch the physicians' steam rise.

While N.P.s and P.A.s are often lumped together under the heading of "new health professionals" or "mid-level practitioners," they are different in style and substance, if not desire. A nurse-practitioner profile overview[26] would show that of the more than 20,000 of them in the United States, about 98 percent are female, a majority work in the areas of family practice or pediatrics, and a typical N.P. would have attained a master's degree after a two-year program taught by both physicians and other N.P.s. Their starting salaries are in the low $20,000s, with some top salaries in the high $30,000s. Since 1965, when the nurse-practitioner concept took hold, it has been seen as a step up the medical professional ladder for nurses, as well as a way to cover certain areas of care that were being affected by the one-time doctor shortage.

Nearly two-thirds of the approximately 20,000 physician-assistants in the United States are male, and a number of them were paramedics in the military, especially during the time of the Vietnam War. They, too, have a two-year training program, but are much more plugged in to the M.D. route, and may take classes with the regular medical school students. Similar to N.P.s, the P.A.s work predominantly in the area of family practice, and their starting salaries are also in the low $20,000s. However, possibly because they are more like doctors than nurses, or possibly because they are viewed as a male profession instead of a female one, their top salaries can hover around $60,000.[27]

The two—N.P.s and P.A.s—are different species, and see themselves as such. One nurse-practitioner is quoted as saying: "I am not a physician extender. I'm a family nurse-practitioner. Our training is very different from that of P.A.s, with an emphasis on patient education and wellness that they don't have. They have a more medically oriented direction. We are nurses first."[28] Deborah Huntington Ward, R.N., M.S.N., of Yale University's School of Nursing, adds:

> Nurse-practitioners, of which I am one, are running public health clinics, establishing school health services, and leading political and economic battles against the notion of health care for profit, not people. In my work in a senior health program sponsored by a public health department, I see patients whose concerns range from the side effects of hypertensive medications to coping with cancer to planning for retirement. I perform physical exams, diagnose and treat both minor and chronic health problems. My education—indeed nurses' education nationwide— concentrates on working *with* patients on prevention, on health teaching, on facing up to the frequently harsh realities of illness with support and cooperation.[29]

P.A.s don't exactly like the tag "physician extender," either. And, similar to nurse-practitioners, many of them want to have greater autonomy and even solo practices. Therein lies most of the problem.

Among the original reasons for needing N.P.s and P.A.s, according to Backup and Molinaro, were that:[30]

• Organized medicine wanted to relieve the doctor shortage without losing control over the health care system.
• Consumers wanted more access to care and would not tolerate disparities in care in rural and inner-city areas.
• Patients hoped for a health worker who would be less removed and who would treat them with more understanding and respect.
• Women and minorities demanded to enter the system as health professionals and to receive better care as patients.

• Health workers and ex–military corpsmen were increasingly militant in their demands for upward mobility and jobs.

• Both nurses and medics were already functioning in expanded roles and wanted recognition and legal sanction.

• The government and consumers were concerned about escalating costs. Individual physicians wanted to ease their work load.

• Institutions needed to become less dependent on foreign-trained physicians who, once they gained citizenship, were less controllable and were already seen as "mid-levels" with the added disadvantage of being foreign.

• Individual students saw an alternative to medical school's many years of study, high tuition, technological focus, and elite graduates.

But times have changed, and so have the attitudes, desires, and concerns of physicians on one side and N.P.s and P.A.s on the other. Despite assertions (albeit hollow ones) by N.P.s and P.A.s that they do not practice medicine and are not physicians' competitors, doctors—who supported the institution of N.P.s and P.A.s because they would be aides, not equals—see it differently. Some doctors are feeling a bit taken and betrayed, and they want to "set things right."

Try as they might, though, physicians cannot document their negative criticism of the quality of care provided by these "mid-level practitioners." Harold C. Sox, M.D., analyzed 21 studies "in which care given by nurse-practitioners or physician-assistants was directly compared with that given by physicians," and discovered that "nurse-practitioners and physician-assistants provide office-based care that is indistinguishable from physician care."[31] Salkever et al. noted that "while nurse-practitioners' care is less costly [than physicians'], it is no less effective."[32] Numerous other studies have reconfirmed and reinforced these findings, and have shown that some of the benefits derived by using P.A.s include "decreased waiting time, more time for each patient, increased patient accessibility to health care, better in-house coverage, and high-quality operating room assistance. . . ."[33]

Despite these facts, the substance of which would lead most observers to the assumption that N.P.s and P.A.s can safely practice on their own (with physician consultation, if necessary), physicians still want N.P.s and P.A.s to act in their original roles as the bridesmaids of medical practice. But rather than remain overworked but underpaid bridesmaids, N.P.s and P.A.s have broken off to become brides in their own right, moving into jobs left open by physicians who have left them for greener, more lucrative pastures. These jobs are, for example, in the areas of geriatric care in nursing homes, in HMOs, in corporate health care, in school health care, and in the less glamorous, less remunerative venues that were once occupied by the currently frowned-upon foreign medical graduates.

Physicians are trying to do everything they can to keep P.A.s and N.P.s from becoming direct competitors and from getting hospital privileges. The M.D.s fear that hiring lower-salaried new health professionals could put some of them out of business. One of the most recent points of contention has to do with N.P.s and P.A.s desiring direct reimbursement for their services—from patients and third-party payers—rather than having their pay funneled first through a physician's practice. (This latter method also keeps costs high for patients, who would probably pay less for that N.P. or P.A. in private practice if they didn't have to pay a doctor's fee for that same N.P. or P.A. within the doctor's office structure.) Another battle has been waged over the right of P.A.s and N.P.s to write prescriptions. A score of states have granted that right, but M.D.s' big lobbying guns have kept up a tenacious defense.

In a struggle to acquire independent practices and expanded rights and privileges, physician-assistants and nurse-practitioners will have to face down those big and heavily loaded guns—a formidable task. They must also avoid factional disputes and internecine turf wars, or they will surely all hang separately. The N.P.s and P.A.s will be fighting in a doctor-glut atmosphere in which pronouncements will regularly be made that their independence is not needed and is in fact detrimental to health care, and pressures may be applied to N.P. and P.A. schools to shut down or reduce graduate class sizes. For N.P.s and P.A.s and the patients, it is a time to see if, in the words of Backup and Molinaro, "the self-protecting pressures from organized medicine are stronger than the forces for the rational planning of high-quality care."[34]

The Blues of the Birth

Birth is not a disease process. Many critics fault organized medicine for regarding it as such and for "medicalizing" a natural human event. These and other critics have also looked unfavorably upon the way many obstetricians and gynecologists have waged a protectionist, nearly imperialist war on those outside the M.D. profession who assist women in delivering babies. Midwives are the main target.

Of the two types of midwife—licensed lay and registered/certified nurse-midwife—it is the lay midwife who has come in for the greatest attack. The licensed lay midwife is seen by doctors as little more than an unskilled, anachronistic, backward backwoods woman who presides at home births and is dangerous to mother and child. But for those women with low-risk pregnancies who believe that "physicians' emphasis on physical pathology [has] led gradually to the routine use of medical interventions originally developed for complications"[35]—and who want to give birth at home—the obstacles to the practice of licensed lay midwifery constitute even greater hazards to mother and infant.

Lay midwives "are either self-taught or have attended one of approximately twelve unaccredited schools in this country. Their legal status depends on individual state laws."[36] Most states do not permit them. Recently, despite 600 to 700 annual births at home presided over by lay midwives in the state, Colorado's legislature failed to recommend a bill providing for the licensing and regulation of lay midwives.[37] Thus, all such birth attendences were illegal, and arrests could have been made. The drive against licensure was spearheaded by the Colorado Medical Society, citing health hazards.

This occurred despite national and international evidence to the contrary, and despite the fact that lay midwives attended only spontaneous vaginal births by healthy women who are at low risk and do not require or desire medication. In Arizona, a state where less than 1 percent of births are attended by lay midwives, statistics show little difference in mother and infant outcome among lay midwives, nurse-midwives, and physicians.[38] According to one report, staying out of the hospital is definitely safer for some parents and infants. A study at Stanford University of 1,046 women who had decided to have their babies at home showed that they had "as few stillbirths and brain-damaged babies as a group of similar women with conventional hospital deliveries. But the hospital group had more medical interventions (forceps, cesareans, anesthesia) and suffered more complications (fetal distress, newborn infections, birth injuries)."[39]

Further, writes Marsden G. Wagner, M.D., a physician with the World Health Organization, "the one country in Europe with over one-third of all births taking place at home [Holland] is also the country with the lowest or near lowest mortality figures."[40] And one British midwife, who has delivered thousands of babies, was quoted as saying about midwives in the United States: "In other countries [a midwife] is a well-respected member of the nursing world. But over here, it is a real battle to be recognized as anything other than a relatively dangerous newcomer to the field."[41]

Besides other concerns, physicians point to a high transfer rate involving home births; that is, approximately 20 percent of "seemingly low-risk mothers, by one estimate, have to be transferred from home to hospital during or after delivery."[42] Supporters claim that these transfers occur because (a) the midwives know their limitations and the glee with which physicians would pounce on any error committed by a midwife, and so they play it extremely safe and move women to hospitals at the first sign of any possible problem, such as prolonged labor; and (b) there are laws and restrictions that keep licensed midwives from suturing even minor tears or from giving even a small dose of antihemorrhagic medication, and therefore a hospital is the only route—along with its added expense.[43]

In the words of Judith Rooks, president of the American College of Nurse-Midwives: "There are probably babies who die at home who would not have died in the hospital, and there are probably babies who die in the hospital who would not have died at home."[44]

Despite the apparent relative safety of lay midwives and home births, why are M.D.s working so hard to wipe them off the face of the earth? Some see it merely as a power struggle; "Doctors," writes Wagner, "to remain in control, must work within their own territory, which may be why so many oppose home birth."[45] Others place the movement against lay midwives in the same context as physician drives against other non-physician practitioners: Use of the legislature and medical practice acts to eliminate economic competition.

The thrust, however, goes beyond legalities into the area of peer pressure and fear of ostracism of physicians who break rank and act as medical backups to midwives, especially during home births. As was found in an Arizona metropolitan area, "the local private physicians, with one or two exceptions for selected midwives and clients, refuse to provide pre-natal and back-up medical care for women planning home births."[46] The catch-22 of all this is that the midwives require physician backup to maintain their practices. They are, then, often forced to turn to doctors whose credentials and safety are questionable, and who often do not have hospital privileges. And those M.D.s with hospital privileges risk losing them if they dare "collaborate" and attend home births.

This must be considered a grave medical mistake, one with ramifications beyond the circumstance of one or several births. The mistake is one of judgment, a sin of pride, a dereliction of duty and denial of the basic tenets of medical practice. For, as only about 50 doctors nationwide will agree to attend home births (down from 150 a few years ago) and less than 10 percent of home births have physicians standing by (down from 20 percent in 1980), "the medical campaign against home births may raise the risk to mothers and infants. Parents who continue to choose home birth may be denied the professional support that makes it safe."[47] Physicians should not be forcing parents to choose one, hospital-bound solution over another, particularly since outcome statistics are similar. Instead, physicians should be working to make all births in all places safe and successful. Revenge and spite at the expense of a patient's health should not be components of a physician's black bag.

Sullivan and Weitz report that lay midwives, who "do not regard themselves as complete alternatives [but rather] want to be part of a continuum of health care," believe that if "there was less resistance and if we could all work together, it would improve the quality of health care in the U.S., not lessen it."[48]

Physicians are also much irritated with and espouse strong negative opinions concerning nurse-midwives, especially when these highly trained practitioners work outside the hospital setting in a birthing center or other location.

Nurse-midwives are registered nurses with one or two years of additional training, often a master's degree in maternal-child health nursing, and they always use obstetricians as backups. To be a member of the American College of Nurse-Midwives, it is necessary to provide a formal collaboration agreement with a physician. This does not mean a doctor is always standing at the elbow of the nurse-midwife, just that he or she is on call in case of emergencies.

Nurse-midwives have shown themselves to be safe, expert, and reliable. In one study at San Francisco General Hospital, it was determined that "outcome statistics are comparable to those of the obstetrics department in general."[49] In fact, slightly better: "The perinatal mortality rate of 9/1,000 for the nurse-midwifery services compares to 13/1,000 for the hospital, 18/1,000 for the city, and 24/1,000 for the state."[50] Similarly good statistics came out of a study of the midwifery services at Los Angeles County/University of Southern California Medical Center, Women's Hospital.[51]

So, again, why the physician negativity? Perhaps the questions asked in a *Medical Economics* article are themselves the answers:

> Is the new generation of midwives—college-trained and certified nurse-midwives—a threat to the financial well-being of OBGs and other physicians who deliver babies? Should patients' growing acceptance of midwifery tell physicians that they've been tolerated only because there's been no alternative? Will the granting of hospital privileges to midwives—even as some hospitals limit privileges for physicians—intensify the competition?[52]

Physicians have come down particularly hard on nurse-midwives who practice in birthing centers. The American College of Obstetricians and Gynecologists "believes that all births should take place in hospitals, and while it officially lauds nurse-midwives as important members of the health-care team, it disdains their practicing independently."[53]

Not surprising. Physicians want to keep the upper hand, have the final say, and make the ultimate dollar. With a surplus of up to 8,000 obstetricians and gynecologists predicted by 1990, the last thing these specialty physicians need is a lower-priced competitor with a reputation for high levels of aptitude and caring.

Therefore, to head off the competition, physicians have already begun asserting and reasserting their dominance, in a sort of Stirrup Wars defense that is all offense—often to the detriment of, at the very least, patients' pocketbooks. By attempting to keep expectant mothers away from independent birthing centers and by luring them to hospitals instead, physicians can utilize and benefit from hospital rules (promulgated, in the main, by the physicians themselves). "Some licensing boards and hospitals have established rules that are purportedly directed at insuring quality of alternative health care practitioners, but may be designed solely to enhance physician income," Andrews states. "Many hospitals require a physician's presence at each nurse-midwife-assisted birth, whether the patient's condition merits it or not. In one community, a hospital provides that midwife-attended births must be supervised by physicians between the hours of 7:00 A.M. and 7:00 P.M., but not after 7:00 P.M., even though the nurse-midwives and their practices are the same throughout the day." Andrews also points out that hospitals are less than keen on midwives and nondoctor practitioners because these alternative groups order fewer tests and perform fewer intrusive procedures, thus making less money for the hospitals than the doctors do. She also claims that hospitals may be nervous about their doctors going out on strike to protest the granting of privileges to midwives and other non-M.D.s, since there have already been strikes in some places where osteopaths received hospital privileges.[54]

Doctors' organizations have also mounted public relations campaigns designed to foster the idea that midwife-attended births outside the hospital setting are of a substandard or dangerous nature. For example, Rae Goodell and Joel Gurin report in *American Health* that the American College of Obstetricians and Gynecologists "has taken a stand against any form of out-of-hospital birth, citing government statistics that show three or four times as many stillbirths outside the hospital. But" they add, "these data don't distinguish between planned out-of-hospital births and those that are unattended or those that occur at home by accident."[55]

On another front, medical liability insurance companies have either dropped nurse-midwives' coverage completely or have raised their premiums to levels that are both higher proportionately to salary than that of doctors and unwarranted by malpractice claims against them. According to a *New York Times* story, individual annual premiums of as high as $24,100 have been proposed for certified nurse-midwives who work in hospitals and as much as $72,300 for those who attend births at home—this for practitioners who earn somewhere between $20,000 and $30,000 a year, and who serve only women with low-risk pregnancies. This, too, in addition to the fact that "only 6 percent of the country's midwives have been named in malpractice suits, compared with 60 percent of the obstetricians. . . ."[56] And the 6 percent claims rate has remained steady for the last 11 years.[57]

In addition, there has been the sense in some locales that the malpractice insurance companies, and especially those that are doctor-owned, have worked in cahoots with the doctors to force nurse-midwives out of business. Such a contention by two independent Tennessee nurse-midwives—who claimed in an antitrust case that the doctor-owned malpractice insurer in that state canceled the insurance of doctors who worked as backups with self-employed nurse-practitioners but issued policies to doctors who themselves employed nurse-midwives—was upheld in 1983 by the Federal Trade Commission, who called the company's action an illegal boycott, and stated that the same criteria had to be employed by the company to all doctors who worked with nurse-midwives under any circumstances.[58]

Nurse-midwives' competitive trump cards have always been and should continue to be lower overall cost than M.D. delivery and a more complete, empathetic, and efficient health care package. Births attended by nurse-midwives "result in shorter hospital stays and less frequent use of anesthesia, electronic fetal monitoring and intravenous infusions."[59] Nurse-midwifery, too, "has been largely responsible for the recognition of the importance of the family's role in the delivery process."[60] Nurse-midwives are reluctant to recommend episiotomies and cesarean sections. Also, "the commonality of motherhood is valued by some expectant mothers," while in addition nurse-midwives "often wield a more personal touch including vigilance during long hours of labor."[61] Norton and Nichols relate that at the Yale Nurse-Midwifery Practice, for example, nurse-midwives "consider themselves consumer advocates and are adamant in their efforts to provide nonroutine, individualized care to each woman and couple. When the larger system does not support, or in fact hinders, a patient's individualized goals, the nurse-midwives act as the patient's advocate. The nurse-midwives also see themselves as facilitators—not directors—of their clients' health care."[62]

The quality and economy of care of nurse-midwives is such that in 1983 Group Health, an HMO in Washington, D.C., urged its members to use nurse-midwives to deliver uncomplicated births.[63]

Unquestionably, nurse-midwifery is here to stay. Where it stays and whether it becomes more available will depend on the effectiveness of consumer demand in the pressurized environment of the medical marketplace.

The Privileged Few

Ground Zero for all health care wars is the hospital, and to the victors go the spoils: hospital admitting and practice privileges. In the health care arena, never have so many fought so hard against so many for so much.

Gary Null relates that during a chiropractors versus AMA trial, one of the AMA's attorneys told the jury that patients go to hospitals "for medical care." "The chiropractors's lawyer, George P. McAndrews, replied—and the difference is more than semantic—that patients don't go to hospitals for medical care, they go to hospitals 'to get well'," writes Null. "The hospital is not supposed to be a low-overhead business office of medical physicians."[64]

"Moreover," Null says, "since most hospitals pride themselves on their status as community health-care centers, it seems anomalous that patients can seek health care at such facilities only if they choose health care providers whose trade associations have gained control of the facility."[65]

This is the crux of the matter, and the pivot around which whirl all recent antitrust trial cases and distant regulatory rumblings.

There are two aspects to the privileges brouhaha. On the one hand, the hospital privilege scene is shrinking—the physician population between 1977 and 1982 increased 15 percent while the percentage of physicians with admitting privileges dropped 2.9 percent.[66] With a doctor glut or surplus, hospitals don't need or want them all, and are in a position to pick and choose among them. On the other hand, there has been a simultaneous movement among nonphysician practitioners, psychologists, nurse-practitioners, nurse-anesthetists, and podiatrists among them, to get full hospital admitting and practice privileges. Thus, they are often vying for slots M.D.s also want and indeed may have felt it was their right to get. So, the M.D.s find themselves fighting not only their own colleagues but also the non-M.D. outlanders for a minislice of a contracting pie.

And they are fighting the Federal Trade Commission (FTC), too, for the FTC has fanned the antitrust and monopoly flames, and sent a fearful AMA and its close ally, the Joint Commission on the Accreditation of Hospitals (JCAH), back to the drawing board to draft new accreditation guidelines that would tolerate the inclusion of nonphysicians on hospital staffs, with privileges.

After nearly four years of bitter and divisive give-and-take, the JCAH came up with a new chapter in its hospital accreditation manual. For nonphysician practitioners, it was a door opened just a crack—hardly an endorsement, ringing or otherwise, and certainly no open-armed greeting of professional respect. In the new chapter, hospitals have the option of allowing nonphysician practitioners on their medical staffs. The nonphysicians are still second-class citizens—though this is a step up from their previous noncitizen status—because the JCAH manual states that all patients admitted by nonphysicians must be examined by an M.D. or D.O. (who will be able to get a fee for doing so), and that, furthermore, the new standards also stipulate "that a majority of the medical staff's executive committee, which makes recommendations on privileges and credentials, must be fully licensed physicians."[67] This is certainly handy and advantageous to the physicians, who will be able to give a thumbs up or thumbs down on any and every nonphysician applicant.

In other words, the new JCAH manual chapter allows hospitals to pass the accrediting process successfully even though they have nonphysicians on staff, but it hands to physicians the continued and utter dominance of all matters, including whether there should be nonphysicians on staff at all. And despite still holding all the cards, the AMA and other physicians have made statements proclaiming that nonphysicians on staff will most certainly dilute the quality of care now present in American hospitals.

Gary Null writes: "One may ask if the time has come for either the state or federal government to seriously consider whether an accreditation body like the JCAH should be allowed to continue to function. It represents only one licensed-provider group (medical physicians) and excludes from its deliberations consumers and patient representatives, in addition to all other licensed-provider groups (podiatrists, clinical psychologists, optometrists, and chiropractors). At least the accreditation group should have to sever its ties with private trade associations that seek to control its functions, or be opened to broader influences in the public interest."[68]

"Modern medicine has systemically shorn its consumers of belief in their recuperative powers," Rick Carlson writes. "It has fostered a pervasive and pitiable dependency. This is why healers operating outside traditional American medicine have always had a marginal but formidable claim upon the loyalty of many of those who are ill. . . . Modern medicine has successfully isolated and denigrated nonallopathic practitioners and practice. But as more people turn to other strains of healing, as often as not because of the failure of modern medicine to heal them, the pressure on medicine to adapt will intensify."[69]

11

BONDAGE AND DISCIPLINE

"Thoughtful public discussion of the iatrogenic pandemic, beginning with an insistence upon demystification of all medical matters, will not be dangerous to the commonweal. Indeed, what is dangerous is a passive public that has come to rely on superficial medical house cleanings."

—Ivan Illich

Airline pilots are accountable to the public, and so are policemen. Bus drivers, too. When these workers, whose responsibilities include the safety of the populace, are found to be in violation of that trust, when crashes occur due to negligence or substance abuse, when unjustifiable shootings occur or brutalities exist, the violators are held up to the scrutiny of that injured populace. And so it is with many other professionals. They are disciplined in full view of the public they have endangered or harmed, and the punishment (which may be standardized and by the book) is made to fit the crime.

Not so with doctors. Whereas faulty airline pilots are exposed to very visible investigatory panels, physicians' hearings and subsequent reprimands (if any) are kept away from the eyes and ears of the citizenry, and records of such meetings are secret and unavailable. Whereas police personnel alleged to have committed "conduct unbecoming" may face the questions of citizen advisory boards, physicians face boards made up of their colleagues—even perhaps of close personal or professional friends—but with few or no members of the public on these panels. Whereas incompetent bus drivers involved in death-dealing accidents are vilified and condemned in the daily press and broadcast media, incompetent physicians and the accidents they perpetrate rarely see the light of a headline because of the secrecy of disciplinary sessions and the publicity lid on malpractice suit out-of-court settlements. And not only do the physician's own patients never find out about his carelessness, his malpractice, but a bad news blackout agreed to by attorneys for both the plaintiff and the defendant also usually keeps the medical licensing boards themselves in the dark. The facts of the cases are not transmitted to the boards for disciplinary measures, or even for informational files.

Like the customers of a famous fast-food chain, doctors have had it their way and continue to do so, and the public and the courts and the lawmakers have let them. With an inviolable, hands-off autonomy—a freedom that has been corrupted by the medical profession into a presumption of a "legal, moral, and intellectual mandate to determine for the individual and society at large what is healthy, moral, ethical, deviant, normal, or abnormal"[1]—physicians have kept their dark secrets to themselves. And, in the matter of licensing and disciplining the "rotten apples," they have provided the classic case of the inmates running the asylum . . . or, better still, to use Stanley J. Gross's image, of foxes guarding the hen house.

No other workers so involved in the health, welfare, and safety of their clients, the public, have so arrogantly fought public accountability. This would not be so bad if the medical profession were doing a good job of weeding out the bad and allowing only the qualified to enter into the fold, and to remain there. But they are not doing that. They are not even coming close. "As a consequence of self-regulation," Gross notes, "they have been able to ignore the substantial amount of evidence that has rejected the assumption that self-regulation has safeguarded the public."[2]

License

What a medical license gives a doctor is what a Senate confirmation gives a Supreme Court justice nominee: a practically unassailable job for life. There is a difference, though. The Supreme Court justice has had to go to law school, pass a bar exam, get a job, do well enough at it, attain a position of high standing—a judgeship, say, or a place in academia—do well enough at it, and catch the eye of a person in a lofty government office. It's a long haul. One usually gets a Supreme Court job for life only after one has paid his dues.

On the other hand, a physician has merely to get through four years of medical school, pass one licensing exam (with an average passing score of as low as 75 out of 100, and in some states with an even lower score[3]), successfully complete an internship somewhere, and "possess acceptable personal attributes,"[4] whatever that means. And that's it. Minimal qualifications. Job for life. The only dues a doctor has to pay are the annual kind for license renewal—*if* he happens to be practicing in a state that even requires an annual fee. Some don't. Simply being alive and having once passed a licensing exam is all that's needed to have carte blanche in the field of medicine. As Illich points out, it is only in rare instances that proficiency or experience are prerequisites for getting a license, or competent or successful work conditions for keeping one.[5] Short of killing someone (or, more likely, a string of someones), once a doctor always a doctor.

Medical licenses so freely dispensed are, then, much more than a scandal. They are a danger, because they lead the doctors' customers to presume competence when that sheepskin on the wall means no such thing. Perhaps at one time, in the beginning of careers, it did—a passable, greenhorn competence. The license does not indicate continued competence or a keeping up with new developments. It is said that medical science changes every seven years.[6] If that is the case, what presumption of competence does a 20-year-old sheepskin and blind, periodic, rubber-stamp license renewal imply?

In 1986, New York Governor Mario Cuomo proposed a stringent licensing and relicensing program for his state, one that would require doctors to pass regularly scheduled examinations of their competency in order to keep their licenses. (Right now, fewer than 20 states require their physicians to attend annual continuing education classes—a sham in themselves—to retain their licenses, whereas, interestingly enough, more than 40 states require that chiropractors and optometrists do so.[7]) The passage of this law would make New York the first state to institute such a reevaluation program—a program the state's health commissioner likened to the one airline pilots must experience every six months. "Other professions undergo recertification, required retraining, or similar continuing education," Cuomo stated, while noting that "there is absolutely no continuing requirement now in place for members of this life-and-death profession."[8]

And there never will be, if certain influential lobbying organizations and vested interests have their way. Cuomo's proconsumer, proquality control, anti-incompetency proposal was immediately attacked by the profession's guardian of autonomy, the American Medical Association. It was also criticized by Otis R. Bowen, the U.S. Secretary of Health and Human Services, himself an M.D. Both the AMA and Bowen felt that the procedures for licensing already in place more than adequately did the job of protection. But the question arises, who is being protected—the public or the practitioners?

The argument has been made that professional specialty boards and organizations keep their members in line and up-to-date through continuing education and recertification procedures. This is only partly true. It is true that 337,000 of the nation's nearly 500,000 physicians are certified as specialists—a mind-boggling statistic in its own right—but only about half of these specialists are ever faced with having to be recertified.[9] Board-certified plastic surgeons have to be recertified periodically, as do practitioners in the fields of orthopedic surgery, pediatrics and pediatric surgery, emergency medicine, obstetrics and gynecology, and family practice, among some others. But specialists in anesthesiology, ophthalmology, radiology, colon and rectal surgery, and dermatology, to name just a few others, have no mandatory recertification process. Then, too, an M.D. needn't be board certified to practice these specialties: "Any physician with an M.D. degree can offer himself in private practice as a specialist in any branch of medicine. An otolaryngologist can offer himself as a plastic surgeon; a general practitioner can say he's a specialist in radiology";[10] and so recertification would not even apply to them. Neither would continuing education seminars, themselves often seen merely as chances to get away from the office and socialize, or as necessary evils required to attain specific credits, as much as they are seen as serious information-gathering sessions.

Also, those who go for specialty recertification and flunk, or are thrown out of their specialty society for some reason, do not lose their licenses or their ability to practice medicine. They merely lose membership in the specialty society. For the most part, that means only that they'll receive fewer professional magazines that they never read anyway, and next year maybe they'll have to change their listing in the Yellow Pages. Maybe. As noted before, any doctor can call himself a specialist at anything without having acquired a residency, fellowship, or any specialty training in that field. The only limitations placed against a physician calling himself a specialist without benefit of specialty training are the physician's *chutzpah* quotient and his regard for or disregard of the risk of malpractice suits.

One might be moved to suggest or believe that the solution to the problem, postmedical school, lies in regular retesting of physicians for license renewal, and also perhaps national standards for doctoring qualifications, rather than the state-by-state hodgepodge of licensing laws that have wild diversity and questionable quality as their hallmarks. But these "solutions" beg the bigger question: Is licensing in its present form, even with the addition of modest cosmetic upgrades, at all valuable in ensuring excellent or even good medical care?

The answer? "There is no convincing evidence from the research on occupational licensure of a tie between licensure and the quality of service," writes Gross.[11] He goes on to emphasize the point that not only does a medical license not ensure the public's safety by ensuring minimal standards of quality but that it may participate with other factors to ensure, instead, much less than adequate care—that, in general, "the norms of professions, supported by the monopoly and autonomy generated by licensing, result in professionals' attitudes that too often lead to shoddy, impersonal and dangerous service."[12]

The medical license, then, as critics see it, protects the license holder and few, if any, others:

• It creates a monopoly and a safe haven for high wage earnings.

• It maintains an unhealthy doctor-patient relationship by legislatively endorsing and legitimizing the mystification of the public.

• It limits the delivery of certain treatment options to doctors, when in fact they may have little or no training in those areas.

• It creates "an inertia that prolongs the use of orthodox but questionable treatments and delays the introduction of unorthodox but useful treatments."[13]

• It puts more weight on tradition than skill, and creates a "credentials mentality" that "puts more stress on where and how people were trained than on what they can do. . . ."[14]

Some critics of the licensing process point out that its long-standing, fatal flaw is that it has always delineated how physicians were to be produced instead of specifying what the product should be, and some have gone so far as to suggest that state licensing examinations should be open to anyone who wants to take them—whoever passes the test would thereby exhibit the minimum requisite skills and standards of doctoring and could (and should) therefore practice. In fact, noted economists Milton and Rose Friedman in their 1980 work, *Free to Choose,* proposed this constitutional amendment: "No state shall make or impose any law which shall abridge the right of any citizen of the United States to follow any occupation or profession of his choice."[15] Such a philosophy—call it a threat—might be sufficient to force the medical establishment and state licensing boards to clean up their acts and devise a real and substantive licensing process. It might also open up the health care field to those not restricted by the tradition of medical education and socialization.

But this is all theoretical and, in some camps, wishful thinking. The nitty-gritty reality that at the moment truly affects the American doctor-going public is this: Licensing does not appear to be a protection against incompetent practice or a means of compelling and ensuring competence. It seems to place in the hands of physicians powers greater than their abilities merit. And, for the patient, the news is worse: Stroman reports that "about 80 percent of today's practicing physicians were licensed [a decade or more ago] under standards and procedures less likely to insure minimum qualifications than today's licensing standards and procedures."[16] Hardly confidence-building news.

"It is not just the current licensing system that is faulty, but that licensure is inherently defective," writes Gross. "Professional licensure is a house of cards that may be tumbled by the wind of consumer information and awareness."[17]

Discipline

Despite all the looseness and loopholes in the licensing process, one might expect that many marginally or thoroughly incompetent doctors would still evidence themselves and be disciplined every year, and that many of them would lose their licenses. But this is not the case—not because the doctors are not so bad but rather because the medical disciplinary process is not so good.

Take, for example, the case of a certain Dr. K. S. This doctor, Robertson tells us,[18] was and probably still is a board-certified orthopedic surgeon in Washington State. Within three years, he twice operated on patients' wrong limbs, and was sued both times. After out-of-court settlements, what penalty was applied to this seemingly incompetent surgeon? What discipline was meted out? Loss of license, perhaps? Probation? Censure? Robertson explains that the doctor was given a choice of two options: either agree to a $50,000 deductible on his insurance policy to cover future surgical foul-ups or find another insurer. He chose the first. And that is the only discipline he received.

But at least it only took two cases to give this physician a knuckle-rapping—a far more efficient record than the one involving Chicago plastic surgeon Annette Lotter. It took 18 malpractice suits between 1972 and 1979 before the disciplinary board in Illinois lifted her license "indefinitely"—or until she could kick her drug dependency and be put back in business.[19]

Far worse even than these two not-isolated, not-unusual cases is the medical disciplinary system's approach to punishing medical researchers who have committed the most serious breach of professional ethics imaginable—that is, falsifying laboratory data. Their punishment? "Demotion" to private practice.[20] In other words, the doctor-patient relationship be damned. A person who commits a "crime" against honesty may not on the one hand be morally or professionally fit enough to work in a research institution but, on the other hand, is just fine for dealing with sick people who desperately need that honesty.

These anecdotes may illuminate, shock, or stir, but they are not nearly as disturbing as the unadorned hard facts and cool statistics concerning medical discipline or the lack of same:

• According to a report by the Inspector General of the U.S. Health and Human Services Department, 20,000 to 45,000 of the nearly 400,000 patient-care doctors in this country "are likely candidates for some level of discipline."[21] Still, only 1,391 disciplinary actions were taken by state medical boards in 1984, the year of the report's study—a situation that led HHS Secretary Bowen to call the level of discipline "nowhere near enough."[22]

• The HHS inspector general's report showed that while the number of disciplinary actions against doctors has risen in the past few years, the rise can be attributed to wrist-slapping over minor infractions. Meanwhile, the number of serious violations acted on by the boards has barely changed over the years.[23] Even with the much trumpeted rise in license revocations in 1985 (406, up from 255 the year before), most of the disciplinary action was in the minor, reprimand categories, and only the medical boards in Nevada, Arizona, and Utah disciplined more than the extremely low statistic of 1 doctor in every 100. The national average for all disciplinary actions in 1985 was a not-very-impressive 4 doctors out of every 1,000.[24]

• In 1983, only 563 American doctors were put on probation or had their licenses revoked, a figure far below what even the most conservative and charitable statistics would predict. Yet, according to a report by Sidney M. Wolfe, M.D., and colleagues at the Public Citizen Health Research Group, "The actual number of instances in which a patient was injured as a result of negligence (the definition of malpractice) was at least 250 times higher."[25] In other words, this report claims that somewhere between 136,000 and 310,000 people a year are injured or killed due to medical mistakes by their doctors (which is almost certainly a conservative figure). Put another way, "out of every 252 times that a patient is injured or killed as a result of doctor negligence, only once is a serious disciplinary action taken against a doctor."[26]

• Though statistics put the percentage of incompetent and dangerous practitioners at anywhere between 5 and 15 percent of the physician population, disciplinary actions occur at a rate of 1.45 serious actions (probation, suspension, or loss of license) per 1,000 physicians—or 1.4 percent.[27] And ten states, comprising nearly 20,000 doctors, took absolutely no serious disciplinary actions in 1983—a fact that led Richard Jay Feinstein, M.D., former chairman of the Florida State Medical Board, to say: "It is difficult to believe that in any given year any state or territory would not have at least one physician per thousand who posed a threat to the health and safety of its citizens. . . . Has the balance of interests in these states tipped too far in the direction of protecting the profession to the detriment of its citizens?"[28]

• When the *Detroit Free Press,* in April 1984, ran a superb seven-part series on bad doctors, it reported that even if incompetent physicians have formal charges brought against them (an unlikelihood in itself), those physicians will continue to treat patients—patients who almost certainly are unaware of the charges—for an average of two and a half years before the case is resolved. The odds of a Michigan doctor keeping his license even after being found incompetent are better than 50-50—and so are the chances of getting a license back once it has been revoked. In fact, so adamant is that board about reinstating revoked licenses and putting offending doctors back to work, 20 percent who come before the board have been there at least once before. And in six years, the board has refused to relicense only one suspended doctor—a physician who was able to coerce two patients to have sex with him. The *Free Press* made this comparison: "Michigan has about the same number of lawyers as doctors—but five times more lawyers lost their license in 1982. And a disbarred lawyer must wait five years to apply for reinstatement; a doctor need wait only a year."[29]

These figures indicate very clearly that not enough doctors are being disciplined, and the disciplinary measures taken are often insufficient or inappropriate. They further imply that autonomy—in practicing without supervision and in being entrusted to discipline colleagues—is not working.

Our Boys Oversee

What are the methods by which the medical profession attempts to discipline its own, and why and where do these methods currently fall far short of their goals—assuming their goals are indeed to discipline?

We are often led to believe that state and county medical and professional societies are concerned about competence and discipline problems, and are therefore bent on taking the situation in hand and curing it. We even come to think of these medical societies as the first and best place to send complaints about bad doctors and medical mistakes. These assumptions couldn't be farther from the truth. For one thing, medical societies are merely clubs, and not every doctor is a member. Medical societies wield no direct power to keep a physician from practicing. All a medical society can do is throw a doctor out of the society, which is more or less like being voted out of your local lodge of the Masons. It's a slight social smudge, but life—and practice—goes on. "Reporting an incompetent or impaired doctor to a county, state or national medical organization is like reporting a bad driver to the American Automobile Association," the

Detroit Free Press writers assert. "The organizations might deplore the behavior, but neither is equipped, legally or politically, to deal with the problem."[30]

In fact, medical societies do not even work very hard to encourage their members to report incompetent or impaired physicians to the proper authorities. Established medicine's strong denial that there is a protective good old boys system that extends to a conspiracy of silence concerning bad doctors and medical mistakes notwithstanding, the facts are to the contrary. For example, of 187 cases brought before the Michigan Board of Medicine between 1977 and 1982, only four were filed by county medical societies, and only one was filed by a professional society.[31]

Further, medical societies may actually bring pressure to bear against physicians who want to report bad doctoring and medical mistakes. In states where the medical society sponsors group malpractice insurance, a doctor who testifies against another doctor in a malpractice case runs the risk of losing his coverage in retaliation. Carl R. Robinson, M.D., J.D., states, "I can assure you that the 'conspiracy of silence' continues,"[32] and goes on to tell of the doctor-owned Mutual Assurance Society of Alabama, which "puts out a monthly newsletter for its shareholders in which current malpractice cases are reported. It makes a point of naming all physician witnesses, both for the plaintiff and for the defense—in effect, telling its members who are the good guys and who are the bad guys in their community."[33]

Peer pressure is a perfectly effective way to chill dissent and defer house-cleaning—and it seems to be working: Over a six-year period, only ten Michigan doctors made formal charges against incompetent colleagues[34]; in New York State in 1983, only 4 percent of complaints to disciplinary bodies came from physicians[35]; in 1984 in New York, the total percentage of referrals by medical societies, individual doctors, and hospitals combined added up to only a meager 11 percent;[36] in a 1987 study, two-thirds of psychiatrists surveyed said they had treated people who claimed they had been sexually involved with other therapists and counselors—a definite professional no-no—and yet these psychiatrists, in some instances mandated by law to file reports on peer sexual misconduct to the proper authorities, did so in only 8 percent of the cases.[37] As one California justice in a case dissent wrote: "Physicians who are members of medical societies flock to the defense of their fellow member charged with malpractice and the plaintiff is relegated, for his expert testimony, to the occasional lone wolf or heroic soul, who, for the sake of truth and justice, has the courage to run the risk of ostracism by his fellow practitioners and the cancellation of his public liability insurance policy."[38]

The American Medical Association is not much better as a disciplinary force. Like the county and state medical societies of which it is a sibling, the AMA has no direct disciplinary powers. Besides, membership in this medical trade and social organization is voluntary, and only about half, or less, of the physicians in the United States care to be members. The AMA is more a force as a lobbyist than as a disciplinarian; it strikes fear into the hearts of politicians much more than it does into the hearts of physicians.

True, under implied pressure from government to straighten up its environment or face the loss of self-regulation, the AMA has made some moves and more noise indicating concern and diligent rectification. It has beefed up its computer file of physicians who have been dismissed from hospital service or had medical board actions taken against them. It has made this information available to hospitals and licensing boards, and has urged medical care institutions to check the files before hiring doctors, and to report to the AMA when the institutions have disciplined or fired a physician. Joseph F. Boyle, M.D., past president of the AMA, in 1985 told a gathering of members of the Federation of State Medical Boards of the United States that "those who violate our professional ethic, whether through incompetence, through physical or emotional impairment, fraud, or something lacking in them as individuals, must be dealt with promptly and forcefully." Boyle went on to tell his audience that "today we have an obligation to see that those who are found guilty of wrongdoing need to be drummed out of the profession, and for good. . . . A physician should expose, without fear or favor, incompetent, corrupt, dishonest, or unethical conduct on the part of members of the profession."[39]

Stirring and noble words. The catch is that although the AMA says it wants to make medicine a clean and heroic profession again (presuming it ever was) it nearly demands that it be done without any outside help, or, as the AMA sees it, interference—meaning government intervention and public scrutiny and input. The AMA wants a total hands-off posture vis-à-vis autonomy and self-regulation, even though it has been shown that leaving the medical profession to police itself has been ineffective. Then, too, are not critics of the AMA justified in their questioning, as the *New York Times* does, "whether the medical association, whose central purpose is to represent the interests of doctors, should take the lead in disciplining them"? And are not the critics further justified in distrusting an association that "maintains there is no correlation between the rise in [malpractice] suits and the number of incompetent doctors"?[40]

Among other attempts to discipline—or, better yet, to educate and improve the performance of—physicians is peer review. This is a watchdog and retrospective critique method of rooting out the bad doctors by having doctors review the work of other doctors to see if all the right steps were taken efficiently and necessarily. The goal is remedial action and the saving of a potentially redeemable doctor.

In theory this is an admirable idea—though only if one believes that autonomy and self-regulation works, which has in no way been shown to be the case. Further, the peer review sentinel system of quality control applies in the main strictly to practitioners working in hospitals. The mass of private practice physicians and their treatment of patients are not monitored in this way. Peer review's scope, then, is limited to a partial universe.

Peer review comes in two general forms. The informal type is just that—an unstructured, private and personal, arm-around-the-shoulder, over-coffee-in-the-cafeteria kind of warning to an errant doc that his sloppiness has been noticed and he's being given an off-the-record chance to get back on track before things really hit the fan. The formal component of peer review involves a routinized exploration of case histories by panels of examining physicians. The Joint Commission on the Accreditation of Hospitals' guidelines mandate peer reviews in the form of tissue, utilization, and audit committees looking into the appropriateness of surgery and tissue or organ removal, length of stays, and services rendered.

But, as Keyser points out, peer review is just not working in many hospitals. For one thing, "not all committee members approach their tasks with zeal."[41] For another, many hospitals do not, after a negative review, restrict the privileges of inept and negligent physicians or cut them off altogether.[42] Peer review becomes an idle threat, at best. "Credential reviews of initial or continuing staff privileges often become pro forma," Robertson notes. "Under some circumstances, when deficiencies are detected, no action follows; and when it does, it is only after considerable time has elapsed."[43]

Stroman relates that in some small hospitals "an untrained surgeon may be the chairman of the committee that reviews his own work. Or the chief surgeon in a proprietary hospital may be one of the owners, so that it is hard to conceive of others questioning his work." The whole process is "a shameful mess of loopholes."[44]

Peer review falls apart when doctors don't want to get involved, either because of their good old boys network or for fear of being sued in retaliation by the doctor they are reporting or disciplining. Peer review falls apart, too, in the very area it is designed to uphold—quality—because "the way things actually work, physicians are almost *never* chastised for undertaking unnecessary procedures," as Keyser points out.[45] In other words, it doesn't matter if the procedure was unnecessary, as long as it was performed well and it followed the accepted method. Process, not necessity or outcome, is what peer review is all about. And a doctor who is good at making his records read as if the operation were an absolute necessity, and who doesn't harm or kill the patient in the process, can play peer review committees like an instrument.

But the real paper tiger of peer review may be vested interest; specifically, that quality control and discipline go down the drain when money and hospital profits are a factor and may be adversely affected by tough peer review committees. "In communities with surplus hospital beds," Keyser writes, "effective peer review programs that result in fewer admissions and shorter hospital stays might lower a hospital's census to the point where its financial status will be jeopardized. . . . Also, when doctors doing the largest amount of unethical surgery happen to have the biggest practices, administrators may be afraid that disciplinary action may lead to the loss of large numbers of hospital admissions and fees."[46] That's just what Roberta Ritter found out during her internship in a Florida hospital, when she discovered a senior doctor overmedicating women in labor, and told the hospital medical director. Instead of getting a pat on the head, Ritter was told to shut up or get out if she didn't like it because that doctor was a "high producer" for the hospital. Ritter did get out. She quit the practice of medicine . . . and became a lawyer—a malpractice attorney fighting for aggrieved victims against incompetent and negligent physicians.[47]

So it boils down to the patient being at risk of being operated on or treated by an incompetent or unethical doctor who is known to be so but is reported to be otherwise via a corrupt peer review system. Ironically, on the other hand, in some cases the patient is no better protected if the peer review system works to perfection, because that patient won't be able to get his or her hands on the information that could save his life or help win his malpractice suit. Courts around the country, most recently in Pennsylvania, have upheld the right of doctors to have their peer review files remain confidential and out of the hands of injured patients and their attorneys, who could use those peer assessments to prove a history of incompetence and malpractice.[48] (The rationalization is that if doctors knew that their opinions could be made public, they'd hedge on them. In other words, only confidentiality breeds physician truthfulness.) So, in essence, for the patient who wants protection or justice, peer review has no more value when it does work than when it doesn't.

With the idealistic peer review concept compromised at nearly every turn, the last resorts for disciplinary intervention are state medical boards. But, as the figures at the beginning of this chapter clearly demonstrate, these boards leave much to be desired . . . unless one is an offending physician. It is nearly a decade and a half since Derbyshire wrote in the *Journal of the American Medical Association,* "To the question, 'Are the boards of medical examiners adequately disciplining unethical physicians?' the answer must be, on the whole, no."[49] Very little if anything has occurred in the intervening years to alter that assessment. In fact, probably the nation's premier disciplining body, the Oregon Board of Medical Examiners, in 1985 had only 85 physicians under close disciplinary supervision—is a mere 1.5 percent of all the physicians practicing in Oregon, and far below the minimum 10 percent of impaired or incompetent physicians one would expect to find. And it seemed relatively content to have disciplined that many.[50]

Some of the blame for the failure must be placed on administrative and fiscal constraints. As many of these disciplinary bodies rely for support on small budgetary grants from the state or just on the usually small licensing fees paid by the physicians, there is frequently a lack of funds to do a proper job. Near-empty coffers also mean minimal or no support staff, and almost never an extant or effective investigatory or surveillance component. Even if the number of complaints were few, a conscientious board is often unable to investigate and follow up. Backlogs occur, as in New York, where the state's board in 1985 had nearly 2,000 complaints backlogged on their files, with some of the complaints sitting in those files since the 1970s.[51] Massachusetts has 20,000 physicians, but only five investigators.[52] Peter Perl in the *Washington Post* has written of "the virtual impotence of the D.C. Commission on Healing Arts, which—due to inadequate funding and staffing, and governmental infighting—has been overwhelmed by a backlog of complaints and clerical duties that leave the commission unable to effectively and promptly police the city's 10,000 doctors."[53] The District of Columbia's board is merely a mirror image of dozens of others. Hearings before the New York State Board for Professional Medical Conduct cost about $2,000 per hearing, a figure that does not include staff salaries and travel costs to get the board appointees to the hearings.[54] Unless and until the states provide more money or physicians' licensing fees are raised, budgetary shortfalls will continue to act as disciplinary detours.

(Critics have further cited possible conflict-of-interest problems with a license fee–supported disciplinary board. It is a situation in which the disciplinarians are, in effect, on the payroll of those who are to be disciplined. Whether this relationship taints judgments is clearly an area for further study.)

Some medical disciplinary boards are also often handcuffed by the guidelines, regulations, and laws under which they must work. In some instances, they are given insufficient penalty options: that is, whereas penalties generally fall into five categories—reprimand, probation, practice restrictions, license suspension, and license revocation—some boards have only harsh or extreme options at their disposal to choose from and impose. This may limit disciplinary efforts, because doctors may hesitate to impose extreme sanctions on colleagues and the punishments may simply not fit the crimes. As Gross indicates, "Boards with more options can be more effective enforcers than those that have only severe sanctions available since they need not overlook less than severe transgressions.''[55] Further-more, in some states ''incompetence'' is not even mentioned in licensing laws and is not grounds for disciplinary actions; but, as Somers and Som-ers attest, ''even where incompetence is specified in the law as a basis for disciplinary action, disciplinary procedures in nearly all the states are so weak and so weighted in favor of the doctor that effective action is virtually impossible.''[56]

A common complaint made against disciplinary boards is that they rarely take action against any doctors except those with addiction prob-lems—a smoke-screen tactic that gives the appearance of activity and dil-igence by singling out only the most visible offenders. Whether or not this represents the majority of cases is unclear, but the problem is a real one. In New Jersey, the insurance commissioner has said that most disciplinary board actions in that state came down on physicians who used or peddled drugs, were alcoholics or mentally impaired, or engaged in nonmedical criminal acts. Between 1980 and 1984, only 7 of 322 board cases in New Jersey dealt with malpractice.[57] A 1986 investigative series in the *Orlando Sentinel* concluded that Florida regulators ''are tough on drunken, drugged, and criminal doctors, but they do little to protect the public from physi-cians who repeatedly lose malpractice claims because they practice poor medicine.''[58]

Some states don't even do a very good job disciplining perpetrators of nonmedical crimes. Pennsylvania is a perfect example. Despite being empowered by the state's medical practice act to refuse, revoke, or sus-pend a physician's license when he or she has been found guilty of a felony or of ''immoral or unprofessional conduct,'' the board has been notably lax in doing so, especially in the area of Medicare and Medicaid fraud. *Philadelphia Inquirer* reporters Edward Colimore and Howard Goodman dis-covered that Pennsylvania doctors defrauded their patients and/or the state and federal governments out of about $13 million in 1985, yet ''34 doctors who are currently barred from the Medicaid program—and who also have been convicted on criminal charges—are still permitted to practice medi-cine in Pennsylvania.''[59] Physicians who have performed unnecessary pro-cedures to accrue Medicaid funds, physicians who have submitted phony bills using other doctors' names, and physicians who have falsified phar-macy records have received, as their punishments from the disciplinary board, license suspensions of a mere 90 days . . . and are still practicing today.

And they are practicing without their patients knowing that these doctors are criminals or untrustworthy or lacking appropriate skills. That is because most medical boards erect what Nat Hentoff calls ''a white wall of silence.''[60] In Pennsylvania, which is by no means alone in this, the board may take years, even a decade, to hold hearings and arrive at a decision in a case. All the while, the doctor is free to keep practicing, shielded by a board-imposed publicity and information blackout. "The public is generally left unaware of a doctor's background, even if he has been convicted," Colimore and Howard report. "Most of them continue to advertise their practices, treating new patients who do not know about their pasts."[61] The *New York Times* reported the results of a 1985 study showing that "about two-thirds of 30 state medical boards surveyed . . . said they tell the public nothing about disciplinary steps until proceedings are complete."[62] To which Kenneth Wagstaff, of California's progressive disciplinary board, is quoted as saying: "If someone is indicted in court, that is public record. We think anyone should be able to get this information."[63] But the "white wall of silence," held together by the mortar of contempt, will keep that information out of the hands of the patients whose lives and money that information might possibly save.

When the *Cleveland Plain Dealer* ran reporter Gary Webb's remarkable week-long exposé of the Ohio State Medical Board—a board not so unlike its counterparts in other states—it uncovered some of the board's reasons for granting leniency to offending physicians who had come before it. Among these rationales were:

• An accused doctor's sincere and honest confession of wrongdoing.
• A doctor's inability to make a living if he were denied his right to practice.
• The embarrassment a doctor had suffered from cases made public, or might suffer if secret proceedings leaked out.
• The belief that just being forced to come before the board is a form of treatment.

These findings led the *Plain Dealer,* in an editorial, to comment:

What nonsense. What crass dereliction of responsibility. What reckless disregard for the human lives they swore to protect. Can anyone imagine judges regularly excusing accused felons because the charges had embarrassed them? Or because the accused would be unable to work if jailed? Or because the defendant had been so contrite when caught? Leniency is one thing, abdication of duty is another. . . . Why has the board been so lax, so craven in its performance? The chief answer is the clout of rich, influential members of the medical profession and their friends. The board also is image-conscious, erroneously thinking it would taint all doctors by publicly disciplining a few.[64]

Adds another editorial, this one in the *New York Daily News:* "Keep quiet, sweep it under the rug, don't sully our good names—those are the whispered words with which the medicos blind themselves to misconduct. . . . The question is, when will they wake up to the situation and begin policing their [profession] for real?"[65]

Even when a bad doctor somehow loses his license, it is no hardship to get it back, because medical boards seem desperate in wanting to help doctors regain their status and incomes, even at the public's expense. That attitude is well expressed in this quote from an article written by representatives of New York's Office of Professional Discipline:

> Millions of dollars have been invested by and on behalf of physicians in obtaining medical educations. Each physician spends many years acquiring experience and expertise. When a physician's license is revoked, is society thereafter to be denied the benefits of his or her knowledge and skill? Does the physician forfeit all the advantages and rewards that are associated with the practice of medicine?
>
> The answer is no. A license, once revoked, can be restored.[66]

The situation is much the same over the country. Despite everything, once a doctor, always a doctor—with a little help from other doctors on medical boards.

So, the response goes, put more civilians on the boards to balance things and air the consumers' viewpoints. In theory, at any rate, that is an excellent idea; medical disciplinary boards, if they have any citizen input at all, are heavily weighted in favor of physician control. But, in practice, a citizen component on medical disciplinary panels does not necessarily help "humanize" or "consumerize" or sharpen the process. Gross explains why:

> The hope has been expressed that public members would be "lobbyists for the people" who would ensure that the views of the public would gain a hearing during board discussions. The reality is that governors tend to see these positions as part of their patronage and fill the vacancies without regard to these exceptions. . . . Public members without special interests or qualifications soon discover the meetings to be dull, the language confusing, the interests at stake submerged, and the prestige and prerogatives to be minimal. If they continue to attend meetings their confusion is often clarified by well-meaning professionals, thus co-opting the special role the public member was to play.[67]

Until the day medical boards stop being impotent political playthings and tools of medical establishment self-regulation and become legitimate panels of investigation and surveillance with teeth and a goodly supply of guts, "discipline" and "medicine" will be the strangest and rarest of bedfellows.

Until the day it is made clear who will mete out punishment and who will define "quality" and the bounds of good practice—the public or the profession—medicine will be a craft enshrouded by the most basic and serious of doubts, and there will be "no support for the claim that licensing agencies hold practitioners accountable to high ethical standards."[68]

Today, immediately, each state's medical disciplinary body, in the words of John H. Morton, M.D., would not "go far wrong by returning to its primary responsibility. Its charge from the state is to protect the public not the profession. Any deviation from this basic principle can lead only to trouble and to protests by protectors of the public interest. If the board is unduly sympathetic to the physician, these protests are fully justified."[69]

"All the evidence suggests," writes *New England Journal of Medicine* editor Arnold S. Relman, M.D., "that most if not all the states have been too lax—not too strict—in their enforcement of medical professional standards."[70]

Or, in the words of United States Attorney for Manhattan Rudolph W. Giuliani, "The medical profession has gotten more immunity than is healthy for society."[71]

12

WHAT DID HE SAY?
WHAT DID I HEAR?
WHAT DID WE DO?

"The secret of caring for the patient is caring for the patient."
—Sir William Osler

The very center of medicine is crumbling. Some say it is already in ruin. And what worries observers is that if the center cannot hold, all the rest surely becomes pointless and worthless, or worse. All that is good in medicine—what makes it work when it works, what makes it safe when it's safe—begins and resides at this center. Greed, negligence, incompetence, and indifference, resulting in avoidable injuries and deaths, all proliferate and rival the benefits when the center comes crashing in on itself.

This center is what has come to be called the "doctor-patient relationship"—a relationship that ideally should be a mutual interrelationship based on trust but that instead has regularly come to resemble an unhappy encounter between the callous and those caught off balance (and purposely kept off balance, some might argue). And it is clear that the first domino that strikes the next domino to start the chain reaction of bad medicine and medical mistakes is toppled by the lack of communication, lack of respect, and lack of caring that typifies many if not most contacts between today's medical providers and the scared human beings who come to them looking for help.

It is doubtful that medical personnel would themselves like to be treated shabbily and impersonally. It is doubtful that they would like to be treated as though they were so unintelligent that it would be useless to bring them into contact with anything even remotely resembling honest and helpful information. It is doubtful that they would like to be treated as voyeurs of their own care rather than participants in their healing experience. In short, it is doubtful that medical personnel would like to be treated the way many of them treat their patients.

"The ideology of modern medical practice has very little to do with the human experience of being sick," writes Louise Lander in *Defective Medicine.* "It has much more to do with the need of physicians for a conceptual framework that will focus and simplify their work and that will justify the segmented, episodic, superspecialized, individualistic character of their work arrangements. It has something to do," she continues, "with justifying as well an enormous societal investment in medical real estate, high-technology hardware, and drugs. It also has something to do with science, but its increasingly apparent scientific weaknesses make clear that its most important purposes have become other than scientific ones, that theory as enlightenment has become ideology as mask."[1]

Lip Service

A few years ago a cartoon in a national magazine showed the cobwebbed, skeletal remains of a beggar, a sign reading "I am blind" around his neck, a bony finger still pressed against the doorbell of the "Home for the Deaf."

Sadly, this bit of line-drawing black humor comes very close to capturing the heart of the failure in doctor-patient communication. It's a skeleton that sits not in the closet but right on the front doorstep of current medical practice.

Study after study, anecdote after anecdote, show that doctors and other medical professionals simply don't communicate well. Every consumer guide to wending one's way through the funhouse of medical care feels an obligation to the reader to provide at least one chapter on deciphering the mumbo jumbo of medicalese—not just a glossary of technical terms you might find on your hospital chart but also translations of that particularly colorful patois that keeps the us-versus-them wall tall and impenetrable.[2]

As one study of patient satisfaction in a family practice center demonstrated,[3] "Because patients obviously cannot follow directions they do not understand, effective communication becomes an essential factor in promoting their compliance with medical regimens." So does personal manner. Since many people tend to weave together their personal feelings about a doctor and their belief in his technical ability—if they like the way he behaves, he's a skilled doctor; if they don't, he's a bungler—"evidence suggests that these judgments influence their subsequent health behavior, such as appointment-keeping.'' And because of this ''important link between patients' perceptions of socioemotional aspects of the physician-patient relationship and their reported satisfaction with medical care,'' that first domino—poor communication and interpersonal skills—invariably sets off the chain reaction that results in that dreaded and frequently avoidable last topple: the malpractice suit. ''Treat your patients like human beings, with care and concern, and you won't get sued'' is a simplification, to be sure, but there is certainly truth in it.

Why is the doctor-patient relationship, and especially that part of it based on communication, in such bad shape? At least part of the blame may lie in the attitudes instilled or reinforced in medical school. Whereas the biomechanical aspects of medical learning get a thorough going over before, during, and after medical school, what to do with the human beings gets short shrift—or no shrift at all. Norman Cousins was troubled by his first encounter with students at the University of California at Los Angeles (UCLA) School of Medicine, where he was a lecturer on the topic of medical humanities; he found that they ''tended to regard the entire area of patient-physician relationships as soft.'' Furthermore, these students ''seemed reluctant to attach appropriate importance to the physician's communication skills, to medical ethics, or to the circumstances of a patient's life.''[4] That was nearly a decade ago, and not much has changed in the schools since then. Even more distressing to contemplate is that those earlier students are now treating (or perhaps mistreating) patients today.

Time is another confounding element. ''Because of the time-consuming nature of the discussion [in the doctor's office],'' writes David Hilfiker, M.D., in *Healing the Wounds*, ''we physicians often are tempted to leave out the description of the process when talking with patients. . . .'' Besides the real danger this can produce, or the lack of compliance it can cause, this time-based communication gap is responsible, especially when the treatment outcome is not all that good, for leaving the patient ''feeling angry and betrayed, sure that the physician was guilty of some gross negligence. For his part, the physician is impatient and angry with the patient's 'unrealistic' expectations and, not infrequently, guilt-ridden for not fulfilling them.''[5] Hilfiker's concerns are certainly as heartfelt as they are apologist, but it is no excuse—and it is no coincidence that doctors, who never have the time to talk, always seem to have the time to do something, to prescribe a drug or perform a test. And is it a coincidence that doctors are paid for doing, not talking? And so they do . . . and do . . . and do.

Some physicians are simply poor communicators, and they would be so if they were bus drivers or businessmen instead of brain surgeons. Some think sharply in medical or scientific terms, but simply can't relay the facts and figures, probabilities, and certain eventualities to the waiting sufferers. They may be excellent technicians, tops in the mental and mechanical and even menial aspects of their jobs but, because of the way they're constituted, can't communicate well with their patients. There are shy doctors just as there are shy people in other professions; there are those who can't frame a coherent sentence or make any helpful sense of anything.

On the face of it, it might not seem all that important: If a doctor is a good doctor, who cares if he or she isn't a verbal whiz kid? It's just this: One isn't a good doctor, a complete doctor, if one's communication skills are lame or nonexistent.

"However well informed a physician may be, and however conscientious about applying his knowledge, if he cannot get his message across to the patient, his competence is not going to be helpful," state Korsch and Negrete. "Moreover, more than half of a physician's working time in patient care, particularly in fields such as general practice, pediatrics and internal medicine, is spent on problems involving primarily psychological factors and the need for communication rather than technical knowledge."[6]

Though it may seem a cruel concept to deny the privilege of becoming a physician to someone with communication difficulties, it is crueler to keep a patient in the dark—or worse, on the wrong therapeutic track—because of such an obstacle.

Perhaps medical schools should do better in selecting the right kinds of students and in instructing young would-be physicians in the art as well as the craft of medical practice. Perhaps the schools should do better in analyzing the qualities of the students they do admit and then track them into areas of the medical discipline to which they are best suited. There are places in the field of medicine for those who can't communicate well, who can't get the satisfactory doctor-patient one-on-one going—research, for one. Unfortunately, they usually don't pay as well as professional practice. So, to the starry-eyed, terribly-in-debt young med student, eager to be a classic doctor, where's the lure? It is also interesting that some of those discussion-deficient practitioners are placed in positions where they teach new students—something else medical schools and teaching hospitals need to monitor.

According to a September 23, 1985, article in *Medical World News,* a study at UCLA's Cancer Rehabilitation Project found that "9 in 10 physicians had never received any formal training in how to disclose a cancer diagnosis [to the afflicted patient]."[7] From that basis of truth comes the anecdote, well known among physicians, about the medical student assigned to keep tabs on a patient in a teaching hospital—the patient being a physician himself. "Doctor," the student said, "you have cancer, and I'm afraid you're going to die." Replied the doctor: "Son, I knew that, but the way you told me hasn't helped me one bit."[8]

Certainly it's a tricky business, dispensing the news of a dire prognosis. In the days of the Greek empire, the messengers of bad tidings were slain, C.O.D.—the unfortunate victims of damnation by association. And so doctors may suffer this same fate, figuratively. But that doesn't justify the fact, as the UCLA study showed, that doctors not only communicate less with cancer patients but may actually go out of their way to steer clear of them. Just when the patients most need guidance and information about available treatment possibilities and alternatives, the physician is nowhere to be found or avoids the important points of discussion and keeps doctor-patient interaction at the small talk, chitchat level—actions that reduce patient compliance and often short-circuit treatment regimens. Interestingly, the study found that those doctors who approached their patients with care, concern, and sensitivity had experienced serious illness themselves or had had it occur within their own families. Doctors make lousy patients, but doctors who have been patients make better doctors.

From a reluctance or inability to deal in a person-to-person, face-to-face, and up-front manner with a patient, it is only a short, simple, and frequently taken slide to dishonesty. This blasts the physician-patient relationship right out of the water. Nothing is more damaging than for the course of a medical transaction to be one of "stabilize, labelize, tableize, fableize."[9] Medical ethicist Sissela Bok, whose *Lying: Moral Choice in Public and Private Life* is the principal work in this field, has noted that physicians (and for years she studied the apparent cream of the crop—those trained at and affiliated with the Harvard Medical School) talk about lying to their patients "in a cavalier, often condescending way . . ."; what they aren't aware of or concerned about is that patients who discover they've been lied to "often have an acute sense of injury and of loss of trust at learning that they have been duped."[10] Bok states that for patients "to be given false information about important choices in their lives is to be rendered powerless."[11] However, according to Thomas Preston, M.D., the physician:

> assumes that his superior knowledge and experience enable him
> to judge what the patient needs. Since the patient is presumed
> to be unable to make an informed decision and likely to choose
> wrongly even if fully informed, it is standard practice for physicians to manipulate information in order to persuade patients

to accept recommendations. . . . Thus the patient is systematically denied the data he needs to make an informed decision.[12]

Medicine is, after all, a game of power plays, and it is clear that if lying and deception are required to maintain the upper hand in the doctor-patient relationship game, doctors will do it.

Bok and others dismiss rather easily and disdainfully the reasons physicians give to justify lying to a patient. For a long time, physicians have claimed that it is impossible to be entirely truthful in medical dealings—that deep down inside, patients really don't want to have bad news about their conditions, and that that information actually hurts them. There is little factual foundation for any of these reasons for deceit, and very good evidence that just the opposite is true.[13] It would be amusing, if it weren't so serious, that physicians who wear the cloak of science and dismiss any contention unsupported by studies, here grasp at the flimsiest of anecdotal straws to buttress their prejudices and maintain their position of power.

Telling patients the truth has never been and is not now considered one of the major supports of the doctor-patient relationship. There is, in the codes and oaths that for centuries have guided the technical and moral activities of physicians, no emphasis at all on telling patients the truth. Look for it even in the "sacred" Hippocratic oath and be prepared to come away empty-handed. It is not there. Except for a few laws with rather loose parameters, doctors can decide on their own just how much or how little of the truth to tell patients. When it comes to ethics, Illich reminds us, the medical profession tends to shape theory so as to be brought into line with actual practice.[14]

Insofar as communicating and truthfulness are concerned, physicians have assumed a strongly paternalistic stance toward their patients. And, as Bok makes clear, "The paternalistic assumption of superiority to patients also carries great dangers for physicians themselves—it risks turning to contempt."[15]

Contempt

The contempt that some doctors show for patients—or certain types or groups of patients—arises not only from dishonesty aimed at the patient but also from being dishonest with themselves.

What it takes to be on top of late-breaking medical developments is more than many doctors can handle easily. There is so much to know, and it is impossible to know it all, or even a large percentage of it. This explosion of medical information "has left all practicing physicians, but especially primary care physicians, in the eerie position of knowing that their skills and knowledge are too often incomplete for the task in which they are engaged.''[16] Physicians are human, and limited; they can't grasp or keep up with everything.

Massive uncertainty—medical practitioners (or at least the ones with an awareness of themselves) are riddled with it. The knowledge gap is one reason—and a reason so many physicians go into specialties and subspecialties: to know a lot about a little, microscopic subset of medical knowledge can be a shelter and a comfort and a way of shutting out uncertainty. It may also shut out challenge, patient contact, and continuous care.

But even for the practitioner who is widely educated and highly skilled, there is another cause of uncertainty: In many cases there is no single way to treat an injury or illness. So much of what a physician does is based on what he *thinks* is going to work, not on what he *knows* for sure will work. Absolute certainty is rarely one of the players in the game of medicine. The 1982 President's Commission for the Study of Ethical Problems in Medicine and Biomedical and Behavioral Research noted this when it reported:

> Even the most mundane case . . . may well have no objective medical criteria that specify a single best way to achieve the goal. A fractured limb can be repaired in a number of ways; a life-threatening infection can be treated with a variety of antibiotics; mild diabetes is subject to control by diet, by injectable natural insulin, or by oral synthetic insulin substitutes. Health care professionals often reflect their own value preferences when they favor one alternative over another; many are matters of choice, dictated neither by biomedical principles or data nor by a single, agreed-upon professional standard.[17]

Despite not knowing everything, despite taking calculated risks, despite the inability to keep up with the newer studies and case histories, despite the very humanness of uncertainty, so many physicians project a force-field persona that says: I know it all. I am in charge. I am in total control. I am not now nor have I ever been uncertain. Such doctors cannot or will not admit a flaw, or a lapse, or a void. And so these doctors cannot or will not be of the greatest help to their patients. In fact, they may do harm. As David Hilfiker, M.D., remarks, "Life *is* uncertain. The physician who conceals that uncertainty with false reassurances ultimately is robbing the patient of her responsibility for her own life."[18]

Such false reassurance and bogus certainty is a sign of pure contempt for the doctor-patient relationship and the social contract that should exist between the "healer" and the afflicted. The presumption that riddles this arrogant certainty is that the physician is superior—not only in medical matters, but in all matters, including moral and intellectual. It represents, as Paul Starr notes in his book, *The Social Transformation of American Medicine,* "the continuing conflict in American life between the democratic respect for common sense and professional claims of special knowledge."[19]

The height of this contempt, this shadow certainty, is the legal domain physicians and their lobbyists have been able to homestead in the name of superiority. "Except for the internal standards set by hospitals and other medical institutions, which vary widely and are often unenforced, any physician, whatever his or her training, can legally do anything in medical practice: perform neurosurgery, counsel people with marital problems, or read X-rays," Victor W. Sidel and Ruth Sidel state. "For physicians who practice largely outside institutions, fear of malpractice suits is almost the only deterrent—other than conscience—to undertaking procedures in which they have had only minimal training or experience."[20]

Contempt for the patient in medical practice takes many forms:

• So little is thought of the patient's ability to think and choose, and so much is made of the physician's superiority, that the patient is usually the last party to get access to his or her own medical records. The records are all about the patient, and what has been done to the patient, and what course of treatment is recommended for the patient, and what is actually wrong with the patient. Despite this, the one person who has the single greatest difficulty in seeing medical records is the patient. Insurance companies can get hold of those records easily, as can numerous employees of the hospital or of the doctor, state agencies, law enforcement departments, and employers of the person receiving treatment. But not the person receiving treatment. In fact, only slightly more than a dozen states assure patients access to their medical records. And even in those states with access statutes, doctors and hospitals can delay turning over the information in medical records—records that are the doctors' or hospitals' property, but in which the data belong to the patients—for years, if they choose, can release edited-down summaries of the records instead of the full report, and can charge a copying fee, to boot.[21]

The point of all the obstruction may be (a) to assert and maintain power and dominance of physician over patient, (b) to make sure diagnostic or treatment mistakes evident on the records do not get into the hands of victims who might in turn want to sue, or even (c) to retain the paternalistic edge in dealings with patients. But it definitely is contempt for basic moral obligations and the right to know, and is put dismayingly but succinctly in a letter to the editor in *Lancet:* "We must maintain a doctor-patient partnership. Better communication, Yes; reading notes, No.''[22]

• In the September 12, 1985, issue of the *New England Journal of Medicine,* a doctor felt the need to denounce to his colleagues—and at the same time announce to a larger reading audience—the tendency for physicians to label as "emotionally disturbed" those patients who come to physicians' offices with written lists of their ailments.[23] *La maladie du petit papier*— the illness of the little piece of paper—is the tag given by doctors to this presumed condition. A major medical text read and absorbed by legions of medical students over the years, E. L. DeGowin and R. L. DeGowin's *Bedside Diagnostic Examination* (London: Macmillan, 1969, p. 17), states that people who bring along notes to refer to during a doctor's visit are psychoneurotic. Writes the article's author, John F. Burnum, M.D., "Some physicians are annoyed by note writing or think it is a joke. Note carriers have become stigmatized." However, Burnum argues that "note writing is a normal, honorable practice that can be used to advantage in patient care." He adds:

> Most notes seem to be written for no devious reasons, because of no lurking Freudian distemper, but because patients and families simply want to get things straight. Anxious, even distraught they may be, but they are seeking clarity, order, information, and control. Some patients tell me that they organize, list their thoughts, and come to the point so as not to waste the doctor's time. If all this is to be labeled compulsion, I say let it be and make the most of it.[24]

It seems patently absurd that a basic organizational technique such as list making should be ridiculed by the medical profession, leading a doctor to the contempt-blinded false conclusion that the patient's complaint is not in the body but merely "in the head." Since, as Burnum notes, more women than men write notes, this plays right into the hands of those doctors who see most "women's conditions" as various forms of emotional disturbance or hysteria, for which sedatives, psychotropic drugs, or even some dangerous and unnecessary surgery is routinely administered as the "cure." (As to this latter "remedy," Gena Corea remembers a particularly chilling example of a woman "whose severe case of peritonitis, caused by a botched sterilization, was at first dismissed by doctors as 'psychosomatic guilt-induced' pain."[25])

Burnum concludes: "Medical care turns on communication. Whatever helps patients express themselves and helps physicians understand patients is acceptable." *If* the physician wants to understand, that is.

• Many doctors have an attitude problem—actually a set of attitudes that affect the doctor-patient relationship—that is primarily one of social and class distinctions. In the aforementioned UCLA Cancer Rehabilitation Project study, researchers found that physicians tended to be more open and to go into greater detail "if a patient was in the middle or upper socioeconomic class, exhibited average or above-average intelligence, was emotionally composed, specifically requested information, and was married or living with someone rather than living alone."[26] A report from Harvard Medical School and Brigham and Women's Hospital and Beth Israel Hospital in Boston entitled "Effects of Patients' Socioeconomic Status and Physicians' Training and Practice on Patient-Doctor Communication," concluded that "there is the risk of less effective communication between patients of lower socioeconomic status and their physicians, and that physicians may be unaware that less effective communication is occurring."[27] These are just two of a wide array of studies that arrive at similar conclusions. Victor and Ruth Sidel in *A Healthy State* show that when a physician or health worker comes in contact with a person whose cultural beliefs are different from his or her own, the result not only is what the patient feels is a cool, uncaring encounter but also may be biases in diagnosis and treatment. "Patients with similar types of psychiatric illness," Sidel and Sidel write,[28] "have been shown to be treated differently—electric shock more likely for the poor, psychotherapy more likely for the affluent—and by different doctors—doctors-in-training more likely for the poor, fully trained and experienced doctors for the rich." The problem is as great or greater, say Sidel and Sidel, in emergency rooms (ERs), where they claim that "much more resuscitative effort is likely to be expended on the man brought in in a suit and tie than on one with dirty, disheveled clothes," and that medical care in the ER is "frequently carried on by doctors who expect—or even hope—never to see the patient again, and who behave accordingly."[29] Even in a less hectic environment than an emergency room, one in which decisions can be made at greater leisure and in which biases could be examined and eliminated, the socioeconomic and cultural biases persist.

And it goes beyond those biases, as well. "Doctors like to feel omnipotent and very capable," explains David Klein, a professor of social science. "When something is beyond the cure of medicine, or if they have difficulty coping with it, they tend to dislike a patient who comes in with that condition."[30] A physician's personal feelings may even be expressed "in aggression towards, or even rejection of, a patient who fails to improve."[31] Adds Roush: "People in helper roles tend to view those whom they help as having inferior status. This tendency may not have great impact on people with short-term problems, but for persons with permanent disabilities the consequences can be profound."[32]

When researchers from the University of Minnesota Medical School and St. Paul-Ramsey Medical Center asked residents and staff physicians about which patient characteristics they disliked, the ones that provoked mostly negative response from both or either group included "marital, family problems," "disheveled, unkempt," "markedly overweight," "markedly underweight," "tearful," "adolescence," "low pain tolerance," and "non–English speaking."[33] These characteristics did not elicit sympathy or pity, as they might in the general population. Negativity is what they received.

"Because they themselves are very self-disciplined, doctors tend to feel that any patient who lacks self-discipline and is willing to indulge himself is, as it were, a bad patient, and culpable for his own condition," explains Klein.

Chronic pain is a major bugaboo of the superior, overcertain physician. Chronic pain, writes Peter J. Nunn, of the Victoria (British Columbia) Stress and Pain Centre, "cannot be measured; there is no convenient blood test that says 'This person has x amount of pain,' and X-ray films are often ambiguous and may even be normal."[34] So, added to their injury many chronic pain sufferers experience the insult of having their condition considered by their doctor to be a manifestation of a neurosis or something they'll just have to learn to live with. Nunn goes on: "When we are confronted by a condition that breaks all the rules and often gets worse despite all our efforts, it is not surprising that we want it to go away. After sending the patient to every specialist in the book it is very tempting to consider that the condition is not real in the sense that it can be treated."[35]

In other words, in the medicalization of society, what the physician can discover and treat is real; that for which he has no knowledge or skills, or for which his science or art contains no tools as of yet, is imaginary. And the patient is a bothersome, complaining crock.

• One might think that the one group sure to avoid being demeaned or held in contempt by physicians would be other physicians. Not so. Hospitalized physicians, too, have had eye-opening nightmare experiences that have been known to change the way they then subsequently behaved toward their own patients.[36]

The death of Hal Lear, as powerfully re-created by his widow Martha Weinman Lear in the best-selling *Heartsounds,* is the worst-case scenario. Plagued with a bad heart, hospitalized numerous times including once for cardiac bypass surgery, Lear not only died in a painful and maddeningly slow physical downhill slide but also had his emotional foundation progressively weakened by the patronizing, smug, smoke-screened attitude of his doctors—who also happened to be his friends and professional colleagues. That he was a well-known and well-liked physician brought him no special treatment. He was treated as poorly as every other patient.

Lear was rarely, if ever, kept informed about what his physicians were thinking about his condition, which was all the more angering because Lear could tell, with a clinician's knowledge, just exactly what was going on inside him. His doctors never told him that neurological problems might result from his bypass surgery, and so his postoperative memory loss was accompanied by the certainty that he was going insane. (And when his psychiatrist turned out to be an insensitive and ineffectual practitioner, and Lear accosted the doctor who had referred the psychiatrist to him, that doctor blushed and replied, "Oh, my goodness. I didn't realize you were asking for *yourself*. He [the psychiatrist] was looking for referrals and I wanted to help him out. He's my wife's cousin."[37] Not good enough for you, Dr. Lear, that exchange made clear, but just fine for any run-of-the-mill patient.) So disdainful of Lear were his friend-physicians that he was actually forced to take his own blood samples at home because the doctors gave no credence to what his body was telling him loud and clear. They never believed what he told them, and they never made him a participant in his own healing.

But where their condescension, even to one of their own, was the greatest was when they made him feel—as they do other patients—that he was responsible for his illness, that he was ultimately to blame for it. Wrote Martha Lear:

Why could no doctor ever say, "It's my fault." . . . Or at least a Maybe. . . . *Maybe* it's our fault, *perhaps*, in some limited insignificant way, we have stirred a drop of culpability into this mess . . . [but] . . . Oh, no. Never. It's Your Fault. Patient gets recurrent hernia, surgeon says, "You got too fat." No clue that he might have botched the surgery. Fracture mends badly, orthopedist says, "You were too active." No hint that the cast was applied incorrectly. Cancer, inoperable, internist tells family, "He should have come to me sooner." No ghost of a suggestion that warning signs may have been missed in the last annual checkup. Cardiac drops dead, cardiologist says, "Well, he never would take care of himself." Never a whisper about the possibility of inadequate medication. Elective surgery, patient dies on table, anesthetist says, "Tch. Difficult case." And who's to know—or who's to tell—that the patient died from too much Pentothal and not enough oxygen? . . . The patient had been blamed for his illness, had been handed back his questions, un-

opened, and had been left feeling rejected, abandoned. . . . You
do not do such a thing . . . to such a patient who comes to you
at such a time, humbled by disease.[38]

The Nondisease Disease

"Most doctors are unable to recognize wellness," the doctor-heretic Robert Mendelsohn informs us, "because they're not trained in wellness but
in *disease.*" He adds: "Because they have sharper eyes for signs of disease
than for signs of health, and because they have no conception of the relative importance of signs of both in the same person, they're more apt to
pronounce you sick than well. As long as the doctor is in control, he can
define or manipulate the limits of health and disease any way he chooses,
narrowly or broadly—depending on *his* intentions and interests. In this
way, he can manipulate the amount of disease."[39]

In other words, doctors see only what they are prepared to look for.
They are prepared to look for biomedical disease. They are prepared to
look long and hard for something, *anything,* and then are more than prepared to move against it. "Like other important actors on the American
scene, the doctor is trained and expected to be an activist, to engage in
active intervention rather than passive observation," writes Louise Lander.[40] And what we get is Rambo, M.D.

The problem with this "activism" is that while society has granted,
or physicians have cannily usurped, the power to define what in our culture is considered a disease, they may not, as Eliot Friedson points out,
have the capacity to deal with those diseases effectively.[41] For one thing,
physicians are not trained to look for, appreciate, or treat many conditions
that are basically socioeconomic and political in nature. For another thing,
a doctor's ostensibly limited time and other personal and professional considerations may lead to a course of treatment that is as much or more
expedient for the doctor than for the patient. Finally, some of those diseases are simply statistical anomalies, deviations from the so-called norm
(and go and try to find somebody who fits all categories of "norm"). They
are not necessarily serious or even worth contemplating, but may occasion
medication and other therapy that in and of themselves may cause a worse
or true illness. Instead of "First, do no harm," the dictum is rather "First,
find something, then do something, but not always necessarily in that
order." And, as Paul Starr quite accurately indicates, "By shaping the
patients' understanding of their own experience, physicians create the conditions under which their advice seems appropriate."[42]

To the reasons doctors may diagnose and treat the nondisease disease—contempt, greed, arrogance, poor or incomplete knowledge, bad doctoring, and unwillingness to appear uncertain, among others—add the old stumbling block: communication. A 1984 George Washington University study showed that doctors firmly believe that patients want to be handed a prescription at the end of an office visit, when in fact 72 percent of the 1,215 adults in the survey said they would rather take a viable alternative home remedy than drugs.[43] The researchers concluded that "patients informed about the risks and benefits of drug and nondrug therapies will prefer the latter if that option is offered." Unfortunately, communication between doctor and patient is often poor to nonexistent, and the home remedy/nondrug option is not even offered. Furthermore, communication or lack of it may be the reason so many women are started down the road to treatment and abuse vis-à-vis their nondisease diseases. "Why do doctors prescribe more mood-altering drugs for women than men?" asks Corea. "One explanation: The doctor misinterprets his female patient's symptoms as imaginary because she speaks in a cultural language that he does not understand."[44] And by treating something that is not there or that he does not quite fathom, or by not treating something that is there because he thinks it is some hysterical hallucination, the doctor endangers the health, if not the life, of his women patients.

Add another reason to the treatment of nondisease disease: physician boredom. Under the reign of specialization and technology and the resultant loss of patient contact, many doctors are getting bored stiff.[45] The bored physician "finds himself droning through the same routines day in and day out" and ends up "masking this essential boredom with feverish activity. . . ."[46] This boredom and its concomitant feverish activity can lead to mistakes of both omission and commission or, at the very least, practice by rote, including perfunctory physical examinations and casual prescribing of medication.

Of course, it wouldn't be fair to put *all* the blame on the individual physician for prescribing for and treating the invisible malady. Doctors are themselves victims of their own profession's publicity and lobbying machines. When the news media tout the latest experimental procedure or the newest wonder drug or the most promising cure for cancer, doctors are inundated by demanding patients with unrealistic expectations. "Medicine has fostered a profoundly dependent public which searches for cures that do not exist," says Carlson.[47] Patients have been conditioned by the medical profession and its media machine to expect that little pill, that invasive technique, and they won't leave, or will go home angry, or won't come back if they aren't prescribed the drug or provided the therapy, however unnecessary.

"Since the advent of antibiotics," states Robert J. Weiss, M.D., "most patients want a 'miracle drug,' so advertised by the media and reinforced by statements of the profession when seeking public funds for research. The misuse of antibiotics is as much a result of consumer pressure as it is a lack of knowledge on the part of the physician. . . . But it is also the fault of the physician who is unable to deal with 'unrealistic' patient demands because to do so would threaten his public and private image of omnipotence. . . . Selected and trained as scientists, and knowing little about the psychosocial needs of patients or appropriate interventions to meet these needs, they have often inappropriately applied their technologies.''[48]

Patients are often their own worst enemies, demanding drugs when none is indicated, lashing out at their physicians for being cautious and doing nothing, which they have been conditioned, by their physician's previous behavior, to equate with uncertainty or ignorance. Still, "Some doctors blame the patients for demanding treatment for conditions that will take care of themselves," says Robert Mendelsohn. "I don't accept this excuse. Patients demand a lot of things, such as more considerate care, more natural healing techniques, and discussion of alternatives—and doctors rarely give in on these issues.''[49]

Weiss sums it up best: "It seems to me that large numbers of physicians who know better but succumb to a patient's demand for a shot of penicillin to treat a cold must be willing to face the responsibility of educating the patient, to explain why this treatment is dangerous. The physician has to be prepared to lose the patient who is dissatisfied with his explanation. Frequently, however, the physician is not willing to accept this responsibility.''[50]

Faith

In medicine, faith is a word you hear a lot, but it is a concept seldom seen in action—and it is here that the doctor-patient relationship and the biomedical model come under the greatest stress and ultimately fail. Many physicians fumble the faith ball in two important ways: They don't know what it means, and they won't permit themselves to believe how important it is in their work.

When physicians think of faith they think of the blind variety. They believe that, ideally, the patient should readily give in to feelings of reverence and submission that allegedly are due a medical power figure. They want, they have been taught to expect, that patients will gladly remove their minds, check them in the nearest cloakroom, disempower themselves, and unthinkingly, unblinkingly, follow the doctor's every order—or else. It is nothing less than a priesthood-populace relationship at work

here. "America has no official religion," state the WNET-TV doc-
umentarians of the *Currents* series, "but if it did, it might be medicine."[51]
(As H. Jack Geiger of the City University of New York notes, there is an
enormous difference between reverence and trust: "Reverence is a one-
way street, trust is a two-way street. And there's a big difference between
trust and accountability."[52])

By faith, we do not mean the selfless belief in a deity (although that
certainly has its place in the medical scheme of things), but rather an
abiding trust, informed by intelligence, that helps one to activate self-
motivated growth, achievement, and a contented equilibrium. As Lander
sees it:

> "Healing," as the character of a relationship, implies trust flow-
> ing from the sick person to the healer, altruistic concern flowing
> from the healer to the sick person. Trust need not inevitably
> involve mystification or awe, just as altruistic concern need not
> inevitably involve authoritarian paternalism. Both together set
> in motion a process in which the sick person, viewing the healer
> with an attitude of expectant faith, grants the healer the oppor-
> tunity to mobilize and bolster the recuperative powers inherent
> in the sick person himself, the healer giving the sick person em-
> pathy and thereby strength, and drawing off the anxieties,
> doubts, and fears that inhibit self-healing. (The process has ele-
> ments of the nonrational, in the sense that it draws on uncon-
> scious forces; on the other hand, it is not irrational, meaning
> against reason, when it does not contradict the sick person's best
> interest but operates to further it.)[53]

The body, according to most physicians, is their "turf." They think
the mind has little or nothing to do with the body and is the province of
what is seen by many physicians as the voodoo branch of modern medicine: psychiatry. To them, the mind and the body are separate. That way
of thinking is where the physicians fail to understand the place of faith in
the healing process, and its central importance in the doctor-patient relationship.

Jacob Needleman believes that "the part of the human psyche that
is most centrally involved in the cure of illness, namely the attention or
will, is not understood in the contemporary era."[54] He continues: "Now-
adays, the only patients who discover will-power in themselves are those
who, through mere chance or through their own exceptional character
development, see with objective horror both their own situation and the
total helplessness of their doctors, and, having no taste whatever for self-
deception, find that there is no place to go but 'up'—that is, inside them-

selves, where they chance to find the existence of a truly higher psycho-physical energy that carries them through either what is called a 'miraculous' cure or an honorable death.''[55]

Only when a physician is willing and able to work with a patient—to communicate well, to be truthful, to banish contempt—in order to mobilize that patient's attention and will, only then is that doctor complete, only then is that doctor doing the best for his patient. "To write prescriptions is easy," Kafka wrote, "but to come to an understanding with people is hard."

It has been said that up until this century, the history of medical treatment can be seen as the history of the placebo effect, a placebo being a pill or an injection or a procedure that has no inherent property that could cause it to improve a medical condition, and yet it may. Why and how? Leon Eisenberg in his 1983 William S. Paley Lecture at the Cornell University Medical School suggests it has to do with the doctor-patient relationship.[56] In fact, since some physicians ridicule the psychosocial aspects of the therapeutic encounter—the placebo being one tool that works with those aspects—Eisenberg suggests replacing the term "placebo response" with "the response to care," or "the healing response," or even "the response to the doctor." By doing so, he acknowledges the key to the placebo: It is not the injection that works, but a relationship of trust with the injector. Or, as Carlson puts it, "The symbols of healing, unadorned with any proven technology, can cure."[57]

Study after study shows that placebos work. Howard Brody, M.D., in *Placebos and the Philosophy of Medicine,* reports findings showing that conditions as serious as angina pectoris and hypertension can be relieved by a placebo response; blood-sugar levels can be made to drop and malignant lymphosarcoma tumors can be made to shrink.[58] The good doctor—the placebo embodied—can rally those emotions to work for, not against, his patient-partner in care. Adds Brody: "It seems reasonable to assume that physicians can unknowingly communicate expectations and attitudes to patients, altering the patients' therapeutic outcomes as a result."[59]

(It is interesting to note that this "response to the doctor" can be so strong that it can work against the patient, too. In a classic study by Bloom and Monterossa, 71 people who had normal blood pressure were mistakenly told that they were hypertensive. They were given no blood pressure medication and were not put under medical care; yet, when compared with people who had normal blood pressure and were told that they had normal blood pressure, the ones who thought they had high blood pressure experienced more symptoms of depression and a worsening of their health in general. This condition—or rather, "conditioning"—has been confirmed by other researchers as well. In other words, the simple act of a physician labeling a person as ill can make it so . . . and ruin a life.[60]

"Given the power of healing responses," says Eisenberg, "their physiological as well as psychological properties, their universality and their antiquity in medical care, it is perverse that 'placebo' has almost become an epithet implying charlatanism rather than a descriptor of a fundamental characteristic of medical practice."[61] To which Brody adds: "The growing body of research on the workings of the importance of the placebo effect demonstrates that the practitioner who holds interpersonal and humanistic skills in disdain is *therefore* an unscientific practitioner."[62]

And as Needleman concludes: "When I say that doctors now have much technique but very little intrinsic skill, I mean that the organic, intuitive intelligence is dying in them while the acquired automatisms of merely mental knowing are spreading like a cancer."[63]

What we are talking about here is not the magic of shamanism, or evangelical faith healing, although it is a kind of healing by faith. We are saying here that the subjective as well as the scientific-rational is important in the care of patients. A good doctor cannot permit himself to lose sight of the forest of the former for the trees of the latter. It is a tightrope walk for the medical practitioner: He cannot overvalue himself and thus err on the side of superciliousness and contempt, but neither can he undervalue himself and the power for good his relationship with his patient can have.

Toward a Better Relationship

There are no tricks, nor are there any shortcuts involved in improving, stabilizing, and indeed salvaging the doctor-patient relationship. A failure in this relationship increases the likelihood of deadly medical mistakes, and of situations in which there are, ultimately and sadly, only victims.

To have an interrelationship based on trust, patients must take responsibility for their own health care. They also need to take fairly large doses of reality and retooled expectations about what medical science and its licensed practitioners can do. Physicians, for their part, must recognize and accept their limitations vis-à-vis the biomedical model on the one hand and deny their limitations vis-à-vis the placebo power of humanism and caring on the other. Physicians must reevaluate their place and power in the healing process, and they must share their uncertainty with their patients; the doctor, along with the patient, must work to break down "what psychiatrists call an 'irrational' or 'narcissistic' alliance, in which the patient approaches the physician as a child to parent rather than as adult to adult."[64] Physician and patient must "deepen their understanding while building a supportive and trusting relationship—a relationship based not on unrealistic certainty but on honesty in facing the uncertainty inherent in clinical practice.''[65] That physicians could fill pages and pages of the *New England Journal of Medicine* in 1985 debating whether it is seemly, convenient, or safe for a doctor to attend the funeral of a patient is evidence that physicians have a long way to go.

"The question," writes Norman Cousins, "is not now—anymore than it has ever been—whether physicians should attach less importance to their scientific training than to their relationships with patients, but rather whether enough importance is being attached to everything that is involved in effective patient care.''[66]

Or, as David Hilfiker says to his fellow physicians: "If we are to begin to regain our balance, we must recognize that inherent in the work of doctoring is the concept of servanthood.''[67]

III

SUMMATION AND CLOSING ARGUMENTS

13

PRESCRIPTION FOR CHANGE

"The Chinese character for 'crisis' is made up of two different characters, one signifying 'danger' and the other 'opportunity'."
—Jacob Needleman

In this book, we have presented evidence—overwhelming, undeniable, frightening, and depressing evidence—indicting many areas and levels of medical care in the United States today. We have tried hard to free the facts from any taint of bias or polemic. Instead we have let experts provide the "testimony" in their own words and paint the bleak picture of a landscape strewn with spent actions and intentions—good, bad, amoral, or indifferent—and ravaged figures of victims.

Now it is time for *our* words, the words of the consumer and consumer advocate, and some solutions to the problem. Because, terrible though the medical mistake situation is today, there are paths to improvement and, in some cases, potential elimination of this national scandal. Certainly the evidence itself suggests some obvious and immediate remedial actions:

• Increased and strictly mandated treatment and discipline of impaired physicians and medical care workers.
• Tougher Food and Drug Administration regulations and oversight of present and emergent medical technology.
• Stricter cleanliness rules and more effective surveillance teams in the fight against nosocomial infections.
• The institution of unit-dose pharmaceutical distribution in all hospitals.
• The undertaking of well-designed and legitimate, academically conducted studies to determine the safety or hazards of reusing of disposable medical equipment.
• Periodic testing, relicensing, and recertification of physicians and other medical care workers.

• The creation of medical "teams" in which the physician is not the head or the sole arbiter, but an equal member in a diagnostic/therapeutic group that includes continuous involvement by and input from nurses, pharmacists, and, of course, the patient.

• The development of governing mechanisms (overseen or operated by government) to replace the failed machineries of medical autonomy. Government must ensure that strong and universal performance standards are developed and applied.

• The redistribution of medical expenditures to include programs of self-care and applied research into the methods of alternative care. Scientific inclinations can no longer be myopic, particularly when notions being considered are based on a form of medicine outside the realm of allopathic. Medical researchers cannot close out that which is not within their sphere of practice or experience. In a truly scientific approach all facts must be open for honest review.

• The creation of medical libraries with access by the public, and with holdings not limited to one school of thought.

• The forcing of public disclosure of doctors' relationships—economic and otherwise—with pharmaceutical and medical equipment companies, hospitals, and clinics. In addition, the development of ethical standards that would ensure no conflict of interest.

• Self-examination by the press to improve its job in identifying and covering stories of medical import. It is critical that those who work for print and electronic media keep a reportorial distance between themselves and the subjects and topics they cover, and that they retain an objective view of the subject and the evidence.

All of these are vital, and yet they are merely surface-level cures— band-aids, if you will, applied to a systemic cancer. Like the medical system they hope to repair, these actions, while important, merely relieve some symptoms without burrowing into and eliminating the underlying, pervasive disease.

What needs to be examined and put into motion to save medical care from itself, and to protect and indeed empower medical consumers, are far deeper and more sweeping systemic reforms—reforms that are humane, that make sense, that bring about real change, and that are long overdue.

Disclosure

Medical doctors and their allied colleagues have systematically denied their clients the information necessary to make informed choices about the course and the nature of their medical care. Further, consumers are regularly denied access to their own medical records, information about the potential side effects of drugs they are taking, and the truth about their own condition.

Rarely do medical practitioners provide evidence about their qualifications to make a particular diagnosis or to perform a certain procedure. Risks of procedures, tests, and treatments are rarely discussed or presented. In fact, one of the most common reasons cited by malpractice insurance underwriters for consumer action brought against a doctor was failure of the doctor to divulge the potential risks and outcomes of the treatment.

Not too many years ago, mostly as a result of the Watergate scandal, the government was "sunshined"; that is, closed meetings, secret hearings, and suppressed documents were made available for public inspection. The general theory behind this full and open disclosure was simple. If matters involving citizens' rights were being discussed or considered, those among the "nonofficial" population who wanted to be active in that discussion were entitled to have access. Furthermore, since citizens were, through their taxes, paying for those meetings, hearings, documents, and the people who conducted or framed them, it was only natural that citizens should expect full disclosure from those on the payroll. With the exception of matters dealing with national security or the jeopardizing of American lives, this doctrine of full disclosure has become the rule in government.

Now it needs to become the rule in the universe of medicine as well.

The most important and significant overall reform necessary in the battle against medical mistakes is full disclosure of critical, quality-related data. These data must be disclosed by practitioners and facilities. Hospitals do not, for example, release infection rates, mortality rates by given procedure, or names of practitioners who have lost privileges or been suspended. Further, they do not divulge publicly the rate of medication error, the rate of adverse medication reaction, or descriptions of clinical trials and clinical experiments proposed or conducted in the institution, including information about any institutional review board determinations made regarding the trials.

While these items may seem technical, the reality is that they and many others provide the bases upon which decisions about care must be made. Individuals can only make informed decisions about the treatments and providers of care with information that addresses quality and competence. Who are we protecting when we keep the name of a doctor in a substance abuse program secret while allowing that individual to continue practicing? Who are we protecting when very few states routinely review practitioner's licenses after they have been found guilty or admitted guilt in a malpractice case? What calling from on high does a medical practitioner have that allows him or her never to be reexamined for competence at any time after receiving an initial license?

Disclosure of health data must be all-encompassing. It cannot be limited to information the medical fraternity decides is of use. It must be all the data and it must be reported in understandable terms. We have granted the medical profession the power to control every facet of medicine without building in safeguards to protect the public it purports to serve. Watergate's implications pale in comparison to the medical mistakes scandal.

Legislating a Cure

Facilities and practitioners are licensed, regulated, and monitored by each state. Although the federal government is involved when the facility or practitioner uses Medicare, Medicaid, military, Hill-Burton, or Veterans Administration funding, medical practice is controlled at the state government level.

To remedy the failure of hospitals to disclose needed quality-related data, the People's Medical Society proposes the following piece of model legislation. We recommend that it, or an enhanced version, be enacted in each state. This model legislation was developed by Lori B. Andrews, J.D., an attorney with the American Bar Foundation and vice-chairperson of the board of directors of the People's Medical Society.

MODEL HOSPITAL DISCLOSURE ACT

PREAMBLE

In order to help lower medical costs, enhance health care quality, and aid informed individual choices regarding health care services, certain information should be provided to the public and to patients.

SECTION I:

All hospitals or health care institutions must provide an annual report, available to the public, which includes the following information:

a) Incidence and outcome of surgical and other diagnostic measures and treatments, including, but not limited to:

  i) Cesarean sections
  ii) Lumbar operations
  iii) Prostate operations
  iv) Hysterectomies
    (Note: In final legislation, others may be added.)

b) Percentage of pathology reports that indicate normal tissue was removed in surgery;

c) Nosocomial infection rate;

d) Number and types of accidents involving staff, patients, and guests;

e) Number and types of workers' compensation claims;

f) Number and types of malpractice claims filed, decided, or settled against the institution in the past year listing the names of physicians or hospital staff named in the suit;

g) Descriptions of the clinical trials and clinical experiments proposed or conducted in the institution during the past year, including information about any Institutional Review Board determinations made regarding the trials and experiments;

h) Morbidity and mortality statistics;

i) A list of tests done routinely on admissions, such as chest X-rays, blood tests, and so forth;

j) A list of in-house training programs and continuing education programs sponsored by the institution for its employees; and

k) A list of names and addresses of the members of the Board of Trustees, the chief administrator of the hospital, and the chief medical officer of the hospital.

SECTION 2:

All health care institutions must have available to the public and to patients before admission a compilation of all forms used in the hospital and those forms shall be updated annually. This should include specific forms developed regarding all the procedures listed in section A.1 which describe the nature of the procedure, its risks and benefits, its success rate generally and in the institution, cost range, number and types of hospital personnel likely to be involved, the type of diagnostic procedures and monitoring procedures used in conjunction with the procedure, a summary of the literature justifying and opposing such proce-

dures, a list of specific references in the literature on the procedure, and whether such materials are available in the hospital
library.

SECTION 3:

All patients upon admission should be given disclosure forms for
all procedures planned to be undertaken on them and potentially
likely to be undertaken on them (e.g., all obstetrical patients
should receive the cesarean section form).

SECTION 4:

All health care institutions must have available to the public a
directory with the education, experience, qualifications, institutional or professional affiliations, and publications of each member of its medical staff.

SECTION 5:

All reports prepared by the health care institutions for filing with
the state should be open to the public. If the reports contain
patient names or other identifying information, that information
should be deleted.

PERSONAL PROCEDURE DISCLOSURE

SECTION 1:

Health care practitioners or institutions shall not proceed with a
drug therapy, or a diagnostic, palliative, treatment, or other
health care procedure before disclosing the nature of the procedure, its risks and benefits, its success rate generally and in the
institution, cost range, number and type of hospital personnel
likely to be involved, the type of equipment likely to be involved,
the type of diagnostic procedures and monitoring procedures used
in conjunction with the procedure, a summary of the literature
justifying and opposing such procedures, a list of specific references in the literature on the procedure, and whether such materials are available in the hospital library.

    This information shall be disclosed at the time an assess-
ment is made that the patient needs the test or treatment in order
to allow sufficient time for a patient to make a decision about
whether to undertake the test or treatment.

    If multiple conditions are being tested (or could be tested)
by a single test, the practitioner shall disclose all such conditions.

SECTION 2:

The patient shall be entitled to a copy of all laboratory reports, including all blood test results and pathology reports, and the facility shall make available to the patient a copy of his or her records.

PRACTITIONER DISCLOSURE

Any practitioner in a health care facility or outside of a health care facility should have available to all patients and the public an annual report with his or her education, experience, qualifications, board certification, institutional or professional affiliations, publications, license information, and a list of states in which he or she is licensed. This report should also include references to any disciplinary actions taken against the practitioner by any health care facilities, state medical organizations, agencies, or any limitations on licensing; any malpractice actions against him or her and their outcome. He or she should also disclose any conditions that make it hazardous for him or her to engage in any particular type of medical practice.

The report should include a list of the cost range of tests and procedures routinely performed as a part of the practitioner's practice.

The report should disclose any financial connection the practitioner has with any health care facility, pharmacy, testing facility, laboratory, or health care supply company.

LABORATORY DISCLOSURE

All health care laboratories, inside and outside of health care facilities or practitioners' offices, shall provide an annual report available to the public, patients, and practitioners regarding each type of testing they offer and the means by which they perform the test, a listing of personnel and their education and experience, costs of tests, and procedures for logging in samples and avoiding contamination.

The report shall also provide a list of the type of equipment used and a list of any types of tests the lab contracts out and what facilities they contract them out to. The report shall also contain a list of each type of test undertaken in the past year, the number of times it was undertaken, the false negative and false positive rates of tests, the equipment failure rate, laboratory accidents, results of any state inspections, any training or continuing education that personnel participated in, and any quality assurance or proficiency testing programs the laboratory participated in and their results.

DUTY OF DISCLOSURE

SECTION 1:

All health care institutions, practitioners, and laboratories (including radiologists, consultants, and commercial and public health laboratories) shall have a duty of direct disclosure to patients. Patients shall not be denied information held about them by any of the above sources.

SECTION 2:

Physicians shall be required to provide the patient (or ensure the dispenser will provide the patient) the package inserts for any medication prescribed.

SECTION 3:

A practitioner must disclose the known side effect of any or all medications he or she dispenses or prescribes or that the patients are taking that have been dispensed or prescribed by anyone else. A practitioner must disclose the interactive effects of the complete regimen of medications.

SECTION 4:

If a previous treatment, diagnosis, or procedure is found to entail a risk not previously disclosed to a patient, the practitioner and the facility must make all reasonable efforts to inform the patient, or former patient, about those risks.

SECTION 5:

There shall be a duty to disclose to the state ombudsman on the part of any health care practitioner or hospital employee suspecting or having knowledge of negligence with respect to a particular patient; infection in a hospital; or a dangerous condition on the part of a practitioner. The individual disclosing shall not be liable for disclosure made in good faith.

SECTION 6:

> A health care practitioner or facility has a duty to disclose to a patient when a procedure or treatment has been ineffective or negligent (or when a procedure or treatment provided by a previous practitioner or facility is identified as substandard).

DISCLOSURE IN CONNECTION WITH SELF-CARE DIAGNOSTICS, TREATMENT, AND EQUIPMENT

> All health care diagnostic tests, treatments, and equipment available directly to the public must provide a disclosure of contraindications, the failure rate, the side effects, and references to literature supporting and opposing the diagnostic test, treatment, and equipment.

WAIVER AND THE USE OF INFORMATION

> Patients should have the right to refuse information after being told of its availability, to refuse any procedure or treatment, or to refuse attendance by any practitioner or any type of practitioner, or leave the health care facility. In order to best exercise these rights, the patient is entitled to the information described in this act.

COMPLAINTS

> All practitioners and facilities shall provide to patients the names, addresses, and phone numbers of the administrative agencies with which a patient may file a complaint about the care or competence of the practitioner or facility.

FINES AND PUNISHMENT

SECTION 1:

> Violation of this act shall be a misdemeanor punishable by up to six months imprisonment and a fine of up to $15,000.

SECTION 2:

> This statute shall give rise to a private cause of action.

SECTION 3:

> The health care practitioner involved in the inadequate disclosure and, if the inadequate disclosure occurs in a health care institution, the administrator and trustees shall be individually and jointly liable.

SECTION 4:

> If a private cause of action is successful, the minimum awarded
> should be $1,000 and double the health care costs of the stay in
> the health care facility (including professional fees) or, in the case
> of an outpatient procedure, double the costs of the procedure
> and all related professional services. Such damages shall be avail-
> able even if the inadequate disclosure has not caused any phys-
> ical risk to the patient.

DISTRIBUTION OF ACT

> All patients of health care practitioners and facilities shall be
> furnished with a copy of this act.

Practitioners, in addition to adhering to most of the principles provided for in the hospital model legislation, should be required by virtue
of their license to do the following:

1. Facilitate a consumer getting his or her medical and hospital record, and provide the consumer a copy of his or her own test results.
2. Inform the consumer of his or her prognosis, including whether
   the condition is terminal or will cause disability or pain, and explain why the practitioner believes further diagnostic activity or
   treatment is necessary.
3. Discuss diagnostic, treatment, and medication options for the consumer's particular problem (including the option of no treatment)
   and describe in understandable terms the risk of each alternative,
   the chances of success, the possibility of pain, the effect on the
   consumer's functioning, the number of visits each would entail,
   and the cost of each alternative.
4. Describe the practitioner's qualifications to perform the proposed
   diagnostic measures or treatments.
5. Inform the consumer of organizations, support groups, and medical and lay publications that can assist him or her in understanding, monitoring, and treating the consumer's problem.
6. Not proceed with treatment until the consumer is satisfied that he
   or she understands the benefits and risks of each alternative and
   has given his or her agreement on a particular course of action.

These last six points are derived from a ten-point Code of Practice developed by the People's Medical Society in 1983, reproduced on page 221.
    When the Code of Practice was first published it became a matter of
some controversy among practitioners. Generally, the criticism was aimed
not at the substance of the provisions themselves, but at the idea that a

CODE
—of—
PRACTICE

As a PMS Code of Practice practitioner, I will assist you in finding information resources, support groups and health care providers to help you maintain and improve your health. When you seek my care for specific problems, I will abide by the following Code of Practice:

Office Procedures

1. I will post or provide a printed schedule of my fees for office visits, procedures, testing and surgery, and provide itemized bills.

2. I will provide certain hours each week when I will be available for non-emergency telephone consultation.

3. I will schedule appointments to allow the necessary time to see you with minimal waiting. I will promptly report test results to you and return phone calls.

4. I will allow and encourage you to bring a friend or relative into the examining room with you.

5. I will facilitate your getting your medical and hospital records, and will provide you with copies of your test results.

Choice in Diagnosis and Treatment

6. I will let you know your prognosis, including whether your condition is terminal or will cause disability or pain, and will explain why I believe further diagnostic activity or treatment is necessary.

7. I will discuss diagnostic, treatment and medication options for your particular problem with you (including the option of no treatment) and describe in understandable terms the risk of each alternative, the chances of success, the possibility of pain, the effect on your functioning, the number of visits each would entail, and the cost of each alternative.

8. I will describe my qualifications to perform the proposed diagnostic measures or treatments.

9. I will let you know of organizations, support groups, and medical and lay publications that can assist you in understanding, monitoring and treating your problem.

10. I will not proceed until you are satisfied that you understand the benefits and risks of each alternative and I have your agreement on a particular course of action.

≡People's Medical Society.

consumer organization had developed them. Those in the medical world who criticized the code felt that consumers had invaded their turf and were telling them how to practice medicine.

Of course, none of the points made in the code tells any practitioner how to practice medicine. Rather, the points discuss how to practice good human relations and deal on an ethical business basis with customers. Many doctors were offended by our suggestion that practitioners disclose their qualifications to perform a proposed diagnostic measure or treatment. Others were upset that their patients should be told about diagnostic and treatment options. They believed that this might undermine the faith and trust consumers must have in their care provider.

One physician, Peter Gott, M.D., a well-known syndicated columnist, devoted an entire chapter to the People's Medical Society Code of Practice in his book, *No House Calls* (New York: Poseidon Press, 1986). In the chapter, Gott went through each provision of the code from his perspective as a practicing physician. While disagreeing with some of the fine points, he generally agreed with what is called for in the code. He also echoed a note of sadness that such a statement is necessary. He concludes the chapter this way:

> I suppose I am saddened by this Code of Practice because of its truths. It is saying: "Doctor, treat patients like people; be understanding, compassionate, considerate, fair, forthright, honest in your self-evaluation, and communicative." Many physicians embody these principles. They go about their active professional lives with skill and confidence, buoyed up by grateful patients; they experience the same fears, disappointments, and insecurities that plague any sane adult. They don't ruminate about PMS [the People's Medical Society] and Codes of Practice because there was a time, not so long ago, when these attributes were taken for granted by every physician who entered the healing profession. What we're talking about here is an issue of manners and decency, two qualities that have become, it seems, in short supply on doctors' shelves. Medical courtesy is not about to be supplanted by the glories of high-tech science. It's humbling to be reminded that the public notices how we behave and sometimes folks out there don't like what they see.

Gott may have a somewhat romantic notion of the past, but his point is clear: It is vital that practitioners be accountable to those they serve. The code was written as a pledge to the consumer by the practitioner. The idea was disclosure, the heart of good consumerism. When practitioners and facilities are forced to disclose data and information, the veil of professional secrecy will begin to rise. When the consumer has information upon which to base his or her own medical decisions, professional accountability will begin to occur. Thus, a consumer-provider relationship can emerge that is one of informed trust, not blind faith.

As a society we examine and publicly disclose almost everything that touches us. We probe and painfully relate the circumstances and causes of airplane crashes. We establish boards of inquiry into alleged police brutality or questionable military incursions. We even go so far as to publish the names and addresses of people who take out a license to marry and later publish their names and addresses when they elect to divorce.

We do this because ours is a nation that believes that the truth strengthens. The more we know about the things that affect us, the better things will be.

Truth is the sine qua non to any solution to the medical mistakes crisis. We, as individuals and as a society, must know the truth. Without it we cannot change that which must be changed. Without public knowledge of where the problems are, who causes them, and when they occur, the entire infrastructure of medicine becomes unstable.

Full disclosure of medical data is the primary means to establishing a truly credible medical system.

Disciplinary Action

Very little in the way of disciplinary action has been taken against practitioners who have harmed the people they serve. The current system of medical discipline has been one established by the medical profession, applied by the medical profession, and evaluated by the medical profession. It is clear that this system has failed to protect the unsuspecting public adequately.

Therefore, the People's Medical Society proposes that the following be adopted in whole or in part by each state as an integral portion of its Medical Practice Act. This proposal would become a chapter in each state law. We urge all states to consider these points. We believe they are comprehensive, fair, and protective of both consumers and good practitioners in the system.

GROUNDS FOR DISCIPLINARY ACTION

(1) The following acts shall constitute grounds for which the disciplinary actions may be taken:

(a) Attempting to obtain, obtaining, or renewing a license to practice medicine by bribery, by fraudulent misrepresentations, or through an error of the department of the board.

(b) Having a license to practice medicine revoked, suspended, or otherwise acted against, including the denial of licensure, by the licensing authority of another state, territory, or country.

(c) Being convicted or found guilty, regardless of adjudication of crime in any jurisdiction which directly relates to the practice of medicine or to the ability to practice medicine or of any felony. This includes any misdemeanor involving drugs or any misdemeanor involving potential harm to persons. Any plea of nolo contendere shall be considered a conviction for the purpose of this chapter.

(d) False, deceptive, or misleading statements to patients, or related to the practice or in advertising.

(e) Deceiving the patient into thinking an unlicensed person is a licensed health care purveyor.

(f) Not meeting the appropriate level of care or skill, or creating an unwarranted risk to the patient.

(g) Performing an unnecessary hysterectomy or cesarean section.

(h) Abandonment of a patient.

(i) Breach of patient confidentiality.

(j) Providing any information about a patient or a patient's condition without the advance written consent of the patient. A blanket consent is valid. Each consent must describe the information to be disclosed and identify the person to whom it will be disclosed.

(k) Failure to post prices.

(l) Failure to abide by the Code of Practice. (See People's Medical Society Code of Practice.)

(m) Violating a patient's rights or failure to comply with the patients' rights statute or the patients' rights statement of the health care facility in which a service is rendered.

(n) Failure to allow the patient to admit a friend or relative into the examining or treatment room.

(o) Advertising, practicing, or attempting to practice under a name other than one's own.

(p) Failure to report to the department any person who the licensee knows is in violation of this chapter or of the rules of the department or the board. When a disciplinary action is taken against a practitioner, based on incompetence or a dangerous condition, all health care practitioners who had reason to know of the practitioner's incompetence or dangerous condition and failed to report may be subject to disciplinary action.

(q) Using an unlicensed person to practice medicine on a patient without disclosing to the patient that the individual is unlicensed and without getting the patient's permission in writing in an acceptable informed consent document. If a licensed practitioner employs an unlicensed person to practice medicine, the licensed practitioner is responsible for ensuring adequate supervision of the unlicensed practitioner.

(r) Failure to perform any valid statutory or legal obligation placed upon a licensed physician.

(s) Making or filing a report which the licensee knows to be false, intentionally or negligently failing to file a report or record required by state or federal law, willfully impeding or obstructing such filing, or inducing another person to do so. Such reports or records shall include only those which are signed in the capacity as a licensed physician.

(t) Paying or receiving any commission, bonus, kickback, or rebate, or engaging in any split-fee arrangement in any form whatsoever with a physician, organization, agency, or person, either directly or indirectly, for patients referred to providers of health care goods and services, including, but not limited to, hospitals, nursing homes, clinical laboratories, ambulatory surgical centers, or pharmacies. The provisions of this paragraph shall not be construed to prevent a physician from receiving a fee for professional consultation services.

(u) Exercising influence within a patient-physician relationship for purposes of engaging a patient in sexual activity. A patient shall be presumed to be incapable of giving free, full, and informed consent to sexual activity with his or her physician.

(v) Making deceptive, untrue, or fraudulent representations in the practice of medicine or employing a trick to scheme in the practice of medicine. This provision does not apply to the use of placebos in circumstances where their value is clearly proven. The burden of proof is on the practitioner to prove the value of the placebo.

(w) Soliciting patients, whether personally or through an agent, through the use of fraud, intimidation, undue influence, or a form of overreaching or vexatious conduct. A solicitation is any communication which directly or implicitly requests an immediate oral response from the recipient.

(x) Failure to keep written medical records justifying the diagnosis and course of treatment of the patient, including, but not limited to, patient histories, examination results, and test results, or failure to provide same to patient upon request of the patient.

(y) Exercising influence on the patient or client in such a manner as to exploit the patient or client for financial gain of the licensee or of a third party which shall include, but not be limited to, the promoting or selling of services, goods, appliances, or drugs and the promoting or advertising on any prescription form of a community pharmacy unless the form shall also state "This prescription may be filled at any pharmacy of your choice."

(z) Performing professional services which have not been duly authorized.

(aa) Prescribing, dispensing, administering, mixing, or otherwise preparing legend drug, including any controlled substance, other than in the course of the physician's professional practice. For the purposes of this paragraph, it shall be legally presumed that prescribing, dispensing, administering, mixing, or otherwise preparing legend drugs, including all controlled substances, inappropriately or in excessive or inappropriate quantities, is not in the best interest of the patient and is not in the course of the physician's professional practice, without regard to his intent.

(bb) Prescribing, dispensing, or administering any narcotic drug by the physician to himself, except one prescribed, dispensed, or administered to the physician by another practitioner authorized to prescribe, dispense, or administer medicinal drugs, in which case the second practitioner would have a duty to report to the disciplinary agency the name of the drug and the name of the practitioner he administered to.

(cc) Being unable to practice medicine with reasonable skill and safety to patients by reason of illness or use of alcohol, drugs, narcotics, chemicals, or any other type of material or as a result of any mental or physical condition. In enforcing this paragraph, the department shall have, upon probable cause, authority to compel a physician to submit to a mental or physical examination by physicians designated by the department. Failure of a physician to submit to such examination when so directed shall constitute an admission of the allegations against him or her, unless the failure was due to circumstances beyond his or her control, consequent upon which a default and final order may be entered without the taking of testimony or presentation of evidence. A physician affected under this paragraph shall at reasonable intervals be afforded an opportunity to demonstrate that he or she can resume the competent practice of medicine with reasonable skill and safety to patients.

(dd) Malpractice or the failure to practice medicine with that level of care, skill, and treatment which is recognized by a reasonable physician as being acceptable under similar conditions and circumstances.

(ee) Performing any procedure or prescribing any therapy without first making an adequate disclosure (as provided in the Disclosure Act) or without first obtaining full, informed, and written consent.

(ff) Failure to maintain an annual report or provide it to an individual on request.

(gg) Practicing or offering to practice beyond the scope permitted by law or accepting and performing professional responsibilities which the licensee knows or has reason to know that he or she is not competent to perform.

(hh) Delegating professional responsibilities to a person when the licensee delegating such responsibilities knows or has reason to know that such a person is not qualified by training, experience, or licensure to perform them.

(ii) Violating any provisions of this chapter, a rule of the board or department, or a lawful order of the board or department previously entered in a disciplinary hearing or failing to comply with a lawfully issued subpoena of the department.

(jj) Conspiring with another licensee or with any other person to commit an act, or committing an act, which would tend to coerce, intimidate, or preclude another licensee from lawfully advertising his or her services.

(kk) Performing, or aiding or abetting in the performing of, an unnecessary procedure of any kind.

(ll) Presigning blank prescription forms.

(2) The disciplinary agency must institute an investigation of any physician:

(a) Whose license is revoked, suspended, or otherwise acted against, including licensure denial, by the licensing authority of another state, territory, or country.

(b) Where any malpractice insurance claim or any judgment against him or her has been rendered.

(c) If a practitioner fails to report (a) or (b) within ten days of its occurrence, there will be an immediate revocation of the practitioner's license.

(3) When the board finds any person guilty of any of the grounds set forth in subsection (1), it may enter an order imposing one or more of the following penalties:

(a) Refusal to certify the department an application for licensure.

(b) Revocation or suspension of a license.

(c) Restriction of practice.

(d) Imposition of an administrative fine of at least $1,000 for each count or separate offense.

(e) Issuance of a reprimand.

(f) Placement of the physician on probation for a period of time and subject to such conditions as the board may specify, including, but not limited to, requiring the physician to submit to treatment, to attend continuing education courses, to submit to reexamination, or to work under the supervision of another physician.

(g) For any disciplinary action that is then to include (a) to (f) above, the identity of the practitioner and the action taken shall be reported in professional and public periodicals.

(h) The board shall not reinstate the license of a physician, or cause a license to be issued to a person it has deemed unqualified, until such time as it is satisfied that he or she has complied with all the terms and conditions set forth in the final order and that such person is capable of safely engaging in the practice of medicine. Before reinstatement, the practitioner must be relicensed.

(i) The board shall by rule establish guidelines for the disposition of disciplinary cases involving specific types of violations. Such guidelines may include minimum and maximum fines, periods of supervision or probation, or conditions of probation or reissuance of a license.

Quality

Quality, in medicine, is in the eye of the beholder. To the practitioner, it means accomplishing the task while adhering to the checklist of professionally approved methods. In other words, if all the right steps are taken, the operation could be a success even if the patient dies. To the federal government, quality has to do with the way facilities and services are utilized. It doesn't matter if the operation is successful or if the patient dies, just so long as the stay in the hospital isn't too long and doesn't cost the taxpayers too much. To the consumer, it all boils down to outcome— quality is when what was set out to be accomplished was accomplished.

Certainly utilization is important. But utilization is only a signal that something is either going right or going wrong. Of course, the practice of medicine is an art, but doing the job well while at the same time losing the patient raises serious questions about the meaning of success.

One, then, does not need an advanced degree to know that the consumer viewpoint is the only correct and rational one. Or that correctness and reason are so difficult to argue with that even the AMA's ally, the Joint Commission on Accreditation of Hospitals, could not deny the wisdom of consumers' desires and demands to alter the way it evaluates hospitals. The new JCAH policy is not only to inspect a hospital's facilities and equipment but also to look at its surgical complication and death rates and its nosocomial infection rate, among other measures of medical outcome. Growing pressure from insurers, business, and, most important of all, consumers, has effected this major change, which shifts the purpose of the heretofore quality outcome–blind JCAH accreditation survey from one that asked the question "Can this hospital provide quality care?" to one that asks *"Does* this hospital provide quality care?"

Although we recognize that exact and exacting standards of excellence may not be attainable, we are certain that benchmarks of quality can be developed. Indeed, there have been numerous studies dealing with the issue of medical quality standards. Most have been funded by the federal government and are now gathering dust in some Washington closet. It is time to dust them off.

It is the recommendation of the People's Medical Society that the secretary of Health and Human Services establish a special quality commission to review all past and current studies relating to medical quality standards. This commission should then develop a set of quality standards for the ten most frequently performed medical procedures. Utilizing those standards, peer review organizations should then be charged to review, over the course of five years, those ten procedures. At the end of that five-year period, a major review of the data should be done and conclusions drawn.

The implementation of this recommendation is an essential first step in the development of standards of quality. We have never had an across-the-board quality application, not even one of the most modest standards. Instead, we have been told that there are regional variations in the rates of operations performed and in their successes and outcomes, when indeed there should be no variations by region. There is no excuse for such variations. A citizen should be able to expect the same outcome in Hospital A as in Hospital Z. A client should have at least a reasonable expectation of a service performance. That is what this book is about—to show that many mistakes are made because there are no standards of quality.

Currently, the United States achieves an almost 30 percent mobility rate; that is, about 30 percent of the population moves every year. The amount of cross-state movement of people really throws into question the implications of individual states having individual criteria applied to their medical care. There is no push here for a national medical practice act . . . yet. However, given the mobility of the American people, it is now very important that there be protection for those people in interstate commerce terms, in much the same way that people receive protection from products that cross state lines. People are crossing state lines, and they are subjecting themselves to substantial risks in the variation of medical care from state to state. If a person falls seriously ill in Mississippi, he should not run a different risk than if he had fallen ill in Massachusetts. The People's Medical Society believes that there should be a federal responsibility for minimum protection of people, somehow utilizing the interstate commerce concept.

Furthermore, it is time to change the way quality is determined from an essentially self-serving opinion of those in the medical profession to one based on fact and acceptable to consumers. The users of health care must ultimately determine what they are willing to accept. Put another, more direct way, consumers must determine the level of medical incompetence they are willing to accept.

A weakness in our current medical monitoring process is the failure to involve consumers. Peer review in medicine is myopic—the only peers involved are those of the practitioner. Too often they are not only peers, but also friends of the party being reviewed.

It is the recommendation of the People's Medical Society that the consumer be involved in the peer review process. Therefore, it is urged that every federally contracted peer review organization have, at a minimum, 50 percent consumer representation on its board of directors.

But that is only the first step. *It is further recommended that at least 50 percent of the members of peer review teams—the groups that actually review medical treatment—be composed of consumers.*

Certainly, this latter recommendation is bound to be controversial, especially because practitioners undoubtedly will argue that an untrained layperson will not know what to look at or how to interpret what he or she sees. But although most consumers will be unable to make a medically educated, fully informed judgment solely from looking at the medical record, they will add a unique and all-important dimension to the review process.

First, by nature, the consumer will be looking at the outcome. Regardless of the mumbo jumbo and technical talk of the professionals around them, the consumer—a concerned citizen, and not just a political appointee or a non-M.D. associate of the physicians—will most assuredly be able to cut through all that to see what happened to the person being served. This will immediately sober professional ego and opinion.

Second, consumer participation will force those professionals on the team to speak and write in language understandable to the public. What good is quality review if it is not understood by the public who pays for it, supposedly benefits from it, and is in dire need of it?

Third, when professionals become aware that consumers are looking at the outcome of their work and will be reporting on it to the public in language the public can understand, the quality of medicine can only improve.

Consumer involvement is so critical to the medical system that it should not and must not be limited to a peer review role. Consumer involvement also needs to be blended into the entire fabric of medicine. For example, the evidence in this book has shown that state medical licensing boards have done little to reprimand or remove incompetent practitioners. It is clear that one of the more important reasons such inaction occurs is because those boards are primarily made up of practitioners, with at most token citizen participants.

Therefore, it is the recommendation of the People's Medical Society that each state's board of medical licensure be composed totally of consumers, with advisory staffs composed of medical professionals.

This is an absolutely essential reform. Medical licensing should be designed to protect the public. Today, however, the nature of medical licensing and the boards overseeing it, in all the states, is to protect the profession.

Once again, we recognize the controversial nature of this recommendation. But the controversy is largely generated by the medical profession. The recommendation assures consumers that the license to practice medicine means something and is citizen-protective.

Functionally, a 100 percent consumer-composed licensing board, with a staff of professionals, would operate much the same way a jury functions in a court of law. The professionals, both staff and those under question, would present either their credentials or their case (depending on the matter at hand) to the board. The board would then review the evidence and make its decision based on that evidence. The professional would be duty-bound to state his or her case clearly, so that it is understandable to consumers and compelling.

The idea of a consumer-oriented licensing board also blends very well with most other state regulatory agencies. In fact, most state regulatory boards are made up entirely of consumers with staff that consists of knowledgeable professionals in fields related to that board's jurisdiction. The boards of education in most states are composed primarily of citizens who are not education professionals. Public utility commissions are similarly composed. The insistence that only medical personnel are qualified to judge the competence of other medical personnel is simply unfounded.

To enhance quality, it is further recommended that:

• Every hospital should institute a direct communications feedback process by which consumers in the hospital can express their concerns with staff, procedures, and care. One way this could be achieved would be to have a meeting once or twice a week on each floor or ward in the facility; participants would be patients, administrators, house staff, nurses from that floor, and other involved and concerned parties. Such a meeting would allow the customers of care to provide direct input into the quality chain.

• All practitioners, HMOs, and other direct providers should institute a quality feedback process by which customers may indicate their concerns in a formal way. This could be done quite easily. It could take a form similar to that of the cards found in motels and hotels requesting satisfaction information. In a medical context, such satisfaction forms could be attached to billing statements.

• Insurance carriers should also institute a quality assessment form that would be sent automatically to each beneficiary with a notice of payment or a bill. The form would ask questions about the beneficiary's (or survivor's) satisfaction with the quality of care at the practitioner and facility level. The insurance carrier would then complete these data and provide them to customers as consumer information in a usable form.

• Similarly, Medicare, the single largest medical payer, must institute a consumer feedback and checkout process in which each beneficiary would be encouraged to provide directly to the Health Care Financing Administration (HCFA) an assessment of his or her care. This could be done through the use of preprinted forms distributed by hospitals and doctors, and sent directly to peer review organizations (PROs). In addition, Medicare should have a financial audit system that allows beneficiaries to dispute payments HCFA makes to providers based on failure to provide services, poor-quality services, or services provided to remedy a medical mistake.

• The Food and Drug Administration must speed up the process of pulling unreliable equipment from use. A citizens' oversight panel should be appointed to monitor this function.

• Operators of any medical equipment should be checked out and certified on all medical equipment they use. Certification on equipment would be part of the personnel record, known to supervisors and administrators and available to consumers upon request.

These recommended reforms are meant to illustrate the numerous changes that need to be made. Quality care must actively involve the perceptions of consumers, the reality of outcomes, and the ever-present vigilance consumers normally have over services provided to them.

Medical Education

It is clear from the evidence that many medical mistakes have their origins in medical education. The isolation, stress, and performance pressure placed upon a young man or woman is comparable to that placed on a political prisoner. It is little wonder, then, that mistakes occur and a denial process develops to cover up these tragedies.

To reduce the occurrence of medical mistakes, the following recommendations are offered:

• Give top priority in medical school admissions to those candidates with previous degrees (advanced) or previous careers. People with an already mature sense of values are less likely to succumb to medical school modeling. Older admittees are in this sense "immunized" against the emergence of cynical attitudes toward consumers/patients.

• Involve consumers in the medical school admissions process and in continuing student progress evaluation. This participation by lay people could also include reviews by patients during the student's residency.

• Reduce the literal and figurative distances between the medical school and the base university. Isolation of the medical school facility in suburbs, for example, creates an environment free of a sense of the broad social context of medicine, thereby creating social distance between medical types and "others."

• Consider the creation of new medical degrees. This would include a bachelor of medicine, a masters of medicine, and a doctor of medicine. Each degree would have a different intent. They would concentrate on the humanities and focus on such areas as history of medicine, medical ethics, and medical organizations, to name just a few subjects. The benefits of such degrees would be twofold: they would allow humanities-influenced academics to enter into discussions of medicine that are impacted upon by nonmedical considerations, i.e., ethics; and they would allow students who wish to be involved in medicine but who are clearly not suited for patient care or research to do so and to make a contribution.

• Require medical students to take classes in clinical epidemiology.

• Invite non-M.D. students to participate in several appropriate classes in the medical school, and have the medical students take regular university classes on the university campus, at least in the first year. This is done, and to good effect, in the United Kingdom.

• Recognize the internal stresses of medical school that exacerbate or even create antisocial behavior and psychological illness. Create a non-M.D., universitywide advisory system to deal with these issues.

• Encourage the development of medical student mutual aid groups that can provide necessary discussions of and help with shared experiences, and help the students gain control over their own circumstances and with their evolving role changes.

• Urge Congress to create a blue ribbon panel to examine the appropriateness of continued funding of education for oversupplied specialties. A surplus or glut of certain specialties can lead to medical mischief and mistakes. It is a social and political mistake as well to perpetuate the problem by educating specialists in overstocked specialty areas and thus maintaining high surplus levels.

There has been as of late a rising concern among medical students, as well as medical consumers, over the long hours such students must be on call during their medical internship and residency. In fact, students who had put in 36-hour days were interviewed on a network television program and made it clear that they consider themselves less than competent practitioners after 12 hours of on-call service. A few states, New York included, have only just limited the number of hours.

The People's Medical Society for many years has advised consumers to ask the medical residents who might be treating them in the hospital how many hours they have been on call. Should those hours seem excessive, we have further advised those consumers to request another, less-overtaxed physician.

Clearly, a reform of this method of education is necessary. *The People's Medical Society recommends that the issue of resident hours be examined carefully by a joint commission of medical students, medical educators, and consumers, and that alterations necessary for the safety of the hospital patient be made immediately. An additional recommendation is that the American Medical Student Association and the Association of American Medical Colleges create a committee or commission a study that would review medical education from the standpoint of consumerism.*

Doing What's Right

Calvin Coolidge said it: "The business of America is business." And medicine is America's business. In fact, it is the biggest single business in America. It accounts for almost 11 percent of the gross national product and is quickly approaching $500 billion per year in expenditures for medical care. In some cities, medical care employment represents the largest block of jobs. Medical professionals with high earnings are often the most regular customers and most monied clients of expensive eateries, country clubs, and boutiques in their communities.

Yet, as consumers, we have not expected of medicine what we have come to expect from any other service/business entity; that is, accountability.

Consumers have not expected information disclosure or uniform standards of quality because we have been lulled into thinking that medicine is "above" such banalities. We have not treated medicine or our encounters with the medical system as a business relationship because those who provide medical care do so in a way that creates illusions of professionalism that lead us to believe it is not a business relationship at all.

The fact is, as currently practiced, medicine is a business and the consumer is a customer. Medical mistakes have occurred and continue to occur because we have been lax customers. Don't believe that medical providers will change because we are right and they are wrong. Don't believe that a presidential commission can be appointed to make doctors, hospitals, and every other provider accountable. Change will come when we as consumers realize our full potential and come to know, as second nature, that those who pay the bills direct the service, demand and receive information—and hold the power.

Until consumer empowerment alters the way medical care is provided in this country—a process that has already begun, as evidenced by the success and influence of groups like the People's Medical Society—there are many ways an individual can protect himself or herself from incompetent practitioners and subpar, dangerous care.

First, ask questions. Question the doctor, question the hospital administrators, question the system. By asking questions, the consumer forces the practitioner to speak. When the practitioner speaks, the consumer should listen and listen carefully. Do the answers make sense? Is he or she using too much technical jargon or too many incomprehensible terms?

Consumers should ask their doctors if their licenses have ever been suspended or if they have ever been reprimanded by a state board of medical licensure. Every consumer should call the board in his own state to see if any complaints have been filed against the practitioner or practitioner-to-be. We use the Better Business Bureau when we are checking up on the integrity of a company we're thinking of dealing with or a workman we're considering hiring. Why not use the medical licensing bodies in a similar fashion when it comes to determining the business record and integrity of a doctor? (The appendix includes the addresses and phone numbers of the medical licensure boards in each state.)

The consumer should ask other practitioners in the community about a doctor he or she might be considering. Nurses and other allied professionals often have informed opinions and observations about doctors. Consumers must be bold in asking about the doctor's competence. It may not be easy to ask questions, but the answers are too important to allow timidity to be a detour or a derailment.

Finally, before a consumer commits himself or herself to a particular doctor, that doctor needs to be examined. The best way to do this is to call up and ask for an appointment interview, or what is known as a "get-acquainted visit." During this visit, the consumer needs to ask questions (and get satisfactory, confidence-inspiring answers) but also must get a feel for the doctor and look for any red-flag danger signs, like shaking hands or the smell of alcohol on the doctor's breath. If anything seems not quite right, question it or get out of the office. Remember, there is a glut of doctors in this country and those numbers are growing every year. One can always find another doctor just as or more competent than the one initially considered.

Friends are often a most valuable asset in defending oneself against incompetent or impaired practitioners. Ask friends about doctors in the community or those under consideration. The consumer should find out about friends' experiences with hospitals and doctors, if those friends, or friends of their friends, have had particular procedures performed or treatments proposed in those hospitals and by those doctors, and if so, how they came out.

The People's Medical Society has always recommended taking a friend or relative into the doctor's office and examining room for any type of treatment or examination. When we formed the People's Medical Society, this was one of the first recommendations we made, and it has proven to be valuable advice to many medical consumers. Not only does this tactic help reassure the possibly ill and thus nervous person, it also provides another set of eyes and ears to see, mention, and remember things in the patient's best interests. A friend who can remember medications the ill person is taking but had forgotten to tell the doctor about could be responsible for avoiding grief on both sides of the doctor's desk. A friend who remembers what the doctor said and can correct any misconceptions the ill person has is a force that can mean the difference between physical improvement and therapeutic failure. A third person in the examining room is also a not-so-subtle reminder to the doctor that he or she had better be on best behavior. Friends acting as witnesses and sentinels are great raisers of medical care quality among private practice physicians, particularly. (And if one does not have a friend who will go along to the doctor, a tape machine set to record the visit and the doctor's diagnosis, prognosis, and medication orders can be nearly as helpful.)

But sometimes, despite asking questions, being wary, having guardian friends along, going to the library to do research on the medications prescribed or the procedures ordered—despite all these home-remedy, first-aid types of safety measures, and no matter how hard one tries—one may still be the victim of a medical mistake caused by an impaired, incompetent, or negligent practitioner, a faulty machine, a medication error, or any of dozens of other practitioner failings and practice pitfalls.

Even though one cannot correct the damage done, one can certainly do something to protect others from having the same thing happen to them. It is essential that if a consumer suspects that he or she has been the victim of a medical mistake due to physician negligence, impairment, or incompetence, he or she must move quickly and boldly to have an investigation launched or action taken against the practitioner, using the medical licensing boards (pitifully impotent though they be), the courts, even the newspapers if need be.

We say it again—and we cannot say it enough—the key to desperately needed medical care reform and the correction of the medical mistakes epidemic is consumerism. What has been proposed in this section, what has been pointed out in infinite detail throughout the entire book, is the absolute necessity for consumers to become empowered and to take charge not only of their own health, but also of the health of the health care system.

The momentum, for the first time in history, is in the consumer's favor. Consumerism in medicine will lead to a partnership between provider and customer. A partnership is what medicine must be about. Medical mistakes too often are the result of the failure of the providers to recognize the dignity and importance of those they serve.

The control of medicine has been in the hands of providers for more than 100 years in this country, and the providers have failed to attain and ensure medical efficacy and consumer safety. We want to retrieve ownership of the health care system. We want to reassert our entitlement to this vital social agency called medical care.

Today's medical care system is like a runaway train. We must get our hand back on the throttle. There is no way that the system itself, without our participation, can self-correct. It can only be corrected through our awareness of the potential for that correction and our powerful economic and social initiative.

We are serving notice that the social charter of medicine is about to be rewritten and reaffirmed as a public responsibility.

APPENDIX:
Where to Seek Redress

If you are unable to reach the agency you desire by using the information listed in the appendix because of a change in telephone number or address, try calling the general state government telephone number at the state capitol. Operators should be able to connect you directly with the appropriate office or provide you with the correct and current telephone and address information.

Dentists

Alabama State Board of Dental Examiners
2308-B Starmount Circle
Huntsville, AL 35801
(205) 533-4638

Alaska State Board of Dental Examiners/Department of Commerce/Division of Occupational Licensing
P.O. Box D
Juneau, AK 99811–0800
(907) 465-2544

Arizona State Board of Dental Examiners
5060 N. 19th Avenue, Room 406
Phoenix, AZ 85015
(602) 255-3696

Arkansas State Board of Dental Examiners
926 Donaghey Building
Little Rock, AR 72202
(501) 371-2085

California State Board of Dental Examiners
1430 Howe Avenue, Suite 85B
Sacramento, CA 95825
(916) 920-7451

Colorado State Board of Dental Examiners
1525 Sherman, Room 128
Denver, CO 80203
(303) 866-5807

Connecticut Department of Health Services/Medical Quality Assurance—Dental
150 Washington Street
Hartford, CT 06106
(203) 566-4619

**Delaware State Board of Dental
Examiners**
  P.O. Box 1401
  O'Neill Building
  Dover, DE 19903
  (302) 736-3029

**District of Columbia Department of
Consumer and Regulatory Affairs**
  614 H Street, N.W., Room 104
  Washington, DC 20001
  (202) 727-7107

**Florida Department of Professional
Regulation**
  130 N. Monroe Street, Suite 225
  Tallahassee, FL 32301
  (904) 487-2395

Georgia Board of Dentistry
  166 Pryor Street, S.W.
  Atlanta, GA 30303
  (404) 656-3925

**Hawaii Regulated Industries
Complaint Office**
  P.O. Box 2399
  Honolulu, HI 96804
  (808) 548-7079

Idaho State Board of Dentistry
  State House Mail
  Boise, ID 83720
  (208) 334-2369

**Illinois State Department of
Registration and Education**
  Attn: Dental Unit
  State of Illinois Building
  100 West Randolph Street
  Chicago, IL 60601
  (312) 917-4531

**Indiana Consumer Protection
Division**
  219 State House
  Indianapolis, IN 46204
  (800) 382-5516

**Iowa State Board of Dental
Examiners**
  Executive Hills West
  1209 E. Court
  Des Moines, IA 50319
  (515) 281-5157

**Kansas State Board of Dental
Examiners**
  4301 Huntoon, Suite 4, Lower
  Level
  Topeka, KS 66604
  (913) 273-0780

Kentucky State Board of Dentistry
  2106 Bardstown Road
  Louisville, KY 40205
  (502) 451-6832

**Louisiana State Board of Dental
Examiners**
  1515 Poydras Street, Suite 2240
  New Orleans, LA 70112
  (504) 524-0777

**Maine State Board of Dental
Examiners**
  Box 104
  West Minot, ME 04288
  (207) 345-3272

**Maryland State Board of Dental
Examiners**
  201 W. Preston Street
  Baltimore, MD 21201
  (301) 225-5858

**Massachusetts State Board of
Registration in Dentistry**
  100 Cambridge Street, Room 1514
  Boston, MA 02202
  (617) 727-7406

**Michigan Department of Licensing
and Regulation/Health
Investigation Division**
  P.O. Box 30018
  Lansing, MI 48909
  (517) 373-9196

Minnesota Board of Dentistry
2700 University Avenue West,
Suite 109
St. Paul, MN 55114
(612) 642-0579

Mississippi State Board of Dental Examiners
P.O. Box 1960
Clinton, MS 39056
(601) 924-9622

Missouri Dental Board
P.O. Box 1367
Jefferson City, MO 65102
(314) 751-2334

Montana Department of Commerce
1424 9th Avenue
Helena, MT 59620–0407
(406) 444-3745

Nebraska State Board of Dental Examiners
Bureau of Examining Boards
P.O. Box 95007
Lincoln, NE 68509–5007
(402) 471-2115

Nevada State Board of Dental Examiners
P.O. Box 12460
Reno, NV 89510
(702) 786-6155

New Hampshire State Board of Dental Examiners
Health and Welfare Building
6 Hazen Drive
Concord, NH 03301
(603) 271-4561

New Jersey State Board of Dental Examiners
1100 Raymond Boulevard, Room 321
Newark, NJ 07102
(201) 648-7370

New Mexico State Board of Dental Examiners
P.O. Drawer 1388
Santa Fe, NM 87504–1388
(505) 827-9933

New York State Education Department/Office of Professional Discipline
622 Third Avenue
New York, NY 10017
(800) 442-8106

North Carolina State Board of Dental Examiners
P.O. Box 32270
Raleigh, NC 27622
(919) 781-4901

North Dakota State Board of Dental Examiners
P.O. Box 1175
Jamestown, ND 58402
(701) 252-1892

Ohio State Dental Board
65 S. Front Street, Suite 506
Columbus, OH 43215
(614) 466-2580

Oklahoma State Board of Dental Examiners
2726 N. Oklahoma
Oklahoma City, OK 73105
(405) 521-2350

Oregon Board of Dentistry
620 S.W. 5th Avenue, Suite 405
Portland, OR 97204
(503) 229-5520

Pennsylvania Bureau of Professional Occupational Affairs/Complaint Department
P.O. Box 2649
Harrisburg, PA 17105
(800) 922-2113

**Puerto Rico Board of Dental
Examiners/Department of Health**
    Call Box 10200
    Santurce, PR 00908
    (809) 723-1617

**Rhode Island Division of
Professional Regulation**
    75 Davis Street, Suite 104
    Providence, RI 02908
    (401) 277-2827

**South Carolina State Board of
Dental Examiners**
    1315 Blanding Street
    Columbia, SC 29201
    (803) 734-8902

**South Dakota State Board of
Dentistry**
    1708 Space Court
    Rapid City, SD 57702
    (605) 342-6228

**Tennessee State Board of Dental
Examiners**
    283 Plus Park Boulevard
    Nashville, TN 37219-5407
    (615) 367-6228

**Texas State Board of Dental
Examiners**
    Capitol Station
    P.O. Box 13165
    Austin, TX 78711
    (512) 834-6021

**Utah Department of Business
Regulations**
    160 East 300 South
    Salt Lake City, UT 84145
    (801) 530-6628

Vermont Secretary of State Office
    Attn: Complaint Department
    Pavillion Office Building
    Montpelier, VT 05602
    (802) 828-2390

**Virgin Islands Department of
Health**
    St. Thomas, VI 00802
    (809) 774-0117

**Virginia State Board of Dental
Examiners**
    1601 Rolling Hills Drive
    Richmond, VA 23229
    (804) 662-9902

**Washington State Dental
Disciplinary Board**
    Department of Licensing,
        Program Management
        Division
    P.O. Box 9012
    Olympia, WA 98504-8001
    (206) 753-1156

**West Virginia Board of Dental
Examiners**
    P.O. Drawer 1459
    Beckley, WV 25802
    (304) 252-8266

**Wisconsin State Board of Dental
Examiners**
    Department of Regulation and
        Licensing
    P.O. Box 8935
    Madison, WI 53708
    (608) 266-1396

**Wyoming State Board of Dental
Examiners**
    P.O. Box 1024
    Powell, WY 32435
    (307) 754-4554

Doctors

**Alabama Medical Licensure
Commission**
    P.O. Box 946
    Montgomery, AL 36102-0946
    (205) 261-4116

**Alaska Department of Commerce
and Economic Development
State Medical Board**
P.O. Box D
Juneau, AK 99811
(907) 465-2541

**Arizona Board of Medical
Examiners**
1990 W. Camelback Road, Suite
401
Phoenix, AZ 85015
(602) 255-3751

**Arkansas Board of Medical
Examiners**
P.O. Box 102
Harrisburg, AR 72432
(501) 578-2448

**California Board of Medical
Quality Assurance**
1430 Howe Avenue
Sacramento, CA 95825
(916) 920-6393

**Colorado Board of Medical
Examiners**
1525 Sherman Street, #132
Denvr, CO 80203
(303) 866-2468

**Connecticut Board of Medical
Examiners**
150 Washington Street
Hartford, CT 06106
(203) 566-1035

**Delaware Board of Medical
Practice**
Margaret O'Neill Building, 2nd
Floor
Dover, DE 19903
(302) 736-4522

**District of Columbia Occupational
and Professional Licensing
Division**
614 H Street, N.W., Room 904
Washington, DC 20001
(202) 727-7480

**Florida Board of Medical
Examiners**
130 N. Monroe Street
Tallahassee, FL 32399–0750
(904) 488-0595

**Georgia Composite State Board of
Medical Examiners**
166 Pryor Street, S.W.
Atlanta, GA 30303
(404) 656-3913

**Hawaii Board of Medical
Examiners**
P.O. Box 3469
Honolulu, HI 96801
(808) 548-4100

Idaho State Board of Medicine
500 S. 10th Street, Suite 103
Boise, ID 83720
(208) 334-2822

**Illinois Department of Registration
and Education**
320 W. Washington Street
Springfield, IL 62786
(217) 785-0800

**Indiana Consumer Protection
Division**
219 State House
Indianapolis, IN 46204
(800) 382-5516

**Iowa State Board of Medical
Examiners**
Executive Hills West
1209 E. Court Avenue
Des Moines, IA 50319
(515) 281-5171

Kansas State Board of Healing Arts
900 S.W. Jackson, Suite 553
Topeka, KS 66612
(913) 296-7413

**Kentucky Board of Medical
Licensure**
400 Sherman Lane, Suite 2222
Louisville, KY 40207
(502) 896-1516

Louisiana State Board of Medical
Examiners
830 Union Street, Suite 100
New Orleans, LA 70112
(504) 524-6763

Maine Board of Registration in
Medicine
State House, Station #137
Augusta, ME 04333
(207) 289-3601

Maryland Board of Medical
Examiners
201 W. Preston Street
Baltimore, MD 21201
(301) 225-5900

Massachusetts Board of
Registration in Medicine
10 West Street
Boston, MA 02111
(617) 727-3086

Michigan Board of Medicine
611 W. Ottawa Street/Box 30018
Lansing, MI 48909
(517) 373-1870

Minnesota State Board of Medical
Examiners
2700 University Avenue West,
Room 106
St. Paul, MN 55114
(612) 642-0538

Mississippi State Board of Medical
Licensure
2688-D Insurance Center Drive
Jackson, MS 39216
(601) 354-6645

Missouri State Board of
Registration for the Healing Arts
P.O. Box 4
Jefferson City, MO 65102
(314) 751-2334

Montana Board of Medical
Examiners
1424 9th Avenue, Building 4

Helena, MT 59620
(406) 444-4284

Nebraska Board of Medical
Examiners
301 Centennial Mall, South/Box
95007
Lincoln, NE 68509
(402) 471-2115

Nevada State Board of Medical
Examiners
P.O. Box 7238
Reno, NV 89510
(702) 329-2559

New Hampshire Board of
Registration in Medicine
Health and Welfare Building
6 Hazen Drive
Concord, NH 03301
(603) 271-4502

New Jersey State Board of Medical
Examiners
28 W. State Street
Trenton, NJ 08608
(609) 292-4843

New Mexico Board of Medical
Examiners
P.O. Box 1388
Santa Fe, NM 87504-1388
(505) 827-9933

New York State Department of
Health
Office of Professional Medical
Conduct
Empire State Plaza
Tower Building
Albany, NY 12237
(518) 474-8357

North Carolina Board of Medical
Examiners
P.O. Box 26808
Raleigh, NC 27611
(919) 833-5321

North Dakota State Board of Medical Examiners
City Center Plaza, Suite C-10
418 E. Broadway Avenue
Bismarck, ND 58501
(701) 223-9485

Ohio State Medical Board
65 S. Front Street
Columbus, OH 47266-0315
(614) 466-3938

Oklahoma State Board of Medical Examiners
5104 N. Francis, Suite C
Oklahoma City, OK 73118
(405) 846-6841

Oregon State Board of Medical Examiners
317 S.W. Adler Street
Portland, OR 97204
(503) 229-5770

Pennsylvania State Board of Medical Education and Licensure
P.O. Box 2649
Harrisburg, PA 17105
(717) 787-2381

Puerto Rico Board of Medical Examiners
Call Box 10200
Santurce, PR 00908
(809) 725-7903

Rhode Island Division of Professional Regulation
75 David Street
Providence, RI 02908
(401) 277-2827

South Carolina State Board of Medical Examiners
1220 Pickins Street
Columbia, SC 29201
(803) 734-8901

South Dakota State Board of Medical and Osteopathic Examiners
1323 S. Minnesota Avenue
Sioux Falls, SD 57105
(605) 336-1965

Tennessee Board of Medical Examiners
283 Plus Park Boulevard
Nashville, TN 37217
(615) 367-6231

Texas Board of Medical Examiners
P.O. Box 13562, Capitol Station
Austin, TX 78711
(512) 452-1078

Utah Department of Registration
160 East 300 South
Salt Lake City, UT 84145
(801) 530-6628

Vermont Board of Medical Practice
109 State Street
Montpelier, VT 05602
(802) 838-2673

Virgin Islands Department of Health
Attn: Licensure
St. Thomas Hospital
St. Thomas, VI 00801
(809) 774-0117

Virginia State Board of Medicine
1601 Rolling Hills Drive
Richmond, VA 23229
(804) 662-9908

Washington State Medical Boards Division of Professional Licensing
P.O. Box 9012
Olympia, WA 98504
(206) 753-2205

West Virginia Board of Medicine
100 Dee Drive, Suite 104
Charleston, WV 25311
(304) 348-2921

Wisconsin Medical Examining Board

1400 E. Washington Avenue/
    P.O. Box 8935
Madison, WI 53708–8935
(608) 266-2811

Wyoming Board of Medical Examiners

Hathaway Building, 4th Floor
Cheyenne, WY 82002
(307) 777-6463

Hospitals

**Alabama Department of Public Health/
Bureau of Licensure and Certification**

654 State Office Building
Montgomery, AL 36130
(205) 261-5113

Alaska Health Facilities Licensing and Certification

4041 B Street, Suite 101
Anchorage, AK 99503
(907) 561-2171

Arizona Department of Health Services/Bureau of Health Care Institutions Licensing

411 N. 24th Street
Phoenix, AZ 85007
(602) 220-6407

**Arkansas Department of Health/
Division of Health Facility Services**

4815 W. Markham Street
Little Rock, AR 72205
(501) 661-2201

California Department of Health Services/Division of Licensing and Certification

714 P Street, Room 823
Sacramento, CA 95814
(916) 445-2070

**Colorado Department of Health/
Division of Health Facilities Regulation**

4210 E. 11th Avenue
Denver, CO 80220
(303) 331-4930

Connecticut Department of Health Services/Hospital and Medical Care Division

150 Washington Street
Hartford, CT 06106
(203) 566-1073

**Delaware Department of Health/
Office of Health Facilities Licensing and Certification**

3000 Newport Gap Pike
Wilmington, DE 19808
(302) 571-3499

District of Columbia Department of Consumer and Regulatory Affairs/Service Facility Regulation Administration

614 H. Street, N.W.
Washington, DC 20001
(202) 727-7190

Florida Department of Health and Rehabilitative Services/Office of Licensure and Certification

2727 Mahan Drive
Tallahassee, FL 32308
(904) 487-3513

Georgia Department of Human Resources/Standards and Licensure Section Complaint Unit

878 Peachtree Street, N.E.
Atlanta, GA 30309
(404) 894-5137

Hawaii Department of Health/
Hospital Medical Services
P.O. Box 3378
Honolulu, HI 96801
(808) 548-5935

Idaho Department of Health and
Welfare/Facility Standards
Program
420 W. Washington Street
Boise, ID 83720
(208) 334-4167

Illinois Department of Public
Health/Division of Health
Facilities
525 W. Jefferson Street, 4th
Floor
Springfield, IL 62761
(217) 782-7412

Indiana Board of Health/Division
of Acute Care Services
1330 W. Michigan Street, Room
236
Indianapolis, IN 46206–1964
(317) 633-8472

Iowa Department of Health/
Division of Health Facilities
Department of Inspections
and Appeals
Lucas State Office Building, 3rd
Floor
Des Moines, IA 50319
(515) 281-4120

Kansas Department of Health and
Environment/Bureau of Adult
and Child Care Facilities
Landon State Office Building,
10th Floor
900 S.W. Jackson
Topeka, KS 66620–0001
(913) 296-1265

Kentucky Cabinet for Human
Resources/Division of Licensing
and Regulation
275 E. Main Street, 4th Floor
East
Frankfort, KY 40621
(502) 564-2800

Louisiana Department of Health
and Human Resources/Division
of Licensing and Certification
P.O. Box 3767
Baton Rouge, LA 70821
(504) 342-6448

Maine Department of Human
Services/Division of Licensing
and Certification
Statehouse Station 11
249 Western Avenue
Augusta, ME 04333
(207) 289-2606

Maryland Department of Health/
Division of Licensing and
Certification
201 W. Preston Street
Baltimore, MD 21201
(301) 225-5430

Massachusetts Department of
Public Health/Division of Health
Care Quality
80 Boylston Street, 11th Floor
Boston, MA 02116
(800) 462-5540

Michigan Department of Public
Health/Patients and Complaints
3500 N. Logan
Lansing, MI 48909
(517) 335-8511

Minnesota Department of Health/
Office of Health Facility
Complaints
717 Delaware Street, S.E.
Minneapolis, MN 55440
(612) 623-5563

Mississippi Health Care
Commission/Division of
Licensure and Certification
P.O. Box 1700, Room 101
Jackson, MS 39215–1700
(601) 960-7769

Missouri Department of Health/
Bureau of Hospital Licensing
and Certification
P.O. Box 570
Jefferson City, MO 65102
(314) 751-6302

Montana Department of Health
and Environmental Sciences/
Medical Facilities Division
Cogswell Building
Helena, MT 59620
(406) 444-2037

Nebraska Department of Health/
Division of Licensure and
Standards
301 Centennial Mall, South
Lincoln, NE 68509
(402) 471-2946

Nevada State Division of Health/
Bureau of Regulatory Health
Services
505 E. King Street, Room 202
Carson City, NV 89710
(702) 885-4475

New Hampshire Department of
Public Health/Bureau of Health
Facilities Administration
6 Hazen Drive
Concord, NH 03301
(603) 271-4592

New Jersey Department of Health/
Division of Health Facilities
Evaluation, Licensing,
Certification, and Standards
CN 367
Trenton, NJ 08625
(800) 792-9770

New Mexico Health and
Environment Department/Health
Services Division Federal
Program Certification
P.O. Box 968
Harold Rennelds Building
Sante Fe, NM 87503–0968
(505) 827-2416

New York Department of Health/
New York State Bureau of
Hospital Services
Empire State Plaza
Albany, NY 12237
(518) 474-5013

North Carolina Department of
Human Resources/Health Care
Facility Branch
701 Barbour Drive
Raleigh, NC 27603
(919) 733-2786

North Dakota Department of
Health/Division of Health
Facilities
State Capitol
Bismarck, ND 58505
(701) 224-2352

Ohio Department of Health/Survey
Operation
246 N. High Street
Columbus, OH 43266–0118
(614) 644-7935

Oklahoma State Department of
Health/Institutional Services
1000 N.E. 10th
Oklahoma City, OK 73512
(405) 271-6868

Oregon Office of Environmental
and Health Systems/Health
Facilities Section
P.O. Box 231
Portland, OR 97207
(503) 229-5686

**Pennsylvania Department of
Health Bureau of Quality
Assurance/Division of Hospitals**
Health and Welfare Building,
Room 532
Harrisburg, PA 17120
(717) 783-8980

Puerto Rico Department of Health
Box 70184
San Juan, PR 00936
(809) 766-1616

**Rhode Island Department of
Health/Facilities Regulation**
75 Davis Street
Providence, RI 02908
(401) 277-2566

**South Carolina Department of
Health and Environmental
Control/Division of Health
Licensing/Bureau of Health
Licensing and Certification**
2600 Bull Street
Columbia, SC 29201
(803) 758-0360

**South Dakota Department of
Health/Licensure and
Certification Program**
523 E. Capitol
Pierre, SD 57501
(605) 773-3364

**Tennessee Department of Public
Health/Division of Health Care
Facilities**
283 Plus Park Boulevard
Nashville, TN 37217
(615) 367-6200

**Texas Department of Health/
Health Facility Licensure and
Certification Division**
1100 W. 49th Street
Austin, TX 78756-3183
(512) 458-7245

**Utah Department of Social
Services/Division of Aging and
Adult Services/Long-Term Care
Ombudsman**
120 North 200 West
Salt Lake City, UT 84145
(801) 538-3190

**Vermont Department of Health/
Medical Care Regulation**
60 Main Street
Burlington, VT 05401
(802) 863-7272, 863-7250

**Virgin Islands Department of
Health**
Attn: Licensure
St. Thomas Hospital
St. Thomas, VI 00801
(809) 774-0117

**Virginia Department of Health/
Division of Licensure and
Certification**
109 Governor Street
Richmond, VA 23219
(804) 786-2081

**Washington Department of Social
and Health Services/Health
Facilities Survey Section**
1112 S. Quince, ET-31
Olympia, WA 98504
(206) 753-5851

**West Virginia Department of
Health/Health Facilities
Licensure and Certification
Division**
1800 Washington Street, E.
P & G
Charleston, WV 25305
(304) 348-0050

**Wisconsin Department of Health
and Social Services/Division of
Health/Bureau of Quality
Compliance**
P.O. Box 309
Madison, WY 53703
(608) 267-7185

Wyoming Department of Health
and Social Services/Division of
Health and Medical Services
  Hathaway Building, 4th Floor
  Cheyenne, WY 82002
  (307) 777-7121

Nurses

Alabama Board of Nursing
  Attn: Legal Division
  500 East Boulevard, Suite 213
  Montgomery, AL 36130
  (205) 261-4060

Alaska Division of Occupational
Licensing
  3601 C Street, Suite 722
  Anchorage, AK 99503
  (907) 561-2878

Arizona Board of Nursing
  5050 N. 19th Avenue, Suite 103
  Phoenix, AZ 85015
  (602)255-5092

Arkansas Board of Nursing
  Tower Building
  1123 S. University, Suite 800
  Little Rock, AR 72204
  (501) 371-2751

California Board of Registered
Nursing
  1030 13th Street, Room 200
  Sacramento, CA 95814
  (916) 322-3350

Colorado Board of Nursing
  1525 Sherman Street, Room 132
  Denver, CO 80203
  (303) 866-2871

Connecticut Department of Health/
Consumer Complaints Division
  150 W. Washington Street
  Hartford, CT 06106
  (800) 842-0038

Delaware Board of Nursing
  O'Neill Building
  P.O. Box 1401
  Dover, DE 19901
  (302) 736-4522

District of Columbia Department of
Consumer and Regulatory Affairs
  Attn: Complaint Division
  614 H Street, N.W., Room 104
  Washington, DC 20001
  (202) 727-7107

Florida Department of Professional
Regulation
  130 N. Monroe Street, Suite 225
  Tallahassee, FL 32399–0750
  (800) 342-7940

Georgia Board of Nursing
  166 Pryor Street, S.W.
  Atlanta, GA 30303
  (404) 656-3943

Hawaii Board of Nursing
  P.O. Box 3469
  Honolulu, HI 96809
  (808) 548-3086

Idaho Board of Nursing
  500 S. 10th, Suite 102
  Boise, ID 83720
  (208) 334-3110

Illinois Nursing Committee
Department of Registration and
Education
  320 W. Washington Street
  Springfield, IL 62786
  (217) 782-7116

Indiana Consumer Protection
Division
  219 State House
  Indianapolis, IN 46204
  (800) 382-5516

Iowa Board of Nursing
  1223 E. Court Avenue
  Des Moines, IA 50319
  (515) 281-3255

Kansas Board of Nursing
900 S.W. Jackson, Suite 551-S
Topeka, KS 66612–1256
(913) 296-4929

Kentucky Board of Nursing
4010 Dupont Circle, Suite 430
Louisville, KY 40207
(502) 897-5143

Louisiana Board of Nursing
150 Baronne Street
New Orleans, LA 70112
(504) 568-5464

Maine Board of Nursing
295 Water Street
Augusta, ME 04330
(207) 289-5324

Maryland Board of Nursing
201 W. Preston Street
Baltimore, MD 21201
(301) 225-5880

**Massachusetts Board of
Registration in Nursing**
100 Cambridge Street
Boston, MA 02202
(617) 727-9961

Michigan Board of Nursing
611 W. Ottawa/P.O. Box 30018
Lansing, MI 48909
(517) 373-1600

Minnesota Board of Nursing
2700 University Avenue, West
#108
St. Paul, MN 55114
(612) 642-0552

Mississippi Board of Nursing
135 Bounds Street
Jackson, MS 39206
(601) 354-7349

Missouri State Board of Nursing
P.O. Box 656
Jefferson City, MO 65102
(314) 751-2334

Montana Board of Nursing
1424 Ninth Avenue
Helena, MT 59620-0407
(406) 444-4279

**Nebraska Bureau of Examining
Boards/Nebraska Department of
Health**
301 Centennial Mall, South
Lincoln, NE 68509–5007
(402) 471-4921

Nevada Board of Nursing
1281 Terminal Way, Room 116
Reno, NV 89502
(702) 786-2778

**New Hampshire Nurses
Registration Board/Division of
Public Health**
Health and Welfare Building
6 Hazen Drive
Concord, NH 03301–6527
(603) 271-2323

New Jersey Board of Nursing
1100 Raymond Boulevard
Newark, NJ 07102
(201) 648-2570

New Mexico Board of Nursing
4125 Carlisle, N.E.
Albuquerque, NM 87109
(505) 841-6314

**The New York State Education
Department**
Office of Professional Discipline
622 Third Avenue
New York, NY 10017
(800) 422-8106

North Carolina Board of Nursing
P.O. Box 2129
Raleigh, NC 27602
(919) 828-0740

North Dakota Board of Nursing
Kirkwood Office Tower, Suite
504
Bismarck, ND 58501
(701) 224-2974

Ohio Board of Nursing
   65 S. Front Street, Room 509
   Columbus, OH 43266-0316
   (614) 466-3974

**Oklahoma Board of Nurse
Registration and Nursing
Education**
   2915 N. Claussen Boulevard,
      Suite 524
   Oklahoma City, OK 73106
   (405) 525-2076

Oregon Board of Nursing
   1400 S.W. 5th Avenue, Room
      904
   Portland, OR 97201
   (503) 229-5653

**Pennsylvania Bureau of
Professional and Occupational
Affairs**
   P.O. Box 2649
   Harrisburg, PA 17105-2649
   (800) 822-2113

Puerto Rico State Board of Nursing
   Colegio de Profesionals de Law
      Enfermario de Puerto Rico
   G.P.O. Box 3708
   San Juan, PR 00936
   (809) 751-9800

**Rhode Island Board of Nursing
Registration and Nursing**
   75 Davis Street, Room 104
   Providence, RI 02908-5097
   (401) 277-2827

South Carolina Board of Nursing
   1777 St. Julian Place, Suite 102
   Columbia, SC 29204
   (803) 737-6596

South Dakota Board of Nursing
   304 S. Phillips Avenue, Suite
      205
   Sioux Falls, SD 57102
   (605) 335-4973

Tennessee Board of Nursing
   283 Plus Park Boulevard
   Nashville, TN 37219-5407
   (615) 367-6232

Texas Board of Nurse Examiners
   1300 E. Anderson Lane,
      Building C, Suite 225
   Austin, TX 78752
   (512) 835-4880

**Utah Department of Occupational
and Professional Licensing**
   P.O. Box 45802
   Salt Lake City, UT 84145
   (801) 530-6628

Vermont Board of Nursing
   26 Terrace Street
   Montpelier, VT 05602
   (802) 828-2396

**Virgin Islands Department of
Health/Board of Nursing
Licensing**
   Knud Hansen Complex
   St. Thomas, VI 00801
   (809) 776-7397

**Virginia Board of Nursing/Health
Regulatory Board Enforcement
Division**
   1601 Rolling Hill Drive
   Richmond, VA 23229
   (800) 533-1560

**Washington Department of
Licensing/Nursing Board
Professional Program
Management Division**
   P.O. Box 9012
   Olympia, WA 98504-8001
   (206) 753-3726

**West Virginia Board of Examiners
for Registered Nurses**
   922 Quarrier Street, Suite 309
   Charleston, WV 25301
   (304) 348-3728

Wisconsin Department of Licensing
Board of Nursing
P.O. Box 8935
Madison, WI 53708–8935
(608) 266-3735

Wyoming State Board of Nursing
Barrett Building, 4th Floor
2301 Central Avenue
Cheyenne, WY 82002
(307) 777-7601

NOTES

||||||
············

1.

1. T. Watkins, "Physicians: A Higher Risk Group." *Medical Tribune,* June 19, 1985, p. 16.

2. "Impaired Physicians: Drug-Alcohol Addiction Afflicts Many." *Phoenix Gazette,* March 30, 1983, p. Rx-13.

3. A. S. Freese, *Managing Your Doctor.* New York: Stein and Day, 1975, p. 19.

4. *Phoenix Gazette,* March 30, 1983, p. Rx-13.

5. "Drug Addiction Casts a Growing Shadow over M.D.s." *Medical Economics,* November 11, 1985, p. 263.

6. W. E. McAuliffe, M. Rohman, S. Santangelo, B. Feldman, E. Magnuson, A. Sobol, and J. Weissman, "Psychoactive Drug Use Among Practicing Physicians and Medical Students." *New England Journal of Medicine,* September 25, 1986, vol. 315, no. 13, pp. 805–810; also, "Poll Finds 40 Percent of Young Doctors Admit Drug Use." *New York Times,* September 25, 1986, p. B8; "Poll Measures Use of Drugs Among Doctors," *Philadelphia Inquirer,* September 25, 1986, pp. 1C, 5C.

7. J. F. Maddux, S. K. Hoppe, and R. M. Costello, "Psychoactive Substance Abuse Among Medical Students." *American Journal of Psychiatry,* February 1986, vol. 143, no. 2, p. 187.

8. D. Hilfiker, *Healing the Wounds.* New York: Pantheon Books, 1985, p. 13.

9. J. Guinther, *The Malpractitioners.* New York: Doubleday, 1978, p. 145.

10. L. M. Simonsmeier and L. A. Fox, "The Law and the Impaired Pharmacist." *American Pharmacy,* June 1985, vol. NS25, no.6, p. 63.

11. *Phoenix Gazette,* March 30, 1983, p. Rx-13.

12. D. L. Breo, "A Doctor Who Beat Addiction Warns of a Hidden Epidemic." *Philadelphia Inquirer,* January 26, 1986, p. 1-I.

13. "Psychiatrist Travels Rough Road to Recovery." *The Home News* (New Brunswick, N.J.), September 25, 1984, p. A9.

14. W. P. Kory and L. A. Crandall, "Nonmedical Drug Use Patterns Among Medical Students." *International Journal of Addiction,* December 1984, vol. 19, no. 8, pp. 871–884.

15. J. D. McCue, "The Effects of Stress on Physicians and Their Medical Practice." *New England Journal of Medicine,* February 25, 1982, vol. 306, no. 8, p. 458.

16. D. L. Breo, *Philadelphia Inquirer,* January 26, 1986, p. 6-I.

17. J. D. McCue, *New England Journal of Medicine,* February 25, 1982, p. 460.

18. E. J. Khantzian, "The Injured Self, Addiction, and Our Call to Medicine." *Journal of the American Medical Association,* July 12, 1985, vol. 254, no. 2, p. 249.

19. R. C. Friedman, J. T. Bigger, and D. S. Kornfeld, "The Intern and Sleep Loss." *New England Journal of Medicine,* July 22, 1971, vol. 285, no. 4, p. 201.

20. R. J. Valko and P. J. Clayton, "Depression in the Internship." *Diseases of the Nervous System,* January 1975, vol. 36, no. 1, pp. 26, 29.

21. R. Paulson, "Fatigue in Medical Personnel." *Journal of the American Medical Association,* July 10, 1981, vol. 246, no. 2, p. 124.

22. W. R. Greer, "New Debate Opens on Doctors' Hours." *New York Times,* August 13, 1987, p. 6-E.

23. D. Hilfiker, *Healing the Wounds,* pp. 78–79.

24. J-H. Pfifferling, "Cultural Antecedents Promoting Professional Impairment," in C. D. Scott and J. Hawk, eds. *Heal Thyself: The Health of Health Care Professionals.* New York: Brunner/Mazel, 1986, p. 5.

25. J. D. McCue, *New England Journal of Medicine,* February 25, 1982, p. 459.

26. E. J. Khantzian, *Journal of the American Medical Association,* July 12, 1985, p. 250.

27. "Luck Saved His Life, Recovering Alcoholic Says." *Phoenix Gazette,* March 30, 1983, pp. Rx-12, Rx-13.

28. G. D. Talbott, K. V. Gallegos, P. O. Wilson, and T. L. Porter, "The Medical Association of Georgia's Impaired Physician Program. Review of the First 1000 Physicians: Analysis of Specialty." *Journal of the American Medical Association,* June 5, 1987, vol. 257, no. 21, pp. 2927, 2930.

29. M. W. Lear, *Heartsounds.* New York: Pocket Books, 1981, p. 42.

30. "How Old Is Too Old to Practice?" *Phoenix Gazette,* March 30, 1983, p. Rx-14.

31. D. A. Lang, "The Challenge of Autonomy—The Impaired Physician." *Federation Bulletin,* May 1985, p. 149.

32. K. Rawnsley, "Helping the Sick Doctor: A New Service." *British Medical Journal,* October 5, 1985, p. 922.

33. D. L. Breo, *Philadelphia Inquirer,* January 26, 1986, p. 1-I.

34. K. Rawnsley, *British Medical Journal,* October 5, 1985, p. 922.

35. "Unfit Dr.s Found in Miss." Associated Press wire service story, September 30, 1985.

36. R. E. Herrington and G. R. Jacobson, "Outlook for Impaired Physicians with Appropriate Treatment," *Journal of the American Medical Association,* December 17, 1982, vol. 248, no. 23, p. 3144.

37. J. Guinther, *The Malpractitioners,* p. 146.

38. R. C. Coe, "Physicians Who Move." *Journal of the American Medical Association,* April 15, 1983, vol. 249, no. 15, p. 2018.

39. C. K. Morrow, "Doctors Helping Doctors." *The Hastings Center Report,* December 1984, p. 32.

40. "Hospitals Cited for Failure to Report Impaired MDs." *American Medical News,* November 4, 1983, p. 8.

41. W. D. Robertson, *Medical Malpractice: A Preventive Approach.* Seattle: University of Washington Press, 1985, p. 193.

42. R. Sullivan, "Doctors Submit to Drug Tests as Alternative to Penalties." *New York Times,* March 13, 1987, p. B2.

43. P. Raeburn, "Doctors Become Patients at Ridgeview Institute." *The Home News* (New Brunswick, N.J.), September 25, 1984, p. A9.

44. C. K. Morrow, *The Hastings Center Report,* December 1984, p. 34.

45. T. Watkins, *Medical Tribune,* June 19, 1985, p. 16.

46. D. A. Lang, *Federation Bulletin,* May 1985, pp. 148, 150.

47. For a good overview, see J. H. Shore, "The Impaired Physician: Four Years After Probation." *Journal of the American Medical Association,* December 17, 1982, vol. 248, no. 23, pp. 3127-3130.

48. H. D. Kleber, "The Impaired Physician: Changes from the Traditional View." *Journal of Substance Abuse Treatment,* 1984, vol. 1, no. 2, pp. 137-140.

49. C. K. Morrow, *The Hastings Center Report,* December 1984, p. 36.

50. D. A. Lang, *Federation Bulletin,* May 1985, p. 149.

51. J. M. Brewster, "Prevalence of Alcohol and Other Drug Problems Among Physicians." *Journal of the American Medical Association,* April 11, 1986, vol. 255, no. 14, p. 1913.

52. "Oregon Foundation for Medical Excellence to Focus on the Problem of Impaired Physicians." *Federation Bulletin,* July 1985, p. 223.

53. D. L. Breo, *Philadelphia Inquirer,* January 26, 1986, p. 1-I.

54. L. Wolfe, "Nurses and Drug Abuse: New Ways to Help." *New York Times,* July 26, 1986, p. 10.

55. P. O'Connor and R. S. Robinson. "Managing Impaired Nurses." *Nursing Administration Quarterly,* Winter 1985, p. 2.

56. M. A. Naegle, "Creative Management of Impaired Nursing Practice." *Nursing Administration Quarterly,* Spring 1985, p. 17.

57. P. O'Connor and R. S. Robinson, *Nursing Administration Quarterly,* Winter 1985, p. 5.

58. L. M. Simonsmeier and L. A. Fox, *American Pharmacy,* June 1985, p. 63.

59. D. A. Bloch, in C. D. Scott and J. Hawk, eds., *Heal Thyself: The Health of Health Care Professionals.* New York: Brunner-Mazel, 1986, pp. viii, xix.

2.

1. L. Lander, *Defective Medicine.* New York: Farrar, Straus, Giroux, 1978, p. 36.

2. P. Zaleski and P. Taylor, "Conversation with a Heretic." *New Age Journal,* November 1985, vol. II, no. 4, p. 79.

3. P. Zaleski and P. Taylor, *New Age Journal,* November 1985, p. 46.

4. P. Zaleski and P. Taylor, *New Age Journal,* November 1985, p. 44.

5. S. G. Wolf and B. B. Berle, eds., *Limits of Medicine: Proceedings of the Totts Gap Colloquium on the Limits of Medicine: The Doctor's Job in the Coming Era.* Held in Totts Gap, Pennsylvania, June 10-12, 1976. New York: Plenum Press, 1978, p. 36.

6. J. Needleman, *The Way of the Physician.* San Francisco: Harper & Row, 1985, p. 109.

7. N. Cousins, "Laymen and Medical Technology," in L. Breslow, J. E. Fielding, and L. B. Lave, eds., *Annual Review of Public Health,* vol. 2, pp. 93–99. Palo Alto: Annual Reviews Inc., 1981, p. 97.

8. B. Dodson, Jr., "Technology for Technology's Sake." *Medical Instrumentation,* November–December 1984, vol. 18, no. 6, p. 329.

9. V. W. Sidel and R. Sidel, *A Healthy State.* New York: Pantheon, 1983, p. 71.

10. I. Illich, *Medical Nemesis.* New York: Pantheon, 1976.

11. L. Lander, *Defective Medicine,* p. 41.

12. L. Lander, *Defective Medicine,* p. 34.

13. B. Dodson, Jr., *Medical Instrumentation,* November–December 1984, p. 329.

14. D. Hellerstein, "Overdosing on Medical Technology." *Technology Review,* August–September 1983, p. 14.

15. J. Needleman, *The Way of the Physician,* pp. 119-120.

16. K. E. Warner, "Effects of Hospital Cost Containment on the Development and Use of Medical Technology." *Millbank Memorial Fund Quarterly/Health and Society,* 1978, vol. 56, no. 2, p. 233.

17. K. E. Warner, *Millbank Memorial Fund Quarterly/Health and Society,* 1978, p. 233.

18. David Hellerstein, *Technology Review,* August–September 1983, pp. 14-15.

19. N. Cousins, "Biochemistry of Emotions." *What's Next,* May/June 1984, vol. 8, no. 3, p. 8.

20. S. G. Wolf and B. B. Berle, eds., *Limits of Medicine: Proceedings of the Totts Gap Colloquium on the Limits of Medicine: The Doctor's Job in the Coming Era,* p. 36.

21. S. G. Wolf and B. B. Berle, eds., *Limits of Medicine: Proceedings of the Totts Gap Colloquium on the Limits of Medicine: The Doctor's Job in the Coming Era,* p. 32.

22. J. M. R. Bruner, "Automated Indirect Blood Pressure Measurement—A Point of View." *Medical Instrumentation,* March–April 1984, vol. 18, no. 2, p. 144.

23. L. Lander, *Defective Medicine,* pp. 55–56.

24. J. M. R. Bruner, *Medical Instrumentation,* March–April 1984, p. 145.

25. G. Bugliarello, "Health-Care Costs: Technology to the Rescue?" *IEEE Spectrum,* June 1984, pp. 97–98.

26. A. S. Freese, *Managing Your Doctor,* New York: Stein and Day, 1975, p. 37.

27. *The Device Experience Network Report,* July 1985. Washington, D.C.: United States Food and Drug Administration, p. 15.

28. *The Device Experience Network Report,* July 1985, p. 41.

29. *The Device Experience Network Report,* June 1985. Washington, D.C.: United States Food and Drug Administration, p. 7.

30. *The Device Experience Network Report,* June 1985, p. 11.

31. *The Device Experience Network Report,* June 1985, p. 53.

32. *The Device Experience Network Report,* June 1985, p. 20.

33. *The Device Experience Network Report,* September 1985. Washington, D.C.: United States Food and Drug Administration, p. 33.

34. *The Device Experience Network Report,* September 1985, p. 51.

35. *Medical Devices: Early Warning of Problems is Hampered by Severe Underreporting.* U.S. General Accounting Office, Washington, D.C., December 1986, pp. 5, 63.

36. K. Simmons, "Device Center Regulates 'Tools of the Trade'." *Journal of the American Medical Association,* October 25, 1985, vol. 254, no. 16, p. 2243.

37. P. L. McGurgan, "Potential Hazard to Cardioversion Patients." *Medical Instrumentation,* July–August 1984, vol. 18, no. 4, p. 237.

38. P. L. McGurgan, *Medical Instrumentation,* July–August 1984, p. 237.

39. P. L. McGurgan, *Medical Instrumentation,* July–August 1984, p. 237.

40. T. S. Hargest, "Teaching the Operation of Medical Equipment: The Potential for Misunderstanding." *Medical Instrumentation,* March–April 1984, vol. 18, no. 2, p. 140.

41. T. S. Hargest, *Medical Instrumentation,* March–April 1984, p. 140.

42. T. S. Hargest, *Medical Instrumentation,* March–April 1984, p. 140.

43. T. S. Hargest, *Medical Instrumentation,* March–April 1984, p. 140.

44. T. S. Hargest, *Medical Instrumentation,* March–April 1984, p. 141.

45. T. S. Hargest, *Medical Instrumentation,* March–April 1984, pp. 141–142.

46. T. S. Hargest, *Medical Instrumentation,* March–April 1984, p. 141.

47. T. S. Hargest, *Medical Instrumentation,* March–April 1984, p. 142.

48. N. Kossovsky, R. Kossowsky, and M. Dujovny, "Artificial Hearts, Fractured Valves, and Other Problems with Medical Devices." *Journal of the American Medical Association,* December 20, 1985, vol. 254, no. 23, p. 3307.

49. P. M. Boffey, "Artificial Heart: Should It Be Scaled Back?" *New York Times,* December 3, 1985, p. C3.

50. R. G. Jennings, "The Problem of Obsolescent and Aging Medical Devices." *Journal of Medical Engineering & Technology,* May/June 1984, vol. 8, no. 3, pp. 99–100.

51. E. D. Robins, "The Cult of the Swan-Ganz Catheter: Overuse and Abuse of Pulmonary Flow Catheters." *Annals of Internal Medicine,* September 1985, vol. 103, no. 3, p. 445.

52. "FDA Threatens Regs for Device Reuse." *Health Policy Week*, October 28, 1985, pp. 2–3.

53. A. L. Otten, "Reuse of Devices by Hospitals and Doctors Stirs Debate over Cost Savings and Safety." *Wall Street Journal*, September 14, 1984, p. 31.

54. *Health Policy Week*, October 28, 1985, p. 2.

55. J. Rowley, "FDA Rejects Senators' Call for Rules on Reusing Kidney Dialysis Filters." *Philadelphia Inquirer*, December 25, 1986, p. 9E.

56. J. Needleman, *The Way of the Physician*, pp. 8, 9.

3.

1. "Anesthetists Are Human." *Lancet*, March 17, 1979, p.593.

2. E. C. Pierce, Jr., "Anesthesiology." *Journal of the American Medical Association*, October 25, 1985, vol. 254, no. 16, p. 2318.

3. J. H. Philip, and D. B. Raemer, "Selecting the Optimal Anesthesia Monitoring Array." *Medical Instrumentation*, May–June 1985, vol. 19, no. 3, p. 126.

4. J. B. Cooper, R. S. Newbower, and R. J. Kitz, "An Analysis of Major Errors and Equipment Failures in Anesthesia Management: Considerations for Prevention and Detection." *Anesthesiology*, January 1984, vol. 60, no. 1, p. 40.

5. W. K. Hamilton, "Unexpected Deaths During Anesthesia: Wherein Lies the Cause?" *Anesthesiology*, May 1979, vol. 50, no. 5, p. 383.

6. J. B. Cooper, R. S. Newbower, and R. J. Kitz, *Anesthesiology*, January 1984, p. 34.

7. J. B. Cooper, R. S. Newbower, and R. J. Kitz, *Anesthesiology*, January 1984, p. 40.

8. J. B. Cooper, "Anesthesia Can Be Safer: The Role of Engineering and Technology." *Medical Instrumentation*, May–June 1985, vol. 19, no. 3, p. 105.

9. E. C. Pierce, Jr., *Journal of the American Medical Association*, p. 2318.

10. M. Weitz, *Health Shock*. Englewood Cliffs, N.J.: Prentice-Hall, 1982, p. 13.

11. J. B. Cooper, *Medical Instrumentation*, May–June 1985, p. 105.

12. J. B. Cooper, R. S. Newbower, and R. J. Kitz, *Anesthesiology*, January 1984, p. 39.

13. M. C. Rogers, "Anesthesiology—The Road Not Yet Taken." *Anesthesiology*, December 1985, vol. 63, no. 6, p. 576.

14. W. Tokarz, "Patient Safety Program Is Launched." *American Medical News*, November 1, 1985, p. 8.

15. J. B. Cooper, R. S. Newbower, and R. J. Kitz, *Anesthesiology*, January 1984, pp. 34–42; J. B. Cooper, *Medical Instrumentation*, May–June 1985, pp. 105–108; and J. B. Cooper, R. S. Newbower, C. D. Long, and B. McPeek, "Preventable Anesthesia Mishaps: A Study of Human Factors." *Anesthesiology*, December 1978, vol. 49, no. 6, pp. 399–406.

16. J. B. Cooper, R. S. Newbower, C. D. Long, and B. McPeek, *Anesthesiology*, December 1978, p. 401.

17. J. B. Cooper, R. S. Newbower, C. D. Long, and B. McPeek, *Anesthesiology*, December 1978, p. 401.

18. R. E. Johnstone, "Unusual Iatrogenic Problems," in F. K. Orkin, and L. H. Cooperman, *Complications in Anesthesiology*. Philadelphia: J. B. Lippincott, 1983, p. 692.

19. J. B. Cooper, R. S. Newbower, C. D. Long, and B. McPeek, *Anesthesiology*, December 1978, p. 401.

20. J. B. Cooper, R. S. Newbower, C. D. Long, and B. McPeek, *Anesthesiology*, December 1978, pp. 401–402.

21. J. B. Cooper, *Medical Instrumentation,* May–June 1985, p. 106; J. B. Cooper, R. S. Newbower, C. D. Long, and B. McPeek, *Anesthesiology,* December 1978, p. 403.

22. R. E. Johnstone, in R. K. Orkin and L. H. Cooperman, *Complications in Anesthesiology,* p. 692.

23. E. L. Lloyd, "Functional Toxicity of Anesthesia," a review of D. L. Bruce, *Scientific Basis of Clinical Anesthesia,* in *Lancet,* February 28, 1981, vol. 1, no. 8218, p. 475.

24. J. H. Philip and D. B. Raemer, *Medical Instrumentation,* May–June 1985, pp. 122, 123.

25. J. H. Philip and D. B. Raemer, *Medical Instrumentation,* May–June 1985, p. 124.

26. R. L. Keenan, and C. P. Boyan, "Cardiac Arrest Due to Anesthesia." *Journal of the American Medical Association,* April 26, 1985, vol. 253, no. 16, p. 2373.

27. G. Taylor, C. P. Larson, and R. Prestwich, "Unexpected Cardiac Arrest During Anesthesia and Surgery." *Journal of the American Medical Association,* December 13, 1976, vol. 236, no. 24, pp. 2758–2760.

28. G. Taylor, C. P. Larson, and R. Prestwich, *Journal of the American Medical Association,* December 13, 1976, p. 2760.

29. J. B. Cooper, *Medical Instrumentation,* May–June 1985, pp. 106–107.

30. J. H. Eichhorn, J. B. Cooper, D. J. Cullen, W. R. Maier, J. H. Philip, and R. G. Seeman, "Standards for Patient Monitoring During Anesthesia at Harvard Medical School." *Journal of the American Medical Association,* August 22/29, 1986, vol. 256, no. 8, pp. 1017–1020.

31. J. H. Eichhorn, J. B. Cooper, D. J. Cullen, W. R. Maier, J. H. Philip, and R. G. Seeman, *Journal of the American Medical Association,* August 22/29, 1986, pp. 1017–1020.

32. P. J. Schreiber, "Anesthesia Delivery Equipment: The State of the Industry." *Medical Instrumentation,* May–June 1985, vol. 19, no. 3, p. 119.

33. P. J. Schreiber, *Medical Instrumentation,* May–June 1985, p. 119.

34. P. J. Schreiber, *Medical Instrumentation,* May–June 1985, p. 121.

35. G. Neufeld, Editorial. *Medical Instrumentation,* May–June 1985, vol. 19, no. 3, p. 103.

36. J. P. Welch, "Clinical Engineering in Anesthesia." *Medical Instrumentation,* May–June 1985, vol. 19, no. 3, p. 110.

37. P. H. Schelkun, "Anesthesia Equipment Standards Seen Curbing Suits." *American Medical News,* November 22/29, 1985, p. 36.

38. J. R. Veale, "Role of the FDA in Regulating the Safety of Anesthesia Equipment." *Medical Instrumentation,* May–June 1985, vol. 19, no. 3, p. 128.

39. P. H. Schelkun, *American Medical News,* November 22/29, 1985, p. 36.

40. R. E. Johnstone, "Equipment Malfunction," in F. K. Orkin and L. H. Cooperman, *Complications in Anesthesiology.* Philadelphia: J. B. Lippincott, 1983, p. 643.

41. R. E. Johnstone, in F. K. Orkin and L. H. Cooperman, *Complications in Anesthesiology,* pp. 640–641.

42. R. E. Johnstone, in F. K. Orkin and L. H. Cooperman, *Complications in Anesthesiology,* p. 643.

43. J. B. Cooper, *Medical Instrumentation,* May–June 1985, p. 108.

44. A. S. Keats, "Role of Anesthesia in Surgical Mortality," in F. K. Orkin and L. H. Cooperman, *Complications in Anesthesiology.* Philadelphia: J. B. Lippincott, 1983, p. 9.

45. E. L. Lloyd, *Lancet,* February 28, 1981, p. 475.

46. B. A. Britt, N. Joy, and M. B. Mackay, "Positioning Trauma," in F. K. Orkin and L. H. Cooperman, *Complications in Anesthesiology.* Philadelphia: J. B. Lippincott, 1983, p. 646.

47. B. A. Britt, N. Joy, and M. B. Mackay, in F. K. Orkin and L. H. Cooperman, *Complications in Anesthesiology,* p. 668.

48. G. R. Neufeld, "Fires and Explosions," in F. K. Orkin and L. H. Cooperman, *Complications in Anesthesiology.* Philadelphia: J. B. Lippincott, 1983, p. 671

49. W. O. Robertson, *Medical Malpractice: A Preventive Approach,* Seattle: University of Washington Press, 1985, p. 161.

50. N. J. Shaw and E. G. H. Lyall, "Hazards of Glass Ampoules." *British Medical Journal,* November 16, 1985, p. 1390.

51. D. Janson, "Deaths at Pennsylvania Hospital Laid to Mixup in Labeling Gases." *New York Times,* August 8, 1977, pp. A1, A10.

52. S. L. Liston, "Ear Wax and the Otolaryngologist." *Anesthesiology,* November 1985, vol. 63, no. 5, p. 566.

53. F. DeFazio, "Open Your Eyes Before Opening Your Mouth." *American Health,* November 1984, vol. 3, no. 8, pp. 92–93.

54. D. Hales, "Ask O.R. Antipollution Action Amid Health Threat Debate." *Medical Tribune,* December 5, 1979, p. 1.

55. D. Hales, *Medical Tribune,* December 5, 1979, p. 38.

56. D. Hales, *Medical Tribune,* December 5, 1979, p. 38.

57. J. H. Philip and D. B. Raemer, *Medical Instrumentation,* May–June 1985, p. 122.

4.

1. R. P. Rapini, "Book Review." *New England Journal of Medicine,* September 4, 1986, vol. 315, no. 10, p. 654.

2. "Medical Malpractice Claims." *Parade,* March 10, 1985, p. 17.

3. N. P. Wray and J. A. Friedland, "Detection and Correction of House Staff Error in Physical Diagnosis." *Journal of the American Medical Association,* February 25, 1986, vol. 249, no. 8, p. 1035.

4. N. P. Wray and J. A. Friedland, *Journal of the American Medical Association,* February 25, 1983, p. 1035.

5. S. Wiener, and M. Nathanson, "Physical Examination: Frequently Observed Errors." *Journal of the American Medical Association,* August 16, 1976, vol. 236, no. 7, p. 852.

6. N. P. Wray and J. A. Friedland, *Journal of the American Medical Association,* February 25, 1983, p. 1035.

7. R. M. Poses, R. D. Cebul, M. Collins, and S. S. Fager, "The Accuracy of Experienced Physicians' Probability Estimates for Patients with Sore Throats." *Journal of the American Medical Association,* August 16, 1985, vol. 254, no. 7, p. 927.

8. S. F. Kronlund, and W. R. Phillips, "Physician Knowledge of Risks of Surgical and Invasive Diagnostic Procedures." *Western Journal of Medicine,* April 1985, vol. 142, no. 4, pp. 565–569.

9. S. F. Kronlund and W. R. Phillips, *Western Journal of Medicine,* April 1985, p. 568.

10. S. F. Kronlund and W. R. Phillips, *Western Journal of Medicine,* April 1985, p. 569.

11. S. F. Kronlund and W. R. Phillips, *Western Journal of Medicine,* April 1985, p. 568.

12. E. J. Zarling, H. Sexton, and Pervis Milnor, Jr., "Failure to Diagnose Acute Myocardial Infarction." *Journal of the American Medical Association,* September 2, 1983, vol. 250, no. 9, p. 1179.

13. Betsy McDonald, "New Autopsy Study: Not Even Practice Makes Diagnosis Perfect." Washington University in St. Louis Feature Service, September 1985.

14. "Diagnostic Errors Cited in Study." *San Jose News* (San Jose, Calif.), April 28, 1983, p. 7A.

15. "Pathologists Build Case for More Autopsies." *Medical World News*, October 14, 1985, p. 75.

16. H. H. R. Friederici and M. Sebastian, "Autopsies in a Modern Teaching Hospital." *Archives of Pathology Laboratory Medicine*, June 1984, vol. 108, p. 520.

17. H. H. R. Friederici and M. Sebastian, *Archives of Pathology Laboratory Medicine*, June 1984, p. 521.

18. J. E. Dimsdale, "Delays and Slips in Medical Diagnosis." *Perspectives in Biology and Medicine*, Winter 1984, vol. 27, no. 2, p. 218.

19. J. E. Dimsdale, *Perspectives in Biology and Medicine*, Winter 1984, p. 218.

20. Robert S. Mendelsohn, *Confessions of a Medical Heretic*. Chicago: Basic Books, 1979, pp. 7–8.

21. L. Berlin, "Does the 'Missed' Radiographic Diagnosis Constitute Malpractice?" *Radiology*, May 1977, vol. 123, p. 523.

22. L. Berlin, *Radiology*, May 1977, p. 523.

23. L. Berlin, *Radiology*, May 1977, p. 525.

24. J. T. Rhea, M. S. Potsaid, and S. A. DeLuca, "Errors of Interpretation as Elicited by a Quality Audit of an Emergency Radiology Facility." *Radiology*, August 1979, vol. 132, p. 278.

25. J. T. Rhea, M. S. Potsaid, and S. A. DeLuca, *Radiology*, August 1979, p. 279.

26. L. Berlin, *Radiology*, May 1977, p. 525.

27. R. G. Swensson, S. J. Hessel, and P. G. Herman, "Omissions in Radiology: Faulty Search or Stringent Reporting Criteria?" *Radiology*, June 1977, vol. 123, p. 563.

28. S. Solomon, "Neurology: Application of Neurology to Psychiatry," in H. I. Kaplan and B. J. Sadock, eds., *Comprehensive Textbook of Psychiatry*. Baltimore: Williams & Wilkins, 1985, p. 154.

29. R. S. Hoffman, "Diagnostic Errors in the Evaluation of Behavioral Disorders." *Journal of the American Medical Association*, August 27, 1982, vol. 248, no. 8, p. 964.

30. R. S. Hoffman, *Journal of the American Medical Association*, August 27, 1982, p. 964.

31. R. S. Hoffman, *Journal of the American Medical Association*, August 27, 1982, p. 966.

32. R. S. Hoffman, *Journal of the American Medical Association*, August 27, 1982, p. 966.

33. M. M. Herring, "Debate Over 'False-Positive Schizophrenics'." *Medicine Tribune*, September 25, 1985, p. 3.

34. D. Goleman, "State Hospital Accused of Wrong Diagnoses, Fueling Debate over Nation's Mental Care." *New York Times*, April 23, 1985, p. C8.

35. D. Goleman, *New York Times*, April 23, 1985, p. C8.

36. C. H. Weingarten, L. G. Rosoff, S. V. Eisen, and M. C. Grob, "Medical Care in a Geriatric Psychiatry Unit: Impact on Psychiatric Outcome." *Journal of the American Geriatrics Society*, December 1982, vol. 30, no. 12, p. 739.

37. C. H. Weingarten, L. G. Rosoff, S. V. Eisen, and M. C. Grob, *Journal of the American Geriatrics Society*, December 1982, p. 743.

38. E. K. Koranyi, "Morbidity and Rate of Undiagnosed Physical Illnesses in a Psychiatric Clinic Population." *Archives of General Psychiatry*, April 1979, vol. 36, pp. 414, 415–416.

39. A. Smith, "Primary Care MDs Overlook 90% of Psychiatric Illnesses." *Clinical Psychiatry News*, February 1984, vol. 12, no. 2, pp. 1, 27.

40. A. Smith, *Clinical Psychiatry News*, February 1984, p. 1.

41. A. Smith, *Clinical Psychiatry News*, February 1984, p. 27.

42. J. D. R. Rose, A. H. Troughton, J. S. Harvey, and P. M. Smith, "Depression and Functional Bowel Disorders in Gastrointestinal Outpatients." *Gut*, September 1986, vol. 27, no. 9, p. 1025.

43. B. C. Coleman, "MDs Flunk Test to Find Cancerous Breast Lumps." *The Home News* (New Brunswick, N.J.), April 19, 1985, p. A6.

44. H. Rasmussen, "Rx for Malpractice Prevention." *The Female Patient,* July 1985, vol. 10, pp. 90, 93.

45. N. Brozan, "Doctors Learning to Diagnose Alcoholism." *New York Times,* December 16, 1985, p. B16.

46. D. Kaul, "What's Up, Doc?" *Philadelphia Daily News,* August 22, 1986, p. 42.

47. S. Rimer, "Aftermath." *Washington Post,* April 17, 1981, pp. A1, A4; see also W. A. Check, "Malpractice Threat: More Tests Not Always the Answer." *Journal of the American Medical Association,* October 24/31, 1980, vol. 244, no. 17, pp. 1886–1887.

48. "Man Awarded $2.5 Million." *Santa Barbara News Press,* November 4, 1983, p. A-6.

49. D. Goleman, *New York Times,* April 23, 1985, p. C1.

5.

1. C. Carver, *Patient Beware.* Scarborough, Ontario: Prentice-Hall Canada, Inc., 1984, p. 37.

2. M. B. Rothenberg and J. Rothenberg, "The Omnipotence-Omniscience Syndrome." *Resident and Staff Physician,* June 1985, vol. 31, no. 6, p. 84.

3. President's Commission for the Study of Ethical Problems in Medicine and Biomedical and Behavioral Research, *Making Health Care Decisions: A Report on the Ethical and Legal Implications of Informed Consent in the Patient-Practitioner Relationship.* Washington, D.C.: U.S. Government Printing Office, 1982, p. 131.

4. R. L. Dickman, R. E. Sarnacki, F. T. Schimpfhauser, and L. A. Katz, "Medical Students from Natural Science and Nonscience Undergraduate Backgrounds." *Journal of the American Medical Association,* June 27, 1980, vol. 243, no. 24, p. 2506.

5. R. L. Dickman, R. E. Sarnacki, F. T. Schimpfhauser, and L. A. Katz, *Journal of the American Medical Association,* June 27, 1980, p. 2506.

6. S. L. Keill, and B. Willer, "Detection of Psychiatrically At-Risk Applicants in the Medical School Admission Process." *Journal of Medical Education,* October 1985, vol. 60, p. 802.

7. P. M. Rabinowitz, *Talking Medicine.* New York: New American Library, 1983.

8. P. M. Rabinowitz, *Talking Medicine,* p. 17.

9. P. M. Rabinowitz, *Talking Medicine,* p. 18.

10. President's Commission for the Study of Ethical Problems in Medicine and Biomedical and Behavioral Research, *Making Health Care Decisions: A Report on the Ethical and Legal Implications of Informed Consent in the Patient-Practitioner Relationship,* p. 131.

11. S. L. Keill and B. Willer, *Journal of Medical Education,* October 1985, p. 800.

12. M. B. Rothenberg and J. Rothenberg, *Resident and Staff Physician,* June 1985, p. 84.

13. S. L. Keill and B. Willer, *Journal of Medical Education,* October 1985, p. 800.

14. S. L. Keill and B. Willer, *Journal of Medical Education,* October 1985, p. 802.

15. C. Carver, *Patient Beware,* p. 37.

16. V. W. Sidel and R. Sidel, *A Healthy State.* New York: Pantheon, 1983, p. 85.

17. C. Carver, *Patient Beware,* pp. 28–29.

18. C. Carver, *Patient Beware,* p. 19.

19. V. W. Sidel and R. Sidel, *A Healthy State,* p. 331.

20. President's Commission for the Study of Ethical Problems in Medicine and Biomedical and Behavioral Research, *Making Health Care Decisions: A Report on the Ethical and Legal Implications of Informed Consent in the Patient-Practitioner Relationship,* pp. 136–137.

21. C. Carver, *Patient Beware,* p. 28.

22. President's Commission for the Study of Ethical Problems in Medicine and Biomedical and Behavioral Research, *Making Health Care Decisions: A Report on the Ethical and Legal Implications of Informed Consent in the Patient-Practitioner Relationship,* p. 138.

23. J. Robinson, "Are We Teaching Students That Patients Don't Matter?" *Journal of Medical Ethics,* March 1985, vol. 11, no. 1, p. 19.

24. T. Mizrahi, "Managing Medical Mistakes: Ideology, Insularity and Accountability Among Internists-in-Training." *Social Science and Medicine,* vol. 19, no. 2, p. 135.

25. T. Mizrahi, *Social Science Medicine,* 1984, p. 135.

26. H. J. Geiger, "Diagnosing the Doctors," *Currents,* WNET-TV, November 21, 1985.

27. G. J. Bazzoli, "Medical Education Indebtedness: Does It Affect Physician Specialty Choice?" *Health Affairs,* Summer 1985, p. 98.

28. "Will Med-School Debts Govern M.D.'s Specialty Choices?" *Medical Economics,* November 11, 1985, p. 264.

29. J. Walsh, "The M.D. Class of '86: Smaller, Deeper in Debt." *Science,* October 3, 1986, p. 21.

30. G. J. Bazzoli, *Health Affairs,* Summer 1985, p. 98.

31. J. P. Winter, "Medical Education Indebtedness." *Journal of the American Medical Association,* July 5, 1985, vol. 254, no. 1, p. 58.

32. V. W. Sidel and R. Sidel, *A Healthy State,* p. 291.

33. C. Carver, *Patient Beware,* p. 156.

34. C. Carver, *Patient Beware,* p. 29.

35. A.L. Siu, S. A. Mayer-Oakes, and R. H. Brook, "Innovations in Medical Curricula: Templates for Change?" *Health Affairs,* Summer 1985, p. 64.

36. President's Commission for the Study of Ethical Problems in Medicine and Biomedical and Behavioral Research, *Making Health Care Decisions: A Report on the Ethical and Legal Implications of Informed Consent in the Patient-Practitioner Relationship,* p. 141.

37. President's Commission for the Study of Ethical Problems in Medicine and Biomedical and Behavioral Research, *Making Health Care Decisions: A Report on the Ethical and Legal Implications of Informed Consent in the Patient-Practitioner Relationship,* p. 130.

38. V. W. Sidel and R. Sidel, *A Healthy State,* p. 332.

39. President's Commission for the Study of Ethical Problems in Medicine and Biomedical and Behavioral Research, *Making Health Care Decisions: A Report on the Ethical and Legal Implications of Informed Consent in the Patient-Practitioner Relationship,* p. 130.

40. V. W. Sidel and R. Sidel, *A Healthy State,* p. 332.

41. R. S. Mendelsohn, *Confessions of a Medical Heretic.* Chicago: Contemporary Books, 1979, p. 181.

42. R. S. Mendelsohn, *Confessions of a Medical Heretic,* p. 181.

43. R. Huet-Cox, "Medical Education: New Wine in Old Wine Skins," in V. W. Sidel and R. Sidel, eds., *Reforming Medicine.* New York: Pantheon, 1984, p. 149.

6.

1. S. G. Wolf, and B. B. Berle, eds. *Limits of Medicine: Proceedings of the Totts Gap Colloquium on the Limits of Medicine: The Doctor's Job in the Coming Era.* Held in Totts Gap, Pennsylvania. June 10–12, 1976. New York: Plenum Press, 1978, p. 48.

2. T. Preston, *The Clay Pedestal.* Seattle: Madrona, 1981, p. 129.

3. T. Preston, *The Clay Pedestal,* pp. 130–131.

4. R. S. Mendelsohn, *Confessions of a Medical Heretic.* Chicago: Contemporary Books, 1979, p. 7.

5. W. O. Robertson, *Medical Malpractice: A Preventive Approach.* Seattle: University of Washington Press, 1985, p. 96.

6. C. Kramer, *The Negligent Doctor.* New York: Crown, 1968, p. 59.

7. S. M. Eby, "How to Question Medical Test Results." *Self,* September 1981, p. 55.

8. P. F. Griner and R. J. Glaser, "Misuse of Laboratory Tests and Diagnostic Procedures." *New England Journal of Medicine,* November 18, 1982, vol. 307, no. 21, p. 1336.

9. M. Napoli, "Pass/Fail Health Tests: 'Test-Happy' Doctors—How to Tell What's Needed, What's Not." *Self,* August 1984, p. 158.

10. M. Napoli, *Self,* August 1984, p. 158.

11. G. D. Lundberg, "Perseveration of Laboratory Test Ordering: A Syndrome of Affecting Clinicians." *Journal of the American Medical Association,* February 4, 1983, vol. 249, no. 5, p. 639.

12. L. Zieve, "Misinterpretation and Abuse of Laboratory Tests by Clinicians," *Annals of the New York Academy of Sciences,* February 28, 1966, p. 571.

13. L. Zieve, *Annals of the New York Academy of Sciences,* February 28, 1966, p. 571.

14. I. G. Stump, "Are Diagnostic Tests Repeated Unnecessarily on Hospital Admission?" *Canadian Medical Association Journal,* May 15, 1983, vol. 128, p. 1186.

15. P. F. Griner and R. J. Glaser, *New England Journal of Medicine,* November 18, 1982, p. 1338.

16. E. T. Wong, M. M. McCarron, and S. T. Shaw, Jr., "Ordering of Laboratory Tests in a Teaching Hospital." *Journal of the American Medical Association,* June 10, 1983, vol. 249, no. 22, p. 3079.

17. E. T. Wong and T. L. Lincoln, "Ready! Fire! . . . Aim! An Inquiry into Laboratory Test Ordering." *Journal of the American Medical Association,* November 11, 1983, vol. 250, no. 18, p. 2511.

18. E. T. Wong and T. L. Lincoln, *Journal of the American Medical Association,* November 11, 1983, p. 2513.

19. E. T. Wong and T. L. Lincoln, *Journal of the American Medical Association,* November 11, 1983, p. 2511.

20. V. Fuchs, "The Growing Demand for Medical Care." *New England Journal of Medicine,* July 25, 1968, vol. 279, p. 193.

21. "Team Approach May Result in Overordering Tests." *Internal Medicine News,* July 15–31, 1984, vol. 17, no. 14, p. 20.

22. "Doctors' Fee Schedules Tied to Ordering of Medical Tests." *New York Times,* April 24, 1986, p. A14.

23. *New York Times,* April 24, 1986, p. A14.

24. C. Carver, *Patient Beware.* Scarborough, Ontario: Prentice-Hall Canada, Inc., 1984, p. 31.

25. M. W. Lear, *Heartsounds.* New York: Pocket Books, 1981, pp. 272–273.

26. L. Lander, *Defective Medicine.* New York: Farrar, Straus, Giroux, 1978, p. 37.

27. E. T. Wong, M. M. McCarron, and S. T. Shaw, Jr., *Journal of the American Medical Association,* June 10, 1983, p. 3079.

28. E. T. Wong, M. M. McCarron, and S. T. Shaw, Jr., *Journal of the American Medical Association,* June 10, 1983, p. 3079.

29. H. P. Russe, "The Use and Abuse of Laboratory Tests." *Medical Clinics of North America,* January 1969, vol. 53, no. 1, pp. 229–230.

30. B. G. Wertman, S. V. Sostrin, Z. Pavlova, and G. D. Lundberg, "Why Do Physicians Order Laboratory Tests?" *Journal of the American Medical Association,* May 23/30, 1980, vol. 243, no. 20, p. 2081.

31. J. W. Mold and H. F. Stein, "The Cascade Effect in the Clinical Care of Patients." *New England Journal of Medicine,* February 20, 1986, vol. 314, no. 8, p. 512.

32. J. W. Mold and H. F. Stein, "Correspondence: The Cascade Effect in the Clinical Care of Patients." *New England Journal of Medicine,* July 31, 1986, vol. 315, no. 5, p. 320.

33. J. W. Mold and H. F. Stein, *New England Journal of Medicine,* February 20, 1986, p. 514.

34. P. F. Griner and R. J. Glaser, *New England Journal of Medicine,* November 18, 1982, pp. 1338–1339.

35. M. Napoli, *Self,* August 1984, p. 160.

36. M. Napoli, *Self,* August 1984, p. 162.

37. I. Molotsky, "Blue Cross Devises Plan to Curb Unneeded Tests." *New York Times,* June 14, 1984, p. B28.

38. R. S. Mendelsohn, *Confessions of a Medical Heretic,* pp. 12–13.

39. A. R. Bradwell, M. H. B. Carmalt, and T. P. Whitehead, "Explaining the Unexpected Abnormal Results of Biochemical Profile Investigations." *Lancet,* November 2, 1974, p. 1071.

40. W. O. Robertson, *Medical Malpractice: A Preventive Approach,* p. 97.

41. W. O. Robertson, *Medical Malpractice: A Preventive Approach,* p. 97.

42. R. L. Dabice, "Pap Test Utility Compromised by Mistakes." *Medical Tribune,* September 4, 1985, p. 19.

43. L. Zieve, *Annals of the New York Academy of Sciences,* February 28, 1966, pp. 563–571.

44. L. Zieve, *Annals of the New York Academy of Sciences,* February 28, 1966, p. 566.

45. H. P. Russe, *Medical Clinics of North America,* January 1969, pp. 226–227.

46. R. K. Riegelman, "The Limits of the Laboratory: Nuances of Normality." *Postgraduate Medicine,* October 1981, vol. 70, no. 4, p. 206.

47. R. K. Riegelman, *Postgraduate Medicine,* October 1981, p. 204.

48. R. K. Riegelman, *Postgraduate Medicine,* October 1981, p. 204.

49. R. K. Riegelman, *Postgraduate Medicine,* October 1981, p. 205.

50. R. K. Riegelman, *Postgraduate Medicine,* October 1981, p. 207.

51. M. Karpen, "Clinical Lab Arriving in MD's Office." *International Medical News Weekly,* October 3, 1984, p. 1.

52. "Physician-Office Lab Results Less Accurate than Those of Licensed Labs, Study Shows." *Medical World News,* April 9, 1984, vol. 25, no. 7, p. 46.

53. *Medical World News,* April 9, 1984, p. 46.

54. *Medical World News,* April 9, 1984, p. 47.

55. *Medical World News,* April 9, 1984, p. 47.

56. R. Crawley, R. Belsey, D. Brock, and D. M. Baer, "Regulation of Physician's Office Laboratories: The Idaho Experience." *Journal of the American Medical Association,* January 17, 1986, vol. 255, no. 3, p. 375.

57. R. Crawley, R. Belsey, D. Brock, and D. M. Baer, *Journal of the American Medical Association,* January 17, 1986, p. 375.

58. R. Crawley, R. Belsey, D. Brock, and D. M. Baer, *Journal of the American Medical Association,* January 17, 1986, p. 376.

59. R. Crawley, R. Belsey, D. Brock, and D. M. Baer, *Journal of the American Medical Association,* January 17, 1986, p. 377.

60. R. Crawley, R. Belsey, D. Brock, and D. M. Baer, *Journal of the American Medical Association,* January 17, 1986 pp. 380–381.

61. R. Crawley, R. Belsey, D. Brock, and D. M. Baer, *Journal of the American Medical Association,* January 17, 1986, p. 381.

62. W. Bogdanich, "Medical Labs, Trusted as Largely Error-Free, Are Far from Infallible." *Wall Street Journal,* February 2, 1987, p. 14.

63. A. S. Freese, *Managing Your Doctor.* New York: Stein and Day, 1975, p. 96.

64. N. Brozan, "Early Detection Is Key in Breast Cancer." *New York Times,* June 21, 1986, p. 52.

65. "Mammography Not Fail-Safe, Doctors Caution." *The Home News* (New Brunswick, N.J.), January 24, 1986, p. A6.

66. J. W. Gofman and E. O'Connor, *X-Rays: Health Effects of Common Exams.* San Francisco: Sierra Club Books, 1985, p. 310.

67. J. W. Gofman and E. O'Connor, *X-Rays: Health Effects of Common Exams,* p. 33.

68. J. W. Gofman and E. O'Connor, *X-Rays: Health Effects of Common Exams,* p. 11.

69. J. W. Gofman and E. O'Connor, *X-Rays: Health Effects of Common Exams,* p. 2.

70. J. W. Gofman and E. O'Connor, *X-Rays: Health Effects of Common Exams,* p. 368.

71. J. W. Gofman and E. O'Connor, *X-Rays: Health Effects of Common Exams,* p. 18.

72. J. W. Gofman and E. O'Connor, *X-Rays: Health Effects of Common Exams,* p. 31.

73. J. W. Gofman and E. O'Connor, *X-Rays: Health Effects of Common Exams,* p. 35.

74. M. Weitz, *Health Shock,* Englewood Cliffs, N.J.: Prentice-Hall, 1982, p. v.

75. J. W. Gofman and E. O'Connor, *X-Rays: Health Effects of Common Exams,* p. 299.

76. J. W. Gofman and E. O'Connor, *X-Rays: Health Effects of Common Exams,* p. 299.

77. J. Whitlow, "Screening for Spine Disorder Raises Questions." *The Sunday* (Newark, N.J.) *Star-Ledger,* November 3, 1985, Section One, p. 97.

78. "Scoliosis Screening—Cause for Alarm." *HealthFacts,* October 1985, vol. X, no. 77, p. 6.

79. J. W. Gofman and E. O'Connor, *X-Rays: Health Effects of Common Exams,* pp. 361–362.

80. J. W. Gofman and E. O'Connor, *X-Rays: Health Effects of Common Exams,* p. 369.

81. J. W. Gofman and E. O'Connor, *X-Rays: Health Effects of Common Exams,* p. 13.

82. M. Weitz, *Health Shock,* p. 89.

83. J. W. Gofman and E. O'Connor, *X-Rays: Health Effects of Common Exams,* p. 13.

84. H. E. Johns and J. R. Cunningham, *The Physics of Radiology,* 4th ed., Springfield, Ill.: C. C. Thomas, 1983, p. 557.

85. J. W. Gofman and E. O'Connor, *X-Rays: Health Effects of Common Exams,* pp. 24–25.

86. J. W. Gofman and E. O'Connor, *X-Rays: Health Effects of Common Exams,* p. 13.

87. M. Weitz, *Health Shock,* p. 89.

88. J. W. Gofman and E. O'Connor, *X-Rays: Health Effects of Common Exams,* p. 36.

89. J. W. Gofman and E. O'Connor, *X-Rays: Health Effects of Common Exams* p. 336.

90. "Fatal Radiation Dose in Therapy Attributed to Computer Mistake." *New York Times,* June 21, 1986, p. 50.

91. A. S. Freese, *Managing Your Doctor,* p. 96.

92. J. W. Gofman and E. O'Connor, *X-Rays: Health Effects of Common Exams,* p. 370.

7.

1. H. H. Keyser, *Women Under the Knife.* Philadelphia: George F. Stickley, 1984, pp. 50–51.

2. H. H. Keyser, *Women Under the Knife,* p. 51.

3. R. G. Schneider, *When to Say No to Surgery.* Englewood Cliffs, N.J.: Prentice-Hall, 1982, pp. vii–viii.

4. M. Weitz, *Health Shock.* Englewood Cliffs, N.J.: Prentice-Hall, 1982, p. 10.

5. G. J. Gennaoui, "Breaking the Oath: Are Some Doctors Performing Unnecessary Surgery?" *Hahnemann University,* Summer 1985, p. 9.

6. E. Eckholm, "Curbs Sought in Caesarean Deliveries." *New York Times,* August 11, 1986, p. A10.

7. E. Eckholm, *New York Times,* August 11, 1986, p. A10.

8. H. H. Keyser, *Women Under the Knife,* p. 48.

9. G. Corea, *The Hidden Malpractice,* New York: Harper & Row, 1985, p. 14.

10. "House Report Says 23 Percent of Lens Implants Not Necessary." *Hospitals,* September 1, 1985, p. 52.

11. L. Rothberg, "About Circumcision" (letter), *New York Times,* October 16, 1985, p. C8.

12. W. E. Schmidt, "A Circumcision Method Draws New Concern," *New York Times* October 8, 1985, p. C1.

13. W. E. Schmidt, *New York Times,* October 8, 1985, p. C7.

14. W. E. Schmidt, *New York Times,* October 8, 1985, p. C7.

15. J. Guinther, *The Malpractitioners.* New York: Doubleday, 1978, p. 128.

16. J. Guinther, *The Malpractitioners,* p. 130.

17. M. I. Roemer and J. L. Schwartz, "Doctor Slowdown: Effects on the Population of Los Angeles County." *Social Science and Medicine,* December 1979, vol. 13C, p. 214.

18. M. I. Roemer and J. L. Schwartz, *Social Science and Medicine,* December 1979, p. 217.

19. M. I. Roemer and J. L. Schwartz, *Social Science and Medicine,* December 1979, p. 215.

20. M. I. Roemer and J. L. Schwartz, *Social Science and Medicine,* December 1979, p. 217.

21. M. I. Roemer and J. L. Schwartz, *Social Science and Medicine,* December 1979, p. 217.

22. T. Preston, *The Clay Pedestal,* Seattle: Madrona, 1981, pp. 134–135.

23. R. Macklin, "Ethical Implications of Surgical Experiments." *American College of Surgeons Bulletin,* June 1985, vol. 70, no. 6, p. 5.

24. "Shortsighted Surgery." *New York Times,* November 13, 1985, p. A26.

25. L. Lander, *Defective Medicine,* New York: Farrar, Straus, Giroux, 1978, pp. 50–51.

26. G. J. Gennaoui, *Hahnemann University,* Summer 1985, p. 11.

27. G. J. Gennaoui, *Hahnemann University,* Summer 1985, p. 11.

28. S. G. Wolf and B. B. Berle, eds., *Limits of Medicine: Proceedings of the Totts Gap Colloquium on the Limits of Medicine: The Doctor's Job in the Coming Era.* Held in Totts Gap, Pennsylvania, June 10–12, 1976. New York: Plenum Press, 1978, p. 65.

29. M. Weitz, *Health Shock,* p. 15.

30. I. M. Rutkow and G. D. Zuidema, "Unnecessary Surgery: An Update." *Surgery,* November 1978, p. 671.

31. G. J. Gennaoui, *Hahnemann University,* Summer 1985, p. 10.

32. G. J. Gennaoui, *Hahnemann University,* Summer 1985, p. 10.

33. D. F. Stroman, *The Medical Establishment and Social Responsibility.* Port Washington, N.Y.: Kennikat Press, 1976, p. 61.

34. V. W. Sidel and R. Sidel, *A Healthy State.* New York: Pantheon, 1983, p. 5.

35. J. L. Breen, "The Forgotten Half of Our Specialty." *The Female Patient,* September 1983, vol. 8, p. 1.

36. L. Shearer, "Most Frequently Performed Operations." *Parade,* September 15, 1985, p. 20.

37. J. L. Breen, *The Female Patient,* September 1983, p. 2.

38. J. L. Breen, *The Female Patient,* September 1983, p. 2.

39. V. W. Sidel and R. Sidel, *A Healthy State,* p. 76.

40. J. Van, "Surgeon Surplus May Dull Skills." *Philadelphia Inquirer,* October 19, 1986, p. 28A.

41. S. Rich, "Surgery Death Rates Compared in Study." *Easton Express,* April 26, 1984.

42. J. Brinkley, "V.A. Finds Errors in Heart Deaths." *New York Times,* August 13, 1986, p. B8; also, "V.A. Under Fire, Will Close Some Heart Units." *New York Times,* August 17, 1986, p. E7.

43. W. Bogdanich and T. J. Quinn, "Heart Surgery Units Break Rules on Safety." *The Plain Dealer,* October 23, 1983, p. 1A.

44. W. Bogdanich and T. J. Quinn, *The Plain Dealer,* October 23, 1983, p. 1A.

45. "Three City Hospitals Fined by State." *New York Times,* June 22, 1986, p. 28.

46. N. P. Couch, N. L. Tilney, A. A. Rayner, and F. D. Moore, "The High Cost of Low-Frequency Events." *New England Journal of Medicine,* March 12, 1981, vol. 304, no. 11, pp. 634–637.

47. M. Waldholz, "Surgical Mistakes Caused Complications for 36 of 2,500 People in Hospital Study." *Wall Street Journal,* March 12, 1981, p. 40.

48. N. P. Couch, N. L. Tilney, A. A. Rayner, and F. D. Moore, *New England Journal of Medicine,* March 12, 1981, p. 635.

49. W. O. Robertson, *Medical Malpractice: A Preventive Approach.* Seattle: University of Washington Press, 1985, pp. 49–50.

50. W. O. Robertson, *Medical Malpractice: A Preventive Approach,* p. 50.

51. L. Lander, *Defective Medicine,* pp. 54–55.

8.

1. M. C. Nahata, "Handwashing Prevents Infections." *Drugs Intelligence and Clinical Pharmacy,* October 1985, p. 738.

2. R. K. Albert and F. Condie, "Hand-Washing Patterns in Medical Intensive-Care Units." *New England Journal of Medicine,* June 11, 1981, vol. 304, no. 24, p. 1465.

3. M. C. Nahata, *Drug Intelligence and Clinical Pharmacy,* October 1985, p. 738.

4. T. C. Horan, J. W. White, W. R. Jarvis, T. G. Emori, D. H. Culver, V. P. Munn, C. Thornsberry, D. R. Olson, and J. M. Hughes, "CDC Surveillance Summaries 1986: Nosocomial Infection Surveillance, 1984." *Morbidity and Mortality Weekly Report. CDC Surveillance Summaries 1986.* pp. 17SS–29SS.

5. R. E. Dixon, "Nosocomial Bacteremia: Etiology, Diagnosis, and Prevention." *Hospital Physician,* July 1985, pp. 17.

6. V. L. Yu, A. Goetz, M. Wagener, P. B. Smith, and J. D. Rihs, "Staphylococcus Aureus Nasal Carriage and Infection in Patients on Hemodialysis: Efficacy of Antibiotic Prophylaxis." *New England Journal of Medicine,* July 10, 1986, vol. 315, no. 2, p. 91.

7. L. S. Elting, G. P. Bodey, and V. Fainstein, "Polymicrobial Septicemia in the Cancer Patient." *Medicine,* July 1986, vol. 65, no. 4, p. 218.

8. S. D. Podnos, G. B. Toews, and A. K. Pierce, "Nosocomial Pneumonia in Patients in Intensive Care Units." *The Western Journal of Medicine,* November 1985, vol. 143, no. 5, p. 622.

9. C. W. Stratton, "Pulmonary Infections in Critical Care Medicine—The Wright State University School of Medicine Symposium: Bacterial Pneumonias—An Overview with Emphasis on Pathogenesis, Diagnosis and Treatment." *Heart and Lung,* May 1986, vol. 15, no 3, pp. 226-244.

10. C. W. Stratton, *Heart and Lung,* May 1986, pp. 226-244.

11. A. Koral, "A Healthier Place to Get Better." *Parade,* December 8, 1985, p. 19.

12. R. A. Garibaldi, S. Maglio, T. Lerer, D. Becker, and R. Lyons, "Comparison of Nonwoven and Woven Gown and Drape Fabric to Prevent Intraoperative Wound Contamination and Postoperative Infection." *American Journal of Surgery,* November 1986, vol. 152, no. 5, p. 505.

13. M. C. Nahata, *Drug Intelligence and Clinical Pharmacy,* October 1985, p. 738.

14. R. J. Albert and F. Condie, *New England Journal of Medicine,* June 11, 1981, p. 1466.

15. D. Rimland, "Nosocomial Infections with Methicillin and Tobyramycin Resistant *Staphylococcus aureus*—Implication of Physiotherapy in Hospital-Wide Dissemination." *The American Journal of the Medical Sciences,* September 1985, vol. 290, no. 3, p. 95.

16. D. Rimland, *The American Journal of the Medical Sciences,* September 1985, p. 95.

17. "Hospital Aides Blamed in Illnesses of 26 Babies." *New York Times,* December 13, 1985, p. A16.

18. A. W. Hastings, "Nosocomial Infections: Washing Away the Problem." *Medical World News,* September 26, 1983, p. 49.

19. A. W. Hastings, *Medical World News,* September 26, 1983, p. 49.

20. R. A. Weinstein and L. S. Young, "Other Procedure-Related Infections." in J. V. Bennett and P. S. Brachman, eds., *Hospital Infections.* Boston: Little, Brown and Co., 1979, p. 503.

21. J. R. Allen and T. K. Oliver, Jr., "The Newborn Nursery," in J. V. Bennett and P. S. Brachman, eds., *Hospital Infections.* Boston: Little, Brown and Co., 1979, p. 110.

22. H. Laufman, "The Operating Room," in J. V. Bennett and P. S. Brachman, eds., *Hospital Infections.* Boston: Little, Brown and Co., 1979, p. 136.

23. M. B. Coyle and J. C. Sherris, "The Clinical Laboratory," in J. V. Bennett and P. S. Brachman, eds., *Hospital Infections.* Boston: Little, Brown and Co., 1979, p. 142.

24. L. Corey and P. G. Spear, "Medical Progress: Infections with Herpes Simplex Viruses." *New England Journal of Medicine,* March 20, 1986, vol. 314, no. 12, pp. 749-757.

25. G. F. Mallison, "The Inanimate Environment," in J. V. Bennett and P. S. Brachman, eds. *Hospital Infections.* Boston: Little, Brown and Co., 1979, p. 89.

26. S. Cohen, "Dental Aide Spreads Herpes Virus," *The Home News* (New Brunswick, N.J.), October 19, 1984, p. A8.

27. A. E. Buxton, "The Intensive-Care Unit," in J. V. Bennett and P. S. Brachman, eds., *Hospital Infections.* Boston: Little, Brown and Co., 1979, p. 102.

28. P. J. Van Den Broek, A. S. Lampe, G. A. M. Berbée, J. Thompson, and R. P. Mouton, "Epidemic of Prosthetic Valve Endocarditis Caused by Staphylococcus Epidermidis." *British Medical Journal,* October 5, 1985, vol. 291, pp. 949-950.

29. R. W. Haley, D. H. Culver, J. W. White, W. M. Morgan, and T. G. Emori,

"The Nationwide Nosocomial Infection Rate," from *American Journal of Epidemiology,* February 1985, excerpted in *Medical Benefits,* February 28, 1985, p. 3.

30. A. Koral, *Parade,* December 8, 1985, p. 19.

31. *Medical Benefits,* February 28, 1985, p. 3.

32. A. Koral, *Parade,* December 8, 1985, p. 19.

33. "Case Records of the Massachusetts General Hospital: Case 31-1985." *New England Journal of Medicine,* August 1, 1985, vol. 313, no. 5, p. 314.

34. R. Platt, B. F. Polk, B. Murdock, and B. Rosner, "Mortality Associated with Nosocomial Urinary-Tract Infection." *New England Journal of Medicine,* September 9, 1982, vol. 307, no. 11, p. 637.

35. J. A. Bryan, "The Hemodialysis Unit," in J. V. Bennett and P. S. Brachman, eds., *Hospital Infections.* Boston: Little, Brown and Co., 1979, p. 93.

36. J. A. Bryan, in J. V. Bennett and P. S. Brachman, eds., *Hospital Infections,* p. 94.

37. E. J. Gangarosa, "Food Services," in J. V. Bennett and P. S. Brachman, eds., *Hospital Infections.* Boston: Little, Brown and Co., 1979, pp. 117-118.

38. G. F. Mallison, "Central Service," in J. V. Bennett and P. S. Brachman, eds., *Hospital Infections.* Boston: Little, Brown and Co., 1979, p. 123.

39. M. B. Coyle and J. C. Sherris, in J. V. Bennett and P. S. Brachman, eds., *Hospital Infections,* p. 142.

40. J. Fierer, P. M. Taylor, and H. M. Gezon, *"Pseudomonas Aeruginosa* Epidemic Traced to Delivery-Room Resuscitators." *New England Journal of Medicine,* May 4, 1967, vol. 276, no. 18, pp. 991-996.

41. W. G. Elliott, "Postoperative Complications." *Western Journal of Medicine,* November 1983, p. 716.

42. L. J. Anderson, L. P. Williams, Jr., J. B. Layde, F. R. Dixon, and W. G. Winkler, "Nosocomial Rabies: Investigation of Contacts of Human Rabies Cases Associated with a Corneal Transplant." *American Journal of Public Health,* April 1984, vol. 74, no. 4, pp. 370-372.

43. P. L. Garbe, B. J. Davis, J. S. Weisfeld, L. Markowitz, P. Miner, F. Garrity, J. M. Barbaree, and A. L. Reingold, "Nosocomial Legionnaires' Disease: Epidemiologic Demonstration of Cooling Towers as a Source." *Journal of the American Medical Association,* July 26, 1985, vol. 254, no. 4, pp. 521-524.

44. H. Laufman, "The Operating Room," in J. V. Bennett and P. S. Brachman, eds., *Hospital Infections.* Boston: Little, Brown and Co., 1979, p. 129.

45. H. Laufman, in J. V. Bennett and P. S. Brachman, eds., *Hospital Infections,* p. 132.

46. H. Laufman, in J. V. Bennett and P. S. Brachman, eds., *Hospital Infections,* pp. 131-132.

47. E. Apgar, "State Closes Surgery Suite for Half-Day." *The Home News* (New Brunswick, N.J.), November 3, 1985, p. B5.

48. R. W. Haley, D. H. Culver, J. W. White, W. M. Morgan, T. G. Emori, V. P. Munn, and T. M. Hooton, "The Efficacy of Infection Surveillance and Control Programs in Preventing Nosocomial Infections in U.S. Hospitals." *American Journal of Epidemiology,* February 1985, vol. 121, no. 2, p. 182.

49. A. Koral, *Parade,* December 8, 1985, p. 19.

50. R. W. Haley, D. H. Culver, J. W. White, W. M. Morgan, T. G. Emori, V. P. Munn, and T. M. Hooton, *American Journal of Epidemiology,* February 1985, p. 182.

51. A. Koral, *Parade,* December 8, 1985, p. 19.

52. J. Graham, "Infection Control Could Save Millions." *Modern Healthcare,* January 4, 1985, p. 104.

53. M. J. Blaser, "Infectious Diarrheas: Acute, Chronic, and Iatrogenic." *Annals of Internal Medicine,* November 1986, vol. 105, no. 5, p. 786.

54. C. B. Inlander and E. Weiner, *Take This Book to the Hospital with You,* Emmaus, Pa.: Rodale Press, 1986, pp. 121–122.

55. A. E. Buxton, in J. V. Bennett and P. S. Brachman, eds., *Hospital Infections,* p. 99.

56. M. J. Blaser, *Annals of Internal Medicine,* November 1986, pp. 786–787.

57. H. N. Beaty, and R. G. Petersdorf, "Iatrogenic Factors in Infectious Disease." *Annals of Internal Medicine,* October 1966, vol. 65, no. 4, pp. 641, 655.

58. S. R. Zellner and L. E. Cluff, "The Pharmacy," in J. V. Bennett and P. S. Brachman, eds., *Hospital Infections.* Boston: Little, Brown and Co., 1979, p. 116.

59. R. Pear, "Need Cited for U.S. Testing for Hospital Disinfectants." *New York Times,* June 22, 1986, p. 16.

60. R. Pear, *New York Times,* June 22, 1986, p. 16.

9.

1. J. Nordheimer, "One Death, Many Questions in Miami." *New York Times,* March 10, 1985, p. 22.

2. J. Nordheimer, *New York Times,* March 10, 1985, p. 22.

3. L. Lander, *Defective Medicine.* New York: Farrar, Straus, Giroux, 1978, p. 27.

4. W. O. Robertson, *Medical Malpractice: A Preventive Approach.* Seattle: University of Washington Press, 1985, p. 86.

5. I. Illich, *Medical Nemesis.* New York: Pantheon, 1976, pp. 27–28.

6. N. M. Davis and M. R. Cohen, *Medication Errors: Causes and Prevention.* Philadelphia: George F. Stickley, 1981, p. 3.

7. N. M. Davis and M. R. Cohen, *Medication Errors: Causes and Prevention,* p. 1.

8. N. M. Davis and M. R. Cohen, *Medication Errors: Causes and Prevention,* p. 1.

9. W. O. Robertson, *Medical Malpractice: A Preventive Approach,* p. 82.

10. W. O. Robertson, *Medical Malpractice: A Preventive Approach,* p. 77.

11. L. Lander, *Defective Medicine,* p. 45.

12. J. A. Miller, "Bad Reactions for Drugged Country." *Science News,* December 17, 1983, vol. 124, no. 25, p. 392.

13. W. O. Robertson, *Medical Malpractice: A Preventive Approach,* p. 110.

14. I. Illich, *Medical Nemesis,* pp. 74–75.

15. M. Weitz, *Health Shock.* Englewood Cliffs, N.J.: Prentice-Hall, 1982, p. v.

16. A. S. Freese, *Managing Your Doctor.* New York: Stein and Day, 1975, p. 143.

17. A. S. Freese, *Managing Your Doctor,* pp. 143–144.

18. L. Lander, *Defective Medicine,* p. 50.

19. R. Sullivan, "Number of Doctors Selling Prescription Drugs Grows." *New York Times,* March 19, 1987, pp. B1, B5.

20. L. Lander, *Defective Medicine,* p. 49.

21. M. W. Lear, *Heartsounds.* New York: Pocket Books, 1981, p. 40.

22. M. Weitz, *Health Shock,* p. v.

23. L. Lander, *Defective Medicine,* p. 45.

24. L. Lander, *Defective Medicine,* p. 45.

25. P. L. Zentler-Munro and T. C. Northfield, "Drug-Induced Diseases: Drug-In-

duced Gastrointestinal Disease.'' *British Medical Journal,* May 12, 1979, vol. 1, no. 6173, p. 1263.

26. R. J. M. Lane and F. L. Mastaglia, "Drug-Induced Myopathies in Man." *Lancet,* September 9, 1978, pp. 562–565.

27. "High Cataract Rate Tied to Daily Prednisone Dose." *Pediatric News,* November 1979, vol. 13, no. 11, p. 24.

28. P. W. N. Keeling and R. P. H. Thompson, "Drug-Induced Diseases: Drug-Induced Liver Disease." *British Medical Journal,* April 14, 1979, vol. 1, no. 6169, pp. 990–993.

29. S. A. Kale, "Drug-Induced Systemic Lupus Erythematosus." *Postgraduate Medicine,* February 15, 1985, vol. 77, no. 3, p. 231.

30. S. A. Kale, *Postgraduate Medicine,* February 15, 1985 p. 242.

31. "Long Term Analgesic May Feed Muscle Headache." *Clinical Psychiatry News,* August 1984, vol. 12, no. 8, p. 20.

32. W. Herbert, "Mental Illness from Psychiatric Drugs?" *Science News,* October 1, 1983, vol. 124, no. 14, p. 214.

33. A. M. Breckenridge, "Drug-Induced Diseases: Drug-Induced Cardiovascular Disease." *British Medical Journal,* March 24, 1979, vol. 1, no. 6166, pp. 793–795.

34. L. A. Savett, "Drug-Induced Illness: Causes for Delayed Diagnosis and a Strategy for Early Recognition." *Postgraduate Medicine,* January 1980, vol. 67, no. 1, p. 155.

35. L. G. Seidl, G. E. Thornton, J. W. Smith, and L. E. Cluff, "Studies on the Epidemiology of Adverse Drug Reactions: III. Reactions in Patients on a General Medical Service." *Bulletin of Johns Hopkins Hospital,* 1966, no. 119, p. 299.

36. K. L. Melmon, "Preventable Drug Reactions—Causes and Cures." *New England Journal of Medicine,* June 17, 1971, vol. 284, no. 24, p. 1362.

37. L. A. Savett, *Postgraduate Medicine,* January 1980, p. 156.

38. K. L. Melmon, *New England Journal of Medicine,* June 17, 1971, pp. 1361–1362.

39. K. L. Melmon, *New England Journal of Medicine,* June 17, 1971, p. 1363.

40. K. L. Melmon, *New England Journal of Medicine,* June 17, 1971, p. 1361.

41. J. Pekkanen, *The American Connection,* Chicago: Follett, 1973, pp. 84–85.

42. W. F. McGhan, G. L. Stimmel, T. G. Hall, and T. M. Gilman, "A Comparison of Pharmacists and Physicians on the Quality of Prescribing for Ambulatory Hypertensive Patients." *Medical Care,* April 1983, vol. 21, no. 4, p. 435.

43. E. B. Larson, D. H. Scott, and H. G. Kaplan, "Inadequate Medical Order Writing: A Source of Confusion and Increased Costs." *Western Journal of Medicine,* July 1983, vol. 139, no. 1, p. 50.

44. D. E. Knapp, D. A. Knapp, M. K. Speedie, D. M. Yaeger, and C. L. Baker, "Relationship of Inappropriate Drug Prescribing to Increased Length of Hospital Stay." *American Journal of Hospital Pharmacy,* October 1979, vol. 36, pp. 1334–1337.

45. L. Lander, *Defective Medicine,* pp. 45–46.

46. Information on the Libby Zion case came from the following sources: N. Hentoff, "Are You Trying to Tell Me My Daughter Is Dead?" *Village Voice,* April 1, 1986, p. 40; Associated Press report, "Writer Sues Hospital Over Daughter's Death," *Times Herald Record* (Middletown, N.Y.), August 27, 1985, p. 24; D. Carmody, "New York Hospital Disputes Allegations on Patient's Death." *New York Times,* January 15, 1987, p. B3; R. Sullivan, "Hospital Admits Fault in Patient's Death." *New York Times,* March 24, 1987, p. B3. Information about Andy Warhol came from the following sources: D. Jacobson, "Hospital Assailed Over Care Given Before Warhol Died," *Philadelphia Inquirer,* April 11, 1987, p. 4A; M. A. Farber, "Warhol Received Inadequate Care in Hospital, Health Board Asserts." *New York Times,* April 11, 1987, pp. 1, 30.

47. K. Kroenke, "Polypharmacy: Causes, Consequences and Cure." *The American Journal of Medicine,* August 1985, vol. 79, no. 2, p. 149.

48. W. O. Robertson, *Medical Malpractice: A Preventive Approach,* p. 187.

49. F. Miller, S. Whitcup, M. Sacks, and P. E. Lynch, "Unrecognized Drug Dependence and Withdrawal in the Elderly." *Drug and Alcohol Dependence,* May 1985, pp. 177–179.

50. "Several Medical Conditions Have High Potential for Legal Difficulties: Drug-Induced Disease Hard to Defend in Court." *Internal Medicine News,* December 1-14, 1983, p. 34.

51. J. Brinkley and R. L. Pierce, "Baby's Death Called Tragic 'Human Error'." *The Courier-Journal* (Louisville, Ky.), December 8, 1982, pp. 1, 12; also R. L. Pierce, "Hospital Defends Safeguards on Drugs." *The Courier-Journal* (Louisville, Ky.) December 9, 1982, pp. B1, B4.

52. N. M. Davis and M. R. Cohen, *Medication Errors: Causes and Prevention,* p. 27.

53. N. M. Davis and M. R. Cohen, *Medication Errors: Causes and Prevention,* p. 28.

54. W. O. Robertson, *Medical Malpractice: A Preventive Approach,* p. 189.

55. W. O. Robertson, *Medical Malpractice: A Preventive Approach,* p. 197.

56. N. M. Davis and M. R. Cohen, *Medication Errors: Causes and Prevention,* p. 28.

57. D. A. Brand, D. Acampora, L. D. Gottlieb, K. E. Glancy, and W. H. Frazier, "Adequacy of Antitetanus Prophylaxis in Six Hospital Emergency Rooms." *New England Journal of Medicine,* September 15, 1983, vol. 309, no. 11, pp. 636–640.

58. D. A. Brand, D. Acampora, L. D. Gottlieb, K. E. Glancy, and W. H. Frazier, *New England Journal of Medicine,* September 15, 1983, p. 636.

59. D. A. Brand, D. Acampora, L. D. Gottlieb, K. E. Glancy, and W. H. Frazier, *New England Journal of Medicine,* September 15, 1983, p. 639.

60. P. H. Peristein, C. Callison, M. White, B. Barnes, and N. K. Edwards, "Errors in Drug Computations During Newborn Intensive Care." *American Journal of Diseases of Childhood,* April 1979, vol. 133, p. 376.

61. G. Koren, Z. Barzilay, and M. Modan, "Errors in Computing Drug Doses." *Canadian Medical Association Journal,* October 1, 1983, vol. 129, p. 721.

62. G. Koren, Z. Barzilay, and M. Modan, *Canadian Medical Association Journal,* October 1, 1983, p. 722.

63. G. Koren, Z. Barzilay, and M. Modan, *Canadian Medical Association Journal,* October 1, 1983, p. 723.

64. G. Koren, Z. Barzilay, and M. Modan, *Canadian Medical Association Journal,* October 1, 1983, p. 721.

65. M. C. Hermansen, R. Kahler, and B. Kahler, "Clinical and Laboratory Observations: Data Entry Errors in Computerized Nutritional Calculations." *Journal of Pediatrics,* July 1986, vol. 109, no. 1, pp. 91–93.

66. O. Morse and D. Duganfor, "When Wonder Drugs Don't Work." *Nova,* Public Broadcasting System, 1986.

67. L. Lander, *Defective Medicine,* p. 49.

68. "Ties Yeast Infection Increase to Iatrogenic Causes." *Family Practice News,* July 1-14, 1983, p. 18.

69. R. S. Mendelsohn, *Confessions of a Medical Heretic.* Chicago: Contemporary Books, 1979, p. 22.

70. J. B. Stamm, D. Schimel, A. H. Postel, and L. E. Bellin, "Typical Diagnostic and Therapeutic Errors in Manhattan Shared Health Facilities." *Bulletin of the New York Academy of Medicine,* May 1983, vol. 59, no. 4, p. 394.

71. O. Morse and D. Duganfor, *Nova,* 1986.

72. "Most Antibiotic Misuse Linked to Use as Prophylaxis in Surgery." *Internal Medicine News,* January 1-14, 1983, p. 1.

73. J. Wang, "Antibiotic Prophylaxis in Surgery—Too Much or Not Enough?" *Mod-*

ern Medicine, September 1, 1975, vol. 43, no. 15, p. 40.

74. J. Wang, *Modern Medicine,* pp. 41–42, 51.

75. C. M. Kunin, "Anti-Infective Therapy: Problems in Antibiotic Usage," in G. L. Mandell, R. G. Douglas, Jr., and J. E. Bennett, eds., *Principles and Practice of Infectious Disease,* 2nd ed., New York: John Wiley and Sons, 1985, p. 308.

76. O. Morse and D. Duganfor, *Nova,* 1986.

77. M. R. Cohen, ed., "Medication Errors." *Nursing 84,* November 1984, p. 25.

78. M. R. Cohen, ed., "Medication Errors." *Nursing 85,* January 1985, p. 20.

79. M. R. Cohen, ed., "Medication Errors." *Nursing 84,* October 1984, p. 70.

80. M. R. Cohen, ed., "Medication Errors." *Nursing 84,* December 1984, p. 24.

81. N. M. Davis and M. R. Cohen, *Medication Errors: Causes and Prevention,* p. 55.

82. N. M. Davis and M. R. Cohen, *Medication Errors: Causes and Prevention,* p. 55.

83. K. N. Barker, R. L. Mikeal, R. E. Pearson, N. A. Illig, and M. L. Morse, "Medication Errors in Nursing Homes and Small Hospitals." *American Journal of Hospital Pharmacy,* June 1982, vol. 39, pp. 987–991.

84. B. C. Wang and H. Turndorf, "Prevention of Medical Error." *New York State Journal of Medicine,* March 1981, p. 395.

85. W. O. Robertson, *Medical Malpractice: A Preventive Approach,* p. 83.

86. L. Lander, *Defective Medicine,* p. 47.

87. S. G. Wolf and B. B. Berle, eds. *Limits of Medicine: Proceedings of the Totts Gap Colloquium on the Limits of Medicine: The Doctor's Job in the Coming Era.* Held in Totts Gap, Pennsylvania, June 10–12, 1976, New York: Plenum Press, 1978, p. 45.

10.

1. L. B. Andrews, *Deregulating Doctoring: Do Medical Licensing Laws Meet Today's Health Care Needs?* Emmaus, Pa.: People's Medical Society, 1984, p. 6.

2. L. B. Andrews, *Deregulating Doctoring: Do Medical Licensing Laws Meet Today's Health Care Needs?* 1984, p. 1.

3. S. Barrett, Comments at Health Fraud Conference, February 13, 1986, New York City.

4. V. W. Sidel and R. Sidel, *A Healthy State.* New York: Pantheon, 1983, p. 314.

5. "Healthcare: Turf Wars." *Currents.* WNET-TV, Newark, N.J., 1986.

6. *Currents,* WNET-TV, 1986.

7. L. B. Andrews, *Deregulating Doctoring: Do Medical Licensing Laws Meet Today's Health Care Needs?* 1984, pp. 17–19.

8. *Currents,* WNET-TV, 1986.

9. *Currents,* WNET-TV, 1986.

10. L. B. Andrews, *Deregulating Doctoring: Do Medical Licensing Laws Meet Today's Health Care Needs?* 1984, p. 19.

11. *Currents,* WNET-TV, 1986.

12. "Proposal to Let Druggists Write Prescriptions Stirs Debate." *Newark Star-Ledger,* June 8, 1986, p. 85.

13. "Chiropractors in This State Can Practice Medicine." *Medical Economics,* August 22, 1983, p. 15.

14. C. Laino, "73 Percent of Those Seeing Doctors Say Pain Is Adequately Treated." *Medical Tribune,* November 27, 1985, p. 8.

15. L. B. Andrews, *Deregulating Doctoring: Do Medical Licensing Laws Meet Today's Health Care Needs?* 1984, p. 7.

16. M. C. Livingston, "Some Facets of Alternative Medicine—Today and Yesterday." *The Western Journal of Medicine,* August 1985, vol. 143, no. 2, p. 270.

17. M. G. Wagner, "Getting the Health Out of People's Daily Lives," *Lancet,* November 27, 1982, p. 1207.

18. L. B. Andrews, *Deregulating Doctoring: Do Medical Licensing Laws Meet Today's Health Care Needs?* 1984, p. 6.

19. L. B. Andrews, *Deregulating Doctoring: Do Medical Licensing Laws Meet Today's Health Care Needs?* 1984, p. 26.

20. G. Null, "Medical Genocide: The War on Chiropractic." *Penthouse,* October 1985, p. 44.

21. P. Mensing, "Judge Rules AMA Tried to Destroy Chiropractic Profession." *Philadelphia Inquirer,* August 29, 1987, p.4-A. This story appeared, in a slightly longer form, as: "Judge Says AMA Led a Conspiracy," *New York Times,* August 30, 1987, p. 27.

22. President's Commission for the Study of Ethical Problems in Medicine and Biomedical and Behavioral Research. *Making Health Care Decisions: A Report on the Ethical and Legal Implications of Informed Consent in the Patient-Practitioner Relationship.* Washington, D.C.: U.S. Government Printing Office, 1982, p. 138.

23. C. Crossen, "Nurses, Tired of Answering to Doctors, Begin to Treat Patients on Their Own." *Wall Street Journal,* January 7, 1986, p. 31.

24. C. Crossen, *Wall Street Journal,* January 7, 1986, p. 31.

25. "A Challenge to Time-Honored Practices?" *Medical Economics,* November 25, 1985, p. 17.

26. M. M. Manber, "NPs, MDs, and PAs: Meshing Their Changing Roles." *Medical World News,* September 23, 1985, p. 61.

27. M. M. Manber, *Medical World News,* September 23, 1985, p. 60.

28. M. M. Manber, *Medical World News,* September 23, 1985, p. 54.

29. D. H. Ward, Correspondence with authors, June 7, 1984.

30. M. Backup and J. Molinaro, "New Health Professionals: Changing the Hierarchy," in V. W. Sidel, and R. Sidel, eds. *Reforming Medicine: Lessons of the Last Quarter Century,* New York: Pantheon, 1984, pp. 201–202.

31. H. C. Sox, "Quality of Patient Care by Nurse Practitioners and Physician's Assistants: A Ten Year Perspective." *Annals of Internal Medicine, September* 1979, vol. 91, no. 3, p. 459.

32. D. S. Salkever, E. A. Skinner, D. M. Steinwachs, and H. Katz, "Episode-Based Efficiency Comparisons for Physicians and Nurse Practitioners." *Medical Care,* February 1982, vol. 20, no. 2, p. 143.

33. M. M. Manber, *Medical World News,* September 23, 1985, p. 60.

34. M. Backup and J. Molinaro, *Reforming Medicine: Lessons of the Last Quarter Century,* p. 215.

35. D. A. Sullivan and R. Weitz, "Obstacles to the Practice of Licensed Lay Midwifery." *Social Science and Medicine,* 1984, vol. 19, NO. 11, p. 1189.

36. D. A. Sullivan and R. Weitz, *Social Science and Medicine,* 1984, p. 1189.

37. "Midwifery Bill in Colorado Loses Again." *American Medical News,* September 27, 1985, p. 31.

38. D. A. Sullivan and R. Weitz, *Social Science and Medicine,* 1984, p. 1192.

39. R. Goodell and J. Gurin, "Where Should Babies Be Born?" *American Health,* January–February 1984, p. 72.

40. M. G. Wagner, *Lancet,* November 27, 1982, p. 1208.

41. D. A. Sullivan and R. Weitz, *Social Science and Medicine,* 1984, p. 1192.

42. R. Goodell and J. Gurin, *American Health,* January–February 1984, p. 74.

43. D. A. Sullivan and R. Weitz, *Social Science and Medicine,* 1984, p. 1195.

44. R. Goodell and J. Gurin, *American Health,* January–February 1984, p. 67.

45. M. G. Wagner, *Lancet,* November 27, 1982, p. 1208.

46. D. A. Sullivan and R. Weitz, *Social Science and Medicine,* 1984, p. 1193.

47. R. Goodell and J. Gurin, *American Health,* January–February 1984, p. 70.

48. D. A. Sullivan and R. Weitz, *Social Science and Medicine,* 1984, p. 1196.

49. R. J. Mann, "San Francisco General Hospital Nurse-Midwifery Practice: The First Thousand Births." *American Journal of Obstetrics and Gynecology,* July 15, 1981, vol. 140, no. 6, p. 676.

50. R. J. Mann, *American Journal of Obstetrics and Gynecology,* July 15, 1981, p. 681.

51. L. D. Platt, D. J. Angelini, R. H. Paul, and E. J. Quilligan, "Nurse-Midwifery in a Large Teaching Hospital." *Obstetrics and Gynecology,* December 1985, vol. 66, no. 6, pp. 816–820.

52. P. Harsham, "Midwifery: The Latest Growth Industry." *Medical Economics,* May 16, 1983, p. 232.

53. P. Harsham, *Medical Economics,* May 16, 1983, pp. 234–239.

54. L. B. Andrews, *Deregulating Doctoring: Do Medical Licensing Laws Meet Today's Health Care Needs?* 1984, p. 10.

55. R. Goodell and J. Gurin, *American Health,* January–February 1984, p. 72.

56. E. Kolbert, "Midwives Face Threat of High Insurance Cost." *New York Times,* September 29, 1985, p. 56.

57. C. Cancila, "Midwives Again Lose Liability Insurance Coverage." *American Medical News,* October 18, 1985, p. 16.

58. "Nurse Midwives Win Another Battle." *Medical Economics,* July 11, 1983, pp. 15–16.

59. "Here Comes a Nurse Midwife Boom." *Medical Economics,* December 26, 1983, p. 150.

60. "Demand for Midwives Increasing," *Health Insurance News,* September 30, 1983, p. 1.

61. F. C. Lee, "M.D. Surplus Could Incite Opposition to Nurse-Midwives' Market Intrusion." *Modern Healthcare,* November 1982, p. 102.

62. S. F. Norton and C. W. Nichols, Champions of Choice. *American Journal of Nursing,* April 1985, p. 382.

63. "Taking More Care Out of Doctors' Hands." *Medical Economics,* August 22, 1983, p. 16.

64. G. Null, "Medical Genocide: Painful Treatment." *Penthouse,* November 1985, p. 120.

65. G. Null, *Penthouse,* November 1985, p. 122.

66. "How Tight Will the Privileges Crunch Really Be?" *Medical Economics,* July 23, 1984, p. 198.

67. M. Curran, "Hospital Staffs Will Be Open to Nonphysicians." *Obstetrics and Gynecology News,* December 1–14, 1983, vol. 18, no. 23, p. 32.

68. G. Null, *Penthouse,* November 1985, p. 124.

69. R. J. Carlson, *The End of Medicine.* New York: John Wiley & Sons, 1975, pp. 69, 70, 72.

11.

1. R. Reiff, "The Control of Knowledge: The Power of the Helping Professions." *Journal of Applied Behavioral Science,* 1974, vol. 10, no. 3, p. 452.

2. S. J. Gross, *Of Foxes and Hen Houses.* Westport, Ct.: Quorum Books, 1984, p. xi.

3. D. F Stroman, *The Medical Establishment and Social Responsibility.* Port Washington, N.Y.: Kennikat Press, 1976, p. 125.

4. "Closing the Circle on Medical Frauds." *Federation Bulletin,* November 1985, p. 341.

5. I. Illich, *Medical Nemesis.* New York: Pantheon, 1976, p. 245.

6. R. Sullivan, "Cuomo Proposes Periodic Reviews for All Doctors." *New York Times,* May 29, 1986, p. B8.

7. J. Brinkley, "U.S. Industry and Physicians Attack Medical Malpractice." *New York Times,* September 2, 1985, p. 10A.

8. R. Sullivan, *New York Times,* May 29, 1986, p. B8.

9. R. Sullivan, *New York Times,* June 9, 1986, p. A19.

10. L. Shearer, "Intelligence Report: Ask the Doctor." *Parade,* October 3, 1982, p. 8.

11. S. J. Gross, *Of Foxes and Hen Houses,* p. 3.

12. S. J. Gross, *Of Foxes and Hen Houses,* pp. 4–5.

13. S. J. Gross, *Of Foxes and Hen Houses,* p. 157.

14. S. J. Gross, *Of Foxes and Hen Houses,* p. 158.

15. M. Friedman and R. Friedman, *Free to Choose.* New York: Harcourt, Brace and Jovanovich, 1980, p. 305.

16. D. F. Stroman, *The Medical Establishment and Social Responsibility,* p. 126.

17. S. J. Gross, *Of Foxes and Hen Houses,* p. xiii.

18. W. O. Robertson, *Medical Malpractice: A Preventive Approach.* Seattle: University of Washington Press, 1985. p. 152.

19. "A Controversial Surgeon Loses Her License." *Medical Economics,* May 2, 1983, p. 16.

20. S. J. Lee, "Fraud in Medical Research." *Journal of the American Medical Association,* January 13, 1984, vol. 251, no. 2, p. 215.

21. "Medical Discipline, Peer Review Weak, HHS Study Finds." *Medical Liability Advisory Service,* February 1986, p. 3.

22. R. Sullivan, "Tighter Reviews of Doctors Urged." *New York Times,* June 6, 1986, p. A13.

23. R. Sullivan, *New York Times,* June 6, 1986, p. A13.

24. J. Brinkley, "State Medical Boards Disciplined Record Number of Doctors in '85." *New York Times,* November 9, 1986, p. 26.

25. S. M. Wolfe, H. Bergman, and G. Silver, "Medical Malpractice: The Need for Disciplinary Reform, Not Tort Reform." *Public Citizen Health Research Group Report,* August 1985, p. 2.

26. S. M. Wolfe, H. Bergman, and G. Silver, *Public Citizen Health Research Group Report,* August 1985, p. 5.

27. "Doctor Discipline: A Necessary Cure for the Malpractice Crisis." *Health Letter,* November/December 1985, p. 6.

28. R. J. Feinstein, "The Ethics of Professional Regulation." *New England Journal of Medicine,* March 21, 1985, vol. 312, no. 12, p. 803.

29. "A System Whose Ills Can Be Fatal." *Detroit Free Press,* April 1, 1984, p. A1.

30. "Doctors Seldom Tell on Doctors." *Detroit Free Press,* April 6, 1984, p. 12A.

31. *Detroit Free Press,* April 6, 1984, p. 12A.

32. C. R. Robinson, "Why the Conspiracy of Silence Won't Die." *Medical Economics,* February 20, 1984, p. 180.

33. C. R. Robinson, *Medical Economics,* February 20, 1984, p. 183.

34. *Detroit Free Press,* April 6, 1984, p. 12A.

35. J. M. Morrissey, "Professional Misconduct." *New York State Journal of Medicine,* December 1984, p. 609.

36. J. Brinkley, "Medical Discipline Laws: Confusion Reigns." *New York Times,* September 3, 1985, p. B6.

37. D. Q. Haney, "Psychiatrists Mum on Peers' Sexual Misconduct." *Philadelphia Inquirer,* April 8, 1987, pp. 1C, 5C.

38. S. Bok, *Lying: Moral Choice in Public and Private Life.* New York: Pantheon, 1978, p. 304.

39. J. F. Boyle, "The 1985 Walter L. Bierring Lecture." *Federation Bulletin,* November 1985, vol. 72, no. 11, pp. 326–327.

40. L. Masnerus and K. Roberts, "AMA Takes on Inept Doctors." *New York Times,* July 6, 1986, p. E7.

41. H. H. Keyser, *Women Under the Knife,* Philadelphia: George F. Stickley, 1984, p. 6.

42. H. H. Keyser, *Women Under the Knife,* pp. 14–15.

43. C. R. Robertson, *Medical Economics,* February 20, 1984, p. 50.

44. D. F. Stroman, *The Medical Establishment and Social Responsibility,* p. 134.

45. H. H. Keyser, *Women Under the Knife,* p. 15.

46. H. H. Keyser, *Women Under the Knife,* p. 16.

47. M. Sauer, "Former Doctor Criticizes Peers." *San Diego Union,* April 6, 1983, p. 14.

48. R. Kirkpatrick, "Peer Reviews by Doctors Confidential, Court Says." *Philadelphia Inquirer,* March 25, 1987, p. 3B.

49. R. C. Derbyshire, "Medical Ethics and Discipline." *Journal of the American Medical Association,* April 1, 1974, vol. 228, no. 1, p. 62.

50. "Oregon Foundation for Medical Excellence to Focus on the Problem of Impaired Physicians." *Federation Bulletin,* July 1985, p. 223.

51. J. Brinkley, *New York Times,* September 3, 1985, p. B6.

52. F. Warshofsky, "A Cure for Doctors Who Are Hazardous to Health." *Reader's Digest* reprint, 1987.

53. P. Perl, "Swamped Agency Has Little Time to Police Doctors." *Washington Post,* May 22, 1983, p. C1.

54. J. Post, "Professional Medical Conduct in New York State." *Bulletin of the New York Academy of Medicine,* November 1985, vol. 61, no. 9, p. 836.

55. S. J. Gross, *Of Foxes and Hen Houses,* p. 151.

56. A. R. Somers and H. M. Somers, *Health and Health Care: Policies in Perspective,* Germantown, Md: Aspen Systems Corporation, 1977, p. 29.

57. J. Whitlow, "Board of Examiners Focuses on Licenses, Continuing Education." *Newark Star-Ledger,* June 1, 1986, Section One, p. 93.

58. R. Goudreau and A. Beasley, "No Rx in Sight for Some Bad Doctors." *Orlando Sentinel,* April 16, 1986, p. A-1.

59. E. Colimore and H. Goodman, "Still Practicing Medicine on an Unwitting Public." *Philadelphia Inquirer,* August 24, 1986, p.8-A.

60. N. Hentoff, "The White Wall of Silence," *Village Voice,* April 6, 1986, p. 41.

61. E. Colimore and H. Goodman, *Philadelphia Inquirer,* August 24, 1986, p. 8-A.

62. J. Brinkley, "Should Doctors Be Given a More Thorough Examination?" *New York Times,* November 10, 1985, p. 10E.

63. J. Brinkley, *New York Times,* November 10, 1985, p. 10E.

64. "Doctoring the Truth." *Cleveland Plain Dealer,* April 14, 1985, p. 4-B.

65. "The Medical Code of Silence." *New York Daily News,* March 4, 1983, p. C17.

66. W. L. Wood, Jr., and A. Z. Scher, "Restoration of the License to Practice Medicine." *New York State Journal of Medicine,* December 1984, p. 605.

67. S. J. Gross, *Of Foxes and Hen Houses,* p. 99.

68. S. J. Gross, *Of Foxes and Hen Houses,* p. 151.

69. J. H. Morton, "Medical Board Disciplinary Action." *Federation Bulletin,* August 1985, p. 240.

70. A. S. Relman, "Professional Regulation and the State Medical Boards." *New England Journal of Medicine,* March 21, 1985, vol. 312, no. 12, p. 785.

71. R. O. Boorstin, "Disciplining Incompetent Doctors: Slow and Complex Process in the State." *New York Times,* January 22, 1986, p. B1.

12.

1. L. Lander, *Defective Medicine,* New York: Farrar, Straus, Giroux, 1978, pp. 78–79.

2. One such section appears in the authors' *Take This Book to the Hospital with You.* Similar explanations of medicalese appear in, among other books: R. Gots and A. Kaufman, *The People's Hospital Book.* New York: Avon, 1978; B. Huttman, *The Patient's Advocate.* New York: Penguin Books, 1981; and J. Nierenberg and F. Janovic, *The Hospital Experience.* New York: Bobbs-Merrill Co., 1978.

3. M. R. DiMatteo and R. Hays, "The Significance of Patients' Perceptions of Physician Conduct: A Study of Patient Satisfaction in a Family Practice Center." *Journal of Community Health,* Fall 1980, vol. 6, no. 1, pp. 18–19.

4. N. Cousins, "How Patients Appraise Physicians." *New England Journal of Medicine,* November 28, 1985, p. 1422.

5. D. Hilfiker, *Healing the Wounds.* New York: Pantheon Books, 1985, p. 67.

6. B. M. Korsch and V. F. Negrete, "Doctor-Patient Communication." *Scientific American,* August 1972, p. 66.

7. "Reluctant Bearer of Bad News." *Medical World News,* September 23, 1985, p. 73.

8. D. Sifford, "Good Doctors and Bad News." *Philadelphia Inquirer,* February 2, 1986, p. I-1.

9. M. W. Lear, *Heartsounds.* New York: Pocket Books, 1981, p. 317.

10. S. Bok, *Lying: Moral Choice in Public and Private Life.* New York: Pantheon, 1978, p. xvi.

11. S. Bok, *Lying: Moral Choice in Public and Private Life,* p. xvii.

12. T. Preston, *The Clay Pedestal,* Seattle: Madrona Press, 1981, p. 73.

13. T. Preston, *The Clay Pedestal,* pp. 226–238.

14. I. Illich, *Medical Nemesis.* New York: Pantheon, 1976, p. 47.

15. I. Illich, *Medical Nemesis,* p. 227.

16. D. Hilfiker, *Healing the Wounds,* p. 47.

17. President's Commission for the Study of Ethical Problems in Medicine and Biomedical and Behavioral Research. *Making Health Care Decisions: A Report on the Ethical and*

Legal Implications of Informed Consent in the Patient-Practitioner Relationship. Washington D.C.: United States Government Printing Office, 1982, p. 42.

18. D. Hilfiker, *Healing the Wounds,* p. 71.

19. P. Starr, *The Social Transformation of American Medicine.* New York: Basic Books, 1982, p. 32.

20. V. W. Sidel and R. Sidel, *A Healthy State.* New York: Pantheon, 1983, p. 57.

21. J. B. Hull, "Patients Are Often the Last People to See Their Own Medical Records." *Wall Street Journal,* September, 30, 1985, p. 2-23.

22. J. N. Blau, "Patients Reading Their Notes." *Lancet,* January 3, 1987, p. 45.

23. J. F. Burnum, "La Maladie du Petit Papier: Is Writing a List of Symptoms a Sign of an Emotional Disorder?" *New England Journal of Medicine,* September 12, 1985, pp. 690–691.

24. J. F. Burnum, *New England Journal of Medicine,* September 12, 1985, p. 690.

25. G. Corea, *The Hidden Malpractice.* New York: Harper & Row, 1985, p. 14.

26. *Medical World News,* September 23, 1985, p. 73.

27. A. M. Epstein, W. C. Taylor, and G. R. Seage, "Effects of Patients' Socioeconomic Status and Physicians' Training and Practice on Patient-Doctor Communication." *The American Journal of Medicine,* January 1985, vol. 78, p. 101.

28. V. W. Sidel and R. Sidel, *A Healthy State,* p. 94.

29. V. W. Sidel and R. Sidel, *A Healthy State,* p. 91.

30. E. Weiner, "The Doctor Is 'In' (and Wishes You Weren't)." *Executive Fitness Newsletter,* May 1, 1982, p. 3.

31. E. Stonehill, "Keep on Taking the Weedkiller?" *Gut,* October 1986, vol. 27, no. 10, p. 1117.

32. S. E. Roush, "Health Professionals as Contributors to Attitudes Toward Persons with Disabilities: A Special Communication." *Physical Therapy,* October 1986, vol. 66, no. 10, p. 1552.

33. I. B. Harris, E. C. Rich, and T. W. Crowson, "Attitudes of Internal Medicine Residents and Staff Physicians Toward Various Patient Characteristics." *Journal of Medical Education,* March 1985, vol. 60, pp. 193–194.

34. P. J. Nunn, "Is Chronic Pain a Real Condition?" *Canadian Medical Association Journal,* December 15, 1984, vol. 131, p. 1435.

35. P. J. Nunn, *Canadian Medical Association Journal,* December 15, 1984, p. 1436.

36. There are many good examples of this; one of the best is F. Mullan, *Vital Signs.* New York: Farrar, Straus & Giroux, 1983.

37. M. W. Lear, *Heartsounds,* p. 98.

38. M. W. Lear, *Heartsounds,* pp. 268–269, 272.

39. R. S. Mendelsohn, *Confessions of a Medical Heretic,* Chicago: Contemporary Books, 1979, p. 11.

40. L. Lander, *Defective Medicine,* p. 38.

41. E. Friedson, *Profession of Medicine.* New York: Dodd, Mead, 1970, p. 251.

42. P. Starr, *The Social Transformation of American Medicine,* p. 14.

43. G. J. Povar, M. Mantell, and L. A. Morris, "Patients' Therapeutic Preferences in an Ambulatory Care Setting." *American Journal of Public Health,* December 1984, vol. 74, no. 12, pp. 1395–1397.

44. G. Corea, *The Hidden Malpractice,* p. 85.

45. W. E. O'Donnell, "Why 'Me First' Is Ruining Medicine." *Medical Economics,* September 27, 1982, pp. 29–39.

46. J. Needleman, *The Way of the Physician.* San Francisco: Harper & Row, 1985.

47. R. J. Carlson, *The End of Medicine.* New York: John Wiley & Sons, 1975, p. 38.

48. S. G. Wolf, and B. B. Berle, eds., *Limits of Medicine: Proceedings of the Totts Gap*

Colloquium on the Limits of Medicine: The Doctor's Job in the Coming Era. Held in Totts Gap, Pennsylvania, June 10-12, 1976. New York: Plenum Press, 1978, pp. 29, 31.

49. R. S. Mendelsohn, *Confessions of a Medical Heretic,* p. 15.

50. S. G. Wolf and B. B. Berle, eds., *Limits of Medicine: Proceedings of the Totts Gap Colloquium on the Limits of Medicine: The Doctor's Job in the Coming Era,* pp. 29, 31.

51. "Health Care: Turf Wars," *Currents.* Produced by J. Petroff, directed by B. Morris, executive producer S. Weinstock. WNET-TV, Newark, N.J., 1986.

52. *Currents,* WNET-TV, 1986.

53. L. Lander, *Defective Medicine,* pp. 93-94.

54. J. Needleman, *The Way of the Physician,* p. 75.

55. J. Needleman, *The Way of the Physician,* p. 74.

56. L. Eisenberg, "The Subjective in Medicine." *Perspectives in Biology and Medicine,* Autumn 1983, vol. 27, no. 1, pp. 48-61.

57. R. J. Carlson, *The End of Medicine,* pp. 19-20.

58. H. Brody, *Placebos and the Philosophy of Medicine.* Chicago: The University of Chicago Press, 1980, p. 11.

59. H. Brody, *Placebos and the Philosophy of Medicine,* p. 17.

60. J. R. Bloom and S. Monterossa, "Hypertension Labeling and Sense of Well-Being." *American Journal of Public Health,* November 1981, vol. 71, no. 11, pp. 1228-1232.

61. L. Eisenberg, *Perspectives in Biology and Medicine,* Autumn 1983, pp. 57-58.

62. H. Brody, *Placebos and the Philosophy of Medicine,* p. 129.

63. J. Needleman, *The Way of the Physician,* p. 173.

64. T. G. Gutheil, H. Bursztajn, and A. Brodsky, "Malpractice Prevention Through the Sharing of Uncertainty." *New England Journal of Medicine,* July 5, 1984, vol. 311, no. 1, p. 50.

65. T. G. Gutheil, H. Bursztajn, and A. Brodsky, *New England Journal of Medicine,* July 5, 1984, p. 51.

66. N. Cousins, *New England Journal of Medicine,* November 28, 1985, p. 1424.

67. D. Hilfiker, *Healing the Wounds,* p. 202.

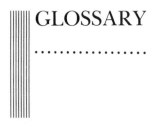

GLOSSARY

Acupuncture. A method of health care treatment created by the Chinese that involves the insertion of needles into specific points on the body that, according to tradition, lie along "meridians" or bodily pathways that are the conduits of the life force, *c'hi.* By placing needles into various locations along the streams of *c'hi,* so the theory goes, a body that is out of balance may be brought back into balance. Acupuncture has made inroads into modern Western medical practice, although it is still seen as an exotic, yet-to-be-proved therapeutic entity, and is used in the West primarily as an experimental pain reliever and mild anesthetic. Acupuncturists have a difficult time getting the right to set up solo private practice; in most instances, they are either an adjunct to a physician's medical practice or are themselves physicians who have received some training in the discipline. In the West, the needles are very often electrified.

Adenocarcinoma. Cancer involving a gland or glands.

Allopathic. A term that describes a form of disease treatment that uses drugs or other medicinal agents to produce effects in a patient that are different from those of the disease being treated. This theory opposes that of *homeopathy,* and describes the system of disease care that we call modern, Western medicine.

Alternative practitioners. Those purveyors of healing arts who are not medical doctors, and are therefore seen as being less than legitimate in the eyes of the establishment medical profession. While chiropractors, homeopaths, herbologists, and other seemingly outré practitioners are clearly alternative health care providers, some unyielding M.D.s often lump them together with osteopaths, nutritionists, nurse-midwives, and psychologists, among others. In other words, for the medical profession, anything that isn't in the M.D. fold is an alternative practitioner, with the negative connotations that that term carries with it.

Ampule swap. An anesthesia error in which containers of anesthetic agents are confused, misidentified, and then wrongly administered because they look like other ampules or containers or because they have been placed on the anesthesiologist's worktable in an order that is different from the one he or she is used to.

Analgesic. Simply, a drug designed to relieve pain; a form of painkiller.

Anaphylactic shock. An extremely serious state of bodily shock brought on by an unusual and heightened sensitivity or allergic reaction to a normally safe and harmless drug or some substance that suddenly behaves like a poison. Sometimes people experience anaphylaxis upon receiving an antibiotic, local anesthetic, insulin, X-ray contrast material, vaccines, or the sting of a bee, wasp, or hornet. The symptoms of anaphylactic shock are often similar to the sudden onset of an asthma attack, and the affected person, if untreated, could die of respiratory failure or shock.

Anesthesia. A general or local loss of feeling, sensation, or pain, artificially produced by specific anesthetic drugs or agents for the benefit of doctor and patient during certain medical procedures. Anesthetic drugs may be administered by inhalation, intravenous, intramuscular, or other invasive methods. A general anesthetic causes unconsciousness in the patient; a local anesthetic merely deadens the senses in a limited area.

Anesthesiologist. A physician who is a specialist in the medical field of anesthesiology, which concerns itself with anesthesia administration and care and monitoring of the patient who is under the influence of anesthesia.

Angina pectoris. A suffocatingly painful attack felt in the chest and caused by diminished blood supply to the heart muscle. Angina is not a disease in itself, but is rather a symptom of diseases of the arteries going to the heart, usually the artery-clogging atherosclerosis ("hardening of the arteries"). Angina pectoris is often seen as a sign of an oncoming heart attack, or myocardial infarction.

Antibiotics. Chemical substances, produced by various microorganisms and fungi, that have the ability, when used in dilute solutions, of killing or inhibiting the growth of bacteria or other microorganisms. The pure definition of the word "antibiotic" is "destructive of life."

Arrhythmias. Abnormal and potentially dangerous variations—too fast, too slow, without regularity—from the normal rhythm of a person's heartbeat. Medications as well as devices such as cardiac pacemakers are used to normalize arrhythmias.

Arteriovenous fistula. An abnormal and possibly congenital or injury-produced tubelike passage within body tissue between an artery and a vein. Fistulas in the body may be caused by diseases or infections, and may themselves become the sites of infections. Also, an arteriovenous fistula may be surgically created as an access to the vascular system of a person who is undergoing or is about to undergo *hemodialysis*.

Arthroplasty. The repair of a joint using techniques involving prostheses—artificial substitutes for missing body parts.

Aspiration. Simply, the act of taking a breath, or inhaling. The aspiration of vomit or other substances while one is under the influence of a general anesthetic can lead to a choking death.

Attending physician. The doctor who admits a patient into a hospital and is responsible for that patient's continuing care there. The attending physician orders tests and medications, and may often be the patient's regular private practice doctor.

Autonomy. A state in which one or a group is independent and self-governing; the autonomy of the medical profession, and its desire to remain free of any societal impositions besides those coming from within the medical community, is the basis for much criticism from those outside the profession who believe that restraints, as well as watchdog and regulatory functions, need to be provided by government, citizen groups, or other external bodies.

Autopsy. The examination, inspection, and, usually, dissection of a body after death to determine the cause of death; also known as a post-mortem examination or necropsy. An autopsy is ordered and performed by coroners or medical examiners or their staffs.

Bacteremia. A condition in which bacteria is found in the blood.

Bilateral destruction or occlusion of fallopian tubes. A female sterilization procedure during which both fallopian tubes may be cut, cauterized (so as to create tube-blocking scar tissue), or clipped shut to prevent the fertilization of eggs and the resulting pregnancy.

Biomechanical model. A way of thinking about how the body works by applying the laws of mechanics to the bodily functions of a living being.

Biopsy. The surgical removal of small, even microscopic, portions of tissue from a live body for the purposes of examination, frequently to determine the status (benign or malignant) of a tumor.

Board-certified. The designation given a physician who has applied for and passed examinations permitting him membership or fellowship in a national board of a medical specialty. There are some inferior doctors who manage to attain board certification and some excellent doctors without board certification; board certification, however, is one of a very few indicators of knowledge and quality in the medical field that a patient can look to when looking for a physician.

Burnout. A state of mental and physical job-caused and -related exhaustion that may be responsible for many on-the-job errors or attitudes of noncaring detrimental to the successful completion of the job duties. Burnout among medical personnel is frequent and dangerous.

Bypass surgery. Any procedure in which a shunt or surgically created pathway circumventing the normal and anatomical pathway is utilized. While bypasses may be used in the intestine (to induce malabsorption of food in order to correct obesity) or to redirect blood flow around an atherosclerosis-blocked artery between the abdominal aorta and the femoral artery, the operation most commonly referred to as a bypass is the open-heart surgery known as coronary artery bypass graft (CABG), which ordinarily uses veins stripped from the legs as shunts to open blood flow to the heart, replacing atherosclerotic coronary arteries.

Cardiac arrest. A major emergency situation in which the heart suddenly stops working, usually because of unexpected heart flutter or rapid, uncontrollable heartbeat, or because of a malfunction in the centers that control the heart's normal contractions. A person who falls victim to cardiac arrest usually has another, underlying heart problem, probably coronary artery disease. The response by medical personnel and others to cardiac arrest in a patient is the immediate application of cardiopulmonary resuscitation (CPR) and emergency cardiac care.

Cardiology. The specialty branch of medicine that deals with the function of the heart and its diseases.

Cardiovascular system. The heart and its blood vessels, including the coronary arteries.

Cardioversion. A method of applying an electric shock to a patient who is experiencing sudden, severe heart rhythm malfunctions, and by doing so to depolarize the heart muscle and allow the heart's own built-in natural pacemaker to retake control. Cardioversion may be performed by opening the afflicted person's chest and applying the electrical shock equipment directly on the surface of the heart, or by placing cardioversion paddles on the chest surface.

Cataract (lens implants). A clouding up of the eye's lens, at first causing dimmed and blurred vision, and ultimately loss of vision. Cataracts are formed in many ways, including radiation, injury, heredity, and the aging process. To treat cataracts, a surgeon removes the milky, opaque lens and provides a new lens. This new lens may be in the form of glasses, contact lenses, or a surgically implanted permanent lens in place of the one extracted.

Catheter. A tube used as an adjunct to medical treatment that acts as a conduit either for removing fluids from (such as those commonly utilized in the urinary tract), or for adding fluids to, bodily cavities.

CAT scan (or CT scan). The abbreviation for computerized axial tomography scan, a method of viewing body tissue by seeing it visualized in "slices" about 1 millimeter thick. Besides this benefit over typical X-rays, a CAT scan is fast and does not require contrast material or media for its imaging. It is a marvel of technology that may possibly be overused, sometimes in order to run up billings and pay back the machine's high cost.

Cerebrospinal fluid. The fluid that is produced by the brain and flows in the spinal cord and portions of the brain. Cerebrospinal fluid acts as a liquid shock absorber for the brain and spinal cord, and may be removed as a diagnostic aid by inserting a needle into the spinal canal and withdrawing a sample of the fluid.

Cesarean section. A surgical technique for delivering a baby believed to be in distress or in danger of dying before or during birth; the fetus is removed through an incision made in the mother's abdominal wall and uterus. The rate of cesarean deliveries in the United States has soared over the past two decades, and many critics believe there are many unnecessary cesareans, being performed more for the doctor's convenience than the mother's or baby's well-being.

Chemotherapy. In its broadest sense, a mode of treating disease using chemical agents. The term can apply to many treatments, but is most commonly used to describe a form of therapy for cancer.

Chiropractic. A system of therapy based on the belief that the root of illness is blockage or impingement of nerves, leading to interference with nerve function. Further, the belief is that the remedy is manipulation and adjustment of the vertebral column so that the body's organs may once again receive their proper neural stimulation. The practitioner of this nonmedical discipline is known as a chiropractor.

Chromosome. A threadlike substance that is found in the nucleus of cells and carries genetic information. Chromosomal damage may be caused by, among other things, radiation, thus skew or destroy the genetic information, leading to cancers and birth defects, among others. There are 46 chromosomes in the nucleus of a normal human cell.

Circumcision. The surgical removal of the prepuce, or foreskin, of the penis, usually performed when the male is an infant.

Collimation. The precise lining up and sizing up of a field of radiation exposure for the taking of X-rays. Field is the size of the area of the body that is exposed to the X-ray, and the field is often too large because radiology technicians do not collimate properly, sizing things up to film size instead of to the body part that is being X-rayed, thus increasing the risk of organ and chromosome damage.

Contrast material or media. An opaque substance introduced into the body to create conditions allowing X-rays to visualize bodily structures.

Controlled substance. The designation given by a federal law to dangerous and addictive drugs, such as narcotics, hallucinogens, and stimulants; the prescribing and dispensing of these drugs are (or should
be) strictly regulated, and stringent record keeping is required.

Cytology. The branch of biology and biomedicine that studies the for-
mation, structure, and functions of cells.

Defensive medicine. The name given to a type of medical practice behavior typified by a physician ordering many and perhaps excessive
tests and procedures, all to avoid the possibility of a patient instituting
a lawsuit.

Defibrillator. A machine that delivers an electric shock to the heart to put
an end to fibrillation, a type of cardiac arrhythmia. See *Cardioversion.*

Dementia. Severe loss of intellectual function and personality integration.

Diabetes. Technically, not one, but a number of disorders. The term
diabetes is most usually used in place of *diabetes mellitus,* a disease that
negatively alters the body's ability to use sugar (glucose), causes sugar
to appear in the urine, and is typified by excessive urination and
thirst. These are secondary to a malfunction of the insulin-producing
beta cells of the pancreas. People with diabetes often have to take
insulin, orally or by injection, to normalize their sugar levels.

Dialysis. See *Hemodialysis.*

Dilation and curettage. Known as *D&C,* this procedure, used as an abortion technique and also for other uterus-related conditions, involves
the expansion of the external opening of the cervix of the uterus into
the vagina so that the walls of the uterus may be scraped.

Disinfectant. A chemical used on an inanimate object—it is usually too
caustic to be applied directly on living tissue—that inhibits the growth
of infection-producing organisms or kills them.

Elective surgery. An operation the patient elects or chooses to have on
his or her own; it is not an emergency or a medical imperative.

Electrocardiogram (EKG). A record of the heart's electrical action, produced by an electrocardiograph machine, which amplifies the heart's
electrical impulses thousands of times and then traces those amplifi-
cations onto a chart in the form of curves and waves. An electrocardiogram is a diagnostic tool that can show, during the course of a
normal physical examination, previously inflicted heart damage and
heart rhythm irregularities, among other things. It should not, however, stand alone as a means of diagnosis or prognosis; rather, it
should be used in conjunction with other tests. Also, it cannot accurately predict future heart problems.

Electroencephalogram (EEG). A record of the brain's electrical action,
produced by an electroencephalograph machine, which amplifies the

brain's electrical impulses millions of times and then traces those am-
plifications onto a chart in the form of curves and waves.

Embolism. The sudden blocking of an artery by an embolus, or piece of
foreign matter, usually a blood clot. An embolism most often occurs
at that point in an artery where it branches off in two; the artery
narrows there, and is most susceptible.

Endoscopic equipment. Medical diagnostic tools that are used for a direct
view into the hollow organs and cavities of the body. An endoscope
usually has a place for the medical personnel to look into, as well as
a light source, and sometimes—for diagnosing certain conditions—
forceps to remove tissue for biopsy.

Epidemiology. The study of the causes, spread, frequency, and other
factors relating to human disease and how it relates to the community.

Extubation. The removal of a tube used during and/or after a medical
procedure. The insertion of that tube is known as *intubation.*

Fetal cardiac monitor. Continuous monitoring of the condition of a fetus
to prevent damage and death during labor. The monitoring—often
performed using ultrasound techniques, but sometimes using direct,
invasive electrocardiographic access to the fetus and amniotic sac—
keeps tabs on fetal heartbeat and uterine contractions, and is designed
to alert medical birthing personnel when there is potentially fatal fetal
distress. Some critics say that fetal monitoring is overused and misused, leading to the skyrocketing incidence of *cesarean sections;* others
believe that ultrasound has not been proven a safe technique.

Food and Drug Administration. An agency of the U.S. Department of
Health and Human Services; as it relates to doctors, hospitals, and
things medical, the FDA is empowered to inspect medical devices and
medications to see if they are safe and effective for use on the public.
Critics contend that the FDA is not doing its job well enough to
protect the public from hazardous drugs and technology.

Fractionating (X-ray dose). The theory, held by many radiologists, that
if in the place of one large dose, which might entail some hazard, a
few smaller doses that add up to the same dose are given, there will
be less risk to the patient. Fractionating *may* reduce or eliminate some
side effects of high-dose radiation, but there is evidence that dividing
a dose does *not* reduce the risk.

Field (X-ray). The size of a beam of radiation when it strikes the body
being X-rayed.

Gallbladder. A bodily organ attached to the underside of the liver, which
stores bile. The most common medical conditions to affect the gallbladder are cholecystitis (inflammation of the gallbladder) and gall-
stones.

Gastrointestinal. Having to do with the stomach and intestines.

Gynecology. The branch of medical science that studies the diseases of the female genital tract.

Halothane. A colorless, nonflammable general anesthetic administered via inhalation. In a hypersensitive person, it could be a cause of *hepatitis.*

Hemodialysis. A mechanical, man-made technique for removing toxic wastes from the blood when a person's kidneys can no longer do the job. The blood is shunted from arterial circulation, sent out of the body and through a hemodialyzer's filtering system, then returned to the body to circulate through the veins. A person with kidney disease may need to use hemodialysis equipment two or three times a week.

Hepatitis. In general, an inflammation of the liver, by any of a number of causes, including viruses, sensitivity to drugs, and ingestion of toxins.

Hepatitis B. A virulent, virus-caused, long-lasting form of hepatitis that is sexually transmitted as well as spread through contact with infected blood and blood products or passed on to infants either during pregnancy or after delivery. A person with hepatitis B is at great risk of developing liver cancer and cirrhosis of the liver; about 10 percent of those affected are carriers of the disease. It is considered a close relative of acquired immune deficiency syndrome (AIDS).

Herniorrhaphy. Surgical repair of a hernia, or rupture.

Herpes. Any of a number of skin outbreaks caused by a herpesvirus, it usually is used to refer to herpes simplex (cold sores), herpes zoster (shingles), or the highly contagious, sexually transmitted genital herpes.

Hippocratic oath. A moral code, based on the teachings of Hippocrates, the "father of medicine," which sets down the duties and obligations of physicians. Students take this oath upon graduation from medical school.

HMO. Abbreviation for health maintenance organization; this medical group practice setup is an alternative to the usual fee-for-service practice of medicine. Users of HMOs pay a fixed sum in advance in regular installments, and this entitles them to nearly any medical care they may require. Some HMOs provide all services and tests on the premises; others send their members to outside specialists who participate in the plan. What HMOs provide and what they do not vary with the HMO. HMOs tend to promote preventive health care measures.

Homeopathy. A method of treating disease by using drugs that are capable of producing in a healthy person symptoms similar to those of the disease, but combat the disease in persons afflicted with it. The drugs are normally administered in extremely small doses. Homeopathy was propounded in the late 1700s and early 1800s by Samuel Hahnemann. As a treatment philosophy, it is opposed to *allopathy*.

House officer. A physician who is employed by and works in a hospital. Usually, this is what the interns and especially the residents are called, but it may also refer to a more experienced practitioner who works at the hospital.

Hyperalimentation. Feeding intravenously. Sometimes referred to as parenteral nutrition, this is a method of providing nutrients to a patient whose gastrointestinal system is not functioning properly or who has undergone surgery.

Hypertension. High blood pressure.

Hypovolemia. An unusually diminished or low volume of fluid circulating in the body.

Hysterectomy. Removal by surgery of the uterus, through the vagina or abdomen. The surgery may also include removal of the cervix (known, collectively, as a total hysterectomy) and upper vagina (radical hysterectomy). A cesarean hysterectomy is one in which a cesarean delivery is followed by removal of the uterus. Critics contend that this may be one of the most overdone, unnecessary operations performed in America today.

Hysteria. A mental illness in which the affected person converts anxiety and mental distress into physical symptoms. The term *hysteria* may also be used to describe a state in which a person has uncontrollable outbursts of emotion—laughing, weeping, temper tantrums—as an irrational reaction to fear or stress. Hysteria is so called because it was felt that the source of such symptoms and outbursts was the uterus, and thus hysteria was a woman's disease. Remnants of that false conjecture unfortunately remain among too many male medical practitioners today, who believe that many women's physical complaints are just ''in their heads.''

Iatrogenic. Doctor-caused; a term used to describe an illness or condition produced in a patient by the actions of a physician or of medical care.

Imaging. The production of images of body parts for the purpose of diagnosis. X-rays, ultrasound, CAT scans, nuclear magnetic resonating machines—all are used for the purpose of imaging. Imaging is also a term used to describe a method of utilizing the power of the mind over physical ills. For example, some people with cancer have been able to shrink their tumors or effect a remission by imaging their disease as a visible entity and then imaging something else that destroys that entity—seeing the cancer as a wall, for instance, and visualizing their mental powers to defeat that cancer as a wrecking ball. Imaging is a mind-over-matter therapeutic technique that is receiving much scrutiny these days.

Impaired physician. A medical practitioner who, through addiction, alcoholism, the effects of advanced age, or mental illness, is no longer able to provide satisfactory medical care and is, in fact, a danger to patients.

Internist/internal medicine. A specialist/specialization in the diagnosis and nonsurgical treatment of diseases, especially those of adults. Internists may set up practices in which they act as highly trained family practitioners, but they often subspecialize in many other areas; i.e., cardiology.

Internship. A period of time during which a graduate of medical or dental school works in a hospital to gain working knowledge and on-the-job training before becoming licensed to practice his or her discipline.

Ionizing radiation. The type of energy form that is commonly used for imaging purposes; usually referred to as *X-rays,* although gamma rays are also a form of ionizing radiation. Ionizing radiation, in even small doses, can produce chromosomal damage.

Joint Commission on Accreditation of Hospitals. An organization that sets guidelines for satisfactory hospital operation and then inspects the institutions to see if they come up to standards. Critics believe that the JCAH is flawed, and that its standards and accreditation inspections are tainted by the vested interests involved: The JCAH is a function of the American Medical Association and the American Hospital Association, among other such groups, and critics feel that such an accreditation process ought to be performed by an independent organization. Osteopathic hospitals are inspected and accredited by the American Osteopathic Association.

La maladie du petit papier. The so-called "illness of the little piece of paper." This is a name given by physicians to an alleged condition that manifests itself in a patient bringing lists of questions and complaints to his or her doctor as a memory aid, but which some doctors see as indicative of mental illness.

Legionnaires' disease. A disease caused by a bacterium, spread in a general manner so that epidemics are common, that causes symptoms not unlike those of *pneumonia* (although with additional serious complications like nausea and vomiting, *renal* failure, and permanent lung damage), although the therapy generally used for pneumonia is ineffective with this disease. Legionnaires' disease, named after an outbreak during a 1976 American Legion convention in Philadelphia, most often strikes middle-age and older men who are smokers or whose immunity is lowered.

Leukemia. A cancerous, malignant, and progressive disease in which white cells are excessively produced in the blood and bone marrow, leading to anemia, infections, hemorrhaging, and enlargement and hyperactivity of the spleen, liver, and lymph glands. It is often fatal, and is a major killer of children.

Mammogram. A record of a procedure in which the breast is X-rayed to diagnose certain conditions, including breast cancer.

Mastectomy. Surgical removal of the breast, usually because of a cancerous condition. A simple mastectomy removes only the breast; a radical mastectomy also excises the pectoral muscles and lymph nodes; a modified radical mastectomy usually retains the pectoral muscles. Some critics see the mastectomy as an overused, possibly unnecessary surgery at times, especially now that alternatives like lumpectomy— the removal of the cancerous growth but retention of the breast— have been shown to be effective.

Medicaid. A program, operated by the states, that provides medical care to those with low incomes.

Medicare. A program, operated by the federal government, that provides medical care to senior citizens.

Midwife (licensed-lay). A birthing practitioner who attends and assists at delivery. Licensed-lay midwives are either self-taught or have attended school (unaccredited) to learn the basics of their occupation, and they are not legally able to practice in most states.

Midwife (registered/certified nurse). A registered nurse with one or two years of additional training in midwifery and prenatal and neonatal care. She or he often has a master's degree in maternal-child health nursing, and may work in a hospital setting or in independent birthing centers, but always with a physician backup.

Milwaukee brace treatment. A treatment method used to brace the spine in cases of scoliosis. The brace itself is made up of a leather girdle and neck ring connected by metal struts.

Morbidity. The condition of being diseased; the proportion of sickness or of a specific disease in a geographical locality.

Mutual aid groups. National or local organizations designed to help a person deal with the fears or physical setbacks caused by a condition, disease, or surgery. These groups are usually composed of others who have gone through or are going through the same stresses and anxieties, and who talk out their problems and assist others to come to terms with their situation.

Myasthenia gravis. A sometimes life-threatening autoimmune disease characterized by muscle weakness, especially in the face, tongue, and neck, but with no muscle atrophy involved. Symptoms include difficulty in chewing and speaking, drooping of the eyelid, and double vision. In severe cases, breathing difficulties ensue. No one knows exactly how or why the body begins to attack itself in this way.

Myocardial infarction. A heart attack; the death of heart muscle due to oxygen deprivation to that tissue, caused by a blocking (as by a clot) of the blood supply through the coronary arteries to the heart.

Myopathies. Diseases affecting the muscles.

Necrosis. The death of cell tissue or of a particular portion of an organ.

Neuroleptic. An antipsychotic drug; a major tranquilizer.

Neurosurgery. Surgery performed on nerve tissue and the nervous system, including the brain.

Nitrous oxide. A gas used as a general anesthetic; also known as laughing gas.

Nosocomial infection. An infection acquired during hospitalization, produced by microorganisms in the hospital itself. Nosocomial infections are among the leading causes of death in hospitals, being responsible for the deaths of a minimum of 100,000 people annually.

Nurse-anesthetist. A certified registered nurse who has received additional training in the administration of all forms of anesthesia, and who is used as a surrogate anesthesiologist.

Nurse-practitioner. A registered nurse with additional training allowing him or her to act with greater freedom and independence in assessing the health of a patient and to perform physical examinations and other procedures that were once the sole domain of physicians.

Obstetrics. The branch of medicine concerned with childbirth and the care of women in connection with childbirth.

Oophorectomy. An ovariectomy, or the surgical removal of one or both ovaries. In a salpingo-oophorectomy, one or both fallopian tubes are also removed.

Ophthalmology. The branch of medicine that deals with the anatomy, functions, and diseases of the eye.

Optometry. The nonmedical profession whose practitioners test vision for defects in order to prescribe prescription corrective lenses.

Organic brain syndrome. A mental illness caused by brain tissue dysfunction. It may be caused by injury, infection, drugs, malnutrition, or other factors.

Orthopedics. The correction or cure of deformities and diseases of the spine, bones, joints, and other parts of the musculoskeletal system.

Osteopath. Common term for a doctor of osteopathy, a non-M.D. medical doctor who, along with taking typical medical school courses, also learns osteopathic healing. Osteopathic healing involves manipulative therapy, whereby muscles, bones, joints, nerves, and tissue are in some way manipulated or have pressure applied to them in order to effect some beneficial change in a patient's condition. Osteopathy holds that if the body is properly aligned and in normal structural relationship, it has the ability to fight disease and heal itself. Except for manipulation, there is very little difference these days between an M.D. and a D.O.

Otolaryngology. Also, otorhinolaryngology; the branch of medicine that deals with the anatomy, functions, and diseases of the ear, nose, and throat.

Pacemaker (electronic cardiac). An electrical device that takes over the task of keeping the heartbeat regular when the heart's own natural pacemaker (called the sinoatrial node) is not functioning properly. It works by sending electrical impulses to the heart muscle, to which it is connected. Pacemakers may be temporary or permanent, external or implantable, fixed rate or on demand.

Pap smear. Officially known as the Papanicolaou test, for its inventor, George N. Papanicolaou, M.D. This test detects early uterine and cervical cancer through microscopic study of samples of vaginal fluid.

Paramedic. An emergency medical technician.

Pathology. That branch of medical science that studies the origin, essential nature, and course of disease, and especially the changes that occur in organs and body tissue that cause or are caused by disease.

Pediatrician. A physician who specializes in diseases of children and child development.

Peripheral nervous system. The nervous system throughout the body not including the brain and spinal cord.

Peritonitis. Inflammation of the membrane lining the abdominal and pelvic cavities and the enclosed organs. Causes of this potentially fatal condition include gastric ulcers and perforated gallbladder. It is an infection that can be treated with antibiotics.

Pharmacokinetics. The study of the way drugs move through the body and are absorbed or eliminated.

Pharmacology. The science of drugs' preparation, uses, and effects.

Physician-assistant. A non-M.D. practitioner who can perform tasks that were once restricted to physicians. Many such practitioners are former military paramedics, and as such are used frequently in the role of assistant in surgical situations as well as as an aide to a physician in primary care.

Physiologist. One who specializes in that branch of science that deals with the way living organisms or their parts function and with the physical and chemical factors and processes involved.

Placebo. A substance that has no value in a real therapeutic pharmacological sense, but actually helps a patient who believes it will work. Placebos are often given to patients who psychologically require a pill (and sometimes do quite well after taking it) or as part of clinical trials to test the effectiveness of new drugs. The placebo effect is a classic example of the mind-body relationship.

Pneumonia. An infection and inflammation affecting the lungs, caused by bacteria (predominantly the *Streptococcus pneumoniae* bacterium) or viruses; despite antibiotic usage (or because of antibiotic misuse and overuse, leading to the development of bacterial resistance), pneumonia is still a major killer, and is a serious nosocomial infection.

Podiatrist. A medical specialist in podiatry, the study and care of the feet.

Polypharmacy. The dispensing of too many drugs together to patients.

Prosthesis. An artificial part used to replace a missing body part. Artificial limbs and dentures are both examples of prosthetic devices.

Psychoneurosis. Also sometimes known simply as neurosis; an emotional disorder in which the personality is debilitated by feelings of anxiety and obsessive-compulsive behavior. It also causes or seems to cause physical illness. It is a milder form of mental illness than psychosis.

Psychotropic. Descriptive of a type of drug that influences the way the mind works and alters a person's mental state by relieving anxiety and combating depression, psychotic disorders, and other mental problems. Valium is a well-known antidepressive psychotropic drug.

Rabies. An infectious disease present in animals that is transferred to human beings by the bite or lick of a rabid creature such as a dog, bat, or other mammal. The virus is often present in the saliva of the affected animal. This is a usually fatal disease that attacks the central nervous system. There is no cure, and if symptoms become apparent, death ensues in less than a week.

Renal. Having to do with the kidney.

Residency. The status of a graduated and licensed physician who remains in a hospital to continue training in a specialty.

R.N. Registered nurse; a nurse with more training and education (a baccalaureate degree and possibly a master's) than licensed practical nurses, who is registered and licensed to practice nursing by a state agency.

Rubber-band hemorrhoidectomy. Also known as a Barron ligation; an alternative to surgery, in this procedure the blood flow to the hemorrhoid is cut off by a tightly applied rubber band or ligature. After a few days, the hemorrhoid falls off.

Salmonellosis. An infection caused by the *Salmonella* bacterium and usually spread by the eating of contaminated, unrefrigerated, or inadequately refrigerated eggs, meat, poultry, and dairy products. Normally, cooking easily kills the salmonellae.

Schizophrenia. The umbrella term for a number of psychotic disorders in which the person affected exhibits bizarre and withdrawn behavior, delusions, auditory hallucinations, and general intellectual deterioration. Also known as dementia praecox, schizophrenia is frequently treated with a combination of *neuroleptics* and psychotherapy; hospitalization may be required.

Scoliosis. Curvature of the spine, which can be *postural,* meaning that it is not severe, does not involve a twisting of the vertebrae, and may be correctable through exercise, or *structural,* which means that the vertebrae have rotated. Structural scoliosis may be congenital, neuromuscular (caused by muscle weakness or neurological problems), or idiopathic (of unknown cause). It can be inherited, happens most often during adolescence, and strikes girls more than boys. Surgery is a treatment, as are various corrective braces, such as the *Milwaukee brace.*

Somatic. Having to do with the body.

Strep throat. A condition manifesting itself as a sore throat, caused by a *Streptococcus* bacterium that may also cause scarlet and rheumatic fevers. Other streptococci are responsible for meningitis, pneumonia, and *peritonitis.* Strep throat may be accompanied by high fever, lymph node swelling, and a rash.

Subclavian. Located below the clavicle (collar bone), as with a subclavian catheter.

Syringe swap. Medical mistake occurring during the administration of anesthesia, when two syringes containing anesthetics are confused or interchanged and the wrong drug is actually or nearly given. It can occur when a doctor reaches for one syringe but grabs another.

Systemic lupus erythematosus. An inflammatory disease—caused by heredity, reactions to certain drugs, infections, sunlight or ultraviolet radiation from sunlamps, and hormonal influences—that manifests itself in injuries to the skin, joints, kidneys, nervous system, and mucous membranes. It strikes women primarily, and although what it is is not exactly clear, it seems to be an autoimmune disease. Treatment includes avoiding sun and ultraviolet light, using steroids, and taking medications to relieve pain. When lupus affects the muscles, physical therapy may need to be instituted to prevent structural deformities.

Ultrasound. A method, using radiation of a frequency that is beyond the audible range of human beings, to create pictures of body structures deep below the surface. Used to get pictures of organs, it is also currently being used on pregnant women to gain information about the fetus, despite continuing controversy over its possible long-term negative effects on the unborn child.

Unit-dose. A system of drug dispensing utilized in many hospitals, in which an individual supply of medication is made up for each patient and is replenished every 24 hours. Each drug is in a unit-of-use form (if a patient is to receive 500 mg of a certain drug four times a day, a drawer in the pharmacy with the patient's name on it will contain four separately wrapped, properly labeled 500-mg tablets of that drug). After every 24 hours, the drawer should be empty. Unit-dose, in other words, is an attempt at quality assurance in medication dispensing. It has succeeded in greatly reducing medication errors wherever it has been instituted.

Urologic. Having to do with diseases of the urinary system, as well as with the organs of reproduction in men.

Uterus, prolapsed. A condition in which the uterus drops down from its usual location until the cervix is either inside or outside the vaginal opening or the entire uterus is outside the vaginal opening.

Vascular. Having to do with the blood vessels.

Workup. What is done in a doctor's office or a hospital to get enough information to arrive at a diagnosis. A workup includes taking a medical history, a physical examination, and a variety of tests such as blood tests and urinalysis, as well as taking an *electrocardiogram* and possibly *X-rays*.

X-ray. Electromagnetic radiation used to create pictures of the body's internal structures.

INDEX